MARCELLA CUCINA

BY MARCELLA HAZAN

———— ❧ ————

The Classic Italian Cookbook

More Classic Italian Cooking

Marcella's Italian Kitchen

Essentials of Classic Italian Cooking

- Poi mettere 2½ cup di acqua e un dado.
- Cuocere finché le fa alcune patate mescolando in di tanto - aggiungere acqua se si vede che diventa molto fitta
- Quando tutto è ben cotto deve essere cremoso non troppo fitto.
- Si aggiusta di sale, si mette abbondante pepe nero e il basilico e il parmigiano - burro
- Si serve calde.

Scalops con sedano rosmarino pomodoro

per 4 persone

① 2 lb di scalops
② 4 Tb di olio d'oliva
③ 4 ts di aglio tritato fine
④ 12½ Tb di rosmarino tritato fine
⑤ 2/3 cup di pomodori pelati con succo, o pomodori freschi
⑥ un buon pizzico di peperoncino
⑦ sale.

- Con un coltellino affilato cercare di togliere quella piccola striscia un po' dura traslucida che c'è in ogni scalops.
- Lavarle e asciugarle in uno straccio.
- In una padella finissato grande (dove poi le scalops staranno quasi di un solo strato) mettere l'olio

For, and because of, Victor

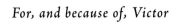

MARCELLA CUCINA

Marcella Hazan

PHOTOGRAPHY BY ALISON HARRIS
DESIGN BY JOEL AVIROM

HarperCollins*Publishers*

HarperCollins books may be purchased for educational, business, or sales promotional use. For information please write: Special Markets Department, HarperCollins Publishers, Inc., 10 East 53rd Street, New York, NY 10022.

FIRST EDITION

DESIGN ASSISTANT: JASON SNYDER
DESIGN COORDINATOR: MEGHAN DAY HEALEY

Library of Congress Cataloging-in-Publication Data

Hazan, Marcella.
    Marcella cucina / by Marcella Hazan. — 1st ed.
        p.   cm.
    Includes index.
    ISBN 0-06-017103-0
    1. Cookery, Italian.   I. Title
TX723.H3426   1997
641.5945—dc21   97-1253

97 98 99 00 01 ❖/RRD 10 9 8 7 6 5 4 3 2 1

Contents

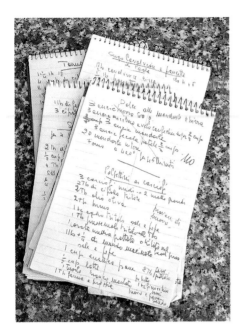

Introduction

An Italian speaker glancing at the title of this book would see the second word, *Cucina*, as a verb, third person singular, thus reading the title as *Marcella Cooks*. That is precisely what this new work of mine is about: What I cook and how I cook. And a little bit about why I cook.

Although at first as a wife, and then as a teacher and writer, I have devoted a large part of my life to cooking, I never deliberately made that choice. It was not I who chose cooking; it happened the other way around. I was trained as a biologist, and until after I married, I had never come close enough to a kitchen stove to turn on the gas. I came to America a few months after our wedding and there I was, having to feed a young, hard-working husband who could deal cheerfully with most of life's ups and downs, but not with an indifferent meal. At home, in Italy, I would not have wasted time thinking about it. My mother cooked, my father cooked, both my grandmothers cooked, even the farm girls who came in to clean could cook. In the kitchen of my New York apartment there was no one. It could not have been a kitchen of unusual size, but stamped in my recollection is the impression of a cavernous space that I entered each day fearing, or perhaps even hoping, that it would swallow me up and I would not be heard from again.

As it turned out, I was not alone in the kitchen. My husband had bought me a cookbook, an early edition of Ada Boni's *Talismano della Felicità*, with scores of tantalizing recipes set down in telegraphic style, their instructions seldom encumbered by fussy attention to measurements or to details. But as useful a guide as Ada was to me, I charted my course by an even more valuable set of directions, the taste memories of the food that I grew up eating.

When you tell a friend an anecdote out of your past, it may happen that details of the event emerge—how people looked, what they were wearing, how they spoke, something about the color of the sky that day, or the way the air felt on your skin—that you were not aware could still be so fresh in your recollection. When I was growing up, going to a university, taking my degrees, embarking on a career, discovering love, the food I was eating was not something I paid attention to. Yet when I began to cook, I found I could fully recall the flavors of the dishes I had had in those years. Then I made an even more remarkable discovery: The flavors themselves pointed to the commonsense ways of preparing and cooking ingredients that would reproduce those dishes. Eventually I learned that some of the methods I adopted were idiosyncratically my own, but for most of them I found corroboration in the practices of traditional Italian cooks. What mattered was that the taste of what I cooked began to correspond to the flavors that had been stored in my mind during my first three decades of life in Italy.

I knew no one then, I spoke no English, my friends and family were thousands of miles away, and I was cooking just for my husband, or rather for the two of us. We didn't even have a dining table, just an old bridge table whose top sagged precipitously in the middle so that, when serving soup, I could never fill more than a quarter of the bowl at a time. We always had multiple servings of soup, which I chose to attribute to the merits of the cooking rather than the shortcomings of the furniture.

Every evening I produced a complete dinner in the Italian family style, first course, second course, and a vegetable side course. When I was in particularly good form, I'd add an appetizer and, much less frequently, a dessert. As my husband and I sat down we approached the results of each new trial circumspectly, even fearfully, but then, when the tastes proved to be satisfying, apprehension gave way to celebration. Virtually our entire conversation was about what we were eating. I described how I made each dish, my husband complimented me on the ones that were successful and, happily less often, consoled me when they were not, suggesting how they might be improved. On those occasions when it seemed that my efforts had been especially triumphant, he would rush out of his chair and throw his arms around me.

There are never enough wooden tools. The long fork is for stirring pasta, the straight-edged spatula for risotto.

In my girlhood dreams of romance I could not have imagined that, as a new bride, I would spend my evenings at a rickety bridge table discussing food with my spouse. After my husband left in the morning the days were long and lonely and often I was desperate, but when he returned and it was time for dinner, my early domestic achievements were greeted with encouragement so tender, and the food I had cooked brought us so much joy, that as I think back on that time, daunting though it was, I am nonetheless filled with warmth.

Forty years have passed and much in our lives has changed, but all the recipes that have earned a place in the book that you are now holding in your hands had to pass inspection at meals that differed very little from those my husband and I once ate alone. In my forty-second year of marriage, I still cook to please my husband. When I am developing recipes for a book, I do not follow what I understand to be the common practice of working on a chicken chapter, or a fish chapter, or any chapter whatever. I cook a meal that my husband and I eat. One day there may be soup and meat, another day pasta and fish; some days it may be just a single course simply because we cannot eat as much every day as when we were young. But the dishes must be tested in the intimate circumstances of a true family meal, and they must satisfy the lively taste expectations that those circumstances arouse. If they do not, they are never served again and they do not go into the book.

I have different ways of finding dishes to cook. When I travel outside my region, I find them in small restaurants and *trattorie* or, when I am lucky, in someone's home. I find them in regional cookbooks and occasionally, when I am at the hairdresser's, I spot a promising idea in one of the many women's weeklies that are published in Italy. If I chat with someone sitting in the same compartment of a train or shopping alongside me at the butcher's or in the fish market, I might come home with several new things to try. I am equally interested in a dish that has been handed down through several generations and in an improvisation not older than a day. Sometimes I find a good one right in my head.

Wherever the dishes I find may come from, my only concern is how they are going to taste. When, in my mind, I have conjured up their taste, I discard any recipe whose imagined flavors do not arouse me or fail to speak to me with a convincing Italian accent. I am not interested in fusion or cross-cultural culinary hybrids, in rootless, inconsequential cooking that does not communicate a clear sense of identity, of place. Once the taste I am looking for is firmly in my sights, I home in on it and let it lead me to the methods that seem most likely to capture it. First comes the taste, then the technique. Cooking must express taste, not technique, because technique alone does not communicate anything. To study it otherwise than as a function of taste is an arid academic exercise; it is like mastering the grammar of a language in which you have nothing to say. It happens too often when I eat the food of highly trained chefs, food that is ingeniously contrived, elaborately described in the menu, and eye-catchingly presented, that virtually nothing registers on my palate. Such occasions remind me of a plea that the composer Richard Strauss once made to an orchestra he was rehearsing: "Gentlemen, you are playing all the notes perfectly, but please, now let me hear some music."

OPPOSITE: *Slotted and perforated steel spatulas for sautéing and frying.*
ABOVE: *Two forks for beating thick mixtures. A scaloppine pounder. The food mill purees vegetables and potatoes. The indispensable tomato peelers. A wire* retina *spreads the flame of a gas burner for even cooking or for charring bell peppers.*

We all agree that taste is subjective and variable, but I do not agree with the old saw that it cannot be discussed. It can indeed be discussed and I do want to discuss it because it is critically important to the kind of cooking you do. Taste is not produced by just any capricious assortment of flavors. Taste is real; it is a potent sensory encounter that has a deep and satisfying reach; it is a powerful emotion that you experience through your taste buds and that you can store, more perfectly than almost any other, in your memory. The home cooking that has been evolving in regional Italian kitchens over the centuries has amassed an inexhaustible hoard of these gustatory emotions. They exist independently of the countless generations of cooks and diners who have experienced and recorded them, they reside in certain intuitively combined flavors and textures, and they are reignited every time one cooks Italian food with a respectful sense of those flavors and those textures.

Of course, everyone in Italy has a different idea of taste. What pleases a delicate Venetian palate is not identical to what may excite the taste buds in Parma, or Florence, or Naples, or Palermo. The silken refinement of Piedmontese cooking is replaced in Abruzzi or in Apulia by flavors that are earthier, more homespun. The pleasure that in Milan one may take in risotto is equaled in Siena by the joys of a bean and cabbage soup; or in Amalfi by spaghetti with mussels and ripe tomatoes; or in Bologna by handmade tagliatelle with meat sauce; or in Genoa by trenette with pesto, boiled potatoes, and green beans; or in Sondrio by buckwheat noodles with soft cheese and Savoy cabbage. Not least among the matchless attractions of Italy's food is its variety. Yet, however dissimilar the cooking traditions may be—as sharply dissimilar indeed as are the cultures, the physical types, the dialects of the many peoples who crowd this small country—it is possible to recognize some common features that make of the disparate brood a family.

The universal quality that Italy's regions can claim for their cooking is that it is kind to the palate. It is food that charms the palate with flavors that are fresh, clear, plain-spoken, direct often to the point of artlessness, and even bold, but not overbearing. Let me give you some examples. Italians, particularly those of the center and south, frequently use chili pepper—*peperoncino*—but scrupulous cooks will use just enough of it to tease the taste buds, not torch them. Except on pasta, there are no sauces as such, just the unlabored juices that issue spontaneously from making a roast or a stew or a fricassee. On pasta itself, sauce is used with restraint, to coat, not to blanket. What you can expect of careful Italian cooking, whatever its regional provenance, is a mannerly approach to garlic: It is never employed with intemperate profusion nor so overbrowned that its presence becomes obtrusive, oafishly shouldering aside that of other ingredients in the dish. If there are green beans or asparagus they will be cooked until they are tender enough to release the flavor sealed within them, not until they are mushy, of course, yet not so maniacally underdone that they taste raw, like blades of grass just pulled out of the ground. If there is fowl it will have been cooked long enough for the juicy flesh to slip easily off the bone and yield meltingly to the bite. If there are herbs they will be handled judiciously, which is to say sparingly, to avoid drugging the food with more fragrance than it needs. If there is olive oil, whether it is pungent in the Tuscan manner or sweet like the oil of Liguria, it must deliver the palpable flavor of its olives.

A dish may be made with two ingredients or with twenty, but every one of them will have been called upon for a good reason. Whether the dish is plain or elaborate, the choices a thoughtful Italian cook makes are governed by a rigorous economy of means. No ingredient, no condiment, no herb or spice gets by on whimsy. Nothing unnecessary ought to be on the dish or enter your mouth. If its taste and texture cannot deliver anything essential, it stays out. What you keep out is as significant as what you put in.

I hope the reader finds in this book not just recipes that sound good, but recipes that will taste good. I have cooked each many times, both in my kitchen in Venice and in American kitchens. Once I was satisfied that they could work for others, I wrote out the recipes by hand, with as much attention to useful detail as I was able to bring to the task, striving to make each one wholly self-contained and accessible even to someone lacking a background in Italian food or, for that matter, advanced cooking experience of any kind. I have tried to supply clues to the taste considerations that guided me as I made my choices about ingredients and procedures so that each recipe is as faithful an account as I can render of what took place when I was cooking it. All these are now just notes on a page, waiting for you to bring them to life. When you do, don't just play the notes, please. Think taste. Make music.

To the Market

AL MERCATO

We go to a food market with one of two objects in view: Either to buy what we have already decided to cook or to choose what, on that day, might be most desirable to cook. For convenience's sake, the first purpose can be satisfied by a good supermarket whose food department, reliably stocked with standard items, we use the way we would a hardware store. It has what we want and we want what it has. On the other hand, when we browse the stalls of an Italian street market, such as the great fish and produce market at Rialto, in Venice, we may not know what we are looking for until we see it, but it will have to be something we won't be able to resist taking home to cook.

We do not go there entirely clueless, because a street market's fidelity to seasonal cycles provides reassuring familiarity. One year's spring crop is expectedly like another's, just as it is predictably different from the winter's crop that preceded it and the summer harvest that will follow it. But a traditional Italian market also depends for the quality of its provisions on such imponderables as sudden or prolonged shifts in the weather, the enterprise—or lack of it—of the stall keepers, the variable temperaments and skills of the supplying farmers, and the uncertainties of the night's catch at sea. Seasonal continuity is paired with daily chance. Each morning there is change and every day there is a fresh choice to make.

In My Market

THE PRODUCE

I spend the richest hours of my life in Venice when I cross the tall bridge at Rialto and reach the stalls on the other side of the Grand Canal where the fruit and vegetable vendors display their wares. It is as difficult for me to pass a single stall by as it would be for a child to ignore any of the windows of a street lined with toy shops.

There may be thousands of zucchini, but every batch looks different: some are slender, some plump, some a deep, almost bottle green, some a green so pale it is nearly callow. When the zucchini are exceptionally fresh, not 24 hours out of the ground, the grower and the vendor may leave their blossoms on. These are the female blossoms, not good to cook, but by their brightness and firmness they are there to show how recently the vegetable has been picked. The male flowers, marvelous when opened up flat and fried with a thin flour-and-water batter, grow attached not to the zucchini, but to a stem, and are gathered, several in a bunch, to make bold orange-yellow posies that outshine anything in the market.

You don't need a calendar to know that spring has come to Rialto. It will have been announced by the appearance of asparagus and young artichokes. The stalls display asparagus of various sizes and colors. There are the spindly stalks of *asparagina*, with more taste than flesh, ideal for omelets or risotto. There is the fancy white asparagus of Bassano and the brawny, meaty green one of Badoere, both from the Veneto's hinterland. The white is the one many people moon over, and often pay more for, but I much prefer the sweeter, more positive taste of the green. A recent addition is the delicious purple variety that originated in Albenga, on the Italian Riviera, but is now produced also in the Veneto's Badoere. Late in the spring comes the asparagus grown closest to home, on the islands of the lagoon, whose lean green spears are less remarkable for their appearance than for the unsurpassed intensity of their flavor.

Had Venice nothing else to offer, it would be worth the trip to be here for *castraure* and *canarini*, the first locally grown artichokes to appear in the spring. Before full-grown artichokes begin to sprout from the plant's lateral stems, a tiny bud sprouts at the top, capping

it somewhat the way a star does the Christmas tree. It is snipped off to become *castraure*, the product of the plant's "castration." A student of mine taking a tour of the market with me dubbed it "artichoke foreskin." *Castraure* are miniatures, so tender there is nothing to trim, each *castraura*, when sautéed in olive oil with garlic and parsley, yielding a concentrated biteful, or two at most, of artichoke essence. *Canarini*, little canaries, are pale golden-green artichokes picked very young from shade-grown plants. They are the tenderest and mildest of their kind, even smaller and more expensive than the already pricey *castraure*.

With one exception, all the artichokes I see, whether full-grown or immature, are the shape of rosebuds, some of them with spiny tips. But for a few short weeks in the spring, the Roman *mammola*, a large, stout variety similar to the globe artichoke produced in California,

appears in some stalls. Like the California globe, it is meatier and blander, less astringent than the rosebud-shaped artichokes. Toward the end of the *mammola*'s growing cycle, when its leaves become fibrous and unchewable, it is turned into a Venetian specialty, *fondo di carciofo*. Sitting by their stalls, the artichoke sellers cut off the stems and whittle away all the leaves down to the base, piling the discarded leaves waist-high, dropping the only part that remains, a half-inch-thick disk, into a basin of water acidulated with white vinegar to keep the *fondi* from turning black. *Fondi* can be breaded and fried, sautéed in olive oil with garlic and parsley, stewed with potatoes and onions, or used in risotto.

I am fascinated by the number of greens in the market that are called radicchio. Some bear no visible resemblance to each other, but they all belong to the chicory family and share, in varying degrees, the intriguing bitterness that is the family's trait, and that is so agreeable to an Italian palate.

The radicchio best known abroad, the one with a tight, round, cabbage-like head of crisp, white-veined purple leaves, is known as *rosa di Chioggia*. It comes around in the fall, is best at wintertime, but remains available through the spring. There is a true spring radicchio, with a clump of small, flat, round-tipped leaves, loosely overlapping like a fully opened rose, and gathered at the root end. It can be green or dark red, and when very fresh is splendidly crunchy and nutty in salads. Another salad radicchio known as *radicchietto* appears late in the spring and is abundant all summer and early fall. Like field lettuce, it has single, small, rounded, dark green leaves, and it is this numerous family's most tender and sweetest offshoot.

The noblest members of the family—*radicchio di Castelfranco, radicchio di Treviso, tardivo di Treviso*—make an eagerly awaited entrance around November. All of them are extravagantly good in salads, but they are bred for loftier uses in the kitchen: in a risotto, in a pasta sauce, braised with a roast, with seafood, or best of all perhaps, just on their own, grilled or baked.

Castelfranco has a large, loosely packed head of soft, dappled leaves, tinged here and there with a lovely pink hue that recalls orchids. It once used to exit the scene with the arrival of spring, but now I can find it much later on, although I prefer it in the cold months. Treviso radicchio has the shape of a small romaine lettuce, its tapered leaves a deep shade of purple with clear white markings. The greatest of the three and, in my opinion, the most magnificent vegetable grown, is Treviso's dazzling *tardivo* or late-harvest radicchio.

Tardivo's leaves are but a narrow, fiery red ruffle fringing the edges of spear-like glossy white ribs that, like overgrown fingernails, curl inward. They are attached at the base to an elongated root from which, flame-like, they spread out and up. On a misty late fall day, the

displays of *tardivo* in the stalls flare like fireworks against the backdrop of the market's seasonally somber produce.

But even without the glamorous presence of radicchio at the end and beginning of the year, I would enjoy the market then no less than at any of its warmer periods. Of course I do look forward to the luscious, ripe taste of summer; to the mounds of red and yellow peppers in the stalls; to six or more kinds of tomatoes, some for salads, some for sauce; to eggplant with purple, mauve, or white skin. And how could I not be thrilled by those few weeks in fall when the wild mushrooms arrive? When I come upon a basket of adorably chubby porcini that might have been modeled by Disney, their fawn-colored stems supporting chocolate-dark tops, I am immobilized by desire struggling against indecision. Shall I make risotto, or a sauce for homemade pasta, or shall I do a roast with porcini *trifolati*, the mushrooms sliced very thin and sautéed in olive oil with garlic and parsley? Or are the caps large enough to grill? Or, if I manage surreptitiously to squeeze them while the vendor isn't looking, do they feel so firm that we can eat them raw, with slivers of Parmesan and white truffle?

But many other wonderful things grow only when the approaching chill of winter puts its bite on autumn's tail. There are the blue-green broccoli Venetians call *amorini*, sold with their leaves on, which are so good in soup. There is purple cauliflower, and fist-size white cauliflower, for either one of which there is no preparation so perfect as boiling it and serving it warm, tossed with wine vinegar and fruity olive oil. And there is red cabbage, with which I make one of my very best chicken fricassees. There is the purple-green cardoon, typical of the Veneto, resembling a celery in appearance, but an artichoke in taste. I braise it or gratinée it with butter and grated Parmesan. There is the dark green, corrugated Savoy cabbage, and *cime di rapa*. The latter is superb for pasta sauces; or I shred and chop the two and sauté them together in olive oil and garlic and serve them over *piadina*, the flat bread of my native Romagna. This is the time of the year for the crispest, sweetest *finocchi*, not just for salads, but for braising in oil or for breading and frying. And at last, nut gatherers from the hills bring burlap sacks bulging with *marroni*, the fine, shiny, potbellied chestnuts with which at Christmastime I make my chocolate and chestnut Monte Bianco dessert.

THE FISH

The comparatively shallow waters of the northern Adriatic, freshened by cool Alpine streams, are populated by an edible marine life that, for its variety and flavor, is unsurpassed, possibly unmatched, elsewhere on the planet. Venice is the queen of the Adriatic, and the queen of fish markets is at Rialto. The lofty Gothic arches of the open-sided *pescheria* hall provide covering for some of the fishmongers' stalls, but not for all. There are too many and the others are strung along outside. The abundance of the display would be astonishing even if the market were servicing a metropolis of millions, but Venice has less than 70,000 residents. On any morning from Tuesday to Saturday, between 8 A.M. and 1 P.M., most of those 70,000 seem to be coming through with their shopping carts. Venetians are mad for seafood. But even if one weren't, it would be impossible to resist the call of the fish market.

These are not just vegetables that have been laid out; they are creatures, as fantastically diverse in expression, shape, size, and color as only creatures of the mysterious deep can be. There are the suave, elegantly tapered blue-backed, white-bellied sea bass; the ferocious monkfish, its tooth-bristling jaws sprung open; and the choleric-looking orange-red scorpion fish, so good for a fish soup. There are skate wings spread out like delicate pink fans; small shark whose skin has been stripped off, exposing the blushing crimson flesh; black and silver sardines evoking thoughts of their dark meat smoking on a charcoal grill, producing the most seductive aroma of the seafood world, as well as their more silvery cousins, the fresh anchovies, born to be floured and fried. There are living shells of all shapes and

markings: scallop shells, razor clams, little white sea snails, small conch, sacks of mussels and clams. And there are baskets of desperately clawing crab, trays of somersaulting shrimp, tubs of sinuous eel ceaselessly doing their snake dance. There is no livelier show in town.

The best known of Adriatic creatures is scampi, which, notwithstanding having its name misappropriated by that over-garlicked standard of Italian-American menus, shrimp scampi, is not a shrimp at all. It is a small, orange-pink, lobster-like crustacean, whose sweetness and tenderness surpass those of lobster itself. Were I to find freshly caught scampi and porcini on the same morning I might well grab some of both to make *risotto con scampi e porcini*.

There is seafood in the Rialto market that you rarely find elsewhere, and it is so freshly caught that often it is still alive when you buy it. *Schile*, pronounced "skee′yeh," is a minute gray shrimp that does not turn red when cooked. The very tiniest ones are fried whole in their shell and popped into the mouth like chips. Or they are patiently shelled after boiling and served with warm, soft polenta.

There used to be many kinds of crab, including one, *granzoporo*, the flavor of whose claws used to make me think of Florida's stone crab. Overfishing and pollution have nearly extinguished all but two or three varieties. The most striking of the survivors, *granzevola* ("grahn-sey′oh-lah"), is a large vividly rose-colored crab with long, spidery legs. At home you would boil it, crack it, and spend the next hour picking out the flesh and coral. Restaurants make it very simple for you: after cooking it, they scoop clean the beautiful rosy shell and fill it with the picked-over body and claw meat. For the pure in palate it is good enough to eat without any seasoning, but waiters usually moisten it with a few drops of olive oil and lemon juice.

Soft-shell crabs, about one quarter the size of their East Coast equivalent, are so local that there is no word for them in Italian: Their name, *moleche* ("moe-ey′keh"), is Venetian. Also Venetian are *folpeti* ("foe-pey′tee")—miniature octopus that you boil and serve whole, still warm, drizzled with olive oil and two drops of vinegar, and *garusoli* ("gah-roo′-zoh-ee"), very small conch. (If you have been following this, you will have noticed that in Venice people like to drop their l's.)

The cuisine of Venice bears no larger debt than the one it owes to a single product of its waters, the cuttlefish and its ink, *la seppia e il suo nero*. In appearance, cuttlefish vaguely resembles squid, but it has a meatier flesh and more complex flavor. The most significant difference, however, is in the ink, *il nero*. Venetians would never make their superb black risotto or their black pasta with any ink but that of the cuttlefish, a satiny, dense, warm-tasting substance immeasurably richer than the squid's thin and pungent dye. One of the dishes that is most popular with Venetians, both at home and when they go out with the family, is *seppie alla veneziana*, cut-up cuttlefish and their ink stewed with sautéed onions, wine, and tomato paste and served over bricks of grilled polenta. If you were to have it in midsummer, when baby cuttlefish no larger than a thumbnail are in season, you would have chosen very well indeed. In the vast seafood repertoire of Italy's maritime regions there is not another combination of flavors more savory than this one.

Small size is one of the factors that contribute to the exceptionally fine flavor of Adriatic seafood. The Adriatic sole, the firmest and nuttiest of all soles, is the size of a small hand. I come from a fishing town on the Adriatic where I grew up eating sole, and now no other gives me comparable pleasure. When working with fish from American waters, the Atlantic, the Gulf, the Pacific, I have found many whose flavors and textures are adaptable to Italian dishes, but I have never been satisfied with sole or, except for young halibut, with any other indigenous flatfish.

Our sole are so small that when I fry them for my husband and myself I buy no fewer than ten. Red mullets, fresh sardines, and fresh anchovies are even smaller. Most other fish, such as bream, gray mullet, mackerel, and monkfish, are just large enough for a single portion, although there are baby monkfish of which you'd need at least a pair. *Branzino*, the very fine Adriatic bass, may be of a size for two persons, as may a *rombo*, the native turbot.

Venetians don't buy fillets; they buy whole fish or, occasionally, fish steaks. Except for small Adriatic shark, indigenous steak fish is not abundant at the Rialto market. You do see swordfish and tuna, but they are not caught locally.

"Local" is the most powerful selling word in the market, and it is never taken in vain. In Italian it is *nostrani* or *nostrane* (depending whether you are using the masculine or feminine form), whose literal meaning is "ours." To shoppers, "ours" means it's better because it has traveled a short distance to the market, hence it's fresher. An underlying, more emotional secondary message is that it will be more satisfying because the taste is the comfort-

ing one of home. People pay more, much more, for "ours." A trayful of baby cuttlefish caught perhaps not a mile from the market and bearing a sign with the magic word *nostrane* will bring three or four times the price per kilo of a stupendous salmon, just flown in from Norway. Nor is it only the fishmongers who follow this practice. Fruit and vegetable vendors are even more explicit: they write out signs naming the specific farm island, among those that ring the Venetian lagoon, where the green beans or zucchini or figs may have been grown.

LOOKING, ASKING, SELECTING

A skeptic might see room for deception, but no one who tries to practice deception of this kind would have steady customers for long in Venice. Venetians know their produce and their fish, they know the places these come from, they know their market and its vendors. Nothing is accepted unquestioningly.

To understand how they shop, let us follow a svelte, smartly dressed woman who is going from stall to stall, peering intently only at radicchios and lettuces, and *rucola*, and onions. It is a sultry summer morning and evidently she has decided that all she is going to make for lunch is a salad. To the various greens and sweet onions that she is looking for, she will probably add chunks of very good tuna packed in olive oil; some anchovies that she has bought loose under salt and will clean, fillet, and soak in olive oil herself; and a hard-boiled egg or two. Stay on her heels and eventually you'll see that she settles on what appears to be the most promising of the stalls, where she waits her turn. When it comes she will not order until she has asked the vendor, and received reassuring answers to, such questions as, "This isn't yesterday's radicchio, is it? Is the *rucola* really wild, not cultivated?

Is that S. Erasmo [one of the farm islands] lettuce? Is this truly—*veramente*—Tropea onion [very sweet red onion from Calabria, in the south]?" Not wanting to lose esteem by showing untoward credulity and shaking her head as if questioning the veracity of the replies, she will finally commit herself: A quarter pound of that please, and a head of the other, one of those, and a bunch of this. If it seems like a lot of trouble to take over a salad, it is food that she is going to put on the table, isn't it, and what could be more important? There are no decisions she will make, either that morning or in her life, to which she is likely to give more deliberate thought.

Knowing Your Market

When I have visitors whom I take to see Rialto, I know in advance that some will remark on how lucky I am and what would I ever do without such a market. I would do as I have always done and as I still continue to do when I am cooking away from Venice. I'd shop carefully, wherever I happened to be.

An encouraging development in America is the appearance of farmers' markets in cities and the proliferation of farmstands near agricultural communities offering vegetables and fruit that are local, *nostrani*. Some of the produce I have bought at such markets and farmstands, although limited in variety, need not envy—and sometimes may even surpass—the freshness and flavor of what I can get at Rialto.

It has been my practice, however, whenever I am testing a recipe that I hope to publish or cooking for a demonstration either live or on television, to use only products that would be available to most of my readers and my audience, and thus I often rely on selective shopping at the local supermarkets. A genuine farmers' market can certainly provide better access to recently picked

produce, but if you can't get to one when you need to cook, it would be foolish to wring your hands in discouragement and dismiss a supermarket's resources. They can be quite valuable if you do as my neighbors do at Rialto: Get to know the market.

Not all supermarkets are the same; look for the best one in your area and be willing to travel a little farther, if necessary, to get to it. Rely on your eyes rather than on a shopping list. Even in the best produce department, the produce is not of identical freshness and quality every day. Take a long look before you decide.

You have an immense advantage over the shoppers at Rialto: You can touch, feel, and choose. Do so. Bear in mind that moisture is an essential component of freshness and when a vegetable's fibers begin to lose it, just as our skin does when it ages, the vegetable deflates and begins to sag.

If you had eggplants in your plans, make sure their stem is a bright green, their skin lustrous and taut, and that they don't feel too heavy in the hand, which would mean they have too many seeds. Should they be otherwise, change your plans. Green beans should be even and clear in color, with no mottling. They should snap sharply. Test an artichoke by bending back one of its leaves. If it is fresh it will offer resistance and remain erect; if long in the tooth it will yield limply. Asparagus tips should be firmly closed. Broccoli florets must be tightly clustered and bright green, with no trace of yellow. A pea pod should be dewy green with no spots. Crack one open; it should open crisply. Taste a pea; it should be juicy and sweet, not starchy. Bell peppers should be very firm, their skin tightly stretched, with no bruises, punctures, or soft spots. For Italian cooking, mature peppers—that is, red or yellow—are preferable to the green ones, which are unripe. Zucchini ought not to be overgrown. Their flavor is sweetest when they are young, that is, small. Their skin should be glossy, and they must absolutely not droop. Choose them all of a size, so that the zucchini will cook uniformly. Garlic heads should be as heavy as possible. They get lighter as they dry out, and as they dry out they become sharper. If you can help it, do not buy what you won't be able to cook very soon. There is no point in making the effort to bring home the freshest possible vegetables and then keeping them in a refrigerator for a week.

The Venetian men and women who go to Rialto every day know their market as though it were their own backyard plot. You can get to know your markets and your farmstands with the same thoroughness and soon you will be able to detect what has been trotted out of cold storage for several days running and what, on that day, has come in fresh.

The people behind the stands or at the farmers' market are easy to approach and they are a priceless source of knowledge about their products. But supermarkets too have people who know. I always try to make the acquaintance of the manager of the produce department, of the butcher, and of the man in charge of the fish. It's in their interest to satisfy a steady and educated customer. I have found good butchers at many supermarkets who will cut the meat as I want it or, if they don't have it, get it for me, often just in a day. Leave your telephone number with the fishmonger if what you are looking for isn't there in the case, and on the day it comes in, you can be the first to know. The only things I have never been able to find in a supermarket are a really first-rate piece of cheese in good condition and a superior olive oil.

If you are in an area that has specialty food shops, you can apply the same "look, ask, and select" strategy there. Some shopkeepers and clerks are unforthcoming, but generally they are grateful to establish a relationship with someone who is as interested as they are in the products they sell. One of the words to which the electronic age has given wide circulation is "interactive." I am not quite sure I understand how it works when applied to a computer program, but interactive is exactly what thoughtful food marketing should be, whether you practice it at Rialto or at a suburban supermarket.

On returning from the Rialto market, Victor and I pause in the 16th-century courtyard of our house.

Three Elements of Taste

OLIVE OIL, PARMESAN, SALT

In cooking there is an uninterrupted sequence of choices, and every single choice made, whether it is deliberate or instinctive or forced upon you, affects the taste of the dishes you prepare: The freshness of the vegetables, of the seafood, of the herbs, of the ground pepper; the ripeness of the tomatoes; the match-up of pasta and sauce; the type of rice; the cut of meat; the pans you use; the heat you work with; and, of course, the judgment you exercise as you sauté, braise, boil, fry, gratinée. In setting down the recipes that follow, I have tried to anticipate many such choices and supply the kind of guidance that I would be ready to offer if I were standing by your elbow when you shop and cook. There are, however, three staple components of taste whose use suffers chronically from insufficient consideration, from a willingness to compromise, from improper handling, or, as is the case with salt, from fear. To these I hope to draw your extended attention.

OLIVE OIL

An olive oil snob I am not. I believe passionately in the equality, by which I do not mean interchangeability, of all good ingredients. There is no more room for intolerance in cooking than in anything else, and I am dismayed by the misguided attitude of those who champion olive oil over butter as though it were a cause. How do they make the sauces for their homemade pasta, I'd like to know, or the bases for most risottos? How do they gratinée anything? There is a place of honor for butter in Italian cooking and there is a large and significant one for olive oil. When it comes to buying butter, our choices are few and the differences negligible. In selecting an olive oil, however, the choices that we face are infinite, the information on which we base them regrettably inadequate, the differences crucial.

The taste of a dish for which you need olive oil will be as good or as ordinary as the oil you use. A sublime one can lift even modest ingredients to eminent heights of flavor; a dreary oil will pull the best ingredients down to its own level. Partial clues to the quality of the olive oil you are buying are supplied by the label and the price, but ultimately, the only way to determine which one, among those available, is right for you is to taste and compare.

Extra Virgin The very least you must ask of an olive oil is that it be "extra virgin," a double-barreled term. It is *virgin* when the olives' oil is extracted solely by cold mechanical pressure, unsullied by solvents or other chemicals. *Extra* refers to the percentage of free oleic acid it contains. *Free* means the acid has been knocked loose from its bond with other compounds in the oil by rough handling of the olives or the use of fruit that is damaged, well past its prime, or even partly spoiled. For an oil to qualify as extra, the percentage of free oleic acid must be less than 1 percent. The healthier the olives, the lower the free acid and, when the oil itself is of high quality—a most important "when"—the aromas and flavors that play such a significant role in those dishes where olive oil is present will be more clearly expressed.

Provenance Choosing would be so easy if extra virgin alone meant high quality. Unfortunately, it does not. Wherever you have a Mediterranean climate you can grow olives and make extra virgin oil, but only those olives grown on exceptional sites will yield exceptional oil. The quality of the olives, and consequently the quality of their juice, is an expression of the climate, altitude, soil, of the terroir, to use a wine term, in which they are produced.

The most richly endowed sites for growing fine olives for oil are in Italy. To the outside world, the best known of these are in the hills of central Italy, in Tuscany, but there are other equally qualified hills and plateaus, those overlooking the Italian Riviera or the shores of Lake Garda, the slopes of Umbria, the Sabine hills of Rome, Apulia's Andria rim, Abruzzi's Moscufo and Pianella zones, or up in the Hyblean altitudes above Syracuse in Sicily, all of whose groves can give birth to oils of great distinction.

Unhappily, our efforts to learn from the label the true territorial identity of the bottle's contents are likely to be fruitless. The overwhelming majority of Italian olive oils in the market, and certainly all the familiar brands with broad national distribution, come from large packers and shippers. The address on the label may carry the name of a town in Tuscany—Lucca, for example—or Imperia on the Riviera, because that is where the packer's plant is located, but most of the oil in the bottle may come from Apulia or even from Spain, Greece, or North Africa. Italy bottles considerably more oil than it grows olives for, but as long as the oil is processed and packed in the country it can be labeled "product of Italy."

A project is under way to establish officially recognized and guaranteed appellations of origin for up to a dozen major zones. High-quality producers from small subzones want to draw the boundaries of their districts as tightly as possible and, once their legitimate hopes are finally reconciled with the aims of the European Union, whose policies are formulated to benefit industrial-size plants and hence favor broad geographic areas, we shall have labels that will tell us if the oil is from Garda, the Riviera, Tuscany, and several other zones.

As I write, the most clearly documented Italian olive oils on the market are those of the Tuscan producers, virtually all of whom are also producers of wine, many of them with an international reputation. You must still read the label carefully, however, because the recognizable name of a Tuscan wine estate does not necessarily mean the oil is made from the estate's own olives. It may only mean they've packed it. To determine if the olives were grown by the same people who bottled the oil, look for one of these phrases preceding the producer's name: *Prodotto e Imbottigliato da*; *Imbottigliato all'Origine da*; *Prodotto dall'Azienda Agricola*; and occasionally in English, *Produced and Bottled by*. Remember, the words *Prodotto* or *Produced* standing alone without further qualification reveal absolutely nothing about the territorial origin of the oil.

PRICE You should be as careful about paying too little as about paying too much. Careful hand-harvesting of olives on hillside groves and getting them to the mill in pristine condition is, in a country with Italy's very high labor costs, the most expensive of agricultural undertakings. Some producers price their oil at cost orF a little over, simply out of respect for the cultural significance of a crop that has been a part of the history and landscape of Italy for at least 3,000 years. It's unlikely that you will find authentic Italian extra virgin oil with claims to better than average quality for less than $15 a ¾-liter bottle (about 24 ounces). For a choice oil of estate-bottled quality, $20 would probably be the lowest feasible price, and $30 would not be at all unreasonable.

Even at these prices, the cost of fine Italian olive oil is comparably less steep today than it used to be. Earlier in this century, when no other vegetable oils were in common use, olive oil in Italy cost five times the price of the equivalent weight of the choicest meat. Decades ago, when my father produced both excellent red wine and olive oil, he sold his wine for 10 cents a liter, and his oil for $1.50.

How do you justify using an oil that may cost $25 or more a bottle? Let us do some figuring. Assume you have yielded to temptation and have brought home a 1-liter bottle of olive oil that cost you $30. In 1 liter there are 72 tablespoons, each one of which costs you just under 42 cents. Every time you toss a salad or sauté spinach or make a tomato and garlic sauce or drizzle a few drops of oil over a bean soup or dress a grilled or steamed fish, for 42 cents a tablespoon you are bestowing priceless flavor on your dishes. Except for onion, garlic, parsley, or salt and pepper, no other ingredient you might be using costs you so little, and none delivers so much. Had you spent half as much for the oil, or even a third—and you should be wary of paying any less—you would have saved a few pennies, but lost an irreplaceable moment in your life in which to enjoy, in the dishes you bring to the table, the pleasure of fully achieved taste.

FILTERING   It is as true for oil as it is for wine that filtering strips it of some of the substances that carry flavor. Wines that are meant to develop in the bottle may profit from the presence of those substances, but unlike some wines, no olive oil gets better as it gets older. The dark vegetable water which, because of its weight, drops to the bottom of a bottle of unfiltered oil will eventually develop undesirable odors and befoul that oil. If you can get oil that is only a few months old, an unfiltered example will deliver fuller taste, but if it is much older, it is safer to choose one that has been filtered. If you have a bottle of very good, expensive oil that has thrown off a murky deposit, use the filtering method that one of my producer friends himself employs: Put absorbent cotton into a funnel and strain the oil through it into a clean, dry bottle.

COLOR   Except for the rare, very mild, spring-harvested Ligurian *biancardo*, no fine extra virgin oil is ever pale, but dark green is not necessarily the color of quality. Intensely green oils may acquire their hue through the unscrupulous addition of chlorophyll or through the use of a coarse, dark oil known as *verdone*.

AGE   New oil, *olio nuovo*, when it is less than a month old, has a distractingly scratchy, throat-searing taste that I don't prize. I like it when it is still lively, but after the initially rough edge has worn off. For me, oil is probably at its best between its third and sixth month. As it ages further it becomes mellower, and a sealed bottle kept in a dark, cool place will stay in good condition for a year or two. Exceptions are those oils from Liguria and from southern Italy that may be produced from ripe or overripe olives and that begin to turn rancid during their second year.

A few estate bottlers disclose the year of production on their labels. Most others give an expiration date that falls 18 months later, so you have to calculate backward to determine when it was made.

STORAGE Once you have started a bottle, use it up; it's not an heirloom to keep, no matter what it cost you. Keep it tightly closed when not using it, and away from the heat of the stove or the light from a sunny kitchen window. You may note from the photographs of my kitchen that I do keep my oil near the stove, but I use up a bottle in less than a week. Nonetheless, when I am not cooking, I cover it with a corrugated sleeve taken from a wine carton.

Unless you have a pizza shop, do not transfer the oil into one of those picturesque cans with a spout. They cannot be closed tight, so they accelerate rancidity. Do not keep olive oil in the refrigerator, because condensation will produce drops of water that contaminate the oil and make it rancid. Do not buy oil from a shop that keeps it in a show window or on a shelf under hot lights.

THE TASTE OF OLIVE OIL The character of an olive oil varies, reflecting the territory where the olives were produced. If you like somewhat bitter oil that prickles, scratches, that seems to explode at the back of your mouth as you swallow, you will enjoy some of the Tuscan oils, particularly when they have just been bottled. If you prefer a warm, creamy, intensely fruity sensation, your choice might be directed toward an Umbrian oil. If you respond to a sweet and delicate touch on the palate, you should reach for an oil made from *taggiasche* olives in Liguria, the Italian Riviera. If it is a graceful combination of fruit and elegant texture that satisfies you, you will find it in the rarer, but possibly most harmonious of all oils, the one from the shores of Lake Garda.

No one can dictate which oil you should use, because that is a decision only your palate can make, one of the many decisions that allow you to put your own stamp on your cooking. Try as many good oils at one time as you can handle, tasting them with your friends so that you may share equally in the discovery as well as the cost. Unless you want to slurp oil in your mouth, sucking in air, as professional tasters do, drizzle a few drops of each over a separate slice of warm boiled potato. You'll be astonished and pleased to find how clearly you can perceive the differences.

When you find an oil whose flavor really satisfies you, do as Italian cooks do at home, and stick to that one for all your olive oil needs, both for cooking and for salads. It makes no sense to clutter your kitchen cupboard with opened bottles of different oils which may well become rancid while waiting their turn to be used.

PARMESAN

"Parmesan" is the most carelessly used and imprecise term in the entire Italian culinary vocabulary. It refers to grating cheese, and it can be either the magnificent cow's milk cheese Parmigiano-Reggiano, or, unhappily more frequently, any hard cheese that you grate, not necessarily from Italy, and sometimes not even made of cow's milk.

Parmigiano-Reggiano

Parmigiano-Reggiano is made from the milk of cows that are raised in a small zone of northern Italy, most of it lying within the administrative limits of two provinces, those of Parma and Reggio Emilia in the Emilia-Romagna region. The unique properties of that environment lead to the production of cow's milk that, when made into cheese, ferments and ages like no other. At the end of an 18-month process, unchanged during the seven centuries in which it has been practiced, true Parmigiano delivers into the mouth the richest sensations of any hard cheese, immensely fragrant and deeply layered flavor with a bracing, faintly bitter backtaste like that of apricot or peach pits. It has unequaled melting properties that seamlessly bond the cheese to any ingredient with which it is cooked. When it is called for as a grated topping on risotto or pasta, it has an elevating effect comparable to that of an outstanding olive oil on vegetables and greens; the flavors of the dish appear to soar and expand, taking on force and volume. Nothing else you can use does it like Parmigiano-Reggiano.

Selecting Parmigiano-Reggiano   When there is a choice, ask that it be cut from the wheel, rather than taking a plastic-wrapped wedge of Parmigiano from the cheese case. The advantages for you are that the cheese you get will be fresher, and, moreover, you will be able to see the branded letters Parmigiano-Reggiano covering most of the rind, which guarantee its authenticity. You do not always find the letters on precut fragments, because some of them are cut from a portion of the wheel, the bottom or the top or one small section on the side, where the rind is never branded.

Look over the cheese you are about to buy. It should be a buttery, amber color, uniform throughout except for white speckles the cheesemakers call snowflakes. Look where the cheese meets its rind: You should find a gradual progression in color from the amber of the cheese to the tawny, leathery one of the rind. If the two are separated by a chalk-white band, the Parmigiano has been stored badly and is drying out. If the band is very broad, the cheese is seriously dehydrated and will taste dry and sharp.

Storing Parmigiano-Reggiano   The vitality of the cheese depends on moisture; when it loses moisture, it begins to die. A totally dried-out Parmigiano crumbles as though it were made of compacted sawdust. For that reason, never grate the cheese long in advance of using it. If you need to grate it an hour or two before working with it or serving it at table, keep it in a saucer or small bowl tightly covered with plastic film. It follows that you ought not to buy packaged grated cheese, unless you like the taste of sawdust.

If you have a conveniently located and reliable source of Parmigiano-Reggiano, don't buy more than you need on a short-term basis, and keep what you buy wrapped first in wax paper, then in heavy foil. Don't use plastic film, which suffocates the cheese, except for very brief periods. Store it on the bottom shelf of the refrigerator or in a vegetable drawer, if you have one to spare.

If your source of Parmigiano is hard to get to often, buy a large piece—4 or 5 pounds, say—and then cut it into several smaller chunks, every one with part of the rind attached and each sufficient to last you for a week or two of cooking. Slice off the corners to blunt them so they won't puncture the wrapping. Wrap each piece of cheese tightly with wax paper, fastening the paper with masking tape, then wrap it in heavy-duty aluminum foil. Store on the bottom shelf of the refrigerator or in the spare vegetable drawer. I have kept

Parmigiano wrapped thus for several months, but it is necessary to unwrap it and examine it after 3 weeks or so. If it is developing some chalky-white patches, moisten a piece of cheesecloth, wring it so that it is only slightly damp, then fold it around the Parmigiano, leaving no part of the cheese exposed. Run cold water over your hand and shake the water off over the cheesecloth. Wrap the cheese in foil and refrigerate for 2 or 3 days, then unwrap it, discard the cheesecloth, rewrap the cheese as described earlier with wax paper and aluminum foil, and return it to the refrigerator. Never freeze Parmigiano.

OTHER HARD CHEESES

Grana Padano. *Grana* is the generic colloquial Italian name for all hard grating cheese, Parmigiano-Reggiano included. Padano is a particular kind of *grana*. Like Parmigiano, it is made from cow's milk, but unlike its competitor, it is produced over a vast zone, embracing twenty-seven provinces in five northern regions. It is consequently far more variable in quality, a variability further accentuated by the two size formats that are permitted, whereas all Parmigiano wheels are of a size. With rare individual exceptions, Grana Padano is aged 12 months, 6 less than Parmigiano. Unarguably, Parmigiano-Reggiano is the richer and more complex cheese, but a good, fresh piece of Padano can be an acceptable, even if not equally satisfying, substitute for Parmigiano.

Pecorino Romano. *Pecora* is the Italian for sheep, hence pecorino is any cheese made from the milk of sheep; or, more precisely, ewes. A few pecorinos, in particular some of those produced in southern Tuscany and on the island of Sardinia, are in the front rank of whatever grouping one likes to make of the world's great table cheeses. Romano, with the sharpest bite of any hard grating cheese, is not among them.

Romano has a limited but attractive role when coupled with those pasta sauces that benefit from its piquancy. It is indispensable in *amatriciana* sauce, a little of it ought to be combined with Parmigiano-Reggiano in pesto, and it is often the cheese to use in olive oil–based sauces for macaroni and other factory-made pasta tossed with such vegetables as broccoli, rapini, and cauliflower.

As the name indicates, Romano was originally a product of the Roman countryside. The best examples of the cheese are still made there, and the outstanding maker is Sini

Fulvi, on the Via Cassia in the province of Viterbo. Today, however, most of the production takes place in Sardinia. Although Sardinians are happy to produce and sell Romano, it is at the bottom of the list of their preferred pecorinos. Eighty percent of the production is absorbed by the American market, a taste legacy from the early days of Italian-American cooking.

There is a splendid, hard Sardinian ewe's milk cheese known as *fiore sardo*, aged 12 months or more, which, unlike Romano, is cooked at low heat and salted very lightly. It deploys flavor no less potent than Romano's, but in a less barbed, more polished style.

SALT

The flavor of nearly all the ingredients we work with lies largely immobile within them, sluggishly waiting to be drawn out. Cooking clears the way for it to emerge, but the magnet, the driver that gets it moving out where our taste buds can capture it, is salt. Nothing is so necessary to the production of taste as salt.

The fear of salt has caused most of the dishes that are set before us to be inexpressive, to be dumb in flavor. To stave off boredom, cooks resort to the immoderate employment of strongly emphatic agents, such as herbs, spices, chilis, and garlic, which substitute their own flavor for that of the ingredients, defeating the care with which one has marketed and cooked. Salt, when used judiciously but confidently, does not replace the natural taste of the food you're cooking or the salads you're tossing, but causes it to bloom.

The magnetic power of salt also affects the intensity of color and the secretion of fluid. If you liberally salt the water in which you are cooking any green vegetable, that vegetable will emerge with a vivid and natural green hue. If you are making a pasta sauce in which the tomatoes are not cooked, sprinkle them with salt well in advance, and they will release a substantial and useful quantity of juice with which to coat the pasta. Conversely, when browning, boiling, or grilling meat, add salt later in the cooking to avoid the early loss of liquid that would make the meat dry. On the other hand, if you wait until the dish is on the table before salting it, the salt will not have time to dissolve evenly and there won't be a full flowering of flavor.

WHICH SALT? As the late Danny Kaye once said during a memorable class session, there are two kinds of salt, salty salt and not so salty salt. I use the salty kind, sea salt.

By the stove I keep two large-mouthed ceramic jars, one for fine salt, one for coarse. I use the coarse when I need a fistful of it to drop quickly into a pot of boiling water, whereas the fine I pinch between my fingertips so I can scatter it over the food, taking time to distribute it as evenly as possible. If you acquire a physical sense of quantity by salting with your hand or fingertips, you will learn to salt more accurately and the comfortable direct contact may help you overcome any lingering fear.

Even among sea salts, however, there are lesser and greater kinds. In the kitchen I use a pure Sicilian salt and at table, whenever a friend from England brings a box to Venice, the delicious Maldon salt from the North Sea. Look at the ingredients list on any box of salt you buy and make sure there are no additives.

Appetizers

APPETIZERS
Antipasti

———— ❧ ————

Crisp Cheese Wafers Friuli-Style

Sardinian Sheet Music Bread

Osimo's Easter Cheese Bread

Ligurian Soft Chickpea Focaccia with
Onion and Rosemary

Ligurian Raw Fava Bean Spread
(or Pasta Sauce)

Cooked-Down Onion for *Crostini*

Mara's Quick-Pickled Zucchini

Frittatas

Basil Frittata

Pancetta Frittata

Frittata with Potatoes, Onion,
and Rosemary

Savoy Cabbage Frittata

Red Bell Pepper Halves Stuffed with Tuna

Three Ways to Stuff Tomatoes

Baked Stuffed Tomatoes Bari-Style

Baked Tomatoes Stuffed with Salmon,
Garlic, and Capers

Baked Tomatoes Stuffed with Ham,
Green Olives, and Parmesan

Venetian-Style Liver Pâté

Savoy Cabbage Rolls with Pork, Rice,
and Spinach

Breaded Eggplant Balls with Mozzarella
Centers

Poached Fresh Tuna Marinated
with a Caper and Anchovy Sauce

Piedmontese Chicken Made Tuna-Style

Venetian-Style Sandwiches

Gorgonzola and Mâche Sandwich

Hard-Boiled-Egg Sandwich
with Anchovies and Capers

Celery and Ham Sandwich

Venetian Meat and Potato Balls,
Bacaro-Style

*Preceding photograph (left to right): Basil Frittata;
Onion Crostini; Venetian Meat and Potato Balls,
Bacaro-Style; Venetian-Style Sandwiches; and
Crisp Cheese Wafers Friuli-Style.*

In English, a word that starts with "anti" usually refers to something that counteracts or blocks or even demolishes what follows, such as antifreeze or antibiotic or antimissile missile. It is the same in Italian, but the language also employs that prefix more peacefully, simply to signify what goes "before," as in *antipasti*, because, as appetizers, you consume them before the *pasto*, the meal. *Antipasti* can be so—how else to put it?—so appetizing that, if one has indulged too well, and finds that they have occupied most of the room required to accommodate the principal courses to which they were meant to serve just as an introduction, one may feel that the other use of "anti" was indeed the one intended.

The appetite-snaring charm of *antipasti* is a tribute to the endless inventiveness of Italian cooks but no less to the skill of Italy's pork curers: Can anything set the juices flowing more copiously than a platter of salmon-pink prosciutto, or of salami from Varzi or Felino, or Venice's *soppressa*, Bologna's mortadella, Zibello's *culatello*, Parma's *coppa*, Bolzano's *speck*, and the olive oil–cured sausages of Tuscany or the wine-cured ones of Piedmont?

When you eat out in Italy, even the most modest trattoria will have a selection of *antipasti* available, which may be as simple as an assortment of good local cold cuts and homemade pickled vegetables. Venice's traditional wine bars serve nothing but *antipasti*, known as *cicheti*. There is a region, Piedmont, where the procession of little dishes with which the meal begins can easily overshadow the substantial courses that follow. A dozen or more of them used to be the standard offering in the restaurants of the beautiful Piedmontese wine country, whereas now three or four are considered as much as the modern diner has the stamina for.

At home, it is only on celebratory occasions—Christmas, Easter, an anniversary, or a birthday—that an Italian cook is expected to prepare a full-scale menu, from appetizers to dessert. The noon meal, the main one of the day in Italy, will omit appetizers and start with pasta or rice or soup. In the evening, however, one craves lighter fare, and what would be considered *antipasti* in a formal setting can become an ideal source of casual snacks that satisfy without being too filling.

Although the *antipasti* repertory has its roots in the once elaborate dining rituals of upper-class houses, I find it extremely useful to a contemporary cook. Because many of the dishes are served lukewarm or at room temperature, one or two of them are ideal for a simple summer lunch. Moreover, precisely because they can be done ahead of time and rarely need to be warmed up, they cannot be improved upon as party dishes, to be served with little fuss buffet-style.

You can put together a splendid party just with the dishes in this chapter. With drinks, when your guests arrive, you can offer *Frico*, the lacy cheese wafers from Friuli, and shards of the Sardinian Sheet Music Bread, *Pane Carasau*, seasoned as described in the recipe. Then set a table with the Basil Frittata, the Quick-Pickled Zucchini, any or all of the stuffed tomatoes, the Savoy Cabbage Rolls, the Piedmontese Chicken Made Tuna-Style, the Venetian-Style Liver Pâté, and a stack of the Venetian sandwiches, *tramezzini*. Also look into the salad chapter, where you'll find two of the most ravishing seafood salads ever, the one with oranges and shrimp on page 404, and the Sardinian Salad with Seafood and Couscous on page 406.

Most of the above would be a good choice for a light lunch or late-night supper, but you'll find specific recommendations throughout this chapter and in recipes elsewhere in the book identifying those dishes that are suitable in such contexts.

Crisp Cheese Wafers Friuli-Style

FRICO

½ teaspoon polenta flour

⅓ cup loosely packed
　grated Montasio cheese

*One 7- to 8-inch wafer for
2 persons*

A nonstick 9-inch skillet

Frico looks like old lace, but it is made of cheese, and it is wonderfully uncomplicated to do. The only component of the batter is grated cheese. No fat is required because the cheese, as it melts, supplies its own. You do need a little bit of polenta flour to keep the wafer from sticking to the pan.

The cheese that works best is Montasio from Friuli. It is a golden, firm cheese, vaguely resembling a fine Cheddar in taste. Should you be unable to find Montasio, use Parmigiano-Reggiano instead.

Serve *frico* with drinks if you are having a cocktail party, or as an appetite teaser when guests arrive, before they sit down for dinner or begin to help themselves from the buffet table.

1.　Turn the heat under the skillet to medium low and sprinkle ½ teaspoon of polenta flour into the pan.

2.　Immediately sprinkle ⅓ cup grated cheese over the polenta, distributing it evenly. Cook for 1½ to 2 minutes, running the edge of a spatula under the perimeter of the wafer as the cheese melts and hardens to loosen it from the pan.

3.　Remove from heat and let it settle for 1 minute.

4.　Using toaster tongs or a large tweezer and a spatula, lift the wafer from the skillet and turn it over. Return to heat for 1 more minute.

5.　Transfer the cheese wafer from the pan to a platter. If it should break it doesn't matter because you must break it up anyway to eat it.

6.　Before repeating the operation, wipe the skillet clean with brown butcher paper or paper towels.

AHEAD-OF-TIME NOTE: The wafers will keep crisp for a few hours, but they taste best the moment they are done.

Sardinian Sheet Music Bread

PANE CARASAU OVVERO FOGLI DI MUSICA

2½ cups semolina flour, often sold as pasta flour, plus more for sprinkling dough and work surfaces

1 cup plus 1 tablespoon lukewarm water

1½ teaspoons active dry yeast OR, if you wish to shorten rising time by about ½ hour, quick-acting yeast

¼ teaspoon sugar

1 tablespoon salt

---

16 wafer-thin round sheets of carasau bread

At least 1, preferably 2, large baking stones

A baker's peel (paddle) or a rimless baking sheet

The crackling, paper-thin, flavorful bread that Sardinians call *carasau*, "cooked twice," has many uses. In its native island, you will find it on every table, both at home and in restaurants. It will be offered to you plain, in full-size sheets, crisp and warm from the oven, or broken into shards and drizzled with a mixture of olive oil, chopped rosemary, chopped garlic, and cracked black pepper, or slivers of another Sardinian specialty, the luxuriously delicious dried mullet roe, *bottarga*, will be sandwiched between two irregular, cracker-size pieces of it spread with butter. It can even be cooked like pasta and served with a lamb *ragù* (see page 206).

I have never seen a good workable recipe for making *pane carasau* at home, either in Italian or in English, and I can't conceal my pleasure at having succeeded in developing one, a pleasure that I hope will be yours too when, by following the directions, you will have made it in your own oven.

The traditional bakers of the bread are the women of the Barbagia, a rugged, austerely handsome mountainous district of eastern Sardinia. I went there, to a village called Oliena, to watch them do it. Four or five women meet once a week at the house of one of the group who has a wood-burning oven. There they bake bread to sell to restaurants and shops as a source of small supplementary income. To produce enough to make it worth their while they start at midnight, fulfilling the quota they have set themselves shortly before noon.

Not counting the building of a blazing wood fire in the oven, there are five stages from the kneading of flour and yeast to the stacking of the finished circular sheets of bread. First, golden hard-wheat flour is kneaded with yeast and water into a ball and set aside to rise. By the time the last of the dough is kneaded, the first ball is ready to be rolled out into a thin disk—the second stage. At this point the oven is red-hot and the first disk is slipped in on a long-handled paddle—the third

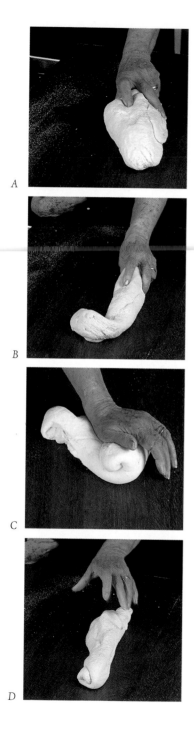

A

B

C

D

stage. On contact with the fiery brick oven floor, the disk swells into beach-ball size, the edge of the original disk forming a seam around its middle. Fourth, it is immediately retrieved and pulled apart at the seam to produce two circular sheets. When all the dough has gone through these four steps, the fire is banked, the heat of the oven is allowed to abate slightly, and then, one by one, the partly baked disks are placed on the oven's brick floor to toast briefly—the fifth stage.

It was obvious why this is called "twice cooked," but why "sheet music," *fogli di musica*? I asked. One woman replied that it was because of the snapping sound it made when you bit into it. Another came up with a lovelier explanation. When they used to work into the early evening to make great quantities of bread, there were stacks of it everywhere, even in the bedroom, waiting to be wrapped on the following day. After the family had gone to bed, the stacked, still tepid disks contracted as they felt the cool mountain air, making crackling "night music."

1. Put the 2½ cups flour, water, yeast, sugar, and salt in the bowl of a food processor. Run the steel blade for about 1 minute, until the ingredients combine into a soft, but not sticky mass. If portions of the dough are stuck to the processor's bowl, loosen them with a spatula to incorporate them into the mass. If the dough is not soft enough, add 1 more tablespoon of water, running the blade again briefly. The dough should be soft, but not so gummy that it sticks to your fingers.

2. Turn the dough out from the processor's bowl onto a work counter. If it is very soft and somewhat sticky, sprinkle a little flour over the counter. Knead the dough briefly with your hands (*photo A*), shaping it into an oblong, slightly tapered mass.

Pick up the mass, holding it by one of the tapered ends, lift it high above the counter, and slap it down hard several times (*photo B*), stretching it out in a lengthwise direction to a length of about 10 to 12 inches. Reach for the far end, fold the dough a short distance toward you, then push it away with the heel of your palm (*photo C*), flexing your wrist. Fold it and push it away again, gradually rolling it up and bringing it close to you. Turn it 90 degrees, reach once again for the far

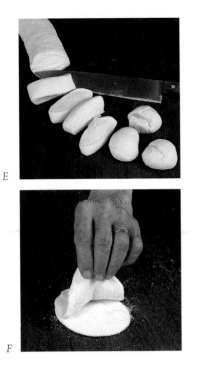

E

F

end, lift it up, and slap it down again on the counter (*photo D*). Then repeat the kneading motion with the heel of your palm and your wrist, bringing the mass close to you once more. After working the dough in this manner for 5 minutes, shape it into a salami-like roll, about 15 inches long and 2 to 2½ inches thick.

3. Divide the roll of dough in half, then divide each half into two, and continue thus until you have sixteen small, equal lumps (*photo E*). Shape each lump more or less evenly into a ball.

4. Sprinkle flour lightly over a surface, or if more convenient, over one or more trays where you can accommodate all the balls of dough, keeping them about 2½ to 3 inches apart. Cover the balls with one or more overturned large mixing bowls, using as many bowls as you may need to cover all of them. Allow the dough to rest for about 3 hours. It will rise to somewhat less than double its original volume.

5. At least 30 minutes before you are ready to bake, put the baking stone on a rack placed in the upper third of the oven. If you have two baking stones, put one on a rack placed in the lower part of the oven and the second one on a rack placed as high up in the oven as it will go. The two stones refract heat between them in a manner that approximates that of a brick oven. Turn the oven on at the highest baking setting your thermostat allows.

6. Dust a pastry board with flour, place one of the balls of dough on it, and using a rolling pin, thin it out into a flat disk about 4 inches in diameter.

7. Take another ball of dough and repeat the operation.

8. Sprinkle about ½ teaspoon of flour over one of the thinned-out disks, place the other one on top of it (*photo F*), and roll both disks out as one, more than doubling its diameter so that it is now over 9 inches wide. (Sardinian women slip a single sheet of dough into the oven, relying on the wood-burning oven's intense heat to puff it up. I devised the double-layer-of-dough method to achieve the same result in a home oven.)

(continued)

9.   Repeat the operation until you have used all the remaining dough. As you finish rolling out each double disk, slip it inside a folded dish towel or another cloth. Once covered by a towel, the disks can be stacked.

10.   Sprinkle very little flour on the baker's peel or the rimless baking sheet, remove one of the disks from the towel, place it on the wooden peel or metal sheet, and slip it into the very hot, preheated oven. Perform this step without keeping the oven door open too long, so as not to lose too much heat.

11.   Remove the dough after 1 minute and 20 seconds. It should swell up like an inflated ball (*photo G*). Although it is scalding hot, you must quickly pry apart at least a small section of the two sides at the edge to let all the hot air escape (*photo H*). Sardinian women use a paring knife to separate the edges of the two sheets of dough, but I have found it easier to trim away a sliver all the way around the edge using scissors. As soon as you can comfortably handle the hot dough, separate the two halves completely, helping yourself by using a knife to loosen them at those places where they are stuck together. Shake any loose flour away and stack them with what was their inner side facing up (*page 38*). Press them down lightly to flatten them.

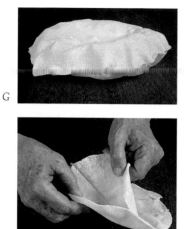

G

H

Alternate Baking Method: (*I discovered this more comfortable method by accident during the photography session.*) When you have removed the inflated ball of dough after the initial 1 minute and 20 seconds, do not open it yet. Wait 8 to 10 seconds, letting it deflate slightly, then return it to the hot oven for another 10 seconds. Remove it, and if it deflates again, return it to the oven after 8 to 10 seconds and bake it another 10 seconds. When you remove it, it should maintain its shape without deflating. Let it cool off until it is very comfortable to handle, and pry it apart. You may not even need scissors.

12.   After you have done three or four of the disks in succession (do not sprinkle more flour on the paddle after you have done it the first

time), wait a few minutes before doing more to let the oven's heat build up again to maximum.

13. When all the disks have been done and pried apart into separate rounds, turn the oven thermostat down to 325°. As soon as the oven's heat has fallen to 325°, place as many of the rounds inside as will fit on the baking stone(s) without overlapping. Toast them for 1 to 4 minutes until they have become crisp, remove them, and repeat the operation until all the bread has been done.

AHEAD-OF-TIME NOTE: When the bread has cooled down completely, it can be stored in a cardboard or tin box or even in a plastic bag. In a dry environment, it will keep perfectly for many months. In very humid climates, however, keep it no more than 1 month. Before using it, whether you are having it simply as a cracker bread or in one of the ways suggested in the introductory note to the recipe, crisp it in a 400° oven for approximately 5 minutes.

Osimo's Easter Cheese Bread

LA CRESCIA PASQUALE DI OSIMO

3¾ cups all-purpose flour

8 ounces (3 cups) freshly grated Parmigiano-Reggiano cheese

4 ounces (1½ cups) grated pecorino cheese (see headnote)

5 eggs

¼ cup extra virgin olive oil plus a little more for oiling the mold

1 teaspoon salt

Black pepper ground fresh

½ teaspoon granulated sugar

1 tablespoon active dry yeast

½ cup barely warm milk

8 ounces Swiss cheese, cut into ¼-inch dice, about 1⅔ cups

---

1 cylindrical loaf of Easter cheese bread

A 2-quart charlotte mold OR *an 8 by 3¾-inch springform* panettone *pan*

My husband and I accepted an invitation, one Easter, to spend the holiday weekend in Osimo with Carlo and Carla Latini, the producers of Italy's best-tasting spaghetti and other factory-made pasta. Osimo is in the heart of the Marches, a pastoral and hospitable land in central Italy that climbs up the Apennine mountain range on the west while it rolls out to the Adriatic shore on the east.

Every day of that Easter weekend at the Latinis' we had a delicious cheese bread called *crescia*, which we ate as an appetizer at table or snacked on in between meals. It looked as though it had been baked in a flowerpot, narrow at the base and expanding curvaceously at the top. I had no such container when I worked on it later at home, but I was satisfied with the results I obtained from using both a charlotte mold and a narrow, high springform pan used for making *panettone*, the Milanese Christmas cake.

The *crescia* tasted wonderfully cheesy and I saw that there were pieces of Swiss cheese distributed within it, but it also had the flavors of other cheeses that I learned were Parmesan and a local, mellow pecorino, sheep's milk cheese. The latter is considerably mellower than Romano, the one Italian sheep's milk cheese most commonly available in North America. If you have no alternative, use Romano, but if you can find either a good Tuscan *caciotta* firm enough to grate or *fiore sardo*, a Sardinian pecorino, both of which are less pungent than Romano, you should choose those.

My husband, Victor, who, with his morning espresso, prefers things that taste of salt rather than sugar, suggested we have *crescia* for breakfast, and it has proved very satisfying. It is also nice to serve before dinner with a glass of wine—Verdicchio if you want to do it in authentic Marches style.

1. Put the flour, Parmesan, pecorino, eggs, ¼ cup olive oil, salt, liberal grindings of pepper, and sugar into a food processor bowl.

2. Dissolve the yeast in the barely warm milk, then add it to the other ingredients in the processor. Run the metal blade for about a minute, until the dough masses into a large ball, or possibly several smaller balls.

3. Knead the dough by hand for a few minutes into a single smooth ball. Put it in a bowl covered with a slightly damp cloth, and let it rise in a warm corner of the kitchen for about 4 hours, until the dough has doubled in volume.

4. Preheat the oven to 425°.

5. Cut a wax paper disk to fit the bottom of the mold or springform pan, then thinly smear the bottom and sides of the mold or springform pan with oil.

6. Remove the dough from the bowl, put it on a work surface, and work the diced Swiss cheese into it, trying to distribute it as uniformly as possible. If some of the bits of cheese bulge through the surface of the dough it's no cause for worry.

7. Place the dough into the oiled mold or pan and bake in the pre-heated oven for about 50 minutes until it rises, mushroom-shaped, above the rim of the pan.

8. Let it settle for several minutes, but unmold it while it is still luke-warm, placing it on a cake rack to cool completely.

AHEAD-OF-TIME NOTE: The taste of this cheese bread is at its best the day it is made, but it is very good even 2 or 3 days later.

Ligurian Soft Chickpea Focaccia with Onion and Rosemary

FARINATA

2½ cups water

1 teaspoon salt

½ pound fine chickpea
flour, about 1⅓ cups

¼ cup extra virgin olive oil

⅓ cup very thinly sliced
onion, soaked in cold
water

1 tablespoon fresh
rosemary leaves stripped
from the branch

Black pepper ground fresh

---

8 to 10 appetizer portions

An 11 by 7 by 2-inch black
baking pan

When I am on the road in Italy, if no other indication were available, I could probably tell where I was by the local attitude to beans. If the overruling passion is for the cranberry bean to the exclusion of every other legume, I am in the northeast. If *cannellini* are the principal object of affection, it is Tuscany. If it is chickpeas that clamor for attention, I could be in various places, in the south, in Sicily, but my first guess would be Liguria, the Italian Riviera.

It is chickpea flour rather than the whole pea that two classic Ligurian preparations are based on, but they take it in divergent directions. One produces a warm, spoon-soft, polenta-like chickpea porridge, usually known by the name of *panissa* or *paniscia*. I have seen people stir into it sliced raw onion, sautéed mushrooms, or cut-up browned sausage. It ends up being an alternative to polenta, but a more laborious one to prepare, with less rewarding flavor. I much prefer *farinata*, which is like a thin, very soft focaccia, and is consumed more casually, either as a snack, as an appetizer with drinks, or at a buffet.

1. Put the water and salt in a mixing bowl. Pour the chickpea flour into the bowl, passing it through a strainer to eliminate any lumps in the flour. Add 2 tablespoons of olive oil and stir thoroughly with a fork or whisk. Let the mixture mature at room temperature for at least 4 hours, or even 6.

2. Preheat the oven to 350°.

3. Before you change the water in which the onion is soaking, squeeze the onion with your hand; this eliminates some of its sharp, milky fluid. Drain the onion into a strainer, refill the bowl with cold water, and drop the onion back into it. Repeat this operation three or four times during a 45-minute to 1-hour period. At the end, drain the

onion, transfer it to a small bowl, add 1 tablespoon olive oil, and stir to coat the onion evenly.

4. Add the rosemary leaves to the chickpea-and-water batter, distributing them uniformly.

5. Smear the bottom of the baking pan with the remaining tablespoon of olive oil. Pour the chickpea batter into the pan, leveling it off. Scatter the onion over the batter, distributing it as evenly as you can. Bake in the upper level of the preheated oven for about 40 minutes. The *farinata's* edges should turn brown and become crisp.

6. Remove from the oven, lift the *farinata* carefully out of the pan, cut into diamond-shaped pieces, and sprinkle with coarse ground black pepper.

AHEAD-OF-TIME AND SERVING NOTE: As the recipe indicates, you can and must complete step 1 several hours in advance. Once baked, the *farinata* tastes best while still warm from the oven, but it will continue to have good flavor for many hours, at room temperature. Don't keep it overnight. *Farinata* should be served as is, alone as a snack or with a glass of wine or as part of a larger selection of appetizers. It doesn't need any dressing up, but if you wish you can top it with a little *rucola*—arugula—or mâche or serve it along with a mixed green salad.

Ligurian Raw Fava Bean Spread (or Pasta Sauce)

MARÒ

1¼ pounds unshelled fava
  beans (see Note below)

2 tablespoons grated
  Romano cheese (see step
  2 below)

½ teaspoon very finely
  chopped garlic

⅓ cup extra virgin olive oil

1½ tablespoons freshly
  squeezed lemon juice

6 fresh mint leaves

Black pepper ground fresh

*About 1½ cups marò spread
or sauce*

If you are vacationing in an exquisitely romantic place, spending your days by a spectacular pool overlooking a picture-perfect harbor, what do you discuss with the terrifically good-looking, friendly pool attendant? If the place is Portofino on the Italian Riviera, and the pool belongs to a hotel called the Splendido, and the pool attendant happens to be Danilo Solari, the answer is: You talk about food; what else?

Danilo's overruling passion is the food of his native Liguria—the region whose jagged coast forms the Riviera. It's indeed a cuisine to fall for. No other cooks in the country have such a bold, high-spirited way of using vegetables and herbs and of making pasta sauces. It is cooking with an impish touch that combines dynamic contrasts of flavor with provocative aromas. Hard to resist, but who would want to?

We were talking about fava beans, the most alluring of fresh beans, regrettably limited to a short period in early spring. I love to use them in soup, or stewed with pork jowl in the Roman style, but what I most look forward to, when the season is at hand, are the first young, tender fava that I shell and eat raw, sprinkling them with a little coarse salt, and accompanying them with a choice Tuscan or Sardinian pecorino. Danilo agrees, but he asks: Have you ever used raw fava to make *marò*? I hadn't even heard of it, let alone made it. The following day Danilo brought me an old Ligurian recipe book from his collection, and there it was. And here it is.

Marò, a creamy emulsion of raw fava beans, cheese, garlic, and olive oil, can be used as an appetizer spread on crackers or bread; as a condiment for boiled meats, cold baked ham, or roast beef; as a dip for raw oysters; over steamed mussels; or as a pasta sauce. The density of the *marò* made from the recipe here is intended for use as a spread or dip. If used as a condiment, it should be loosened with a little more olive oil. If you want it on pasta, hold back some of the water in which you cooked the pasta and add a tablespoon or two to the *marò*, when tossing it with the pasta. A boxed factory-made dry pasta such as spaghettini, thin spaghetti, or fusilli would be the one to choose.

1. Shell the beans out of their pods and slip your fingernail or the tip of a small paring knife under the pale skin of each bean to peel it away. You should obtain about 1½ cups shelled and peeled beans.

2. Before proceeding, taste the grated Romano cheese. If it is exceedingly salty, reduce the quantity slightly. A Sardinian pecorino cheese of grating consistency such as *fiore sardo*, if it is available, is a mellower and desirable alternative to Romano.

3. Put all the ingredients into the bowl of a food processor and process to a creamy consistency.

NOTE: It's difficult to determine exactly how many beans a given weight of unshelled pods will yield because some thick and heavy pods may contain fewer beans than others. If you end up with more or less than 1 cup, adjust the proportion of the other ingredients accordingly.

SERVING SUGGESTIONS: As an appetizer or snack or with an aperitif, spread over rounds of grilled or toasted crusty bread. As a condiment, spoon over boiled meats or fish, or over cold sliced roast beef.

Cooked-Down Onion for *Crostini*

CROSTINI DI CIPOLLA

1 fresh, ripe, firm plum
tomato

4 cups very thinly sliced
yellow onion

2 tablespoons extra virgin
olive oil

Salt

⅛ teaspoon chopped chili
pepper OR to taste

4 or more basil leaves,
hand-torn into pieces

*Onion spread for 6 medium-size
crostini*

I'd love to be able to tell you that I found the recipe for these *crostini* in a fifteenth-century Florentine manuscript written backward, but the truth is that the history of the dish begins in my own kitchen. I had got carried away slicing onion and made a lot more than I needed for something I was cooking. I cooked it all anyway, and to the surplus I added some diced tomato and chili pepper, processed it to a creamy consistency, mixed in some basil, and I had onion spread.

The trick in cooking thin sliced onion like this is to cook it very slowly with salt in a covered pan. The salt causes the onion to release liquid, which in turn steams the onion, making it very soft. Stir from time to time, and eventually all the liquid will evaporate. When that happens, remove the lid from the pan and stir the onion until it becomes colored a very light nut brown. It may take between 25 and 30 minutes. This is a useful technique because you can use it in many dishes, including a pasta sauce made solely with onions.

1. Skin the tomato raw with a peeler. Cut it in half lengthwise, scoop out the seeds, then cut it into small dice.

2. Put the sliced onion, the olive oil, and some salt in a small pan; cover the pan and turn on the heat to low. Cook the onion down to a very soft, pale pulp.

3. Add the diced tomato and the chili pepper, uncover the pan, and cook for 10 more minutes, stirring occasionally.

4. Transfer the contents of the pan to a food processor, add the basil, and process to a creamy consistency.

SERVING SUGGESTION: Spread over rounds of crusty bread, which need not be toasted or grilled if one enjoys a tender consistency. The spread can be prepared hours in advance, but it tastes better at room temperature, or even still lukewarm, rather than refrigerated.

Mara's Quick-Pickled Zucchini

LE ZUCCHETTE SOTTACETO VELOCI DELLA MARA

1 pound young, very firm
    zucchini

3 garlic cloves, lightly
    mashed

⅓ cup extra-virgin olive oil

⅓ cup red wine vinegar

Salt

10 fresh mint leaves

4 to 6 portions pickled zucchini

It was Sunday morning at the farm that Mara and Maurizio Martin, of Venice's Da Fiore Restaurant, own on the mainland. We were going to have a barbecue, and as Maurizio was collecting the wood for the fire, Mara asked whether I'd like some pickled zucchini with the meat. "Sure," I said. "When did you make them?" "I haven't yet," she replied. Starting from scratch, she was, to my surprise, putting pickled zucchini on the table by the time her husband was putting meat on the grill.

1. Soak the zucchini for about 20 minutes in a basin of cold water and clean as described on page 162. After trimming away the ends, slice them lengthwise in half, then cut them into thin sticks, ¼ inch wide or less.

2. Put all the ingredients except the mint in a 10-inch skillet, turn the heat to low, and cook at very low heat for 30 minutes, until the vinegar has completely evaporated and the zucchini are tender but still somewhat firm.

3. Turn the contents of the pan into a bowl. Toss with the mint.

AHEAD-OF-TIME NOTE: Although you can eat the zucchini immediately, I must admit they are even better after 5 or 6 hours. They won't keep as long as regular pickles, but a week or more in the refrigerator does them no harm.

FRITTATAS

It's curious about the idioms we use: We rarely think to question their appropriateness. Inexplicably, eggs seem always to be associated with failure. Someone has a flop and you say he has laid an egg. Why should that be when nothing is so perfect as an egg? Italian has a similar expression—if you bungle whatever you are engaged in doing, you hang your head and say, "I've made a frittata." Yet, a frittata is one of the most popular things you can make in the kitchen, a sure fire hit.

It has been 25 years since I began teaching people how to make frittatas, and in the interim the word has entered English-language dictionaries. In looking back I find that among all the different frittatas in my previous books—with cheese, with all manner of vegetables, with spaghetti, even one that you cut into noodles and sauce and toss like pasta—two basic ones are missing. They are the classic summer one with basil and potatoes, and the Italian version of bacon and eggs, frittata con la pancetta. The time has come to remedy that oversight and, while I have the opportunity, I'm adding two new ones I've been making. There is a frittata with potatoes and rosemary that incorporates potatoes thin as chips cooked with onion, and a winter frittata I am particularly fond of, with Savoy cabbage.

If you haven't yet got around to making frittatas, let me repeat what I have said in the past: Their texture, their appearance, and the cooking procedure are quite unlike those of other types of omelets. Instead of being creamy or runny, they must be firm and set, although not to the point of being stiff and dry. They are never folded over into a thick, padded, tapered shape; they are flat, thin, open-faced, and round like the bottom of the pan in which they are made.

A traditional frittata is cooked very slowly on both sides. More acrobatic cooks than I cook it entirely over the stove flipping it in midair, like a flapjack. Others turn the pan over onto its lid and slide the frittata from the lid back into the pan. My own less dramatic method is to cook it in an all-metal skillet over the stove until the eggs are set and thick and it is runny only on top, then run the skillet briefly under the broiler, taking it out the moment the top side of the frittata has set, but before it has browned. I have also flirted with cooking it entirely in the oven, hoping this would spare me some of the concentration the over-the-stove method requires, but it is no use. The only way you get the thinness and consistency that make frittatas such a pleasure to eat is to do them on the stove.

Frittatas are as good at room temperature as when they are hot or just warm, but they are simply dreary when eaten cold out of the refrigerator. They make a lovely lunch when served with a good salad. Italians would have one at supper, having taken the larger meal at midday. When serving frittata as an appetizer, either at table or as part of a buffet, cut it like a pie, into wedges.

Basil Frittata

FRITTATA AL BASILICO

---

2 medium potatoes, about
¾ pound

2 tablespoons butter

⅓ cup chopped onion

4 eggs

Salt

Black pepper ground fresh

½ cup fresh basil, cut into
very thin strips

½ cup freshly grated
Parmigiano-Reggiano
cheese

---

*For 4 persons or, if served as a
small appetizer, for 8*

A 12-inch nonstick skillet with
a flameproof handle

1. Boil the potatoes with their skins on, drain when done, peel them, and puree them into a bowl using a food mill or a potato ricer.

2. Turn on the broiler.

3. Put two tablespoons of butter and chopped onion in a small skillet, turn on the heat to medium, and cook the onion, stirring from time to time, until it becomes colored a deep gold. Empty the contents of the pan over the potatoes in the bowl.

4. Lightly beat the eggs in a deep dish, then put them in the bowl with the potatoes. Add salt and pepper, and turn over the contents of the bowl with a fork and spoon to amalgamate them.

5. Add the basil and Parmesan and mix thoroughly once more.

6. Put 1 tablespoon of butter in a 12-inch nonstick skillet and turn on the heat to medium. Do not let the butter become colored, but as soon as it begins to foam, pour the egg and potato mixture into the pan. Turn the heat down to very low. When the eggs have set and thickened, and they are creamy only in the center of the pan, run the skillet briefly under the broiler. Take it out the moment the surface of the frittata has set, but not browned.

AHEAD-OF-TIME NOTE: You can prepare the frittata batter hours in advance, but not overnight. Cover the bowl with plastic wrap, and if cooking it much later, refrigerate.

Pancetta Frittata

FRITTATA CON LA PANCETTA

1 cup finely chopped
   pancetta

6 eggs

6 tablespoons freshly grated
   Parmigiano-Reggiano
   cheese

Salt

Black pepper ground fresh

1 tablespoon butter

---

*For 4 persons or, if served as an
appetizer, for 8*

A 12-inch nonstick skillet with
a flameproof handle

1. Turn on your broiler.

2. Put the chopped pancetta in a small skillet, turn on the heat to medium, and cook, stirring from time to time, until it becomes deeply colored and has shed much of its fat. Do not let it become crisp. Lift the pancetta from the pan using a slotted spatula in order to separate it from the liquefied fat, and put it into a bowl. Discard the fat in the pan.

3. Add the eggs, grated Parmesan, salt, and liberal grindings of pepper to the bowl and mix thoroughly with a fork or whisk.

4. Put 1 tablespoon of butter in a 12-inch nonstick skillet, turn on the heat to medium, and proceed to make the frittata following the directions for Basil Frittata on page 53.

Frittata with Potatoes, Onion, and Rosemary

FRITTATA CON LE PATATE, CIPOLLE, E ROSMARINO

½ pound potatoes

2 tablespoons extra virgin olive oil

2 medium or 1 large yellow onion sliced very thin, about 1 cup

Salt

½ tablespoon fresh rosemary leaves, chopped very fine

5 large eggs

Black pepper ground fresh

For 4 persons or, if served as an appetizer, for 8

A 12-inch nonstick skillet with a flameproof handle

1. Peel the potatoes, wash them in cold water, and slice them as thin as possible, potato-chip thin if you can. If you have a mandoline, this would be an appropriate use for it.

2. Put the olive oil and onion in a skillet, sprinkle with salt, and turn on the heat to low. Cook at low heat, turning the onion over occasionally, until it is very soft, but do not let it become brown.

3. Add the potatoes and the rosemary, turn over all ingredients three or four times, and cover the pan. Cook at low heat, turning the potatoes over from time to time, until they are tender, about 30 minutes.

4. Turn on the broiler.

5. While the potatoes are cooking, break the eggs into a bowl, add salt and several grindings of black pepper, and beat the eggs until the whites are indistinguishable from the yolks.

6. When the potatoes have become tender, pour the eggs into the skillet. Cook, uncovered, at very low heat. When the eggs have set and thickened, and they are creamy only in the center of the pan, run the skillet briefly under the broiler, proceeding as described in the directions for Basil Frittata on page 53.

Savoy Cabbage Frittata

FRITTATA DI VERZA

---

4 to 6 Savoy cabbage leaves,
  depending on their size

Salt

2 tablespoons extra virgin
  olive oil

1 tablespoon very finely
  chopped garlic

5 large eggs

Black pepper ground fresh

---

*For 4 persons or, if served as an
appetizer, for 8*

A 12-inch nonstick skillet with
a flameproof handle

1.   Wash the cabbage leaves in cold water. Bring a pot of water to a boil, add salt, and put in the cabbage leaves. Cook at a moderate boil until tender, then drain. As soon as they are cool, chop them fine.

2.   Turn on the broiler.

3.   Put the oil and the garlic in the skillet, turn on the heat to medium, and cook the garlic, stirring frequently, until it becomes colored a pale gold.

4.   Add the chopped cabbage, turn it over several times to coat it well, cook for 2 or 3 minutes, then turn off the heat.

5.   Break the eggs into a bowl, beat them with a fork until the whites are indistinguishable from the yolks, then transfer the cabbage to the bowl. Add liberal grindings of black pepper. (Do not clean the skillet.) Turn the contents of the bowl over several times to combine the cabbage and beaten eggs into a well-integrated mixture.

6.   Empty the bowl into the skillet, and cook, uncovered, at very low heat. When the eggs have set and thickened, and they are creamy only in the center of the pan, run the skillet briefly under the broiler, proceeding as described in the directions for Basil Frittata on page 53.

Red Bell Pepper Halves Stuffed with Tuna

PEPERONI ROSSI FARCITI DI TONNO

2 large red bell peppers

Salt

4 ounces tuna packed
　Italian-style in olive oil,
　drained

¼ pound unsalted butter

2 teaspoons cognac or other
　grape brandy

4 stuffed pepper appetizers

In the wine districts of Piedmont in Italy's northwest corner, hospitable tables are laid with a great variety of appetizers, among which figures one version or another of stuffed peppers. Unlike conventionally hollowed-out and stuffed whole peppers, these are roasted, peeled, and flattened into broad fillets that are exceptionally luscious because they have been peeled. The fillets are folded over the stuffing, enclosing it in a kind of pouch. Like Piedmontese and other Italian cooks, I rarely use the oven's broiler.

If You Have Gas

1. Place the peppers directly over the gas burner or over a grill made specifically for cooking over gas burners.

If You Don't Have Gas

Light the broiler of your oven and when it is hot, place the peppers on the grilling pan under it, rather close to the source of heat.

　Whichever method you use, roast the peppers until the skin is blackened on one side, then turn them with tongs. Keep turning until the skin is charred all over. Cook them as briefly as possible to keep their flesh from becoming too soft. When all the skin is charred, put them in a plastic bag, twisting it tightly shut, and as soon as they are cool enough to handle, pull off the charred peel with your fingers.

2. Cut the peeled peppers in two, lengthwise, completely flattening them. Remove stems, core, and seeds; pat dry with paper towels.

3. Put the tuna, butter, and cognac in a food processor and whip to a creamy consistency. Remove the mixture from the bowl and divide into four equal portions.

4. Place the four flattened pepper halves on a serving dish, their inner side facing up. Spread one portion of the tuna mixture over half the surface of each halved pepper, then fold the uncoated remaining half over it. Serve at room temperature.

THREE WAYS TO STUFF TOMATOES

There are other vegetables—peppers, zucchini, mushrooms, eggplant—that can take up the role of container for various stuffings. But none, I think, does it so gracefully as the tomato. Its own flavor is forward enough to play a significant part, yet it concedes full expression of character to the stuffing. The recipes that follow illustrate three aspects of tomato's versatility.

My mother, who died at 101 in 1996, liked her food to be tasty and she was lucky that Romana, her companion, was able to provide it. Romana is from Bari, in Apulia, and the first of the stuffed tomatoes is hers. There is nothing shy about the components of the stuffing—anchovies, capers, oregano—whose depth of flavor and prominent fragrance clearly deliver a stimulating southern message, tempered by the sweetness of the onion and brought into harmony by the juicy tomato flesh that wraps it up.

Salmon, the principal ingredient of the recipe that follows Romana's, is certainly not indigenous to any Italian region. Until not too long ago, fresh salmon was a rare and expensive item in the market, and most of the salmon that ended up on Italian tables was tinned, a sad thing to do to the noble fish and to one's palate. More recently, farming in Norway has made salmon plentiful and inexpensive, exceeded in price by many locally caught fish. Like most Italians, I love fresh salmon, and I particularly like the way it adapts itself to preparations with a recognizably Italian flavor that here is provided by the capers, olive oil, and garlic. This is one of the most richly satisfying ways to stuff tomatoes I have found. It begs for special attention and, although it would certainly dignify a buffet table, it is worth serving as part of an elegant sit-down seafood dinner or even alone, as a light single-course meal.

The ham and the Parmigiano-Reggiano in the third recipe give it away as representative of a northern approach. The style is that of Mantua, a corner of Lombardy whose cooking is closer to that of Emilia-Romagna than to its own region's. The flavors are certainly full-blown, but expressed with delicacy.

NOTE: Unless you are making tomato juice, don't squeeze a tomato. To remove the seeds, scoop them out gently with a small spoon.

Baked Stuffed Tomatoes Bari-Style

POMODORI FARCITI ALLA BARESE

8 medium fresh, ripe, firm, round tomatoes

¼ cup extra virgin olive oil plus a little for smearing the baking pan

⅓ cup chopped onion

6 flat anchovy fillets, preferably the ones prepared at home as described on page 148, chopped to a pulp

½ cup fine, dry, unflavored bread crumbs

1 tablespoon chopped capers

½ teaspoon chopped oregano

2 tablespoons chopped Italian flat-leaf parsley

Salt

Black pepper ground fresh

---

8 appetizer portions or 4 servings as a light lunch

1. Turn on the oven to 400°.

2. Wash the tomatoes. Using a serrated knife or sharp paring knife, slice the top of each tomato, but do not cut it completely off: Leave one end still connected to the bottom by the skin so that it will function as a lid, with the skin its hinge. Hollow out the tomato bottoms, removing the seeds and core. Place them in a pasta colander, turning them cut side facing down, to let all the runny juices drain away.

3. Put 3 tablespoons of olive oil and all the chopped onion in a small skillet, turn on the heat to medium high, and cook the onion, stirring from time to time, until it becomes colored a light gold.

4. Turn the heat down to very low and put in the chopped anchovies, stirring with a wooden spoon until they dissolve.

5. Transfer the contents of the skillet to a small mixing bowl; add the bread crumbs, chopped capers, oregano, and parsley. Turn over all ingredients to blend them into a uniform mixture. Taste and correct for salt, taking into account that the tomatoes have not been salted, and add several grindings of pepper. Stir thoroughly once again.

6. Retrieve the tomatoes from the colander, stuff them with the anchovy and caper mixture, drizzle over it the remaining tablespoon of oil, and close the tomatoes with their own top.

7. Thinly smear the bottom of a baking dish with olive oil, put in the tomatoes, and bake in the upper middle level of the preheated oven for 30 to 40 minutes, depending on the size and wateriness of the tomatoes. They are done when some of the juices have evaporated and the flesh is fully cooked. Serve lukewarm or at room temperature. Do not refrigerate before serving.

AHEAD-OF-TIME NOTE: You can make the tomatoes just long enough in advance for them to cool to room temperature.

Baked Tomatoes Stuffed with Salmon, Garlic, and Capers

POMODORI AL FORNO FARCITI DI SALMONE

1 tablespoon capers,
    preferably packed in salt

1 pound salmon

3½ tablespoons extra virgin
    olive oil

1 tablespoon chopped
    Italian flat-leaf parsley

1 teaspoon very finely
    chopped garlic

2 tablespoons fine, dry,
    unflavored bread crumbs

Salt

Black pepper ground fresh

Two large ripe, firm
    tomatoes, weighing
    approximately ¾ pound
    each

4 individual appetizer servings

1. Drain the capers if packed in vinegar; soak, rinse, and drain if packed in salt; then chop them fine.

2. Turn the oven on to 400°.

3. Remove the salmon's skin, remove any loose membranes, and carefully pick out all bones. Cut the fish into very small dice and put it in a bowl together with 2½ tablespoons of olive oil, the chopped parsley, garlic, capers, 1 tablespoon of bread crumbs, salt, and several grindings of black pepper. Toss thoroughly.

4. Wash the tomatoes, cut them in half horizontally, scoop out all the seeds and the centers to make a cup-like hollow. (If you are cooking anything else that day or the next that calls for fresh tomatoes, use the scoopings in the recipe.)

5. Pat the inside of the tomatoes with paper towels to soak up excess juice, then stuff them with the salmon mixture, pressing it down lightly as you do so. There should be enough to form a mound. Sprinkle the tops with the remaining bread crumbs and drizzle with the remaining olive oil, holding back a few drops to smear the bottom of a baking pan.

6. Place the tomatoes on the baking pan and bake in the upper level of the preheated oven for 35 minutes or until the salmon stuffing has formed a light golden crust. Serve not piping hot, but lukewarm. They are also good later, at room temperature, but not reheated.

Baked Tomatoes Stuffed with Ham, Green Olives, and Parmesan

POMODORI AL FORNO FARCITI DI PROSCIUTTO COTTO E OLIVE VERDI

6 medium-large ripe, firm, round tomatoes, about 3 inches across

2 ounces boiled, unsmoked ham, chopped fine, about ½ cup

⅓ cup very finely chopped onion

12 green olives, pitted and chopped fine

2 tablespoons chopped Italian flat-leaf parsley

⅔ cup freshly grated Parmigiano-Reggiano cheese

5 tablespoons extra virgin olive oil

Salt

Black pepper ground fresh

2 tablespoons fine, dry, unflavored bread crumbs

12 appetizer portions or 6 if served as a first course or as a light summer luncheon course

1. Turn on the oven to 400°.

2. Wash the tomatoes and cut them in half across their width. Scoop out the seeds with a teaspoon to partly hollow out the tomatoes. Do not squeeze them. Place them, cut side up, on a baking pan large enough for them to fit in one layer, snugly if necessary but without overlapping.

3. Combine in a small bowl the ham, chopped onion, olives, parsley, grated Parmesan, 4 tablespoons of olive oil, salt, and very liberal grindings of pepper and mix the ingredients thoroughly with a fork.

4. Stuff the hollowed tomatoes with the ham and olive mixture, distributing it evenly among them. It is all right for it to form a mound. Sprinkle the bread crumbs over the stuffed tomatoes and trickle the remaining tablespoon of olive oil over them. Bake in the upper level of the preheated oven for about 30 to 35 minutes until the tops of the tomatoes become colored a very light brown. Serve while still warm, but not piping hot.

AHEAD-OF-TIME NOTE: You can bake the tomatoes several hours in advance. Reheat in a 350° oven until just lukewarm.

Venetian-Style Liver Pâté

PATÉ DI FEGATO ALLA VENEZIANA

---

3 medium onions, sliced very thin, about 3 cups

Salt

1 pound calf's liver

Black pepper ground fresh

8 tablespoons (1 stick) butter, softened to room temperature and cut up

---

10 or more appetizer portions

A 4-cup loaf pan or other container of no smaller capacity

If you want to serve the pâté in Venetian style, make some polenta ahead of time, cut it into thin slices when it is cold, then grill or fry the slices to accompany the pâté. Good plain toast is fine too.

1. Choose a medium nonstick skillet. Put in the sliced onions and a little salt. Turn the heat to very low, and cover the pan. Cook for 30 or more minutes, turning the onion over from time to time, until it is greatly reduced in bulk and its consistency becomes creamy. Do not let it become colored. Should you find it getting darker as it cooks, add 1 or 2 tablespoons of water.

2. While the onion is cooking, trim the liver of its tough membrane and any tubes. Sometimes the membrane pulls off easily; other times you have to slice it away. Cut the liver into pieces more or less 2 inches by 1 inch. The pieces can be irregular in size, but not wildly so.

3. When the onion has become very soft, uncover the pan, turn the heat up to medium high, and add the cut-up liver, with salt and very liberal grindings of black pepper. Cook for little more than 2 minutes, turning the liver pieces over at least once.

4. As soon as the liver is done, put it with the onions into the bowl of a food processor. Add the cut-up softened butter and run the steel blade of the processor until the mixture reaches a smooth, uniformly creamy consistency.

5. Line the loaf pan or other container with plastic wrap and fill the pan with the liver pâté, leveling it off. Cover with more plastic wrap, patting it down to make it adhere to the pâté's surface. Refrigerate for at least 6 hours. To serve, remove the plastic wrap on top of the pâté, invert the pan onto an oval or rectangular platter, and lift it away.

AHEAD-OF-TIME NOTE: The pâté keeps perfectly, if refrigerated, for a full week.

Savoy Cabbage Rolls with Pork, Rice, and Spinach

INVOLTINI DI VERZA

12 whole Savoy cabbage
　　leaves

1 pound fresh spinach

Salt

¼ cup rice

2 tablespoons extra virgin
　　olive oil

10 ounces boneless pork
　　loin, sliced thin

2 tablespoons finely
　　chopped onion

2 tablespoons finely
　　chopped carrot

1 teaspoon chopped
　　rosemary leaves

Black pepper ground fresh

1 egg yolk

⅛ teaspoon grated nutmeg

¾ cup freshly grated
　　Parmigiano-Reggiano
　　cheese

3 tablespoons butter

---

*12 Savoy cabbage bundles,
serving 6 as an appetizer, or 4
as a light luncheon course*

A 13 by 9-inch baking dish

This simple dish offers a passing glimpse of a noble tradition and of the talents of a great cook. The cook is Lidia Alciati, whose husband Guido presides over the restaurant that bears his name. Guido's is in the Piedmontese castle town of Costigliole d'Asti, just north of Alba, and has long deservingly enjoyed the reputation of offering Piedmont's supreme dining experience.

1. Gently wash the Savoy cabbage leaves without breaking them, and drop them into boiling salted water. Retrieve them as soon as they become tender enough to be pliable, and set them aside.

2. Detach any tough, thick stalks from the spinach, then wash the spinach in a basin, refilling it with many changes of clean, cold water.

3. Bring about 1½ cups of water to a boil in a small saucepan, add salt and the rice. Drain as soon as rice is tender.

4. Put the olive oil in a medium skillet and turn on the heat to medium high. When the oil is hot put in the pork slices and brown them on both sides. Add the chopped onion, carrot, and rosemary, some salt and pepper, and turn the heat down to medium. Cook until the carrot and onion are very tender, then add the spinach.

5. When the spinach becomes tender, turn the contents of the pan over onto a cutting board and chop very fine. You may opt to use the food processor, but do not overprocess. The consistency should be that of chopped, not pureed, ingredients.

6. Put the mixture into a bowl; add the cooked rice, the egg yolk, nutmeg, and ½ cup of Parmesan; and mix thoroughly.

7. Turn the oven on to 400°.

8. Spread the cabbage leaves out flat on a work counter. If all twelve won't fit on your counter, do it in two or more stages. The side of the leaf from which the central rib protrudes should be facing up. With a sharp knife, shave away the thickest part of the rib from each leaf without cutting into and damaging the leaf itself. Then turn the leaves over.

9. Divide the pork and spinach mixture into 12 equal mounds. Place a mound onto the center of each cabbage leaf, then fold the leaf's edges over the center, envelope-fashion. You should obtain flat bundles with sides about 3 inches long, and 1½ to 2 inches thick.

10. Lightly smear the baking dish with ½ tablespoon butter and put the cabbage bundles into it, the side with overlapped edges facing down. Sprinkle the remaining grated Parmesan on top and dot with remaining butter. Bake in the upper tier of the preheated oven for 20 to 25 minutes. Allow the rolls to cool slightly before serving.

Breaded Eggplant Balls
with Mozzarella Centers

PALLINE DI MELANZANA E MOZZARELLA

3 medium eggplants, about
1½ to 2 pounds

Salt

⅓ cup freshly grated
Parmigiano-Reggiano
cheese

¼ cup Italian flat-leaf
parsley, chopped very
fine

2 eggs

Black pepper ground fresh

¼ cup fine, dry, unflavored
bread crumbs plus 1 cup
spread on a plate

1½ tablespoons flour

3 ounces mozzarella, cut
into 1-inch cubes, about
1½ cups

Vegetable oil

For 4 persons

When I wait at the hairdresser or in a doctor's office I always turn to the culinary columns in the Italian women's weeklies that are stacked on the table, but it takes a long wait to come across something appealing. I found this variation on the classic combination of eggplant and mozzarella intriguing, and I thought it worth working on.

When you use eggplant in a composed dish, it is usually fried first, but here it is baked, a somewhat simpler operation. You grind the baked eggplant flesh and mix it with egg, Parmesan, and bread crumbs. This mixture is then formed into balls and mozzarella is inserted in the center. The balls are then breaded and fried and make quite a delicious mouthful.

1. Wash the eggplants and cut them into slices ½ inch thick.

2. Set a pasta colander over a bowl and begin lining it with eggplant slices. When you have covered the inside of the colander with one layer of eggplant, sprinkle it liberally with salt, and continue thus using all the eggplant. Let it steep for 30 to 40 minutes.

3. Turn on the oven to 350˚.

4. Pat the eggplant slices dry with a kitchen towel and spread them on a baking sheet or in a shallow baking pan large enough to accommodate them in a single layer without overlapping. Place the pan in the upper level of the preheated oven and cook for about 40 minutes until the eggplant is tender and dry.

5. Chop the eggplant, using the food processor if you like, but taking care not chop it too fine. Put it in a bowl; add the grated Parmesan, chopped parsley, one egg, liberal grindings of pepper, and the ¼ cup of bread crumbs; and mix thoroughly.

6. Break the remaining egg into another bowl, beat it well, then beat the flour into it a little at a time to obtain a smooth batter.

7. Shape the eggplant mixture into spherical patties just slightly smaller than a Ping-Pong ball. Bury a piece of mozzarella in the center, making sure it is completely covered by eggplant. Turn the balls one at a time in the egg batter, then roll them over the bread crumbs in the plate.

8. Pour enough oil in a medium-size skillet to come at least ½ inch up the sides of the pan, and turn the heat on to high. As soon as the oil is hot—a dab of batter dropped into it should sizzle and float instantly—slip in as many of the breaded eggplant balls as will fit without crowding the pan. As soon as they have formed a golden crust all over, retrieve them with a slotted spoon or spatula and place them on a rack or on a platter lined with paper towels. Proceed thus until you have fried all the eggplant balls. Serve piping hot, or lukewarm, or even at room temperature.

AHEAD-OF-TIME NOTE: You can complete the preparation through to the end of step 7 two or three hours ahead of time, but do not put the breaded eggplant balls in the refrigerator.

Poached Fresh Tuna Marinated with a Caper and Anchovy Sauce

TONNO ALLA MODA DEL VITELLO TONNATO

---

1 celery stalk

1 medium carrot, peeled

½ medium onion, peeled

¼ cup wine vinegar

Salt

1 pound fresh yellowfin tuna, cut into 1-inch steaks

1 teaspoon very finely chopped garlic

2 to 3 flat anchovy fillets, chopped very fine

2 tablespoons chopped capers

¼ cup freshly squeezed lemon juice

⅓ cup extra virgin olive oil

1 teaspoon mustard

Black pepper ground fresh

For 4 persons as a full course, for 8 as an appetizer

Are you familiar with what is easily the greatest of all Italian cold dishes, *vitello tonnato*? It is composed of poached veal sliced quite thin and layered lasagne-style, each successive layer of veal covered with a sauce made of canned tuna (packed in olive oil), mayonnaise, anchovies, and capers. It must marinate at least 24 hours, during which time the flavors of tuna and veal interpenetrate, each dissolving into the other, and producing something that is like no other dish of meat or fish in its tenderness and sweetly piquant taste. (The recipe is in my previous book, *Essentials of Classic Italian Cooking*.)

Finding myself at John Haessler's splendid seafood shop in Long Island's Hamptons at a moment when a side of fresh yellowfin tuna was being sliced, I decided to use the principles of *vitello tonnato* to glorify not a piece of veal, but the tuna itself.

At home I cooked the tuna in a vegetable broth, taking care to cook it briefly and gently so that it would not dry out, which is the fate of overcooked fresh tuna. I prepared a little sauce with olive oil, garlic, anchovies, capers, lemon juice, and mustard. I cut the tuna into domino-shaped pieces, spread the sauce over them, covered the dish tightly with plastic wrap, and left it out to try at dinner, 8 hours later. The tuna was as I had hoped, nearly melting in its tenderness and its taste breezily fresh, lightly piquant, and appetizingly fragrant. Once we started nibbling, it was difficult to hold back. But hold back we did because I wanted to see if, like *vitello tonnato*, it would improve after a day or two in the refrigerator. In fact a similar exchange between the tuna and its condiments took place, and it became an even more perfectly integrated dish. Please, don't eat it icebox cold but at the comfortable temperature of a not-too-warm dining room or a pleasantly ventilated patio.

1. Choose a sauté pan or other shallow broad pan that can accommodate the vegetables and the fish. Put in the celery, carrot, onion, vinegar, a pinch of salt, and enough water to cover the fish later. Turn on the heat to medium high, cover, and boil the water for 10 minutes.

2. Put in the tuna steak; when the water resumes boiling adjust heat so that it simmers gently, set a cover on the pan, and cook for 8 minutes.

3. While the fish is cooking, put in a bowl the chopped garlic, anchovies, and capers, the lemon juice, the olive oil, the mustard, salt, and liberal grindings of black pepper. Beat and stir with a fork to combine all ingredients smoothly.

4. When the tuna is done, retrieve it with a slotted spoon or spatula, pat it dry with kitchen towels, and cut it into slices 1½ inches long.

5. Choose a deep glass or ceramic dish, either rectangular or square, that can contain the tuna in a single layer without overlapping. Lightly smear the bottom of it with some of the caper and anchovy mixture. Put in the tuna slices, laying them flat in a single layer, and cover them with the remaining caper and anchovy sauce, spreading it smoothly with a spatula. Cover with plastic wrap. Leave at room temperature and serve 6 to 8 hours later. It is even better if refrigerated and served 1 or 2 days later. Always return it to room temperature before serving.

AHEAD-OF-TIME NOTE: It may be kept refrigerated for 4 to 5 days.

Piedmontese Chicken Made Tuna-Style

TONNO DI POLLO ALLA PIEMONTESE

A 3-pound chicken

1 carrot

1 celery stalk

1 potato, peeled

1 medium onion, peeled

1 medium fresh, ripe
 tomato OR 1 canned
 Italian plum tomato

The stems only of 3 or 4
 Italian flat-leaf parsley
 stalks

Salt

2 dozen whole black
 peppercorns

4 whole bay leaves

½ cup extra virgin olive oil

3 heads Belgian endive

⅔ cup shredded radicchio,
 preferably the elongated
 Treviso variety

1 teaspoon red wine vinegar

Balsamic vinegar, 1
 teaspoon if of rare
 tradizionale quality, 1
 tablespoon if of good
 commercial grade

---

*For 6 persons as an appetizer,
for 4 as a summer luncheon
course*

In the town of Alba, the capital of the Langhe, the Piedmontese district that produces Italy's most profound red wines, there is a marvelous casual trattoria, Osteria dell'Arco, where producers hang out. The wine list is, as one might expect considering who their patrons are, extensive, but the menu is short. It changes weekly or monthly at the whim of the chef, always featuring three or four traditional dishes that are rarely well known beyond Piedmont.

When dining out in Piedmont one is always torn between yielding to the temptation of the appetizers in which the cuisine excels and the desire to leave room for the other courses. On the day, however, when the Osteria listed as an appetizer a dish described as *tonno di gallina*, which translates literally as "tuna of chicken," I was too intrigued to pass it up. I am so glad I didn't.

The idea behind the dish is to work with chicken as though it were a piece of fresh tuna that you boil and pack under very good olive oil, something Italian cooks used to do at home before they became lazy and started buying commercially canned tuna. Although it is considered an appetizer in Piedmont, I find it quite suitable as an entrée for a light summer lunch, a refreshing departure from standard chicken salads. If you want to save the chicken broth, freeze it. Exactly the same procedure can be applied with great success to boned rabbit.

1. Wash the chicken thoroughly inside and out under cold running water.

2. Into a pot that can later hold the whole chicken covered by water, put 3 to 4 quarts of water and the carrot, celery, potato, onion, tomato, and parsley stems;

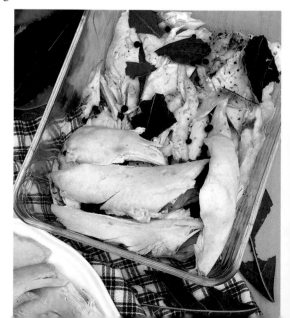

bring to a boil. When it has boiled for 15 minutes, put in the chicken.

3. When the chicken has boiled for 30 minutes, add salt. Cook until the flesh can be lifted easily from the bone, testing one of the legs, but not so long that flesh and bones come apart by themselves.

4. Drain when done, and as soon as it is cool enough to handle, strip away the skin and detach the flesh from the bone, taking care not to break up the meat too much.

5. Put a layer of chicken, starting with the breast, into the bottom of a 3-inch-deep, 5-inch-wide, 7-inch-long ceramic or glass dish—sprinkle with salt, scatter over some peppercorns, a bay leaf, and cover with olive oil, making sure that there is enough oil left to cover the top layer. Repeat the operation using all the chicken. Cover the dish with its own tight-sealing lid, if it has one, or with plastic wrap, and put it in the refrigerator for at least 3 days or up to a week.

6. Return the chicken to room temperature before assembling the salad. Cut the endive into thin strips and put it on a serving plate together with the shredded radicchio. Toss with salt, some of the oil from the dish containing the chicken, and the wine vinegar. Distribute the chicken over the salad greens, discarding the peppercorns and bay leaves. Moisten the chicken lightly with some more of the oil from the dish. Sprinkle the balsamic vinegar over it and serve.

NOTE: Do not discard the oil remaining in the dish, because it can be reused should you wish to make the chicken again within 2 weeks' time. Transfer the oil to a jar with a lid. Tightly close the jar and refrigerate, but for no longer than 2 weeks because after that off-odors may develop.

Tramezzino—which can be translated as "a little something held in between"—was a term coined in Venice to replace the foreign word "sandwich." But a *tramezzino* is a particular kind of sandwich whose most distinctive characteristic is that it is soft: Soft is the white bread and soft is the filling.

Each *tramezzino* is actually the triangular half of a sandwich cut diagonally, its cut side turned to expose the filling bulging in the center. Nearly every café and wine bar in Venice makes

tramezzini, displaying them in stacks. They are often found served thus at the smart parties in the palazzi, showing their stuffing to spare guests the unpredictability of a blind choice.

The filling varies with the fancy of the maker. It can be composed of prosciutto, bresaola, or any of the other splendid Italian cold cuts; of tuna, hard-boiled eggs, anchovies, fried eggplant—but whatever else is contains, it is sure to include one or more of the wonderful greens grown on the farm islands of the Venetian lagoon.

Gorgonzola and Mâche Sandwich

TRAMEZZINO CON GORGONZOLA E GALLINELLA

¼ pound Gorgonzola cheese, kept at room temperature for at least 2 hours

3 tablespoons extra virgin olive oil

¼ pound mâche

8 slices good white bread, trimmed of their crust

8 Gorgonzola and mâche tramezzini

1. Put the Gorgonzola in a small bowl, break it up into small pieces with a fork, add the olive oil, and mash with a fork to obtain a creamy mixture.

2. Detach the longer and tougher stems of the mâche, wash it in several changes of cold water, then shake in a towel or spin.

3. Put the mâche in a bowl and add the Gorgonzola and olive oil mixture a little bit at a time, turning the ingredients gently with a fork until the mâche is evenly coated with Gorgonzola.

4. Place one quarter of the mâche and Gorgonzola filling in the center of one of the bread slices, making a mound. Top with another slice. Hold a knife diagonally across the slice of bread, place your other hand over it with the fingertips holding down the bread by the corners so that you do not flatten the center, then slice the sandwich diagonally to produce two *tramezzini*.

Hard-Boiled-Egg Sandwich with Anchovies and Capers

TRAMEZZINO CON LE UOVA SODE

Romaine lettuce

2 hard-boiled eggs

10 flat anchovy fillets

2 tablespoons capers

3 tablespoons mayonnaise

Black pepper ground fresh

8 slices good white bread,
  trimmed of their crust

---

8 hard-boiled-egg tramezzini

1. Detach the lettuce leaves from the head, wash them in several changes of cold water, shake in a towel or spin in a salad spinner until dry, then shred them very, very fine. Shred enough to make 2 cups.

2. Shell the hard-boiled eggs, put them in a food processor with the anchovies and capers, and chop, pulsing on and off, to a coarse consistency.

3. Put the egg and anchovy combination in a bowl; add the mayonnaise, the shredded lettuce, and several grindings of black pepper; and toss thoroughly to combine all ingredients uniformly. With the mixture, stuff the sandwich to make *tramezzini* as described in Venetian-Style Sandwiches (facing page).

Celery and Ham Sandwich

TRAMEZZINO DI SEDANO E PROSCIUTTO COTTO

1 cup not too finely
  chopped celery

¼ pound boiled, but not
  smoked, ham, chopped
  not too fine

3 tablespoons mayonnaise

2 teaspoons mustard or
  more to taste

6 slices good white bread,
  trimmed of their crust

---

6 celery and ham tramezzini

1. Mix the celery, ham, mayonnaise, and mustard, turning with a fork to combine them evenly.

2. With the mixture, stuff the sandwich to make *tramezzini* as described in Venetian-Style Sandwiches (facing page).

Venetian Meat and Potato Balls, Bacaro-Style

LE POLPETTINE DEI BACARI

½ pound boiling potatoes

3 tablespoons vegetable oil plus oil for frying

1 teaspoon chopped garlic

½ teaspoon chopped rosemary

1 pound ground beef chuck

Salt

Black pepper ground fresh

½ cup whole milk

3 thin slices firm white bread, trimmed of their crust

2 tablespoons chopped Italian flat-leaf parsley

2 eggs

½ cup freshly grated Parmigiano-Reggiano cheese

1 cup fine, dry, unflavored bread crumbs, spread on a plate

Approximately fifty 1-inch meatballs

A wire draining rack

The meatballs made by Venice's *bacari*—the city's wine bars—are delightfully soft because they contain a large proportion of mashed potatoes. *Bacari* make them early in the morning and serve them throughout the day at room temperature. Some people ask for them to be warmed up in the microwave, but they are quite good cold, although they never taste better than when they are hot. The traditional version calls for a ground mixture of three meats—beef, veal, and pork—in equal parts, but I find the all-beef variation I have adopted here to be more succulent.

1. Wash the potatoes, put them into a pot of cold water with their skins on, and bring to a steady but gentle boil.

2. Into a 10-inch skillet put 3 tablespoons of vegetable oil, ½ teaspoon chopped garlic, and ½ teaspoon chopped rosemary, and turn on the heat to medium high. Cook, stirring frequently, until the garlic's scent begins to rise. Before the garlic can become lightly colored, add the meat, breaking up and spreading the mass with a wooden spoon.

3. Add salt and pepper; turn the meat over from time to time with a wooden spoon, cooking it until it is evenly browned throughout.

4. Pour the contents of the skillet into a colander or strainer set over a small bowl to let all the fat drain away. When there is no more fat draining, turn the contents of the colander over into a clean, medium-size bowl.

5. Put the milk into a small bowl and add the sliced bread, letting it steep to absorb as much milk as possible.

6. As soon as the potatoes are tender, drain, peel them while they are hot, and mash them through a food mill or potato ricer into the bowl with the meat. Lift the milk-soaked bread with a slotted spoon or spatula, leaving the excess milk behind in the bowl. Add the bread to the

meat together with the remaining ½ teaspoon of chopped garlic, the parsley, 1 egg, and the grated Parmesan. Combine all ingredients into a homogeneous mixture.

7. Break the remaining egg into a small bowl or deep saucer, add 2 tablespoons of water, and beat it lightly.

8. Make 1-inch balls out of the meat mixture, taking care not to squeeze tightly. Dip the balls first into the beaten egg, lifting them one at a time to let excess egg flow back into the dish, then turn them in the bread crumbs. Place them on a platter, where they can stay for even an hour before you begin to fry them.

9. Put enough vegetable oil in a 12-inch skillet to come at least ½ inch up the sides of the pan. Turn the heat on to high; it is hot enough when a bit of meat dropped in sizzles immediately. Put in as many meatballs as will fit loosely in one layer. Cook them, turning them as they become browned on one side, until they are evenly browned all over. Transfer them, using a slotted spoon or spatula, to a wire draining rack set over a tray or paper towels. If you do not have a wire rack, use a platter thickly lined with paper towels. Proceed thus in batches until all the meatballs are done. Serve immediately from a warm platter if you like them piping hot, or let them cool to room temperature.

AHEAD-OF-TIME NOTE: You can cook the meatballs up to 6 or 8 hours before serving.

Soups

SOUPS

Minestre

———————— ❧ ————————

Artichoke and Potato Soup

Broccoli and Potato Soup

Ligurian Fava Bean and Lettuce Soup

Friuli Basil Soup with Vegetables,
    Beans, and Barley

Swiss Chard, Cannellini Bean,
    and Barley Soup

Barley, Broccoli, and Cannellini Bean Soup

Savoy Cabbage and Cannellini Bean Soup

Cranberry Bean and Cime di Rapa Soup

Cranberry Bean and Chicory Soup

Simplest Leek and Chickpea Soup

Bergamo-Style Savoy Cabbage Soup
    with Chickpeas

Asti-Style Soup with Pork Ribs,
    Chickpeas, and Potatoes

Mussel Soup with Cranberry Beans,
    Celery, and Basil

Sardinian Clam Soup with Couscous

*Preceding photograph: Friuli Basil Soup
with Vegetables, Beans, and Barley*

Soup is *zuppa*, but there is another word for it in Italian, *minestra*, a word that resonates more deeply within the Italian soul than any other in the language. When Italy was a poor country, *minestra*, which existed long before pasta, signified more than a dish—it was, for most of its people, the whole meal. *Minestra* was synonymous with survival, with one's lot in life, and it became a word overlaid with immemorial travail.

One could say of one's job that one is working for *la minestra*. We would describe a person who is free to act as he wishes as someone who can have any *minestra* he likes. A warmed-over *minestra* is the attempt, without hope of success, to do what one has failed at before. When we have used up all our options we say, *O mangiar questa minestra o saltar dalla finestra*, "It's either swallow the soup or jump out the window."

It follows that Italy's great soups come out of the country's most inspiring gastronomic heritage, the cooking of the poor, *la cucina povera*. Nothing about them is fancy: There are no bisques, not one fussy cream-of-anything soup. Matters of substance were riding on what the *minestra* could deliver, and to this day a good Italian soup can generate a fuller, more profound sense of well-being than any other dish in this cuisine, or possibly in any other.

A film producer researching a scene in a humble Italian kitchen as it might have been lived 100 years ago, or even the day before yesterday, could find the makings of a typical dinner in the ingredients list of the soups in this chapter: potatoes, beans, chickpeas, fava, swiss chard, leek, broccoli, *cime di rapa*, Savoy cabbage, clams, mussels. Meat is absent, except for an occasional piece of salt pork or pancetta and the pork ribs that are required in one soup. The meat broth some of the recipes now call for would have been made at one time with scraps gleaned from the landowner's kitchen.

The ingredients are so modest and the techniques so simple, so unsophisticated, that anyone schooled in more elaborate disciplines might ask, after tasting one of these soups: Where does the rich taste come from? From Providence, probably. Who else used to look after the poor?

Artichoke and Potato Soup

ZUPPA DI CARCIOFI E PATATE

---

5 standard-size artichokes

A lemon, cut in half

¼ cup extra virgin olive oil

½ cup finely chopped onion

1 tablespoon chopped garlic

3 tablespoons chopped
    Italian flat-leaf parsley

1 pound potatoes

1 bouillon cube

Salt

Black pepper ground fresh

For 4 persons

Potatoes do marvelous things to such slow-cooked dishes as soups and stews. Acting like sponges, they draw flavor out of the other ingredients and concentrate it in themselves. In exchange, they give up some of their starch, which adds desirable density to a soup's liquid or a stew's juices. Here the artichoke, which can be rather a retiring vegetable if left to its own devices, finds its flavor broadcast boldly through the potato. If you like potatoes and you like artichokes, this soup can't fail to please. Once you have trimmed the artichokes—and you must do that thoroughly unless you want to end up with unchewable matter in your mouth—there is nothing laborious about the making of the soup.

1. Trim away the hard, inedible parts of the artichokes as described on page 362; then cut them lengthwise into very thin slices, put them in a bowl, cover with water, and add the juice of half the lemon.

2. Choose a pot that can eventually accommodate all the artichokes and potatoes plus enough liquid for the soup. Put in the olive oil and onion and turn on the heat to medium high. Cook, stirring frequently, until the onion becomes translucent. Add the garlic, and stir and cook it until it becomes colored a very pale gold. Add half the parsley, stirring the contents of the pot thoroughly with a wooden spoon. Turn the heat down to medium.

3. Rinse the sliced artichokes in cold water and add them to the pot. Cook, turning the artichokes over in the flavored oil from time to time, until they are tender and lightly browned.

4. Wash the potatoes, peel them and cut in half, and put them in the pot with the artichokes. Add the bouillon cube and enough water to cover. Cook at a slow, gentle boil for 30 minutes or more until they feel tender when prodded with a fork.

5. Remove the potatoes from the pot using a slotted spoon or spatula and mash them lightly on a plate. Don't mash them to a pulp; part of the potatoes should be crushed and part left in small pieces about ½ inch thick. Return them to the pot, which should still be over medium heat.

6. If necessary, adjust the consistency of the soup, which should be rather dense, by adding just a little water. Stir well, add salt and pepper to taste, and with a wooden spoon turn over all ingredients two or three times. Swirl in the remaining parsley and serve at once.

AHEAD-OF-TIME NOTE: You can prepare the soup a day or two in advance, preferably stopping at the end of step 4, when the potatoes are done, but before mashing them. Reheat thoroughly at a lively simmer before proceeding.

Broccoli and Potato Soup

ZUPPA DI BROCCOLI E PATATE

A large yellow onion, sliced
   very thin, about 1½ cups

Salt

¼ cup extra virgin olive oil

3 tablespoons butter

2 pounds broccoli

1 large garlic clove, peeled
   and sliced very thin

4 large boiling potatoes,
   peeled, washed, and cut
   into small dice

2½ cups homemade meat
   broth OR 1 bouillon cube
   dissolved in 2½ cups
   water

Black pepper ground fresh

6 to 8 basil leaves, torn into
   small pieces

½ cup freshly grated
   Parmigiano-Reggiano
   cheese

For 6 persons

My spouse and collaborator loves broccoli stems, the thicker the better, and he loves them best boiled, served still lukewarm and generously doused in olive oil. The florets on the other hand he considers an accident of nature, and he refuses to touch them. I had bought magnificent broccoli one day whose stems I had made, as I have just described, for lunch. But I hated to throw away the florets—they were so fresh, the buds very tightly clustered and their color a deep bluegreen. So I acted on the thrifty Italian cook's principle that you can make a good soup out of anything.

In truth, I didn't have just anything. I had excellent meat broth in the freezer, lovely waxy boiling potatoes in the kitchen's potato basket, basil growing in a sunny window, a fresh piece of Parmesan, and those perfect broccoli florets. I prepared a base of onion sliced thin and cooked very slowly to absolute softness in olive oil and butter. Why use both? Because the oil does terrific things for green vegetables such as broccoli, whereas the butter imparts a luscious quality that helps all the flavors come together. Many cooks in the farm country of my native Romagna do the same.

The garlic was sliced very thin and I let it just steam briefly, buried in the faintly moist onion, so that it stayed very sweet, which is the flavor accent I wanted in this soup. The potatoes were cut into small dice so that they dissolved as they cooked and contributed silken texture. Just before bringing it to the table, I swirled in a little raw butter, the basil, and the Parmesan. Broccoli florets notwithstanding, Victor greeted the soup with applause.

1. Put the onion, a large pinch of salt, all the olive oil, and 1 tablespoon of butter in a saucepan; turn on the heat to medium low, and cover the pan. Cook until the onion is completely tender and has become colored a light nut brown.

2. Detach the broccoli florets from the stems, keeping the stems aside to use as suggested in the headnote above. If you want to use the stems in the soup, wash them, pare away their tough outer layer, and cut them into ¼-inch pieces. It will, however, become a different soup in consistency as well as appearance. Wash the florets under cold running water.

3. When the onion is cooked, add the sliced garlic and leave the pan uncovered. Cook, stirring, for about 1 minute, without letting it become colored. Add the broccoli florets and a generous pinch of salt, and cook, turning the florets over from time to time, until they feel tender at the pricking of a fork.

4. Add the diced potatoes and cook for about 5 minutes, turning them over frequently. Then add the broth or 2½ cups water together with the bouillon cube. Cook until some the potatoes dissolve as you stir them. Add 1 or 2 tablespoons water if you find the soup becoming too dense. The final consistency should be loosely creamy, rather runny than thick.

5. Taste and correct for salt, and add liberal grindings of black pepper. Swirl in the basil, the freshly grated Parmesan, and the remaining 2 tablespoons of butter, and serve at once.

AHEAD-OF-TIME NOTE: You can prepare the soup several hours in advance, but serve it the same day you make it. Reheat gently and swirl in the basil, Parmesan, and butter just before serving.

Ligurian Fava Bean and Lettuce Soup

ZUPPA LIGURE DI FAVE E LATTUGA

A large head of Romaine
  lettuce

2 to 2½ pounds fresh fava
  beans

1 medium potato

¼ cup extra virgin olive oil

1½ cups very thinly sliced
  onion

2 cups homemade meat
  broth OR 1 bouillon cube
  dissolved in 2 cups
  lukewarm water

Salt

Black pepper ground fresh

½ cup freshly grated
  Parmigiano-Reggiano
  cheese

½ teaspoon chopped
  marjoram

For 4 persons

When I was discussing fava with Danilo Solari in Portofino (see *Marò* on page 48), another fragrant specialty of the cooking of Liguria came up, this soup with fresh fava and Romaine lettuce. It is a textbook example of the Riviera's culinary style, combining gentleness and boldness, gentle in the sweetness of the lettuce and the fresh fava beans, bold in the fragrance of the marjoram alighting on the soup just as you are about to bring it to the table.

Youth and freshness, always of consequence when cooking with vegetables and herbs, become particularly significant here. Like that other delicacy that comes in a pod, early peas, fava is full of sugar and juice when young and freshly picked, but starchy as it matures. Look for slenderness in the pods, an indication that it encloses youthfully small beans, and a clear light green color unblemished by black spots. If you can, open a pod and taste the fava. It should be dewy, not floury. As for the marjoram, need I insist? Fresh.

1. Detach all the leaves from the lettuce head, discarding any bruised or withered ones. Take a thin slice off the butt end of the root and cut the remainder into thin rounds. Wash leaves and root in two or three changes of cold water, then cut the leaves into very narrow shreds. They should amount to approximately 2½ cups.

2. Shell the fava beans, discarding the pods. If the beans are rather large, pare away their thin but tough green skin. You should have about 2 cups of beans. Wash them in cold water.

3. Peel the potato, wash it, and cut it into four wedges.

4. Put the olive oil and onion in a large saucepan, turn the heat on to medium high, and cook the onion, stirring three or four times, until it becomes colored a pale gold. Add the shredded lettuce with the sliced lettuce root and cook for about 1 minute; then add the potato and the fava beans and cook for a few seconds, turning over all ingredients.

Add the broth or dissolved bouillon cube, turn the heat down to very low, and cover the pot.

5. Cook at a very gentle but steady simmer until the fava beans are tender; about 30 minutes, depending on the youth and freshness of the beans. Retrieve the potato wedges using a slotted spoon, mash them on a plate with a fork, then return them to the pot. Add salt and liberal grindings of pepper, stir thoroughly, and cook for another 5 minutes or so.

6. Off heat, just before serving, swirl in the grated Parmesan and the marjoram. Taste and correct for salt and pepper.

AHEAD-OF-TIME NOTE: The soup may be cooked several hours in advance, but add the Parmesan and marjoram only after you have reheated it, just before serving. It may also be frozen, but it may need to be thinned with a little broth or water when reheated.

Friuli Basil Soup with Vegetables, Beans, and Barley

ZUPPA FRIULANA CON L'ORZO E IL BASILICO

½ cup barley

3 medium zucchini

1½ pounds Swiss chard

2 medium potatoes

1 medium onion, peeled

1 medium carrot, peeled
and cut into medium-
size pieces

1 cup whole celery leaves

1 whole, peeled garlic clove

Salt

Black pepper ground fresh

1 cup dried cranberry or
white *cannellini* beans,
soaked overnight as
described on page 401 OR
about 1 pound unshelled
fresh cranberry beans

¼ pound green beans

½ cup shelled fresh peas OR
frozen peas

⅓ cup extra virgin olive oil

½ cup fresh basil leaves,
chopped very fine just
before serving

2 tablespoons butter

For 6 persons

For a long time I used to think that nothing could compare with a Tuscan soup, but after accompanying my husband on visits to the wineries of Friuli, the northeasternmost Italian region, I found that there Tuscany had met its match.

The recipe for this soup came from Patrizia Felluga, of the winery at Russiz Superiore. Think of it as a broad anthology of flavors and textures. There are vegetables of both the green and the root kind, two kinds of beans, and the favorite Friuli grain—barley—all pulled together by the rousing fragrance of fresh basil. You will have a number of pots going because there are so many different things to cook, yet all of them are very easy to do, demanding nothing beyond a certain investment in time. You can make it whenever time is not a problem; freeze it, all but the basil; and have it whenever you want to put something substantially satisfying on the table.

1. Put the barley in a saucepan with 1½ cups water, bring to a slow boil, and cook at a gentle simmer for about 45 minutes, until the barley is tender but not mushy. Drain when done, reserving its cooking liquid for possible later use.

2. Soak and clean the zucchini as described on page 162, trim off the ends, and cut them into 1-inch pieces.

3. If using mature chard with fleshy stalks, detach the stalks and cut them into 1-inch pieces. If it is young chard, detach and discard the spindly, spinach-like stems. Look all the leaves over for any that are blemished or withered and discard them. Soak the leaves and, if you have them, the cut-up stems in a basin with several changes of cold water to remove all traces of soil.

4. Wash the potatoes, peel them, and cut them along with the onion and the carrot into 1-inch pieces.

5. Put the drained chard; the pieces of zucchini, potatoes, onion, and carrot; the celery leaves; and the garlic into a soup pot. Add salt and 2½ cups of water. Turn the heat on to medium, cover the pot, bring its contents to a slow boil, and cook at a gentle simmer for at least 45 minutes until all the ingredients are very, very soft and their flavors merge. Add several grindings of black pepper when the vegetables have cooked for about 15 minutes.

6. If you are using dried beans that have been soaking overnight, drain and rinse them. If using fresh beans, shell them and wash in cold water. Put the beans in a pot with enough water to cover by 2 or 3 inches, and cook them over very low heat until tender—45 minutes or so. Drain, reserving the cooking liquid.

7. While all the pots are going, wash the green beans, snap off the ends, and drop them into a pot of boiling salted water. Cook them until tender, about 10 minutes or so, then drain them.

8. If you are using shelled fresh peas, cook them as you did the green beans, even using the same pot if you like, in boiling salted water. If you are using frozen peas, no preliminary cooking is required.

9. When the vegetables in the soup pot are completely tender, puree them in a food processor, then return them to the pot. Add the drained barley, the cooked dried beans, the green beans, the peas, and the olive oil. Cook at a gentle simmer, stirring from time to time, for 10 or 15 minutes. If the soup becomes too dense, thin it with some of the beans' reserved cooking liquid and, should it prove necessary, some of the barley's liquid. Just before serving, chop the basil very fine, swirl the butter into the pot, then add the basil and stir thoroughly.

AHEAD-OF-TIME NOTE: The soup may be completed a few hours in advance, but add the basil and butter only after reheating, when ready to serve. If using the same day, do not refrigerate. If you want to keep it longer, it is better to freeze it. When frozen, the soup thickens and it may be desirable to add a little water when reheating.

Swiss Chard, Cannellini Bean, and Barley Soup

ZUPPA DI BIETE, CANNELLINI, E ORZO

---

1 pound Swiss chard

¼ cup extra virgin olive oil

1 cup finely chopped onion

½ cup finely chopped celery

⅓ cup chopped, peeled fresh tomatoes OR canned imported Italian plum tomatoes, cut up with their juice

Salt

½ cup pearl barley

1½ cups canned *cannellini* beans, drained, OR ¾ cup dried white kidney beans, soaked overnight as directed on page 401 and drained

Black pepper ground fresh

Freshly grated Parmigiano-Reggiano cheese for the table

For 4 to 6 persons

If you are in Italy and see a soup with *orzo* on the menu, then you are likely to have come to one of the two northeast regions, Trentino or Friuli, where barley, *orzo* in Italian, is a popular soup ingredient. Don't mistake it for the pasta shape by the same name, which is more common in Middle Eastern than in Italian cooking.

I have based this chard and barley soup on various models, all from Friuli. Some may have had spinach instead of chard or cranberry beans instead of *cannellini*, or omitted the tomatoes, or added garlic—all of them choices that you too can make. I am happy with my version: I like tomatoes in a soup—they add a fresh, sharp taste—and although I certainly don't shrink from using garlic, I don't have to have it always. It's possible, too, to substitute rice for barley, but I would miss the barley if it weren't there. There is such a satisfyingly chewy quality to barley, and moreover there is something about its pearl-like shape that feels very good in the mouth. It takes a long while to cook, between 40 and 45 minutes, although you can cook it less if you want it firmer. Be careful, however; don't go overboard on firmness, because the tenderness of fully cooked barley is very appealing.

1. Soak the chard in a basin of cold water for about 10 minutes, drain, then wash in several changes of cold water. If it is mature chard with broad stalks, detach the stalks and cut them across into short, very thin strips approximately ⅛ inch wide. Cut the leaves into narrow strips about ¼ inch wide.

2. Put the olive oil and the chopped onion in a soup pot and turn on the heat to medium. Cook the onion, stirring from time to time, until it becomes colored a light gold, then add the chopped carrot and celery. Cook for 6 to 7 minutes, stirring occasionally; then add the tomatoes, turning them over once or twice.

After another 6 minutes or so, add the cut-up chard leaves and stalks and some salt. Turn the contents of the pot over to mix them well, cover the pot, and turn the heat down to the lowest setting.

3. In the meanwhile, bring 4 to 5 cups of water to a boil in a medium saucepan, put in the barley, and cook at a gentle but steady simmer for about 40 minutes—more if you like the barley very tender, or possibly slightly less if you like it chewy. Drain the barley into a small bowl, but do not discard the water in which it cooked.

4. Taste the chard leaves and stalks. When both are quite soft, add the cooked barley and the drained beans. Turn over all the contents of the pot to mix them thoroughly, and cook for 2 or 3 minutes longer, always at low heat.

5. Add as much of the water in which you boiled the barley as you deem necessary to bring the soup to a desirable consistency. This soup is meant to be rather on the dense side, but you can thin it to taste by adding additional water if required. Add salt and a few grindings of pepper, stir, and cook just long enough to heat up the liquid you have just added. Serve with grated Parmesan available on the side.

AHEAD-OF-TIME NOTE: You can cook the soup entirely in advance several hours before serving, as far ahead as early morning if you are serving it for dinner.

Barley, Broccoli, and Cannellini Bean Soup

MINESTRA D'ORZO, BROCCOLI, E CANNELLINI

⅓ cup pearl barley

Salt

1 pound broccoli

⅓ cup extra virgin olive oil plus some for trickling into the soup when serving

1½ tablespoons chopped garlic

1 cup canned *cannellini* white beans, drained, OR ½ cup dried, soaked and boiled as directed on page 401

1 beef bouillon cube

Black pepper ground fresh

For 6 persons

Here is another soup from the northeastern region of Friuli that relies on the textural satisfactions of barley. Unlike the version on page 88, this is a "white" soup, no tomatoes are present, and the base on which its flavor rests is pared down to garlic sautéed in olive oil. I have tinkered a little with it, substituting for cauliflower, which a Friuli cook had used, a southern vegetable, broccoli, whose deeper, lengthier taste seemed to me to find a suitable niche in the elemental structure of the soup. You can try it with cauliflower, if you are so inclined, or even with a recent addition to that family, broccoflower.

1. Put the barley in a soup pot; add enough water to cover by 3 inches and a large pinch of salt. Put a lid on the pot, bring the water to a slow but steady simmer, and cook for about 45 minutes or until the barley is fully tender. Drain when done, collecting the water in a bowl for possible use later in the soup.

2. While the barley is cooking, detach the florets and any small leaves from the broccoli and put them in a bowl of cold water.

3. Pare away from the broccoli's main stems, and from the florets' stems as well, the hard, dark green rind and any other tough stringy part.

4. Wash the stems under cold running water, and the florets in several changes of cold water.

5. Bring a pot of water to a boil, add 2 tablespoons salt and the thick, main broccoli stems. The salt is to keep the broccoli green and it will not make it too salty. Cook for 7 or 8 minutes, then add the florets. When the water returns to a boil, cook for another 10 minutes or so, then drain. Chop the broccoli rather fine and set aside.

6. Put the olive oil and garlic in a soup pot, turn on the heat to medium, and cook the garlic, stirring frequently, just until it becomes colored a deep ivory.

7. Add the broccoli and cook for 2 or 3 minutes, turning it over from time to time to coat it well.

8. If you used dried *cannellini*, drain them when cooked. If using canned *cannellini*, drain and discard the liquid. Add the drained *cannellini* beans and barley and stir once or twice.

9. Add enough of the barley's water, and if insufficient, plain tap water, to cover by at least 2 inches. Put in the bouillon cube and several grindings of pepper, and stir for 15 or 20 seconds. Cook at a steady but gentle simmer for about 5 minutes. Taste, and correct for seasoning, transfer to a serving bowl, and bring to the table. Trickle a little olive oil into each plate after serving the soup.

AHEAD-OF-TIME NOTE: You can cook the barley and store it, drained, under plastic wrap and cook and drain the broccoli and store it separately, without chopping it, under plastic wrap, but in a cool place outside of the refrigerator, for several hours before completing the soup. Don't forget to save their respective cooking waters.

Savoy Cabbage and Cannellini Bean Soup

ZUPPA DI VERZA E CANNELLINI

A large head of Savoy
    cabbage

⅓ cup extra virgin olive oil
    plus additional olive oil
    for the table

⅓ cup chopped onion

1 tablespoon chopped garlic

Salt

2¼ cups canned *cannellini*
    white beans, drained, OR
    ¾ cup dried, soaked and
    boiled as directed on
    page 401

1 beef bouillon cube

Black pepper ground fresh

Thick-sliced, crusty
    country-style bread,
    1 slice per serving

Parmigiano-Reggiano
    cheese, grated fresh at
    the table

6 ample or 8 standard servings

My native Cesenatico, in Romagna, is a fishing town and in the summer months a crowded beach resort, but pressing at the opposite edge of town from the beach, there is farm country, broad and luxuriant. My father had land there all his life where he kept some cows and grew wheat, sugar beets, and excellent *sangiovese* red grapes that were highly sought after by local wine producers.

Every morning, black-kerchiefed women come into town from the farms with fresh vegetables and fruit they have grown. Once, but sadly no longer, they used to bring a delicious runny cow's milk cheese called *scquaquarone*, made at break of day. Set aside for them is a small open site in the oldest part of town where they conduct the littlest outdoor market I have ever seen. All of us know them, just as they know us, and hardly a morning passes by that we don't stop to pick up not just some fresh vegetables, but the conversational thread whose beginnings coincide with their beginnings and ours.

The produce the farm women sell is rigorously seasonal and I recall their saying of Savoy cabbage that it isn't ready to pick until it has felt the first hard chill of the year. I was there after such a chill to choose a head of cabbage, with the deeply ridged, dark green outer leaves of perfectly achieved maturity. The woman who sold it to me explained how I could use it to make the soup described below. Here you have a textbook example of the warm, mellow flavor of *minestra* in Romagna. A base of sautéed onion is the invariable point of departure, with spiced and aromatic notes conspicuously absent, and the *minestra* reaches completion at table with the almost obligatory condiment of the region, a shower of freshly grated Parmesan.

1. Discard the tough outer leaves and any bruised ones the Savoy cabbage may have, then shred the cabbage very, very fine. You should have about 10 to 12 cups, but slightly more or less won't affect the results too much. Soak in a basin of cold water and drain.

2. Put the olive oil and onion in a soup pot, turn on the heat to medium, and cook the onion, stirring frequently, until it becomes colored a rich gold. Add the garlic, continuing to cook and stir until the garlic becomes colored a very pale gold.

3. Add the shredded cabbage and a large pinch of salt and, using a long wooden spoon, turn the cabbage over several times during 2 or 3 minutes to coat it well. Pour enough water into the pot to cover by about an inch, turn the heat down to low, and cover the pot. Cook for about 3 hours, occasionally turning the cabbage, until it has become very soft. If during this time it should become necessary to replenish the cooking liquid to keep the cabbage from sticking, add 2 or 3 tablespoons of water when needed. There should be no liquid left, however, when the cabbage is done. Should you find some, uncover the pot, turn the heat up to high, and boil away all liquid, turning the cabbage frequently.

4. If you used dried *cannellini*, drain them when cooked, but hold back the liquid to use in the soup. If using canned *cannellini*, drain and discard the liquid. Add the drained *cannellini* beans, turning them with the cabbage for a minute or two.

5. Pour enough liquid—either water or the reserved liquid from the boiled *cannellini* or a combination of both—into the pot to cover by a full inch and add the bouillon cube. Turn the contents of the pot over with your wooden spoon once or twice, put the lid on, and cook at a gentle but steady boil for about 30 minutes. Add black pepper and taste and correct for salt.

6. For each plate of soup that will be served, toast a slice of bread in a 450° oven or grill it under the broiler. Place the bread in the individual soup plates, trickle some olive oil on it, pour the hot soup over it, sprinkle grated Parmesan on top, and serve.

AHEAD-OF-TIME NOTE: The soup can cooked entirely in advance, even a day or two ahead. Reheat in a covered pot at a gentle simmer.

Cranberry Bean and Cime di Rapa Soup

ZUPPA DI FAGIOLI BORLOTTI E CIME DI RAPA

2¼ pounds fresh unshelled
   cranberry beans OR 1½
   cups dried, soaked and
   boiled as described on
   page 401

Salt

1½ pounds *cime di rapa*
   (also known as *rapini* or
   broccoletti di rape)

¼ cup extra virgin olive oil

1 tablespoon chopped garlic

¼ pound salt pork,
   chopped fine, about 1
   cup

For 6 persons

Like other soups in this chapter this is a duet, two ingredients harmonizing and setting off each other's strengths. I love the powerful simplicity of the approach. The *cime di rapa*—also known as *broccoletti di rape* or *rapini*—acts as a vehicle for the flavors of the garlic and salt pork sautéed in olive oil, and contributes tenderness together with a bracing hint of bitterness. The beans bring body to the soup and with their mellow taste balance the slight austerity of the *broccoletti*. Although this is a soup out of Apulia, in Italy's southeast, I deliberately used a northern bean, the cranberry, whose richness of flavor I think is not unwelcome.

If Using Fresh Beans:

1. Shell them, put them in a pot with enough cold, unsalted water to cover by about 2 inches, bring the water to a gentle simmer, cover the pot, and cook at a slow, steady pace until tender, about 45 minutes to 1 hour. After 30 minutes of cooking have elapsed, add salt. Let the beans steep in their liquid until you are ready to use them.

If Using Dried Beans:

Soak them overnight or for at least 6 hours, drain, then boil them in a fresh change of water. After 30 minutes of cooking have elapsed, add salt. Let them steep in their liquid until ready to use.

2. Peel away the tough outer layer of the *cime di rapa* stalks, particularly all the larger ones. Wash the vegetable in several changes of water; then put it in a saucepan, add 2 cups of water, cover the pan, and bring to a boil over high heat. Add salt and cook at a steady boil until the thicker stalks of the *cime di rapa* feel fully tender when prodded with a fork. Drain and wipe the saucepan dry so you can use it for the soup.

3. As soon as the *cime di rapa* is cool enough for you to handle, chop it coarsely.

4. Put the olive oil, garlic, and salt pork in the saucepan, and turn on the heat to medium high. Cook the garlic, stirring frequently, until it becomes colored a pale gold. Add the chopped *cime di rapa* and cook briskly for about 5 minutes, turning it over frequently with a wooden spoon to coat it well.

5. Retrieve the cooked beans, using a colander or slotted spoon. Do not discard the cooking liquid. Puree half the beans directly into the saucepan, turn over with the wooden spoon, and add the remaining beans and enough of their cooking liquid to make the soup's consistency medium dense. Continue cooking for another 10 minutes, stirring from time to time. Taste and correct for salt, transfer to a warm serving bowl, and bring to the table.

AHEAD-OF-TIME NOTE: The soup may be cooked several hours in advance, but not the day before. A night in the refrigerator will give the vegetable a grassy, metallic taste.

Cranberry Bean and Chicory Soup

ZUPPA DI FAGIOLI BORLOTTI E CATALOGNA

1½ pounds fresh unshelled cranberry beans OR 1 cup dried, soaked overnight, and boiled as described on page 401

½ pound boiling potatoes

¼ pound *catalogna* chicory (see headnote)

2 tablespoons extra virgin olive oil

⅓ cup chopped onion

1 large or 2 medium garlic cloves, peeled and chopped very fine

1 tablespoon chopped Italian flat-leaf parsley

½ cup diced celery

3 cups homemade meat broth OR 1 bouillon cube dissolved in 3 cups lukewarm water

Salt

Black pepper ground fresh

1 cup freshly grated Parmigiano-Reggiano cheese

1½ tablespoons butter

For 4 to 6 persons

A small dose of bitterness is a desirable thing, Italians have long since found. Like the chili in Thai cooking, it sends a quickening shock of energy coursing through the palate, but unlike the most potent chilies, it is meant not to step out front but to slip its message into the dialogue conducted by the other ingredients. Such is *catalogna*'s role in this soup. Yet another member of the prolific chicory family to which the many varieties of radicchio belong, *catalogna* is a tall vegetable with a loose bunch of slender stalks spreading outward from their common base, bearing saw-toothed leaves like those of dandelion, which you can use if *catalogna* is not available. The stalks and leaves are tender and you use both together.

If Using Fresh Beans:

1. Shell them, discard the pods, and set the beans aside for later.

If Using Dried Beans:

Soak them overnight or for at least 6 hours, drain, then boil them in a fresh change of water, using no less than 5 cups water. After 30 minutes of cooking have elapsed, add salt. Cook until tender; then, off heat, let them steep in their cooking liquid until ready to use.

2. Wash the potatoes, peel them, and cut them into large dice.

3. Detach the chicory leaves from their root, wash them in several changes of cold water, then cut them into strips ½ inch wide.

4. Choose a saucepan that can comfortably accommodate all the ingredients. Put in the olive oil and chopped onion, and turn on the heat to medium. Cook, stirring from time to time, until the onion becomes translucent but not colored. Add the garlic and parsley and cook, stirring frequently, until the garlic becomes colored a very pale gold. Add the diced celery and cook for about 1 minute, turning it over

to coat it well. Add the diced potatoes and continue cooking for another minute, turning over the potatoes two or three times.

If Using Fresh Beans:

5. Put in the shelled beans together with the meat broth or the water with the dissolved bouillon cube. Turn over the contents of the pot two or three times, using a wooden spoon, then cook at a gentle but steady simmer. After 30 to 35 minutes, add the cut-up chicory, the salt, and liberal grindings of pepper, and turn over all ingredients three or four times. Cook at a gentle simmer for 1 hour.

If Using Dried Beans:

Drain them but, unless you are using meat broth, do not discard the water they have cooked in. Put them into the pan adding either the broth or 3 cups of the water they cooked in with a bouillon cube dissolved in it. Turn over the contents of the pot two or three times and bring to a steady, gentle simmer. After a minute or two, add the cut-up chicory, the salt, and liberal grindings of pepper, and turn over all ingredients three or four times. Cook at a gentle simmer for 1 hour.

6. Off heat, swirl in the grated Parmesan and butter, then bring the soup to the table in a serving bowl.

AHEAD-OF-TIME NOTE: You can make the soup several hours in advance, keeping it covered but not refrigerated. If you are not serving it the day you make it, refrigerate it in a tightly sealed container, but bear in mind that cooked greens tend to acquire a metallic taste in the refrigerator. Do not add the Parmesan and butter until after you have thoroughly reheated the soup.

Simplest Leek and Chickpea Soup

SEMPLICISSIMA DI PORRI E CECI

2½ pounds leeks

3 tablespoons extra virgin
  olive oil

Salt

One 16-ounce can
  chickpeas, drained

A beef bouillon cube

Black pepper ground fresh

½ cup freshly grated
  Parmigiano-Reggiano
  cheese

---

4 ample, 6 moderate portions

We had the briefest of honeymoons, Victor and I, a single winter night in a *pensione* in Sirmione, a narrow peninsula at the southern end of Lake Garda, a tongue-like extension of land impudently stuck into the underbelly of the huge lake. Sirmione has since been devastated by tourism and the cheap shops and souvenir stalls that cater to it, but it was empty then, and the most romantic of places. We clambered over the ruins of a Roman bath, past a grove of olive trees planted before the birth of Christ, to reach the lake's icy edge, our exhalations dissolving in the wintry mist as we gaily chucked stones to see who could send them bouncing farthest over the water.

The evening we arrived the *pensione* served us leek and potato soup, an event that to this day Victor seems to recall more sharply than anything else that took place during our stay. It was, admittedly, a splendid soup, and both of us have adored leeks ever since.

I use leeks in many ways, nearly always in combination with another vegetable, such as the dish of leeks and artichokes in one of my previous books, a great favorite of ours. None of the things I do, however, is so simple as this aptly named "simplest" soup. Except for trimming the leeks and slowly cooking them in olive oil—not a daunting task for even the least expert of cooks—the most difficult things you have to do are opening a can of chickpeas and grating some Parmesan.

There is something about the flavor of chickpeas that yearns to be coupled with a member of the onion family. There are many such matches, but none more congenial than this one.

1. Trim away the root end of the leeks and any part of the green tops that is wilted, bruised and discolored, or dry. Cut the remainder into thin disks. Soak in several changes of cold water. Drain and spin or shake dry.

2. Put the leeks in a medium saucepan, add the olive oil and salt, turn on the heat to medium low, cover the pan, and cook the leeks at a slow pace, turning them over from time to time, until they are nearly dissolved.

3. While the leeks are cooking, skin the chickpeas by squeezing off the peel between your fingers. When the leeks are very soft and creamy, add the chickpeas, enough water to cover by 1 to 2 inches, and the bouillon cube. Turn over the contents of the pot with a wooden spoon, put back the lid, and cook for another 15 minutes.

4. Take two or three ladlefuls out of the soup and puree them back into the pot through a food mill, or chop briefly in a food processor. Add liberal grindings of black pepper to the pot, swirl in the grated Parmesan, cook for 5 minutes longer, taste and correct for seasoning, and serve. In the final stage of cooking, adjust density to suit you. This soup tastes best to me when it is neither too thick nor too runny.

AHEAD-OF-TIME NOTE: You can prepare everything even a day in advance, up to, but not including, the moment when you add the pepper and Parmesan. When resuming cooking, warm up thoroughly before executing that last step.

Bergamo-Style Savoy Cabbage Soup with Chickpeas

ZUPPA DI VERZA ALLA BERGAMASCA CON I CECI

— ❧ —

A medium of head Savoy
    cabbage

3 tablespoons extra virgin
    olive oil

2 ounces chopped pancetta
    OR salt pork

⅔ cup chopped onion

½ cup chopped carrot

½ cup chopped celery

⅔ cup dried chickpeas,
    soaked overnight and
    cooked as described on
    page 401, OR 2 cups
    drained canned
    chickpeas

Salt

Black pepper ground fresh

¼ cup freshly grated
    Parmigiano-Reggiano
    cheese

For 4 to 6 persons

Compare this Savoy cabbage soup from Bergamo, in Lombardy, with the one from Romagna on page 92. They both start with the cabbage and end with the Parmesan, but what different roads they travel in between! This one is spicier, thanks to the pancetta; more aromatic, courtesy of the celery; and faintly muskier, a quality derived from the chickpeas.

I have left the choice of dried or canned chickpeas to the reader. For reasons I can't fathom, the canned are excellent, often better than the dried, which can be variable. When it comes to other legumes such as *cannellini* or cranberry beans or lentils, if I have the choice, I prefer to use the dried rather than the canned kind because their consistency and flavor are so much better. Nevertheless, given the impulsive, unpremeditated nature of Italian cooking, if there is no time for soaking and cooking dried beans, I'd sooner use canned ones than forgo making the dish.

One step I don't try to save time on is peeling chickpeas. It's not such a nuisance as it may seem and goes very quickly once you get the knack of squeezing the peel off between thumb and forefinger, and the result is a soup free of the pesky, papery, distractingly dry, and wholly useless bits of peel. Nothing belongs in what you eat that doesn't bring some pleasure.

1. Detach the outer leaves of the cabbage, discarding any that may be bruised or discolored. Wash them briefly in cold water, then shred them very fine together with the rest of the head. You should get about 6 cups, but slightly more or less does not matter.

2. Put 2 tablespoons of olive oil in a soup pot, add the chopped pancetta or salt pork and chopped onion, and turn on the heat to medium high. Cook, stirring frequently, until the onion becomes col-

ored a pale gold, then add the chopped carrot and celery, turning them over to coat them well.

3. Stir from time to time and when the color of the carrot and celery has become darker, add the shredded Savoy cabbage. Turn it over and over to coat it well, then cook, stirring from time to time, until all the cabbage has wilted. Add just enough water to cover the cabbage, put a lid on the pot, and turn down the heat to low. Cook for about 1 hour.

4. Squeeze the skins off the drained chickpeas. (You may omit this step if you really don't mind having the skins in the soup.) Add the chickpeas to the soup pot; add salt and liberal grindings of black pepper; and with a wooden spoon, turn over the contents of the pot two or three times. Add just as much water as may be necessary to cover, put the lid back on the pot, and cook at a gentle but constant simmer for 2 more hours. If you find that the soup is short of liquid, add 2 or 3 tablespoons of water when needed. When ready to serve the soup should be rather dense.

5. Just before transferring the soup to a serving bowl, add the grated Parmesan and the remaining tablespoon of oil, stirring them thoroughly into the soup.

AHEAD-OF-TIME NOTE: The soup is excellent when prepared a day in advance and reheated. Hold back the grated Parmesan and the last tablespoon of oil, stirring them in just before serving after reheating the soup.

Asti-Style Soup with Pork Ribs, Chickpeas, and Potatoes

ZUPPA ASTIGIANA CON COSTICINE E CECI

Two 16-ounce cans chickpeas

2 medium potatoes

2 tablespoons extra virgin olive oil

1 cup very thinly sliced onion

1 tablespoon very finely chopped garlic

3 bay leaves

1 tablespoon rosemary leaves, chopped very, very fine

1 pound pork short ribs, cut into 1-inch pieces

Salt

Black pepper ground fresh

For 4 persons if served as a one-course meal, for 6 if the first of two courses

One of the major events of the year on many Italian farms, taking place as the season begins to cross the bridge between fall and winter, is the butchering of a pig. The Italian expression is *fare il maiale*, "do the pig." Some farmers "do" it themselves; others hire a specialized crew. The law prescribes that the pig be dispatched instantly, but there are those who ignore that requirement and bleed it slowly to death, a procedure whose details I shall spare you. The justification for it is that if the hog loses most of its blood before it expires, there will be less of it in the meat, which will then taste better.

Once dead, the carcass is immediately divided into parts that suit various purposes: the hind thighs for prosciutto, the shoulders and neck for salami and sausage, the jowl and some lean meat for *cotechino*; selected parts of the fat are rendered to make cooking lard; the belly is spiced and rolled up or pressed down flat for pancetta. Many remaining cuts, the liver, the tenderloin, the ribs, are consumed later at a feast that celebrates the occasion as well as the end of a day that began at dawn.

My husband was in Piedmont on one of his periodic visits to wine producers, it was early December, and a family that had just "done" a pig asked us to join them for the dinner. Many came; several generations and branches of the family were represented, as well as a few friends. There were enough people for a large Handel chorus, and they certainly could have outshouted one, but every single mouth was needed because much was served: salami and prosciutto from the previous year, soup, risotto with fresh sausage, grilled pork liver wrapped in caul fat, breaded pork chops, roast pork tenderloin in red wine. I am sure you don't want to hear about the peripheral courses, the home-made pickles, the three kinds of potatoes, the salads, the desserts.

The soup was this one, with fresh ribs. Alone, it is an amply satisfying meal for four.

1. Drain the chickpeas, and squeeze off the peel from each one. Set aside.

2. Peel and wash the potatoes, and cut them into medium dice. You should have about 1 cup.

3. Put the oil and sliced onion in a large saucepan and turn on the heat to medium. Cook the onion, stirring frequently, until it becomes colored a pale gold.

4. Add the garlic. Cook, stirring frequently, and when the garlic becomes colored a pale gold add the bay leaves, chopped rosemary, and ribs. With a wooden spoon, turn over all ingredients several times to coat them well.

5. Add the skinned chickpeas, diced potatoes, salt, and liberal grindings of pepper, turning them over a few times with the other ingredients.

6. When the contents of the pot begin to simmer, add enough water to cover, put a lid on the pot, and adjust heat to cook at a gentle but steady simmer. Cook for at least 1½ hours. Turn the soup's ingredients over from time to time. If you should find, during the cooking, that the liquid needs replenishing, add ½ cup water whenever needed. When done, the soup should be liquid enough to eat with a spoon, but it ought to be dense rather than runny. Taste and correct for salt and pepper and, before serving, retrieve and discard the bay leaves.

AHEAD-OF-TIME NOTE: You can make the soup a full day in advance. Reheat at a slow simmer, adding 1 or 2 tablespoons of water if required.

Mussel Soup with Cranberry Beans, Celery, and Basil

ZUPPA DI COZZE CON FAGIOLI BORLOTTI

1½ pounds cranberry beans, fresh in their pods, OR ⅔ cup dried, soaked overnight as described on page 401

3 pounds live mussels

⅓ cup extra virgin olive oil

⅓ cup very finely chopped onion

1 tablespoon finely chopped garlic

1 cup canned Italian plum tomatoes with their juice

Chopped fresh or dried chili pepper, to taste

1 loosely packed cup chopped celery leaves

Salt

Black pepper ground fresh

12 large basil leaves, cut into very narrow strips

For 4 to 6 persons

There is a restaurant in Italy that seems never to have a free table, and it is not in one of the celebrated cities, but in Olbia, a shabby port town in northeastern Sardinia, on the ground floor of a modest hotel. It is Rita D'Enza's Gallura. How to describe the flavor of Rita's food? Intense, yet subtle; penetrating, yet gentle; surprising, yet comforting; sprightly, aromatic, surging from deeper sources of savor than anyone else seems to have tapped.

I adapted this mussel and bean soup from one of hers, and when I was working on seafood recipes one summer in the Hamptons on Long Island, it was the one dish that, once tasted, my friends asked me to make again and again. Even the photographer who came to shoot a story for *Food & Wine* magazine, and claimed he never ate at work, wiped the pot clean.

The procedure can be summed up simply: the beans are cooked separately; the mussels are steamed open; a base of olive oil, onion, garlic, and tomatoes is prepared and combined with the beans and mussel meat. The liquid for the soup comes from the bean broth and the mussel juices. Chili pepper, in minute quantity, adds spice with restraint; the distinctive fragrance is that of celery leaves and basil.

There is a lovely logic to the sequence by which the flavors of the soup are built up, each element of taste and texture layered over the other until they fuse into a delicious whole. Master the pattern, understand its sense, and you will be able to spin off from it versions with other legumes, with other seafood, with or without onion, with whole garlic cloves rather than chopped, with herbs other than celery leaves and basil.

1. Put the fresh or reconstituted dried cranberry beans in a saucepan with enough water to cover by at least 2 inches. Put a lid on the pot and

bring to a steady but gentle simmer over medium low heat. Cook until tender.

2. Soak the mussels in several changes of cold water, scrubbing them vigorously each time with a stiff brush. Cut off any protruding whiskery tuft. Discard any mussel that does not clamp shut.

3. Put the mussels in a large sauté pan, turn on the heat to high, and cover the pan. As soon as their shells swing open, transfer them to a bowl and set aside, pouring over them any liquid they may have shed. The pan should accommodate the mussels in a single layer. If it is not large enough to do so at one time, perform the operation in two or more stages.

4. As soon as the mussels are cool enough to handle, pry the shells completely open and detach the meat, discarding the shells. Work right over the bowl that contained them so that all of their liquid flows back into the bowl into which you'll put the meat. When you have shelled them all, retrieve the mussel meat from the bowl using a slotted spoon and put it into a smaller bowl. Slowly pour the juice in the bowl over the mussel meat, being very careful not to pour with it the sand that will have settled at the bottom of the bowl.

5. Choose a lidded saucepan large enough to contain later all the beans and mussels and enough liquid for the soup. Put in all the olive oil and chopped onion and, without covering the pot, cook the onion over high heat, stirring from time to time, until it becomes colored a deep, tawny gold.

6. Add the garlic, stirring and cooking it just until you begin to notice its aroma, taking care not to let its color become any darker than a very pale gold.

7. Add the tomatoes with their juice and cook, always over high heat, for about 10 minutes, stirring occasionally. Add the chili pepper and the chopped celery leaves, turn everything over two or three times, and cook for 2 or 3 more minutes.

8. Retrieve the mussel meat from its bowl using a slotted spoon, and put in the pot, turning it over with the pot juices for 2 or 3 minutes.

9. Drain the cooked beans, but save their liquid, and add them to the pot. Turn them over with the other ingredients for a minute or two.

10. Line a strainer with a sheet of paper towel and pour the mussel liquid through it and into the pot. Stir once or twice.

11. Add to the pot enough of the beans' cooking liquid to achieve a soupy, but not too runny, consistency. Stir well, turn the heat down to low, taste and correct for salt, add liberal grindings of pepper, and simmer gently for 10 more minutes. Just before transferring the contents of the pot to a serving bowl or tureen, swirl in the shredded basil.

AHEAD-OF-TIME NOTE: You can make the soup a few hours in advance, stopping short of adding the basil, which you will do after reheating it.

Sardinian Clam Soup with Couscous

ZUPPA ALL'ORISTANESE CON VONGOLE E FREGOLA

———————— ❧ ————————

3 dozen littleneck clams

Salt

4 tablespoons extra virgin
   olive oil

½ cup couscous (precooked
   medium-grain semolina)

1 tablespoon very finely
   chopped garlic

3 tablespoons chopped
   Italian flat-leaf parsley

¼ teaspoon chopped chili
   pepper OR to taste

————————————————

For 4 persons

On a fine May morning in Sardinia I discovered three wonderful things. We were in Cabras, on the western coast, to have lunch, but we were early, so my husband and I decided to drive to the nearby beach of Is Arutas for a walk that we hoped would stir our becalmed appetites. We went as far as was permitted by car, and began to cross the seemingly scrubby ground that separated us from the beach. I looked down to see that, like a princess in a fairy tale, I was walking over what could have been a tightly woven carpet made of wildflowers unimaginable in their variety and numbers. Approaching the beach, I was startled by its brilliance. When I scooped up a palmful of the "sand" I found spilling from my hand a multitude of minute polished quartz fragments, dazzling in their whiteness. My third discovery was this soup.

Gigi Ledda has a restaurant in Cabras, Sa Funtà, where he cooks only on special order, and since, on any given day, you may be the only customer, it is necessary to let him know at least 24 hours in advance that you are coming. All of the dishes we had that day were new to me, and most had ingredients that I would have difficulty finding in mainland Italy—"the continent," as Sardinians call it—let alone elsewhere. But the entrancing soup Gigi made with couscous-like nuggets and clams could clearly be replicated anyplace. Aside from procuring those two ingredients, a quick browse through the recipe will reveal that no seafood soup makes such simple demands of its cook.

1. Soak the clams in a basin of cold water for 15 minutes, then empty the basin and, under cold running water, scrub the clams vigorously, rubbing one against the other, rinsing them in two or three changes of water.

2. Choose a skillet or sauté pan that can contain the clams no more than two layers deep. If you don't have a large enough pan, do half the clams at one time, performing this step in two stages. Put in 3 cups of water, cover the pan, and turn on the heat to high. After 2 or 3 minutes,

uncover the pan and turn the clams over, bringing up the ones on the lower level. As they begin to open, remove them from the pan, using a slotted spoon or spatula or tongs, and transfer them to a bowl. Proceed thus until all the clams have opened up and have been put in the bowl. Pour all the liquid remaining in the pan over the clams.

3. As soon as the clams are cool enough to handle, detach the meat from the shells, putting it in a small bowl and discarding the shells. Slowly pour the juices in the original bowl over the clam meat, tipping the bowl with care so that the sand that has settled on the bottom does not get poured out with the juices. Let the clam meat steep in its liquid for 20 to 30 minutes.

4. While waiting for the clams to finish steeping, put ⅔ cup of water in a small saucepan together with a pinch of salt and 1 tablespoon olive oil, and bring it to a boil. Add the couscous, cover the pan, and remove from heat. After 5 to 6 minutes, uncover the pan and stir the couscous, which is now ready for the soup.

5. Retrieve the clam meat from the bowl, using a slotted spoon or spatula; chop each piece into four smaller pieces; and put them all back into the bowl for 5 minutes. Working very gently to avoid stirring up any sand that may still be in the juices, retrieve the chopped clam meat, once again using a slotted spoon or spatula, and transfer it to a plate. Line a strainer with a sheet of single-ply paper towel and pour the clam juices through it into a clean bowl.

6. Put 3 tablespoons of olive oil and the chopped garlic into a medium saucepan and turn on the heat to medium. Cook the garlic, stirring it two or three times, and the instant it becomes colored a very pale gold, add the chopped parsley. Stir once or twice, then add the filtered clam juices. Let the liquid bubble for 1 or 2 minutes, then add the couscous, stirring it thoroughly. When the liquid bubbles again, put in the clam meat and continue cooking for another minute or two. The finished consistency of the soup should be somewhat runny. If you find it becoming too thick, add a little water. Serve piping hot.

Pasta

PASTA
La Pasta

SAUCES

Celery and Tomato Pasta Sauce

Ligurian-Style Pasta Sauce
    with Raw Tomatoes, Olives, Capers,
    and Anchovies

Scallion, Cherry Tomato,
    and Chili Pepper Pasta Sauce

Sardinian-Style Raw Tomato Sauce
    for Pasta

Spinach and Tomato Pasta Sauce,
    Romagna-Style

Eggplant Sauce with Bell Pepper,
    Tomato, and Basil

Broccoli and Mozzarella Pasta Sauce

Pepper and Anchovy Pasta Sauce

Pepper, Pancetta, and Parsley Pasta Sauce

Porcini-Style Shiitake Mushroom
    Pasta Sauce

Rosemary and Sage Pasta Sauce

Hunter-Style Pasta Sauce with Herbs,
    Pancetta, Tomato, and White Wine

Zucchini, Tomato, and Basil Sauce
    for Pasta

Ligurian-Style Pasta Sauce with Zucchini
    and Carrots

Zucchini Sauce for Pasta with Tomato,
    Parsley, and Chili Pepper

Zucchini and Thyme Pasta Sauce

Pasta Sauce with Peas, Ham, and Cream

Goat Cheese, Chive, and Chili Pepper
    Sauce for Pasta

Bell Pepper and Goat Cheese Sauce
    for Pasta

Pancetta, Onion, and Parsley Pasta Sauce

Simple Veal Pasta Sauce

Lamb Sauce for Pasta, Abruzzi-Style

Savoy Cabbage and Sausage Pasta Sauce

Quail Sauce for Fresh Pasta

Mara's Broccoli and Scallop Pasta Sauce

Mussel and Basil Sauce for Pasta

Lobster Pasta Sauce Busara-Style

SPECIAL PASTA DISHES

Pleated Ravioli Piedmontese-Style
    Stuffed with Meat and Savoy Cabbage

Rosemary and Sage–Scented
    Homemade Pasta

Homemade Ravioli with Asparagus
    and Scallops

Homemade Ricotta and Mint Tortelloni

Green Ravioli Pesaro-Style Stuffed with
    Lamb and Sauced with Yellow Peppers

Spinach Tonnarelli Sauced with
    Yellow Peppers and Tomato Dice

Sardinian Sheet Music Bread
    with Lamb Sauce

Baked Crêpes Pie with Eggplant
    and Peppers

Pasta is the single most universally captivating dish any cuisine has put on the table. The Chinese do it, the Japanese do it, Hungarians and Germans do it, and even some cooks in France do it, but Italians do it best. Pasta is a simple thing, yet its rewards ought not to be taken for granted. Selecting a promising match of pasta and sauce, judging doneness, and tossing purposefully are a few of the actions that we want to think about when preparing pasta, and if we perform all such actions informed by the results to which they can lead, our life at the dining table will be connected to a source of pleasure without equal. The force of pasta's power to satisfy is beyond explanation. What we can explain is how to tap that power.

PHOTO KEY FOR PAGES 110–11

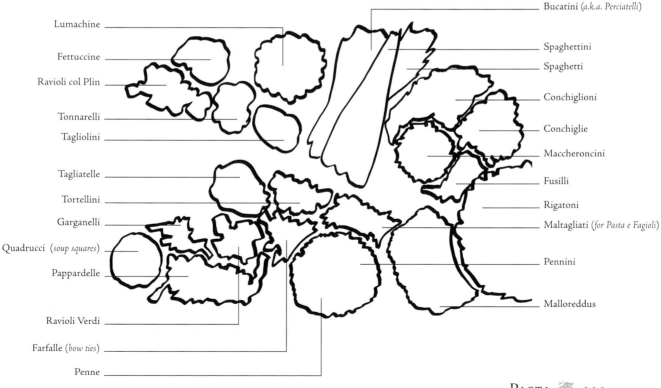

Lumachine

Fettuccine

Ravioli col Plin

Tonnarelli

Tagliolini

Tagliatelle

Tortellini

Garganelli

Quadrucci (*soup squares*)

Pappardelle

Ravioli Verdi

Farfalle (*bow ties*)

Penne

Bucatini (*a.k.a. Perciatelli*)

Spaghettini

Spaghetti

Conchiglioni

Conchiglie

Maccheroncini

Fusilli

Rigatoni

Maltagliati (*for Pasta e Fagioli*)

Pennini

Malloreddus

PASTA 113

THE TWO FUNDAMENTAL KINDS OF PASTA

There are two broad categories within which are grouped all but a few of the regional pasta specialties: There is homemade pasta produced by hand, or with hand-operated tools, using soft wheat flour and eggs; and there is industrially made, boxed pasta produced with semolina—hard wheat flour—and water.

Homemade egg pasta includes all the flat noodles—fettuccine, tagliatelle, *pappardelle*, *tonnarelli*, lasagne—and the stuffed pastas; ravioli, tortellini, *tortelloni*, *agnolotti*, *pansoti*.

When speaking of boxed semolina pasta we refer to such solid shapes as spaghetti, spaghettini, linguine, fusilli, *farfalle* (bow ties), and the hollow or cupped shapes such as penne, *maccheroni*, ziti, rigatoni, *bucatini*, *conchiglie* (shells), *lumache* (snails).

Identifying their attributes, acquiring a sense of which sauces fit them best, anticipating the different taste and texture sensations each can deliver—these are the first necessary steps toward becoming a good pasta cook.

There is a critical difference in texture between homemade egg pasta and store-bought, boxed semolina pasta, a difference that I hope to make clear by reaching for a comparison outside the field of food. Imagine that there are two fabric houses, one specializing in spinning and weaving the fluffiest, most ethereal cashmere, the other producing linen that possesses a splendidly crisp, firm hand. The same designer may acquire cloth from both, but what he cuts and drapes with the cashmere will be different from what he tailors from the linen.

Egg pasta made at home is the cashmere; store-bought, factory-made semolina pasta is the linen. The latter has a hard, impenetrable surface that can carry olive oil–based sauces cleanly without becoming saturated, delivering taste that is lively and fresh. Homemade egg pasta has an almost invisible but open weave; it is porous and absorbent. You would hardly ever want to sauce egg pasta with olive oil, because when it sucks in that oil it develops an unpleasantly slick texture. What it really thirsts for is the luscious butter and cream sauces for which it is the ideal receptacle. Egg pasta embraces sauce; semolina pasta slips it on.

Although there exist deplorably ill-conceived machines for extruding spaghetti, *maccheroni*, and other semolina pasta shapes in your kitchen, that is a product you don't ever want to make at home. Egg pasta, on the other hand, ought never to be made anywhere else.

Making Egg Pasta at Home

What You Need

- A work counter, at least part of it wood, if possible; the wood top, which can be a movable board, is for kneading

- A dinner fork

- A dough scraper

- Several large dish towels

- Plastic wrap or thin plastic in large sheets

- An 8- to 10-inch knife, straight-edged if possible, such as a cleaver

- A pasta machine, either hand-cranked or electrically driven, with thinning rollers and noodle-cutting attachments; OR, if you are making the pasta entirely by hand, a 1½- to 2-inch-thick, 32-inch-long hardwood pin

- Large eggs and all-purpose flour

I don't know of anything you can make in your kitchen that yields such generous returns on as modest an investment of time and effort as egg pasta. It can be produced, from start to finish, in substantially less than 1 hour; you can schedule its making at any time of the day or night convenient to you and cook it even months later. If you choose to roll it out by hand, as described on pages 121–25, you will approach it as you would the mastering of any basic manual craft. If you use the simple cranked machine, no advanced skill is demanded.

How to Begin

Whether making pasta by hand or by machine, you start by incorporating eggs and flour. This is not kneading; it is combining the eggs with as much flour as is required to produce a mass that is neither too dry and crumbly nor too sticky. The basic proportion is two large eggs for 1 cup of flour; but exactly how much flour will be needed is impossible to tell in advance, because it depends on how much of it the eggs you have can absorb and on the humidity, or lack of it, in your kitchen.

Pour flour onto the work surface, shaping it into a mound, and hollow out the center. Break the eggs into the hollow (*photo A*). Scramble the eggs lightly with a fork, drawing some of the flour over the eggs, using the fork to mix it with the eggs until these are no longer runny (*photo B*). With your hands, draw the sides of the mound together but push off some of the flour to the side, where you will keep it until you find you absolutely need

A

B

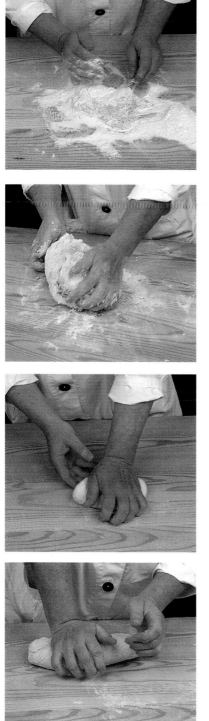

C

D

E

F

it. Work the eggs and flour together, using your fingers and the palms of your hands (*photos C and D*), until you have a smoothly integrated mixture. If it is still moist, work in more flour.

When the mass feels as if it will become too dry if you add more flour, stop, wash your hands, dry them, and perform this simple test: Press your thumb deeply into the center of the mass, and if it comes out clean, without any sticky matter on it, no more flour is needed. Put the dough to one side, wrap it tightly in plastic wrap, and scrape the work surface absolutely clear of any loose or caked bits of flour and of any crumbs. Wash and dry your hands and prepare to knead.

Kneading

Pasta quality depends on how you knead the dough. You can knead it using the rollers of the pasta machine, and you can knead it in the food processor, but to obtain the matchless texture unique to pasta made at home, you must knead it by hand. If the only egg pasta you have had has been the so-called "fresh" kind you buy, or entirely machine-kneaded pasta, whether it is made in a restaurant's kitchen or even in your own, then you have never felt under your teeth the resilient body, the sinew, of true homemade pasta. Dough needs the warmth of your hands and of the wood surface on which you work it. It responds to those as it cannot to the metallic touch of a steel cylinder or blade. The procedure is not as daunting as it may sound. It takes just 8 minutes and, physically, it can be a deeply satisfying rhythmic exercise. It is good not just for the dough, but for you as well.

Place the mass of flour and eggs near you on the work surface. With your fingers bent, push forward against it using the heel of your palm, giving it a lengthened, oblong shape (*photo E*). Fold the mass in half, give it a half turn, press hard against it with the heel of your palm again, and repeat the operation (*photo F*). Turn the ball of dough always in the same direction, either clockwise or counterclockwise, as you prefer. When you have kneaded it thus for 8 full minutes, the dough is ready to be thinned in the machine, or rolled out with the long pasta pin.

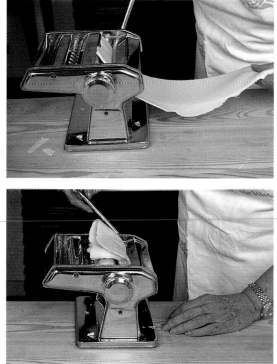

G

H

If you are working with a large mass, divide it into two or more parts and knead one part completely before doing another. Keep any part of the mass you are not working with, or of the dough you have finished kneading, tightly covered in plastic wrap.

Thinning and Cutting by the Easy Pasta Machine Method

Divide the ball of kneaded dough into several parts so that the pasta strips you will end up with will be of manageable size and not stretch across the room. Calculate how many eggs you have used for the ball of dough, multiply by three, and divide the dough into that many parts.

Spread clean, dry, cloth dish towels over a work counter near the machine. If you are making a large quantity of pasta you'll need a lot of counter space and a lot of towels.

Fit the thinning rollers, the pair of smooth cylinders, into the pasta machine and set them at their largest opening. Pummel one of the pieces of dough with your palm to flatten it; then run it through the machine (*photo G*). Fold the dough twice, reducing its length by two-thirds, and feed it by its narrower end through the machine once again (*photo H*). Repeat the procedure, turning the dough back into the machine two or three times, thus duplicating hand kneading. Then lay the strip of pasta perfectly flat over a towel on the counter. Start at one end of the counter, leaving room for the strips to come.

Take another piece of dough and repeat the operation just described above. Lay this second strip next to the preceding one on the towel, but do not allow them to touch or overlap, because they are still moist enough to stick to each other. Proceed to thin all the remaining pieces in the same manner.

NOTE: If you are making ravioli or other stuffed shapes, please see the note about stuffed pasta on page 120.

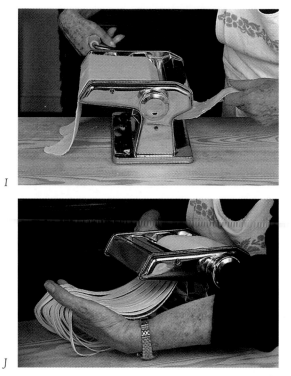

I

J

Close down the opening between the thinning rollers by one notch on the machine. Take the first of the flattened pasta strips lying on the towel and run it once through the rollers, feeding it by its narrow end. Spread it flat on the cloth towel, and move on to the next pasta strip in the sequence.

When all the pasta strips have gone through the narrower opening once, bring the rollers closer together by another notch, and run the strips of pasta through them once again, as described. The strips become longer as they get thinner (*photo I*), and if there is not enough room to spread them out on the counter, you can let them hang over the edge. Continue thinning the strips in sequence, progressively narrowing the opening between the rollers one notch at a time, until the pasta is as thin as you want it. This step-by-step thinning procedure, which commercial makers of so-called fresh pasta greatly abbreviate or skip altogether, is responsible, along with proper kneading, for giving good pasta its body and structure.

For all cut pasta such as fettuccine, tagliatelle, *pappardelle*, and the like, allow the strips spread on the towels to dry for 10 minutes or more, depending on the temperature and ventilation of your kitchen. From time to time, turn the strips over. Do not dry the pasta too much because it must still be pliant enough that it won't crack and split when cut. You can't cut it, however, if it is still too soft and moist, because the noodles would stick to each other.

Use the broader set of cutters on the machine to make fettuccine, the narrower ones for *tonnarelli* (see the recipe on page 203), feeding the pasta strips, one at a time, through the cutter of choice. As the ribbons of noodles emerge (*photo J*), separate them and spread them out on the cloth towels.

Other Noodle Cuts

Pappardelle. The larger surface of this mouth-filling broad noodle is perfectly suited to substantial sauces, whether made with meat or vegetables or a combination of both. The machine has no cutters for *pappardelle*, so you must cut it by hand. Using a pastry wheel—a fluted one produces the prettiest noodles—cut the rolled-out pasta strips into ribbons about 6 inches long and 1 inch wide.

Tagliatelle. The classic Bolognese noodle, and the most appropriate one to couple with Bolognese meat sauce, is a little broader than what the machine's fettuccine cutters produce; hence it must be cut by hand. When the thinned strips of pasta are dry enough to cut, but still pliant enough, to bend without splitting, like soft leather, fold them loosely lengthwise to make a flat roll about 3 inches wide. With a cleaver or another knife, cut the roll across into ribbons about ¼ inch wide.

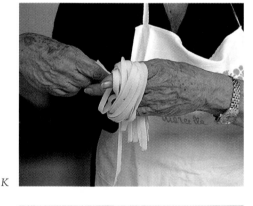

K

L

Drying Noodles for Future Use

If "fresh" means "soft," homemade egg pasta is not necessarily fresh. It is soft the moment it's made and it can be cooked then, but if one waits it will dry, a natural process with which there is no reason to interfere. All the artificial methods by which commercial "fresh" pasta is kept soft—sprinkling with cornmeal, covering with plastic wrap, refrigeration—undermine its structure and consistency. Properly dried homemade egg pasta, when cooked, delivers all the texture and flavor it had when just made. The limp product marketed as "fresh" does not. Once dried, homemade noodles can be stored for weeks in a cupboard, just like a box of store-bought semolina pasta.

When the noodles are cut, gather several strands at a time and curl them into circular nest shapes (*photo K*). Let the nests dry on towels for 24 hours (*photo L*), making sure they do not touch or overlap. They must be absolutely dry because if any moisture remains when they are stored, mold will develop. When dry, place them in a large box or tin, interleaving each layer of nests with paper towels. Handle carefully because they are brittle. Store in a dry cupboard, not in the refrigerator. Allow slightly more cooking time for dried pasta than for the freshly made.

Stuffed Pasta

When pasta is to be cut into wrappers for stuffing, its consistency must be soft and sticky. The procedure given above for making noodles must therefore be adjusted as follows: Take one piece of dough at a time through the entire thinning process and *before* going on to the next piece, cut it and stuff it as the specific recipe describes. While working with one piece of dough, keep all the others that you will subsequently be getting to tightly covered with plastic wrap.

Maccheroni alla Chitarra

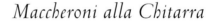

In Abruzzi, noodle dough is cut into ribbons on the taut steel strings of a guitar-like tool. The sheet of dough is as thick as the space between the strings is wide to produce a square noodle. In Rome, the shape is called *tonnarelli*. It can be duplicated on a pasta machine's narrow cutters (page 203).

Rolling Pasta Out by Hand

Producing egg pasta that is not just homemade, but handmade, is a craft. I have seen some of my students master it right away. Others take a little longer. Some never get it at all. Why do it? Because if you succeed, you will possess one of the most precious skills that a cook can command, and from your hands will come a product without compare.

When you roll out egg pasta by hand, you are stretching the dough, with a rapid succession of motions, over the length of the long pin. In the machine method, the dough is compressed between two cylinders. There is a difference in color—the color of hand-stretched pasta is considerably deeper than the color of dough squeezed out by machine—and a more important difference in structure.

The surface of hand-stretched pasta is etched by a minute pattern of intersecting ridges and hollows. When cooked and tossed, the pasta draws in sauce and exudes juiciness. On the palate it has a succulence that no other pasta can match.

If it seems worth trying, get a lumber dealer to supply you with a 1½- to 2-inch-thick, 32-inch-long hardwood dowel. Round off the ends with sandpaper so that there are no sharp edges that might tear the pasta. Into one end, screw an eye hook from which to keep your pin suspended so it won't warp. Protect it from dents. Before using it the first time, wash it thoroughly, dry it with a soft cloth, then rub it lightly with food-safe oil. When the oil has seeped into the wood, rub the pin with flour. To maintain the pin in good condition, repeat the treatment once every dozen times the pin is used.

I asked Carla Grimaldi from Bologna, who has been making pasta since she was twelve, to come up to Venice and demonstrate for the photographer, Alison Harris, the motions involved in making pasta by hand. The illustrations that follow, along with the descriptions, should make the detailed instructions easier to grasp.

When you are just learning to roll pasta, work with dough using two eggs. A one-egg dough would be awkward to handle, but more than two eggs might be a waste. Be prepared to waste quite a lot of eggs and flour, until you find you have made something edible. Keep in mind two important points:

1. Work quickly because as pasta dough dries, it loses its elasticity and cannot be stretched.
2. Never apply downward pressure on the pin. You are going to thin the dough not by pressing it against the table, but by lightly stretching it along the length of the pin. Making pasta on a pin requires not strength, but just quick hands.

Thinning Pasta Dough Using a Long Rolling Pin

Getting the Dough Ready. You will find it simpler to work with dough that is fully relaxed. When you have finished kneading the ball of dough as described above on page 116, cover it with plastic wrap and let it rest at room temperature for at least 15 minutes or as much as 2 hours. Remove the wrapping when you are ready to begin rolling it out. Should you find the dough slightly moist, do not add flour, but knead it briefly until the excess dampness disappears.

Part One. Put the dough within comfortable reach in the center of the work table and with the palm of your hand pummel it two or three times firmly to flatten it slightly. Place the rolling pin across the top of the dough, about one third of the way in toward its center. The pin should be parallel to the edge of the table near you. To open out the ball of dough, push the pin energetically forward, let it roll backward to its starting point, and push forward again, repeating the operation four or five times (*photo A*). Do not let the pin roll onto or past the far edge of the dough. Turn the dough a full quarter turn, and repeat the above operation. Continue to turn the gradually flatter disk of dough after every three or four passes of the pin, at first a full quarter turn, then less, but without changing direction. If this is done correctly, the ball of dough will spread out into an evenly flattened, regularly circular shape. When its diameter reaches about 8 to 9 inches, you are ready for the next movement.

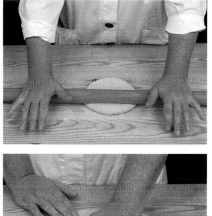

A

B

Part Two. You have flattened the dough; now you must begin to stretch it. Hold the near edge of the dough down with one hand. Place the rolling pin at the opposite, far edge, laying it down parallel to your side of the table. One hand will work the pin while the other will act as a stop, holding down the edge of the dough nearest you.

Curl the far edge of the dough over the pin. Start rolling the pin toward you, taking up no more dough than needed to fit snugly under the pin. With your other hand, keep the near edge of the dough from moving. Roll the pin part of the way back to you, then with the heel of your palm push it forward, stretching the sheet of dough held taut between one hand on the table and the other on the pin (*photo B*). Work rapidly, without interrupting the action. Do not apply any downward pressure whatsoever and do not let the hand working the pin rest on the dough longer than 2 or 3 seconds on the same spot.

Roll the pin back to you, stop, then push it forward to stretch the dough; wrap more dough around the pin, rolling it back toward you, stop and push forward, stretching the dough; continue to repeat this procedure until you have wrapped all the dough around the pin. Then, while the dough is curled around the pin, rotate the pin a full half turn—180 degrees—so that one end points toward you, and unfurl the dough, opening it up flat. Once again, place the rolling pin at the opposite, far edge of the dough, laying it down parallel to your side of the table.

Repeat the rolling and stretching operation you performed before, until the dough is once again completely wrapped around the pin. Rotate the pin another 180 degrees in the same direction as before, uncurl the dough from it, and repeat the full procedure once again. Continue thus until the sheet of dough has been stretched to a diameter of about 12 inches. Proceed immediately to the next phase.

C

Part Three. This is the decisive final step, the one in which you'll stretch the sheet of dough to nearly double its preceding diameter.

The circle of dough is lying flat before you on the table. Place the rolling pin at its far end, parallel to your edge of the table. Curl the end of the dough around the center of the pin and roll the pin toward you, taking up with it about 4 inches of the sheet of dough. Cup your hands lightly over the center of the pin, lifting your fingers to keep them from touching it (*photo C*). Roll the pin forward and away from you, unfurling the dough, and then back toward you, taking up again no more than the original 4 inches of dough. At the same time that you are rolling the pin back and forth, slide your hands, with fingers always uplifted, away from each other and toward the ends of the pin; then slide them back together toward the middle of the pin, quickly repeating the motion a number of times.

As your hands move away from the middle, let the heels of your palms brush against the surface of the dough, dragging it, pulling it, in fact stretching it toward the ends of the pin. At the same time that you are sliding your hands from the middle toward the ends, you must roll the pin back toward you. Bear in mind that the pressure in this motion is directed sideways, not downward. If you press down on the dough, it will stick, not stretch.

The dough can be stretched in only one direction. When the hands move back toward the middle of the pin, they should be floating over the dough, barely skimming it. You want to stretch the dough outward, toward the ends of the pin, and not drag it back toward the middle. While you are bringing your hands back over the middle of the pin, roll the pin forward, away from you.

Your hands must flick out and back very rapidly, making contact with the dough only with the heel of the palm, applying not weight, but pull, as they move outward. All the while, you are rocking the pin forward and back.

D

Take up another few inches of dough on the pin and repeat the combined motion: The hands moving out and in, the pin rocking forward and back.

When you have taken up and stretched all but the last few inches of dough, rotate the pin 180 degrees, unfurl the sheet of dough, opening it up flat, and start again from the far end, repeating the entire stretching procedure described above.

As the sheet of dough becomes larger, let it hang over the near side of the table. It will act as a counterweight and contribute to the stretching action. But do not lean against it, because you might break it. As you take up dough on the rolling pin from the far end, gradually allow the near end of the sheet to slide back onto the table.

When you have rotated the pasta sheet a complete turn and it is all fully stretched, open it up flat on the table. The rim of the sheet is likely to be thicker than the central portion (*photo D*). Run over it with the rolling pin to make it uniformly thin. Should there be creases anywhere, iron them out with the pin. If there are any tears, do not be dismayed; it happens under the most expert hands, and they can be repaired. Gently pull their edges together, narrowly overlap them, and seal the patch either with a moistened fingertip or by running the pin over it or both.

It may take longer to read this than to do it, because the action itself should be executed in 10 minutes or less for a two-egg dough.

Drying a Sheet of Handmade Pasta

Spread a dry, clean, cloth towel on a table or work counter and lay the pasta sheet flat over the towel, being careful to avoid creases. One third of the sheet should hang over the edge. Rotate the sheet every 10 minutes to let a different part of it hang. Actual drying time depends on how moist the dough is and how warm or well ventilated the kitchen is. The dough must shed enough moisture to enable you to fold and

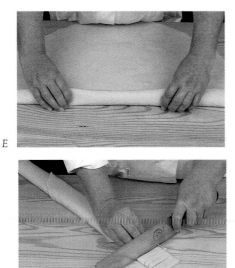

E

F

G

cut it without its becoming glued to itself, but it must stay pliant, not so dehydrated that it becomes brittle. It is usually ready to cut as soon as its surface acquires a leathery look.

Cutting Hand-rolled Pasta into Noodles

When the dough can be cut, roll up the sheet on the pasta pin, remove the towel from the counter, and unroll the pasta from the pin, laying it flat on the work surface. Fold the sheet loosely at 3-inch intervals starting at the edge farthest from you until you have one long, flat, rectangular roll about 3 inches wide (*photo E*).

Cut the roll across into ¼-inch-wide ribbons for tagliatelle, a shade narrower for fettuccine, 1 inch wide for *pappardelle* (*photo F*). Unfold the ribbons and spread them out on a dry, clean, cloth towel (*photo G*). To prepare the noodles for storage, see page 119.

Ravioli and Other Stuffed Pasta from Hand-rolled Dough

Do not let the pasta sheet dry. Cut a rectangle of the size the recipe requires from the freshly rolled-out pasta sheet, keeping the remainder of the sheet fully covered with plastic. Proceed exactly as described for machine-made pasta on page 120.

Store-Bought Boxed Semolina Pasta

In that glorious extravaganza that is Italian pasta cookery, homemade egg pasta and factory-made, boxed, semolina pasta have separate roles, but fully equal billing. The components of boxed pasta, and the methods and place of production, are wholly different from those of the homemade variety; its very structure is different, and as one might expect, it performs differently, though not a jot less brilliantly.

Unlike homemade egg pasta, whose various shapes are cut from flat, thin sheets of dough, semolina pasta shapes are extruded; the tough hard-wheat-and-water dough of which they are composed is forced through dies that mold dough into any form desired. The still soft shape is then hardened in controlled drying chambers. Although the best Italian pasta makers—Martelli, Latini, Giuseppe Cocco—are essentially craftsmen, they must work with industrial equipment, and their product, while of the highest quality, is of necessity factory-made.

Factory-made pasta is chewy and lively. It is the kind to choose when the basic fat in the sauce is olive oil, because it never gets sodden. Since all but a few seafood sauces have an olive oil base, it follows that on most occasions, factory-made semolina pasta is the one to match with seafood. Moreover, because so many sauces with summer vegetables—fresh tomatoes, peppers, eggplants—are made with olive oil, semolina pasta has special warm-weather appeal.

It is possible to match a number of butter sauces to factory pasta, and the result can be very satisfying indeed, but a butter sauce with penne or *maccheroncini* will have a different taste character from that of the same sauce with tagliatelle or fettuccine. The palate sensation can perhaps be described as blunter, more forceful, more direct. Factory pasta makes very frank taste impressions and we are naturally inclined to choose it for less formal, more improvisatory, dynamic eating experiences.

The variety of shapes that factory pasta comes in encourages us to couple it with sauces that can exploit the attributes of each shape. Each sauce recipe in this chapter makes pasta recommendations that I hope will offer useful guidance to the classic choices as well clues to discovering new, appealing combinations.

Cooking, Draining, Tossing, and Serving Pasta

What You Need

- A lightweight aluminum pot holding at least 4 quarts of water; if making pasta for 6 or more, a 6- to 8-quart pot
- A bowl-shaped self-supporting footed pasta colander
- Coarse sea or kosher salt
- A long wooden fork
- When cooking stuffed pasta, a large wire scoop for retrieving it; I use a Chinese scoop
- A cheese grater
- Fresh butter or olive oil, depending on which one was used in the sauce
- Shallow platters and deep broad bowls for serving
- A variety of skillets and saucepans for making sauce

Cooking

For 1 pound of pasta, use 4 quarts of water; and add another quart for each additional half pound. Never use less than 3 quarts, even if you are making a small quantity of pasta just for yourself. Unless you have a lot of experience in handling large pots full of scalding water, do not cook more than 2 pounds of pasta in the same pot.

First fill the pot with cold water. When it comes to a rapid boil put in no less than 1½ tablespoons of coarse sea or kosher salt for every 4 quarts of water. If the sauce is very mild and underseasoned, add a little more salt to the water. Put a lid back on the pot so that the water can quickly return to a full, rolling boil.

Put all the pasta in at one time. If it is a long, factory-made semolina pasta shape such as spaghetti or spaghettini, the moment you drop it into the pot use a long wooden spoon or fork to bend—not break—the strands and submerge them completely. If it is one of the shorter tubular shapes such as penne or *maccheroncini*, stir rapidly with the wooden spoon or fork. When pasta comes into contact with boiling water, part of its starch begins to soften; and if you don't separate the pasta immediately, and don't continue stirring periodically while it cooks, it comes together and sticks, forming gummy lumps.

Cover the pot to get the water boiling fast again. As soon as the boiling water begins to rise to the rim of the pot, either uncover completely or leave the lid on, largely askew. Adjust heat so the water continues to boil but doesn't boil over. While the pasta is cooking, stir it frequently with the wooden fork.

If you are cooking homemade egg pasta, whether it is noodles or one of the stuffed shapes, gather it in a dish towel, hold it high enough above the pot of boiling water to clear it, and while grasping the top end of the towel firmly, loosen the bottom and let the pasta slide into the pot. If you are cooking stuffed pasta, put a tablespoon of olive oil in the pot to reduce the friction that the wrappers produce as they are tossed against each other and thus keep them from splitting and spilling their stuffing. Flat strands quickly become pliant in boiling water, they will not crack, and they have nothing to spill, therefore it is neither necessary nor desirable to add olive oil to the pot in which you cook them. It follows that it is pointless to add olive oil to a pot in which any kind of factory-made semolina is cooking.

Al Dente Pasta must be cooked until it is firm to the bite, al dente. Overcooked pasta becomes leaden and pasty, it loses buoyancy and any ability to deliver briskly the flavors of its sauce. The firmness of factory-made semolina pasta is different from that of homemade egg pasta. The latter can never be as resilient and chewy as the former, but that does not mean one should allow it to become dissolvingly soft: It should always offer some resistance to the bite.

Never just follow the manufacturer's suggested cooking time on the box. Cooking times vary depending on the intensity of the heat, the conductivity of the pot, the proportion of water to pasta, and the altitude. The only way to get it right is to taste periodically while the pasta cooks.

Draining

If you drain pasta when you think it is correctly done, it will probably be overcooked when you get it to the table. You must drain pasta when you think it still needs a few seconds. By the time you have turned off the burner, carried the pot to the sink, poured the pasta into the colander, shaken it well, transferred it to the serving platter or bowl, and tossed it with the sauce, the retained heat will have cooked it just the little while longer that would have been required.

Saucing

Do not let drained pasta sit in the colander waiting for the sauce to be finished or reheated. The sauce must be ready when the pasta is,

Transfer cooked, drained pasta without a moment's delay to a warm serving platter or bowl. For egg pasta, use the broader surface of a platter, because it is too delicate to be piled deep in a bowl. The instant it's in the platter or bowl, start tossing it with the sauce. If grated cheese is called for, add some of it immediately, and toss the pasta with it. The heat will melt the cheese and it will mingle creamily with the sauce. If the fat in the sauce was olive oil, dribble some raw oil over the pasta. If it was butter, add a few dollops of fresh butter.

Tossing

In the sequence of steps that leads to producing a dish of pasta and getting it to the table, none is more important than tossing. Up to the time you toss, pasta and sauce are two separate entities. Tossing makes them one. The oil or butter must thoroughly and evenly coat every strand, reach into every crevice, and with it carry the flavors of the sauce. However appropriate a sauce may be, it cannot merely sit on top of or at the bottom of the bowl. If sauce is not uniformly dispersed, the pasta which is to be its vehicle will have an imperfect load of flavor to deliver.

Toss rapidly, using a fork and spoon or two forks, reaching into the bottom of the bowl or platter to lift the pasta up. Separate it, lift it, drop it, turn it over, swirl it around and back. If the sauce clings thickly together, separate it with the fork and spoon. When the dish is ready to serve, there should be an even distribution of pasta and sauce.

ABOUT PASTA "ROUX"

This applies mainly to factory-made semolina pasta. Home cooks have long known that the water in which the pasta cooked contained some dissolved starch, and they used a spoonful of this water as a thickener, adding it to the sauce, to which they gave a very fast blast of heat and a swirl or two before tossing it with the pasta. Restaurant cooks have gone further. They drain the pasta when it is quite underdone, add the pasta and some of its water to a skillet containing the sauce, and toss it over high heat for a minute or so. It is to my mind a little like using roux, that flour-and-butter fixture of French sauces. I have never cared for roux-thickened sauces and I don't like the fashion for pasta "roux," as I call it. Today, in restaurant after restaurant, it imparts the same tedious, faintly gelatinous texture to what might otherwise have been fresh and lively sauces. When used occasionally and sagaciously—see the Broccoli and Mozzarella Pasta Sauce on page 146—it is to impart a special consistency to that dish. When the practice becomes routine, it ends by being boring.

Sauces

Celery and Tomato Pasta Sauce

SUGO DI SEDANO E POMODORO

3 tablespoons butter

1 tablespoon extra virgin olive oil

⅓ cup finely chopped onion

1 cup chopped celery stalks

1 cup chopped celery leaves

2 cups canned imported Italian plum tomatoes, cut up, with their juice

Salt

Black pepper ground fresh

⅓ cup freshly grated Parmigiano-Reggiano cheese

Enough sauce for 1 pound of pasta, making 4 large or 6 small servings

The aroma of celery, a zephyr-like presence, has a background role in many preparations, from vegetable soups to risottos to stuffings to stews, but in this Roman sauce it gets an up-front opportunity to display all its considerable charm. There is a greater concentration of fragrance in the leaves than in the stalks alone, an important consideration when using American celery, whose scent is usually more muted than that of Italian varieties. To achieve the aromatic intensity I was looking for when cooking in America, I used leaves and stalks in equal proportion, whereas in Italy, if I used leaves at all, it would be in a ratio of one part of leaves to four of stalks.

If you'd like to do as the Romans do, serve the sauce over fine homemade fettuccine.

SUGGESTED PASTA: Homemade noodles are the best foil for this sauce, either fettuccine or the square ones known as *tonnarelli* (see page 118). Boxed dry pasta will also work well if you choose a short tubular shape such as penne or *maccheroncini*.

1. Put 2 tablespoons of butter, the olive oil, and the chopped onion in a medium saucepan and turn on the heat to medium. Cook, stirring from time to time, until the onion becomes colored a pale gold.

2. Add the celery stalks and leaves and cook for about 10 minutes, stirring occasionally.

3. Add the chopped tomatoes with their juice, salt, and liberal grindings of pepper, and turn them over two or three times with the other ingredients. Lower the heat to low or medium low, and cook at a gentle simmer for about 15 or 20 minutes until the fat begins to separate from the sauce.

NOTE: As tomatoes cook down and their watery part evaporates, the fat you have used begins to run clear. When you skim the surface of the sauce with the side of a wooden spoon, or wipe away the sauce with the spoon from the bottom of a skillet, you see clear fat following the spoon's trail, an indication that the tomato is done.

4. Cook and drain the pasta and toss it immediately and thoroughly with the sauce, swirling into it the remaining tablespoon of butter and the grated Parmesan.

AHEAD-OF-TIME NOTE: You may prepare the sauce up to a day or two in advance. Reheat it through and through at a gentle simmer when you are ready to cook and serve the pasta.

Ligurian-Style Pasta Sauce with Raw Tomatoes, Olives, Capers, and Anchovies

SUGO LIGURE COL POMODORO CRUDO, OLIVE, CAPPERI, E ACCIUGHE

1½ dozen whole small black olives

8 whole green olives in brine

1½ tablespoons capers

5 or 6 anchovy fillets, preferably the ones prepared at home as described on page 148

1½ pounds fresh, really ripe, firm tomatoes

10 basil leaves

1½ teaspoons marjoram OR ¾ teaspoon oregano

2 garlic cloves, peeled and chopped very fine

¼ cup very finely chopped Italian flat-leaf parsley

Salt

Black pepper ground fresh

½ teaspoon red wine vinegar

6 tablespoons extra virgin olive oil

Enough sauce for 1 pound of pasta, making 4 large or 6 small servings

Although this sauce is completely raw, you might say that it cooks itself. It is a fine demonstration of the dynamic reaction that ingredients can have to each other, if you give them the chance.

SUGGESTED PASTA: Only boxed factory-made dry pasta is a good match for this sauce, and spaghettini, thin spaghetti, is the most strongly recommended shape.

1. Pit both the black and the green olives. If using capers packed in vinegar, drain them and rinse them in cold water. If using capers packed in salt, run cold water over them, then place them in a bowl of cold water to soak for 30 minutes. Drain them and rinse in several changes of cold water.

2. Chop the pitted olives, the capers, and the anchovy fillets all together. You can use a food processor but do not overprocess to a pulp. Set aside in a small mixing bowl.

3. Wash the tomatoes and skin them raw using a swivel- bladed vegetable peeler. Cut them in half, scoop out the seeds, and cut the tomatoes into narrow fillets about ¼ inch wide. Add them to the bowl.

4. Cut the basil into very thin strips and add it to the bowl together with the marjoram or oregano, the garlic, the parsley, a liberal sprinkling of salt, black pepper, and the vinegar. Toss once or twice, then add the olive oil and toss again, thoroughly. Allow the sauce to steep for at least 1 hour, turning all ingredients over from time to time. Taste and correct for salt and other seasonings.

5. Cook the pasta to a firm, al dente consistency. Drain and toss at once with the contents of the sauce bowl, turning the pasta strands over several times to coat them well. Serve promptly.

WORKING WITH TOMATOES

The tomato—by its presence in appetizers; in pasta sauces; in fish, poultry, and meat courses; in vegetable dishes; and in salads—plays a many-sided, and sometimes commanding, role on the Italian table. To marshal its broad expressive range for your purposes you must get under its skin, and I mean that as literally as I do figuratively.

WHICH TOMATO? Our choice of tomato depends on how we are going to use it and, in Italy, that can depend on regional preferences. When making salads, for example, the south of Italy favors tomatoes that are ripened to a deep red and whose flesh is tender and sweet. Northerners are more likely to select underripe tomatoes that are more pink than red and even partly green, prizing them for their firmness and sprightly, refreshing tartness. Some of the most sought-after salad varieties are the small round ones grown in Pachino, Sicily, and in S. Margherita di Pula in Sardinia. The even smaller *cigliegini*, cherry tomatoes, particularly the kind known as Naomi, have surged in quality and popularity in recent years. Originally from Sicily, they are now grown in every region, as are the large, round, creased-on-top garden variety that are the staple of tomato salads everywhere. Wherever one's personal preference in tomatoes may fall—and when more than one variety is available one may use several in a salad—a tomato that you eat raw should be chosen with the same criteria you apply to fruit. The pulp should be luscious, not woolly, and flavorful juice must spring from it at every bite. Yet it ought never to be decadently soft and overripe.

Although very good salad tomatoes can also be satisfactory cooking tomatoes, and that is certainly the case with the cherry variety, there are some whose properties make them particularly desirable to cook with. Their mouth feel, when raw, may not be quite as luscious as you'd like in a salad, but their density, their meatiness, their delicious concentration of flavor are what you look for when making sauce. Romans use small, deeply furrowed, round tomatoes called *casalini*. Sicily produces excellent, smooth, round tomatoes which are shipped attached in bunches to their branch. They are now available not only all over Italy, but also abroad. The paramount cooking tomatoes, however, are the plum-shaped ones that Italians call perini, little pears. There are several varieties, which go by such names as Roma or San Marzano. There is no better sauce tomato than the latter, particularly if it is grown and ripened on the vines of the plains of Campania, the region whose capital city is Naples. I have found fresh plum tomatoes in nearly every market where I have shopped, but no variety so needs the full heat of summer to ripen fully, and that is the only season in which to buy it fresh.

PEELING. A tomato's peel is a veil which obscures the wonders of its flesh. If you leave it on, the tomatoes will eventually shed their peel as they cook, and later you will either have to pick it out

or, since it is not pleasant to chew on, swallow it. And whether you pick it out or swallow it, it will have faintly tainted the dish with that slight touch of bitterness which, like all vegetable and fruit peels, it possesses. Like many Italians, I even peel tomatoes for salad so that they will taste sweeter. The only tomatoes I don't peel are the tiny cherries because their size makes it impractical and their skin is so thin as to be negligible.

There is more than one way to skin a tomato. If I am using it in a salad or if I am cooking it very quickly for one of the sauces where the tomato pulp must remain fairly firm—in Naples they call such sauce *al filetto di pomodoro*, tomato fillets stripped of their seeds—I use a peeler. The tool I refer to is the one with a movable blade, slotted lengthwise in the center, held loosely by pins at each end. Such a tool requires absolutely no pressure. The swiveling blade

adjusts itself to the tomato's shape and you use it the way you'd use a slicing knife, sawing backward and forward, letting the blade do the work. The moment the blade's edge digs into the skin, slide it along with the lightest of touches and a side-to-side seesawing motion to separate the peel from the flesh. Cut the tomatoes in quarters if you are going to cook them, and if you want just the pulp, scoop out the seeds with a spoon. Do not squeeze them, because that will make them mushy.

NOTE: If you are working with raw plum tomatoes, look to see if they have a single straight furrow on top where they had been attached to the plant. If they do, slice the tomatoes lengthwise in half, cutting perpendicularly to the furrow. You will find that the tomato comes open exactly where its seeds lie, and you can then easily scoop them out.

Dousing tomatoes with hot water enables you to lift off the skin quickly and effortlessly. It will make the surface very slightly soft and moist, but the flesh beneath will still be firm and you can use them in a quick-cooking sauce or wherever you want palpable pieces of tomato as a featured component of the dish. With a paring knife, cut a 1-inch cross into the top, where the tomato had been attached to its branch. Put all the tomatoes you are going to use into a bowl. Bring water to a boil, pour it into the bowl, count to 15, drain and lift away the tomatoes' skin with your fingertips. Cut them in quarters and scoop out the seeds as suggested above.

When the tomatoes' place is in the background of a dish—where its consistency requires no emphasis—it doesn't matter if it undergoes the preliminary softening up that blanching produces. In such an instance you can lower the tomatoes into a pot of boiling water, retrieve them after 5 or 6 minutes, and slip the skin off completely. Chop them and use them as they are, with their seeds and juices.

COOKING. The longer you cook tomatoes the more of their fragrance they lose. For most sauces, 15 to 20 minutes is long enough, and it ought not to be longer than 45 minutes to 1 hour for any preparation. In those dishes that cook longer, such as some stews and meat sauces, the tomatoes are usually added to the pot during the last cooking phase.

STORAGE. Keep tomatoes out of the refrigerator, in a basket or other ventilated container.

Underripe tomatoes will ripen nicely indoors in just a few days. Eat them or cook them before they begin to spoil.

CANNED TOMATOES. The ideal tomato is fresh, firm, ripened on the vine, but even when available, its season is short. Cooking with out-of-season tomatoes, no matter how fetching they may look, will prove a disappointment. You will not be disappointed, however, with high-quality canned tomatoes. The best are the San Marzano variety, and the label should state "packed in Italy," not just "Italian-style." They should be whole, firm, and deep red in color. Do not buy crushed, chopped, or pureed tomatoes, which are made from tomatoes that are not perfect enough to be packed whole. Do not give your preference to cans that contain a basil leaf in addition to the tomatoes. Not that it does any harm; it is merely useless.

Scallion, Cherry Tomato, and Chili Pepper Pasta Sauce

SUGO DI CIPOLLOTTI, POMODORINI, E PEPERONCINO

12 to 14 cherry tomatoes

24 scallions

¼ cup extra virgin olive oil

**2 garlic cloves, peeled and
sliced very, very thin**

**½ jalapeño chili pepper, or
more to taste, cut into
thin rounds**

Salt

---

*Enough sauce for 1 pound of
pasta, making 4 large or 6 small
servings*

Cherry tomatoes have long been around, but it is only in the past decade that their quality has so improved that one is more likely to use them for their flavor than for their appearance. Cultivation under plastic canopies has lengthened their season in Italy, from early spring to fall, and although they are very expensive, we are happy to have them when other varieties of tomatoes, either for cooking or for salads, are not at their peak.

They must be quite ripe, and quite firm, otherwise they make no sense. When I can get away with it, I pop one into my mouth before deciding. If it releases dense, sweet juice and full flavor, I buy; if it is thin, vapid, and acidulous, I go for something else.

The Italian version of this sauce, which I had in Amalfi during a wine event my husband and I attended there, requires both very ripe, sweet cherry tomatoes and young onions, *cipollotti. Cipollotti* are onions at an early stage of development when the bulbs are small and tender. They are sold with their green shoots still on. I have never seen them in an American market, but I always see scallions, which are rare in Italy. Having made that substitution I also opted for jalapeño peppers, rather than the fresh small red chili pepper—*peperoncino*—that Italians are accustomed to using. Jalapeño is an unusual example of a nontraditional ingredient whose fresh and attractive aroma finds a ready welcome in an Italian dish.

SUGGESTED PASTA: A slim shape of boxed dry pasta such as spaghettini or narrow penne.

1. Wash the tomatoes and cut them in half—any particularly large ones in quarters. Set aside.

2. Trim away any roots from the scallion bulbs and any wilted or bruised ends from the green tops. Cut the scallions into 2-inch lengths, dividing the white part in half lengthwise. Soak the pieces in cold water, then rinse under running water.

3. Put the scallions, olive oil, sliced garlic, chili pepper, and salt in a medium skillet and turn the heat on to medium. Cook for 10 or 15 minutes, stirring from time to time, until the scallions are very soft.

4. Add the cut-up tomatoes, turn over all ingredients using a wooden spoon, and cook for 10 or 15 minutes longer, stirring occasionally. Taste and correct for salt and chili pepper.

5. Cook and drain the pasta; toss it immediately and thoroughly with the entire contents of the pan.

AHEAD-OF-TIME NOTE: The sauce may be prepared up to a day in advance, but there is not much to be gained by doing so because it can be made practically in the same time that it takes the water for the pasta to come to a boil and the pasta to cook.

Sardinian-Style Raw Tomato Sauce for Pasta

SUGO DI POMODORINI CRUDI COME A S. MARGHERITA DI PULA

¾ to 1 pound cherry
   tomatoes

½ dozen black, round
   Greek-style olives

3½ tablespoons extra virgin
   olive oil

1 tablespoon aged sheep's
   milk cheese, preferably
   fiore sardo, otherwise
   Romano, crumbled or
   coarsely grated

½ cup thinly slivered
   Parmigiano-Reggiano
   cheese

2 tablespoons chopped
   Italian flat-leaf parsley

½ teaspoon very finely
   chopped garlic

Salt

Black pepper ground fresh

*Enough sauce for 1 pound of
pasta, making 4 large or 6 small
servings*

A serving bowl for pasta and,
preferably (see recipe), another
bowl of larger diameter

In S. Margherita di Pula, on the southern coast of Sardinia, they produce a small, round, deep red tomato, about 1½ inches in diameter, its
top dimpled and marked by splotches of vivid malachite green. When I
saw a basket of these tomatoes for the first time at the market, my gaze
attracted the attention of the vendor, who picked one up, rubbed it with
her apron, and handed it to me saying, "Here, try it." To say it tasted more
of tomato than any other one I had ever had might be correct, but it falls
short of describing the explosive impact its flavor had in the mouth.
When, under the teeth, it burst through its skin, the sensation was overwhelming; it had more than sweetness, more than ripeness; it had force.

Whenever I sat down to eat in Sardinia, I asked if there was any
dish with the tomatoes of S. Margherita, and I had them with fish,
with sausages, in salads, in pasta sauces. In one sauce they were used
raw. It had a denser, spicier flavor than the Ligurian raw sauce on page
134, and as soon as I was back in Venice I tried it with local cherry
tomatoes. It may not have tasted like Sardinia—nothing anywhere else
can—but it was good, and later on I tried it again on Long Island, in
the Hamptons, with marvelous red and yellow cherry tomatoes from
Jim Pike's market in Sagaponack, and it was even more successful.

The tomato is the thing. There is hardly anything to the making of
the sauce, which really consists just of assembling the ingredients and
letting them go to work, but the tomatoes have to be ripe and tasty. If
the cherry tomatoes available to you are watery, use any other kind, as
long as they are ripe and sweet, but skin them with a peeler, and cut
them up into cherry-size nuggets, scooping away the seeds.

SUGGESTED PASTA: In Sardinia I had this with the local pasta, a
short, narrow, tapered handmade shape called *malloredus*, which looks
like a little shell. You could substitute *cavatelli* or fusilli or short, tubular boxed dry pasta shapes such as penne or *maccheroncini*.

1. Wash the tomatoes in cold water, and cut each into four wedges or in half, if very small. Put them in the pasta bowl.

2. Cut the olives' flesh away from the pit in little slices, and add it to the bowl.

3. Add to the bowl 3 tablespoons of olive oil and then all the other ingredients, toss a few times, and allow to steep at room temperature for at least 30 minutes—better, 45 minutes or longer—before cooking the pasta.

4. When ready to cook the pasta, put very hot water into the empty larger bowl and lower the pasta bowl into it, making sure that the water does not overflow into the sauce. You want to take the chill off both the serving bowl and the sauce so that later they won't cool off the pasta too quickly. If you do not have a large bowl that will accommodate the one with sauce, place the latter over a saucepan with barely simmering water. Turn the sauce over from time to time.

5. Cook and drain the pasta, transfer it immediately to the bowl with the sauce, and toss thoroughly, drizzling over it the remaining ½ tablespoon of olive oil. Serve at once.

AHEAD-OF-TIME NOTE: The sauce can be made up to 1½ to 2 hours in advance and kept at kitchen temperature.

Spinach and Tomato Pasta Sauce, Romagna-Style

SUGO ROMAGNOLO CON GLI SPINACI E IL POMODORO

1 pound fresh spinach

2 tablespoons extra virgin olive oil

⅓ cup very finely chopped onion

1½ tablespoons finely chopped pancetta

¼ cup finely chopped celery

¼ cup finely chopped carrot

Salt

Black pepper ground fresh

1 tablespoon butter plus one to two tablespoons for tossing the pasta

1 cup canned imported Italian plum tomatoes, cut up, with their juice, OR ripe, firm, fresh tomatoes, peeled, seeds scooped away, and cut up

¾ cup freshly grated Parmigiano-Reggiano cheese

Enough sauce for 1 pound of pasta, making 4 large or 6 small servings

If you have ever strolled through an Italian street market you will have noticed that it differs from American farmers' markets or country farmstands in one startling regard. Buying vegetables from stalls in America is a little like being in a mime show or watching a video with the sound shut off. A rarely interrupted silence accompanies the process: You pick your produce, hand it to the vendor, the price is mentioned, money is exchanged, someone says thank you, and that is it. An Italian market explodes with sound. The moment you come within earshot of the vendors you are the object of exhortations: "Look at my green beans—they snap like dry kindling! The mushrooms, the mushrooms, they are only 30,000 lire! Have you seen my figs? they are *crepati*—so ripe they are cracking!"

In my hometown of Cesenatico, a small open-air market is held every morning by a few women who come in from the surrounding farms with produce and fruit from their vegetable gardens and orchards. We have all known each other forever and the address becomes more personal. "Signora Marcella!" one of the women cries out, "I picked the spinach this morning. Take it and make a sauce for lunch." "How do you make your sauce?" I ask. Patiently, she tells me. And now, I shall tell *you*.

SUGGESTED PASTA: The spinach and tomato sauce was born to wed the homemade noodles every housewife in Romagna used to make. (My cousin Fabio had them every day of his life.) Tagliatelle or fettuccine (pages 118–19) are a faultless choice, but an even happier union is with the broad noodles known as *pappardelle*, described on page 119.

1. Trim away the longer, tougher stems of the spinach, and soak the leaves in a basin of cold water. Retrieve the leaves with your hands, pour out the water, rinse the basin, refill it, and put the leaves back in again to soak until you no longer find the slightest trace of soil. Chop the spinach rather coarse.

2. Put the olive oil and chopped onion in a 12-inch skillet or sauté pan, and turn on the heat to medium. Cook the onion, stirring it, until it becomes colored a pale gold.

3. Add the pancetta; cook it for about a minute, turning it with a wooden spoon so that it browns on all sides; then add the celery and carrot. Cook these for a minute or two, turning them to coat them well.

4. Begin to add the chopped spinach, a fistful at a time, turning it as it cooks. When the first batch has become limp, add another, and proceed thus until all the spinach is in the pan. Add salt and liberal grindings of pepper, and turn all ingredients two or three times.

5. Turn the heat up to high. Turn the spinach. At first it will throw off the liquid that was clinging to it from the soaking. When the liquid has evaporated, add 1 tablespoon of butter, and cook for 10 minutes, turning the spinach frequently to keep it from sticking.

6. Add the tomatoes and adjust heat to cook at a lively simmer, turning all ingredients two or three times with the wooden spoon. Cook for 5 to 8 minutes longer.

7. Toss in a warm, deep platter with the just cooked and drained pasta, swirling into it 1 to 2 tablespoons of butter—2 tablespoons will taste better than 1—and the grated Parmesan. Serve at once.

AHEAD-OF-TIME NOTE: The sauce can be entirely cooked 2 or 3 hours in advance. Cover with plastic wrap, but do not refrigerate. Reheat at a gentle but steady simmer, adding a little pat of butter.

Eggplant Sauce with Bell Pepper, Tomato, and Basil

SUGO DI MELANZANE

———— 🍇 ————

1½ pounds medium
eggplants

Salt

1 yellow bell pepper

3 tablespoons extra virgin
olive oil plus 1
tablespoon for tossing
the pasta

3 garlic cloves, peeled and
sliced very, very thin

Chopped red chili pepper,
⅛ teaspoon or to taste

2 tablespoons Italian flat-
leaf parsley, the whole
leaves, not chopped

⅓ cup thinly sliced onion

1 cup ripe, firm, fresh
tomatoes, peeled, seeds
scooped away, and cut
up, OR canned imported
Italian plum tomatoes,
cut up with their juice

⅓ cup dry white wine

6 small basil leaves OR 3 to 4
large ones, hand-torn
into smaller pieces

When employed to make a pasta sauce, eggplant is a vegetable that can spring surprises, not all of them invariably agreeable. The flavor can swing from bitterness to cloying blandness. Ivo, the owner-cook of the small restaurant in Venice that bears his name, makes an eggplant sauce that has never wearied or disappointed me. It is authoritatively fragrant and spicy, yet it always delivers a good measure of that lively sweetness that is eggplant's most winning feature. If you are acquainted with *caponatina*, the Sicilian eggplant dish, you'll recognize a touch of it in this sauce, and a touch too of *peperonata*, the pepper and onion combination often served over meat.

Suggested Pasta: Boxed dry pasta is a must. Choose a short tubular shape such as penne or *maccheroncini*. Fusilli would also be a good choice.

1. Cut away the eggplants' green tops, wash the eggplants in cold water, and split them lengthwise in half. If there is a large quantity of seeds, and particularly if these are dark, cut the eggplant halves lengthwise again in half and scoop out the seeds, leaving about 1 to 1½ inches of flesh next to the skin. If there are only a few small, pale seeds, leave them. Cut the eggplant into 3-inch lengths, about 1 to 1½ inches thick.

2. Set a pasta colander over a shallow bowl, place the eggplant pieces inside the colander, sprinkle with salt, toss them, and let them steep for at least 45 minutes to discharge their bitter liquid.

3. Split the pepper in half, scoop out the pith-like core and seeds, and use a peeler with a swiveling blade to skin the pepper. Cut it lengthwise into thin strips.

**6 green olives in brine,
pitted and quartered**

1½ tablespoons capers

---

*Enough sauce for 1 pound of
pasta, making 4 large or 6 small
servings*

4. Put 3 tablespoons of olive oil, garlic, and chili pepper in a 10-inch skillet and turn on the heat to medium. Cook, stirring frequently, just until the garlic's scent begins to rise, but do not let it become colored.

5. Add the parsley leaves, stir two or three times, then add the onion and turn the heat down to low. Cook the onion, turning it over occasionally, until it becomes very soft.

6. Add the pepper strips, and sprinkle with salt. Cook, turning the ingredients over occasionally, until the pepper has become somewhat tender.

7. Add the eggplant, the tomatoes, and the wine, basil, olives, and capers. Turn over all ingredients two or three times to coat them well. Put a lid on the pan and cook at steady but gentle simmer for about 40 minutes. If, while the sauce is simmering, you should find that the cooking juices have dried up and there is danger of the vegetables sticking to the pan, add ⅓ cup water. Do not add too much water too often, or the vegetables will steam rather than stew, and bear in mind that there should be no water left at the end.

8. Cook and drain the pasta. Toss it immediately and thoroughly with the sauce, swirling into it 1 tablespoon of olive oil. Serve promptly.

AHEAD-OF-TIME NOTE: The sauce may be prepared several hours in advance or even the night before. Reheat gently but thoroughly, adding a tablespoon or two of water if needed.

Broccoli and Mozzarella Pasta Sauce

SUGO DI BROCCOLI E MOZZARELLA

½ pound broccoli

Salt

1 tablespoon vegetable oil

2 tablespoons butter

1 tablespoon chopped garlic

¼ pound mozzarella, chopped fine

2 tablespoons coarsely chopped Italian flat-leaf parsley

½ cup freshly grated Parmigiano-Reggiano cheese plus more cheese to grate at the table

Enough sauce for 1 pound of pasta, making 4 large or 6 small servings

There are many vegetables in Italian cooking with which, on occasion, one uses butter: green beans, zucchini, asparagus, spinach, Swiss chard, to name just the ones that come immediately to mind. When I was told that broccoli absolutely had to be cooked in olive oil, I bridled. Absolutely? Why? So here is a sauce where I pulled and stretched some regional borders to include something from the south—broccoli and mozzarella—and something from the north: butter and Parmesan. After all, if in the south of Italy no one cooks with butter, why do all the stores there bother carrying it, as indeed they do?

There is a luscious, clinging texture to this lovely green sauce that works so well with pasta. Note that tossing the pasta with the sauce is completed in the skillet, at which time you add the mozzarella so that as it melts over heat it completes the fusion of pasta and sauce. It's not a technique that I favor indiscriminately, as you will note from my comments on it on page 131, but this is one of those rare instances when there is a compelling reason for adopting it.

SUGGESTED PASTA: With broccoli, boxed dry pasta tastes better than any other kind. You'll be tossing the cooked pasta in a pan at the end, so a short shape such as rigatoni would be the one to choose, for its sturdiness and ease of handling. Also satisfactory are fusilli or penne.

1. Detach the florets and any small leaves from the broccoli. Pare away from the broccoli's main stems, and from the larger of the florets' stems as well, the hard, dark green rind and any other tough stringy part. Cut the thick, detached stems lengthwise in half. Wash the stems under cold running water, and the florets in several changes of cold water.

2. Bring a pot of water to a boil, add 2 tablespoons salt and the thick main broccoli stems. (The salt is to keep the broccoli green and will

not make it salty.) Cook for 6 or 7 minutes, then add the florets. When the water returns to a boil, cook for another 10 minutes or so, until the thickest broccoli piece feels tender when tested with a fork. Drain, and as soon as the vegetable is cool enough to handle comfortably, chop it fine.

3. In a 12-inch skillet put the oil, butter, and chopped garlic, and turn on the heat to medium. Cook the garlic, stirring frequently, until it becomes colored a pale gold.

4. Add the chopped broccoli and a little salt, turn it two or three times to coat it well, then take the pan off heat.

5. Cook the pasta in abundant salted boiling water to a very firm *al dente* consistency. Drain it, collecting in a small bowl better than half a cup of the water.

6. Add the drained pasta to the pan containing the broccoli; turn on the heat to high; turn over the pasta and broccoli three or four times; then add the chopped mozzarella, the parsley, the ½ cup grated Parmesan, and ½ cup of the pasta water that you previously collected. Briskly turn over the pasta until the mozzarella has fused and the water has been entirely absorbed or boiled away.

7. Transfer to a warm bowl and serve at once with additional Parmesan to grate at the table.

AHEAD-OF-TIME NOTE: You can cook the chopped broccoli a few hours in advance to the end of step 4, in which it is sautéed with the garlic. Keep it in the pan, putting a lid over it as soon as it has cooled off. Do not refrigerate. When you resume cooking and the pasta is boiling, warm up the broccoli with a little dollop of butter.

MAKING YOUR OWN ANCHOVY FILLETS

There is no region in Italy that does not use anchovy fillets in some of its dishes. Used wisely, anchovies provide an unseen but firm foundation on which other ingredients can build up flavor. Unfortunately, most prepared and tinned anchovy fillets are of the crumbly, excessively salty kind that have given this precious ingredient a bad name. When you find a brand, either in cans or in jars, whose fillets are well fleshed and whose flavor enriches a dish without masking the other flavors, stick with it.

Whole anchovies packed in salt, sold loose out of a large tin, are the best of all. You needn't buy more than ¼ pound at a time, which you will take home, rinse, bone, and keep under good olive oil until you need them. You may discover that served on buttered crusty bread they make one of the world's most satisfying snacks, and then you will want to buy a larger quantity. Here is how you prepare them:

1. One by one, hold the anchovies under cold, running water, rinsing off the salt which encrusts them.

2. Lay an anchovy down on a washable work surface, or on a plate, grasp it at the tail end, and use a small paring knife to scrape off the skin, going from the tail toward the head. Turn it over and do the other side; then remove the dorsal fin, pulling away with it the tiny bones attached to it.

3. Insert your thumbnail into the end of the anchovy where the head used to be and scrape it along the bone to open the anchovy completely flat, exposing the spine. Snap off the spine at the tail end and pull it away, thus producing 2 spineless fillets.

4. With the paring knife, scrape away the intestines from the anchovy's belly.

5. Most Italians would not be bothered by the small loose bones that may remain because they are so small and soft they are virtually imperceptible. If you are troubled, pick them out with a tweezer.

6. When all the anchovies are done, rinse the fillets under cold running water, then pat dry.

7. Choose a rectangular glass or ceramic container that can accommodate the fillets lying flat. Smear the bottom with olive oil, cover with a layer of fillets, pour olive oil over these, and continue in the same manner using up all the fillets. Their top layer must be fully under oil. Wrap the container with plastic wrap and refrigerate. You could also roll up each fillet and store them all in a jar filled with olive oil. The anchovies are most delicious just at this moment, but they will keep quite well for up to 2 weeks. Bring to room temperature before using.

NOTE: I was delighted to receive some months ago a 2-pound tin of anchovies under salt, but my delight turned to despair when I opened it and began to clean and fillet the anchovies. They were so small that they became infuriatingly difficult to handle. An hour's work produced so few fillets that I gave the rest away. I regret that I cannot recommend buying them, unless to someone far nimbler than I.

Pepper and Anchovy Pasta Sauce

SUGO DI PEPERONI E ACCIUGHE

3 large or 4 medium red or yellow bell peppers

4 tablespoons extra virgin olive oil

4 garlic cloves, peeled and sliced very thin

Salt

8 anchovy fillets, preferably the ones prepared at home as described on facing page

2 tablespoons chopped capers

Hot chili pepper, ⅛ teaspoon or to taste

2 tablespoons chopped Italian flat-leaf parsley

2 tablespoons fine, dry, unflavored bread crumbs

Enough sauce for 1 pound of pasta, making 4 large or 6 small servings

The sauce, unmistakably Apulian, is one that the companion my mother had in her last years—Romana, a woman who emigrated to my hometown from Bari—prepared when her charge used to yearn for something savory.

I have brought to it some small Marcella touches: I peel the peppers raw because that makes them even sweeter, and I slice the garlic cloves very thin rather than smashing them because that releases a gentler scent. Avoid strong, direct heat, which would make it hard to dissolve the anchovies. No Parmesan cheese is used here. In characteristic southern style, fine unflavored bread crumbs take its place.

SUGGESTED PASTA: High-quality boxed spaghetti or spaghettini take precedence over all other shapes, with a strong preference for spaghettini, thin spaghetti.

1. Wash the peppers, split them in half, remove the white core and the seeds, and peel them, using a vegetable peeler with a swiveling blade. Cut the peppers lengthwise into thin strips about ¼ inch wide.

2. Put 3 tablespoons of the olive oil and the sliced garlic into a skillet and turn on the heat to medium. Cook, stirring from time to time, until the garlic becomes colored a light gold.

3. Add the peppers and a pinch of salt and cook, stirring occasionally, until they are completely tender, approximately 15 minutes. Take the pan off heat and let the peppers cool down.

4. Chop the anchovy fillets to a fine pulp. (If you have not chopped the capers separately, you can do both together, even in the food processor.) Add the anchovies, capers, and chili pepper to the skillet containing the peppers and, always off heat, stir them in very thoroughly. Taste and correct for seasoning, adding salt or chili pepper if necessary.

(continued)

5. While the pasta is boiling, and when it is about 1 or 2 minutes away from being done, put the pan back over the burner, turn on the heat to medium low, and gently warm up the sauce, stirring steadily.

6. When the pasta is cooked to a firm, *al dente* consistency, drain and toss at once with the contents of the pan. Add the remaining tablespoon of raw olive oil, the parsley, and the bread crumbs, turning the pasta strands over several times to coat them well. Serve promptly.

AHEAD-OF-TIME NOTE: You can prepare the sauce several hours ahead of time through to the end of step 4.

Pepper, Pancetta, and Parsley Pasta Sauce

SUGO DI PEPERONI, PANCETTA, E PREZZEMOLO

2 large or 3 medium red
  bell peppers

1 tablespoon vegetable oil

1 tablespoon butter plus 1
  tablespoon for tossing
  the pasta

2 tablespoons finely
  chopped garlic

½ cup Italian flat-leaf
  parsley, the whole leaves
  only

Salt

¼ pound pancetta, cut into
  very thin strips

1 cup freshly grated
  Parmigiano-Reggiano
  cheese

*Enough sauce for 1 pound of
pasta, making 4 large or 6 small
servings.*

The influence of small details on flavor can be disproportionately large. Two seemingly inconsequential steps are essential to its taste. The special aroma of the parsley is owed to the use of the whole leaves, without chopping. And the peppers' flesh would not be quite so luscious if you failed to skin them before cooking them.

SUGGESTED PASTA: Although homemade noodles, particularly the broad ones known as *pappardelle,* see page 119, go nicely with this sauce, I find that boxed dry pasta in the shape of fusilli makes the tastiest combination of all. A short tubular shape such as penne or *maccheroncini* also works well.

1. Wash the peppers, split them in half lengthwise, and remove the pulpy white core with all the seeds. Use a vegetable peeler with a swiveling blade to peel the peppers, then cut them lengthwise into strips ¼ inch wide.

2. Into a 10-inch skillet put the oil, 1 tablespoon butter, the chopped garlic, and turn on the heat to medium. Cook the garlic, stirring frequently, just until it becomes no darker than a translucent white.

3. Add the whole parsley leaves with a little salt, turn them briskly three or four times, then add the pancetta strips. Cook, turning the pancetta over occasionally for 2 or 3 minutes, then raise the heat to medium high and add the peppers. Cook, turning the peppers from time to time, until they feel tender, about 8 to 10 minutes.

4. Cook and drain the pasta, toss it immediately and thoroughly with the sauce, swirling into it the remaining tablespoon of butter and the grated Parmesan. Serve at once.

AHEAD-OF-TIME NOTE: You could prepare the peppers 2 or 3 hours in advance, covering them with plastic wrap, but since it will take less time to make the sauce than to bring water to a boil and cook the pasta, there is nothing to be gained by starting it ahead.

Porcini-Style Shiitake Mushroom Pasta Sauce

SUGO DI FUNGHI FRESCHI ALLA MODA DEI PORCINI

¾ pound fresh white
  cultivated mushrooms

½ pound fresh shiitake
  mushrooms

3 tablespoons extra virgin
  olive oil

½ cup chopped onion

1½ tablespoons chopped
  garlic

2 tablespoons chopped
  Italian flat-leaf parsley

Salt

½ cup heavy cream

2 tablespoons butter

Black pepper ground fresh

¾ cup freshly grated
  Parmigiano-Reggiano
  cheese

*Enough sauce for 1 pound of
pasta, making 6 adequate
servings*

Late in spring and early in the fall, puddles bring mushrooms, and mushrooms in Italy bring their gatherers, both professional and amateur, who scour the woods with bent back and a large potato sack in hand. As I am writing this, at the end of September in Venice, baskets full of fresh wild mushrooms are glorifying the Rialto market, displaying porcini (*Boletus edulis*), yellow and black *finferli* (chanterelles), *spugnole* (morels), *chiodini* ("little nails," a long-stemmed, densely clustered variety), and *ovoli* (orange-capped *agaricus*).

When Italian cooks say *funghi*—mushrooms—they are referring to the wild variety, because the cultivated ones are a poorly regarded synthetic version of the real thing. *Ovoli* are highly prized for salads; but to cook with, the intense musky scent and juicy flesh of porcini makes it by far the most desirable of all *funghi*.

When working with cultivated mushrooms, I try to find methods that will excite from them flavor reminiscent of *Boletus*. An example is the combination of dried porcini and fresh cultivated white button mushrooms that I discovered years ago; it is described in my earlier books. Recently I found that I could achieve a comparable result by using white mushrooms and fresh shiitake together. The exchange of flavor that takes place between the two varieties produces such a remarkable evocation of the aroma that one looks for in *Boletus* that, as long as I have shiitake, I am more peacefully resigned to the absence of fresh porcini from American markets.

There is nothing like olive oil for bringing out the woodsy accent from mushrooms, and that is how I start them. But I love to serve mushrooms with homemade pasta, whose porous texture thirsts for butter and cream, so I add the two in the final cooking stage to achieve both objectives, full mushroom flavor from the mushrooms and an elegant sauce for fine homemade egg pasta.

SUGGESTED PASTA: Any of the homemade noodles; the square ones known as *tonnarelli*, see page 118, or *pappardelle*, page 119, or fettuccine.

1. Rinse all the mushrooms quickly under fast-running water. Cut the white mushrooms from cap to stem into thin lengthwise slices, detach and discard the hard shiitake stems, and slice the caps into thin crescents.

2. Put the olive oil and chopped onion in a 12-inch sauté pan, turn on the heat to medium high, and cook the onion, stirring occasionally, until it becomes translucent. Add the garlic and continue cooking, stirring, just until the garlic begins to release its scent, without letting it become colored any darker than a pale gold.

3. Add the parsley, stir quickly once or twice, then add all the mushrooms. Add salt—do not be salt-shy if you don't want a bland-tasting sauce—turn over all ingredients a few times, then cover the pan and turn the heat down to medium. Cook for about 10 minutes or more until the liquid that the mushrooms shed has simmered away.

4. Add the cream, butter, and liberal grindings of pepper to the pan, raise the heat to maximum force, and reduce the cream to half its original volume, stirring frequently.

5. When the pasta is tender but firm to the bite, drain it, and toss it immediately in a warm serving bowl with the mushroom sauce. Add the grated Parmesan, toss thoroughly to coat the pasta well, and serve at once.

AHEAD-OF-TIME NOTE: You can cook the sauce up to the end of step 3 several hours in advance. Reheat briefly before proceeding.

Rosemary and Sage Pasta Sauce

SUGO AL ROSMARINO E SALVIA

---

3 tablespoons extra virgin olive oil plus 1 tablespoon for tossing the pasta

¼ cup chopped onion

4 fresh sage leaves OR 1 teaspoon chopped dried leaves

A sprig of fresh rosemary OR 2 teaspoons very finely chopped dried leaves

2 tablespoons very finely chopped pancetta

2 cups canned imported Italian plum tomatoes, with their juice OR ripe, firm, fresh tomatoes, peeled and seeds scooped away

Salt

Black pepper ground fresh

Enough sauce for 1 pound of pasta, making 4 large or 6 small servings

What delights me most about Italian cooking, and what still excites my interest, even though I have been practicing it for a lifetime, is its infinite resourcefulness, its amazing adaptability. "*Muoio di fame*—I am starved," declared my dear Victor one morning, standing in the kitchen door. "What are we having for lunch?" "I have made lamb stew," said I. "Oh, I am so hungry, but I am really not in the mood for a meat stew." "So, what are you in the mood for?" "Pasta, with something zesty and appetizing on it."

To cook something and not be able to serve it is crushing, but what I find even more discouraging is to watch my husband eat my food dutifully but unenthusiastically. I looked around to see what I had: There was pancetta in the refrigerator, sage in a window box, and rosemary growing on the terrace. In a basket on one of the counters I always keep onions. I had no fresh tomatoes on hand, but I had canned ones in the cabinet. I chopped the onion and the pancetta; sautéed the onion briefly in olive oil; added some sage and rosemary, then the pancetta, and then the tomatoes. I put on water for the pasta, when it came to a boil I dropped in the pasta, and by the time the pasta was cooked, the sauce was done, and for that day at least, my husband staved off starvation.

Admittedly, it went so fast because I was making only enough sauce for two and using canned tomatoes. When I tried it for six on a subsequent occasion, with fresh tomatoes, it took me 15 minutes longer.

SUGGESTED PASTA: Like all sauces using only olive oil as the cooking medium, this one calls for boxed dry pasta. Spaghettini—thin spaghetti—would be the ideal shape to choose, but *bucatini or perciatelli*—thick, hollow spaghetti—will also work well. Nor would you be doing badly if you chose a short tubular shape such as penne or *maccheroncini*.

1. Put 2 tablespoons olive oil and the onion in a 10- or 12-inch skillet and turn on the heat to medium high. Cook the onion, stirring often, until it becomes colored a pale gold.

2. Add the sage and rosemary, and cook for about 1 minute, stirring frequently.

3. Add the pancetta and cook it for about 1 minute, turning it over from time to time.

4. Add the tomatoes, salt, and black pepper, turn over all ingredients with a wooden spoon, adjust heat so that the sauce bubbles at a gentle but steady simmer, and cook for about 20 minutes, until the fat begins to separate from the sauce, as described in the Note on page 133. (If you have used rosemary on a sprig, remove it before tossing the sauce with the pasta.)

5. Toss in a warm bowl with the just cooked and drained pasta, swirling into it 1 tablespoon of olive oil. Serve at once.

AHEAD-OF-TIME NOTE: You can cook the sauce several hours in advance, if you need to, and reheat it thoroughly at a gentle simmer before tossing the pasta. A better time-saving idea, however, would be to chop all the ingredients several hours earlier, but cook the sauce only when you will be ready to use it. It will taste sweeter and fresher.

Hunter-Style Pasta Sauce with Herbs, Pancetta, Tomato, and White Wine

SUGO ALLA CACCIATORA

2 tablespoons extra virgin
olive oil

2 tablespoons butter

1 cup finely chopped onion

½ cup chopped pancetta

½ cup chopped celery, both
stalk and leaves

½ cup chopped carrot

4 whole bay leaves

¼ cup juniper berries

½ cup dry white wine

1 cup canned imported
Italian plum tomatoes,
with their juice, OR ripe,
firm, fresh tomatoes,
peeled and seeds
scooped away

Salt

Black pepper ground fresh

⅓ cup freshly grated
Parmigiano-Reggiano
cheese

*Enough sauce for 1 pound of
pasta, making 4 large or 6 small
servings*

Italian hunters must do a lot of cooking!" exclaimed one of my students when I was introducing yet another dish called *alla cacciatora*, hunter's style. Although some hunters may like to cook and there are certainly cooks who also hunt, the term refers not to them, but to a style of cooking that applies to meats or pasta sauces employing ingredients that would be used in preparing game. Aromatic flavorings such as sage, bay leaves, and juniper are typical components of the *cacciatora* style, as are wine or vinegar, tomatoes, and garlic.

The presence of bay leaves and juniper berries and, through its leaves, the cool scent of celery qualify this richly flavored sauce as a member of the hunter's family of dishes. Game itself, hoofed game in particular, has never been a favorite food of mine and in fact I never cook it, but I love the flavor of the style. It has influenced quite a bit of my cooking, and thus I enjoy some of the pleasures of the hunt without contributing to the premature end of any wild creature.

SUGGESTED PASTA: Good homemade noodles will be quite delicious with this sauce, particularly the broad cut known as *pappardelle*, see page 119. Boxed dry pasta can be equally satisfying if you choose a short tubular shape such as penne or *maccheroncini*.

1. Put all the olive oil and 1 tablespoon of butter in a saucepan with the chopped onion and pancetta, and turn on the heat to medium high. Cook, stirring from time to time, until the onion becomes colored a light gold, then add the celery, carrot, bay leaves, and juniper berries.

2. Cook, stirring frequently, for 4 to 5 minutes, then add the wine. Let the wine bubble away for a minute or two, then add the tomatoes, salt, and liberal grindings of black pepper. Turn the heat down to

medium and cook at a gentle, but steady simmer for 20 minutes or so, until the fat begins to separate from the sauce, as described in the Note on page 133. Remove the bay leaves before serving.

3. Cook and drain the pasta and toss it immediately and thoroughly with the sauce, mixing into it the remaining tablespoon of butter and the grated Parmesan. Serve promptly.

AHEAD-OF-TIME NOTE: The sauce may be prepared several hours in advance. Reheat it through and through at a gentle simmer when you are ready to cook and serve the pasta.

Zucchini, Tomato, and Basil Sauce for Pasta

SUGO DI ZUCCHINE, POMODORO, E BASILICO

6 medium zucchini, about 1 pound

2 tablespoons garlic, peeled and sliced very, very thin

¼ cup extra virgin olive oil

2 cups fresh, ripe, firm tomatoes, peeled and seeds scooped away OR drained canned Italian plum tomatoes, chopped rather coarse

Salt

Black pepper ground fresh

A dozen basil leaves, cut into thin shreds

Enough sauce for 1 pound of pasta, making 4 large or 6 small servings

An elemental vegetable garden taste summarizes what this sauce of zucchini and tomatoes is all about. It is a taste that comes through even more explicitly if you can obtain vine-ripened, fresh, firm tomatoes.

An important component of the light, bright flavor is the way the garlic is handled. It is sliced very thin and aside from a brief, preliminary contact with hot oil, it is simmered in the juices of the tomato so that what emerges of its aroma is the sweetness rather than the pungency.

SUGGESTED PASTA: The most congenial pasta would be high-quality boxed spaghetti or spaghettini.

1. Soak and clean the zucchini as described on page 162, trim off the ends, and shred them into fine julienne strips.

2. Put the garlic and olive oil in a skillet, turn on the heat to medium, and cook, stirring two or three times, just until the garlic becomes colored a very pale blond.

3. Add the chopped tomatoes, turn the heat up to high, and cook, stirring frequently, for about 10 minutes, or slightly longer if the tomato is watery.

4. Add the shredded zucchini, salt, black pepper, and cook for 5 to 6 minutes, turning the ingredients over from time to time. The zucchini should be quite firm—*al dente*—but not raw.

5. Cook and drain the pasta and toss it immediately and thoroughly with the sauce, mixing into it the basil shreds. Serve promptly.

AHEAD-OF-TIME NOTE: The sauce takes so little time to cook and it tastes so much better when freshly made that although you could make it entirely in advance, there is little to be gained in doing so. What you can do is prepare the ingredients—peel and slice the garlic, clean and shred the zucchini, chop the tomatoes—a few hours beforehand.

Ligurian-Style Pasta Sauce with Zucchini and Carrots

SUGO LIGURE DI ZUCCHINE E CAROTE

1 pound young, glossy zucchini, small, but not miniatures

3 medium carrots

2 tablespoons butter plus 1 to 2 tablespoons for tossing the pasta

1 tablespoon vegetable oil

1 cup chopped onion

Salt

Marjoram, 1 tablespoon if fresh, 2 teaspoons if dried

Chopped chili pepper, ⅛ teaspoon or to taste

1 to 2 tablespoons butter

1 cup freshly grated Parmigiano-Reggiano cheese

Enough sauce for 1 pound of boxed dry pasta or ¾ pound homemade fresh noodles, making 4 standard or 6 small servings

While I was staying at the Hotel Splendido in Portofino, my friend Danilo Solari, who was then marking time as the pool attendant but has since opened his own restaurant in Chiavari, suggested that the next time I dined in the hotel restaurant I try the pasta with julienne of zucchini and carrots. I have never been misled by Danilo, nor was I this time.

This is a lovely dish, the thin green and orange strands of the vegetables twining themselves around the pasta. The flavor is delicate, which doesn't mean it's bland. Zucchini is a vegetable with a companionable personality that here makes an excellent match with the carrot and is receptive to the aromatic and spicy touch-ups contributed by the marjoram and chili pepper.

SUGGESTED PASTA: Homemade fettuccine (see page 118) are delicious with this fresh, buttery sauce. High-quality imported Italian boxed dry pasta will also work well. If you choose the latter, the only shape to use is spaghetti.

1. Soak the zucchini for about 20 minutes in a basin of cold water and clean as described on page 162. After trimming away their ends, first slice them in half crosswise, then cut them in half lengthwise. Scoop out and discard nearly all the white seed-bearing core, keeping the green outer part. Slice the green lengthwise into very fine strips, about ⅛ inch wide. You can avail yourself, if you own one, of a mandoline with a julienne blade or of the equivalent attachment in a food processor.

2. Wash the carrots, and prepare them as you did the zucchini, scooping out the paler core and cutting the orange outer part lengthwise into fine strips.

(continued)

3. Choose a skillet that can contain both the zucchini and the carrots without crowding them; put in 2 tablespoons butter, 1 tablespoon vegetable oil, and the chopped onion; and turn on the heat to medium high. Cook the onion, stirring from time to time, until it becomes colored a light gold.

4. Add the carrot strips with some salt and cook, stirring occasionally, for 6 or 7 minutes. Then add the zucchini with a little more salt and continue to cook, turning the vegetables over from time to time, until the zucchini are browned.

5. Add the marjoram, stir well, add the chili pepper, stir again, taste, and correct for seasoning. Toss the sauce in a warm bowl with the pasta, swirling into it 1 tablespoon of butter if you are using boxed dry pasta, 2 tablespoons if using homemade noodles. Add the grated Parmesan, toss thoroughly again, and serve at once.

AHEAD-OF-TIME NOTE: You can prepare the sauce a few hours in advance and warm it up gently while you are cooking the pasta. Add a dab of butter while reheating the sauce. Avoid refrigeration, if possible, because it alters the taste of cooked green vegetables.

Zucchini Sauce for Pasta with Tomato, Parsley, and Chili Pepper

SUGO DI ZUCCHINE CON POMODORO, PREZZEMOLO, E PEPERONCINO

7 or 8 medium zucchini,
about 1¼ pounds

¼ cup extra virgin olive oil

1 tablespoon chopped garlic

2 tablespoons chopped
Italian flat-leaf parsley

Salt

Chopped hot chili pepper,
⅛ teaspoon OR to taste

1 cup fresh, ripe, firm
tomatoes, peeled and
seeds scooped away, OR
canned Italian plum
tomatoes with their
juice, chopped up

8 or 10 basil leaves, torn by
hand into small pieces

---

*Enough sauce for 1 pound of
pasta, making 4 large or 6 small
servings*

At first glance, the ingredients list of this recipe would cause one to think it is going to be a repetition of the one on page 157. Here, however, the zucchini is cooked before it is combined with the tomato. It is cooked by a method that would be called *trifolare* in Italian, letting it cook down at moderate heat until it is very tender. This method both sweetens and lengthens the flavor of the vegetable.

SUGGESTED PASTA: The most desirable choice would be high-quality boxed short macaroni, either the solid fusilli or hollow tubes such as penne, ziti, or *maccheroncini*.

1. Soak and clean the zucchini as described on page 162, trim off the ends, and cut them lengthwise into strips 2 inches long and ¼ inch wide.

2. In a medium skillet or sauté pan put 2 tablespoons of olive oil and the chopped garlic, and turn on the heat to medium. Cook the garlic, stirring from time to time, until it becomes colored a pale gold. Add the parsley and stir quickly for a few seconds.

3. Put in the zucchini strips, a large pinch of salt, and the chili pepper. Turn over once or twice, then put a lid on the pan. Cook, stirring occasionally, until the zucchini are very tender, about 15 or 20 minutes.

4. Add the tomato, turn over all ingredients, bring the tomatoes to a steady simmer, and cook, uncovered, for about 10 or 15 minutes, stirring from time to time.

5. Cook and drain the pasta and toss it immediately and thoroughly with the sauce, mixing into it the torn basil leaves. Serve promptly.

AHEAD-OF-TIME NOTE: You can prepare the sauce through to the end of step 4, reheating it just before the pasta is cooked.

Zucchini and Thyme Pasta Sauce

SUGO DI ZUCCHINE E TIMO

---

3 medium zucchini

1 tablespoon vegetable oil

2 tablespoons butter

3 tablespoons very finely chopped onion

2 cups fresh, firm, ripe tomatoes, skinned with a peeler, seeds scooped away, and cut up, OR canned imported Italian plum tomatoes, cut up, with their juice

Salt

Black pepper ground fresh

1 teaspoon fresh thyme

Freshly grated Parmigiano-Reggiano cheese for the table

Enough sauce for 1 pound of pasta, making 4 large or 6 small servings

Every time I bring to the table pasta with zucchini, my Victor tells me it puts him in mind of a cartoon in *The New Yorker*. A painter is working at an easel set up in front of a pond, and a woman, presumably his wife, is saying "Claude, not another lily pond!" I admit it, I have a zucchini addiction, but if there is sameness I never tire of it, for within it I find, as Monet did in his lilies, infinite variety.

The elements of this sauce are not different from some of the other zucchini recipes in this chapter: zucchini, onion, and tomatoes. But the taste is different, with a clarity and graciousness that is its own, featuring a combination of vegetable and herb—zucchini and thyme—that I have always found especially apt.

SUGGESTED PASTA: Here is a sauce that is equally satisfactory when matched with either homemade or boxed dry pasta. Of the homemade variety, either fettuccine or the square ones known as *tonnarelli* (see page 118), would be the best choice. If you opt for boxed pasta, choose fusilli, spaghetti, or penne. If you can find it, the longer, skinnier penne known as *pennini* would be a highly desirable shape to use.

1. Soak the zucchini for about 20 minutes in a basin of cold water. Scrub them under running cold water using a brush or rough cloth. Cut off both ends, then cut the zucchini lengthwise into narrow strips. You should get about 1½ cups.

2. Put the oil, butter, and chopped onion in a medium skillet and turn the heat on to medium high. Cook the onion, stirring from time to time, until it becomes colored a pale gold.

3. Add the zucchini strips, turn them over with a wooden spoon to coat them well, and cook until they become deeply colored.

4. Add the tomato, turn it over once or twice, add salt, pepper, and thyme, and turn all ingredients over two or three times. Cook at a

steady, but moderate simmer for about 15 or 20 minutes, until the fat begins to separate from the sauce, as described in the Note on page 133.

5. Cook and drain the pasta, toss it immediately and thoroughly with the sauce, and serve at once, with the grated Parmesan on the side.

AHEAD-OF-TIME NOTE: The actual cooking of the sauce should be performed when you are going to serve the dish: It doesn't take too much longer than boiling boxed dry pasta, and it will taste so much fresher than when reheated. You can, however, go through the preliminary preparation of the other ingredients: chop the onion, wash and slice up the zucchini, peel and cut the tomatoes (if using fresh ones) several hours in advance—you can do it in the morning if you are serving the pasta for dinner. Keep all the vegetables covered with plastic wrap until you are ready to proceed.

Pasta Sauce with Peas, Ham, and Cream

SUGO DI PISELLI, PROSCIUTTO COTTO, E PANNA

2 pounds fresh young peas
in their pods OR 1 cup
thawed frozen peas

4 tablespoons (½ stick)
butter

Salt

½ cup chopped onion

¼ pound boiled, unsmoked
ham, cut into strips less
than ¼ inch wide

½ cup heavy cream

Black pepper ground fresh

⅓ cup freshly grated
Parmigiano-Reggiano
cheese

*Enough sauce for 1 pound of
pasta, making 4 large or 6 small
servings*

This ingredients list—ham, cream, butter—is as good as a road map; it tells us we are in Emilia-Romagna, the land of bounteous flavor. We may not be able to or want to eat this way every day, but when we can and we do, it makes us realize how much we miss when we don't.

As a delicious way to acknowledge and celebrate the coming of spring, you would make this pea and ham sauce when very fresh and very young peas become available in a farmers' market near you. You certainly ought not to waste time and work by using older, mealier peas. But if you cannot get the right kind of fresh peas, there is no reason to deprive yourself; you can substitute frozen early peas. This is one of the rare occasions for which I would make such a suggestion, and while the frozen are not quite so entrancing as the fresh, they do work here well enough. It is a better alternative than not having the sauce at all.

SUGGESTED PASTA: A pasta with hollows, such as *conchiglie*—sea shells—or a short tubular shape such as penne or *maccheroncini* would make the most satisfactory match for this pea and cream sauce. If you want to come as close as possible to the original form of this dish, toss the sauce with *garganelli*, the handmade macaroni illustrated on page 110.

1. If using fresh peas, shell them, soak them in a basin of cold water for a few minutes, then drain.

2. Put 2 tablespoons of butter in a medium saucepan, add the peas and ¼ cup water, and turn on the heat to medium high. When the water reaches the boil, adjust heat to cook at a steady but gentle simmer. After 10 minutes, add some salt. Cook until the peas are tender, 15 minutes or much longer, depending on their freshness and youth.

3. While the peas are cooking, put the remaining 2 tablespoons of butter and the chopped onion into a 10-inch skillet and turn on the

heat to medium high. If you are using frozen peas, start the sauce at this point, putting all 4 tablespoons of butter into the skillet with the onion. Cook the onion, stirring frequently, until it becomes colored a light gold, then add the strips of ham. Cook, stirring, for about a minute. If the peas are not yet done, take the pan off heat.

4. If using frozen peas, add them to the pan at this point. If using fresh peas, when they are cooked, transfer them to the skillet, and cook for 5 minutes at medium heat, turning them over from time to time to coat them well.

5. Swirl in the cream, taste and correct for salt, add very liberal grindings of black pepper, turn the heat up to high, and cook down the cream, stirring frequently, until it is reduced to a dense consistency.

6. Cook and drain the pasta and toss it immediately and thoroughly with the sauce, mixing into it the grated Parmesan. If using another tablespoon of butter does not alarm you, swirl it into the pasta. It will greatly enhance the flavor.

AHEAD-OF-TIME NOTE: The freshly made sweet taste of this sauce does not come through so alluringly when you cook it in advance, but if you must, you must. Stop just before it's time to add the cream. You can hold the sauce for a few hours—but not overnight—and warm it gently but thoroughly before adding the cream.

Goat Cheese, Chive, and Chili Pepper Sauce for Pasta

SUGO DI CAPRINO, ERBA CIPOLLINA, E PEPERONCINO

6 ounces creamy goat cheese

¼ cup extra virgin olive oil

2 tablespoons chopped chives

Chopped chili pepper, ¼ teaspoon or to taste

Salt

Enough sauce for 1 pound of pasta, making 4 large or 6 small servings

When Victor goes off to visit wine producers he likes to return with something for me. Once, to my enduring pleasure, he brought back from Alghero in Sardinia a long antique coral necklace, but the mementos of his trips are usually less tangible, often consisting of detailed descriptions of new dishes he had and liked. The goat cheese sauce was on pasta that he had been given at a winemakers' lunch in Piedmont.

I was intrigued by it because goat cheese is such an unusual ingredient in Italian cooking. For both cheese and meat, sheep and lamb wholly eclipse goats in the national preference. Piedmont probably raises most of Italy's goats and its *tume*, the small, soft rounds of goat cheese it makes, are the most luscious I have ever had.

To me, this is an ideal pasta sauce for summer. There is nothing to cook, except for the pasta, and the zestful combination of goat cheese, chives, and chili pepper is a welcome answer to the hot-weather demand for refreshing flavor. The goat cheese you choose should be as creamy as possible to produce an adequate coating for the pasta.

SUGGESTED PASTA: The firm bite and compact texture of boxed dry pasta are just what you want with the goat cheese sauce. The most desirable shape here would be spaghettini, thin spaghetti.

1. Put all ingredients in a small bowl and mix them with a fork until they are smoothly and thoroughly amalgamated.

2. Cook the pasta and drain it, pouring some of the water into the serving bowl. Swirl the water around the bowl to warm it, then pour out all but a tablespoon of it. The water will help the sauce, which is rather dry, coat the pasta more uniformly.

3. Immediately put the drained pasta into the bowl, add the goat cheese mixture, toss thoroughly to spread the sauce and coat the pasta strands well, and serve at once. No additional cheese is required.

Bell Pepper and Goat Cheese Sauce for Pasta

SUGO DI PEPERONI E FORMAGGIO CAPRINO

4 to 5 medium yellow or red bell peppers

4 tablespoons butter (see headnote)

1 teaspoon very finely chopped garlic

Salt

¼ pound creamy goat cheese (see headnote above)

Black pepper ground fresh

2 tablespoons finely chopped chives

Enough sauce for 1 pound of pasta, making 4 large or 6 small servings

I was in the Aliani cheese shop in Venice buying goat cheese for the Piedmontese pasta sauce that precedes this one, and I happened to mention to Signor Aliani that I was going to use it for a very unusual sauce. "How do you make your sauce?" a woman standing near me asked. I told her how. "I am from Menaggio, on Lake Como," she said, "and we make a goat cheese sauce with peppers." "With *peppers?*" I exclaimed, hardly believing that I might be coming into possession of another goat cheese recipe.

Aside from the peppers, her version was totally different from mine, I was delighted to find. It is cooked, whereas mine is raw, and Como being butter country, it has butter rather than olive oil. The butter really works well, helping the goat cheese to reach a consistency that coats the pasta beautifully.

Note that only half the amount of butter listed is cooked; the remainder is tossed raw with the pasta. Do not use lean, crumbly goat cheese; the creamier it is the more smoothly you can integrate it into the sauce.

What I find strongly appealing here is the pairing of peppers and goat cheese, the sweetness and softness of the former balancing the sprightly astringency and graininess of the latter.

SUGGESTED PASTA: Boxed dry pasta in either a short tubular shape such as penne or *maccheroncini*, or the flanged fusilli. Because of the butter base, the sauce is also very appealing over homemade noodles, either ribbon-shaped like fettuccine, or the square *tonnarelli* (see page 118).

1. Wash the peppers, split them in half lengthwise, remove the seeds and pulpy core, and skin them raw using a vegetable peeler as described on page 151. Cut them into very thin strips. You should have about 4 loosely packed cups.

2. Put 2 tablespoons of butter and the garlic in a medium skillet, turn on the heat to medium, and cook the garlic, stirring it frequently, just until it becomes colored a very pale gold.

3. Add the peppers and a little salt, and cook them, turning them over from time to time, until they feel very tender when prodded with a fork, about 20 or 30 minutes.

4. Lower the heat to minimum and add the goat cheese, mashing it with a wooden spoon and turning it over with the peppers. Add liberal grindings of pepper, stir well, and remove the pan from heat.

5. When the pasta is almost done, return the pan to low heat, warming the sauce gently.

6. Cook the pasta, draining it when it is very firm to the bite, toss it immediately in a warm bowl with the remaining 2 tablespoons of butter and the pepper and cheese sauce, swirling into it the chopped chives. Serve promptly.

AHEAD-OF-TIME NOTE: The sauce can be prepared several hours in advance. While the pasta is cooking, warm it gently but thoroughly over low heat, using a wooden spoon to turn over the peppers and cheese frequently.

Pancetta, Onion, and Parsley Pasta Sauce

SUGO DI PANCETTA, CIPOLLE, E PREZZEMOLO

3 ounces pancetta, cut into thin strips, about 1 cup

3 tablespoons extra virgin olive oil

4 medium onions, sliced very thin, about 5 cups

Salt

Black pepper ground fresh

3 tablespoons chopped Italian flat-leaf parsley

⅓ cup freshly grated Parmigiano-Reggiano cheese

Enough sauce for 1 pound of pasta, making 4 large or 6 small servings

Pancetta is what Italians do with bacon. It is not smoked but cured with salt, black pepper, and such spices as nutmeg, cinnamon, cloves, or juniper berries, varying in proportion and assortment according to individual formulas. In the most common version of pancetta, the one usually available abroad, the meat is tightly rolled up after 2 weeks of gradual seasoning. It used to be pressed between boards and sold thus, but that is done now solely for show, and as a pretext to charge a higher price. Everyday pancetta is now wrapped in a casing that in all but the homemade versions is made of synthetic material. It can also be left flat, without a casing. The former is known as *pancetta arrotolata*, the latter, *pancetta stesa*.

There is also smoked pancetta, known as *pancetta affumicata*, similar to American bacon, although less smoky in taste, prepared in slab form and sliced to order by the grocer. It is very popular throughout northeastern Italy, from Venice west to Verona, up north to Bolzano, and east to Udine and Trieste in the Friuli–Venezia Giulia region.

Pancetta arrotolata is fundamental to a wide variety of Italian dishes because it is an indispensable part of many a *battuto*, the chopped mixture of pancetta, onion, and sometimes other vegetables that, when it is sautéed in olive oil or butter, becomes *soffritto*, the flavor foundation of countless pasta sauces, soups, fricassees, and stews. It is fortunate for American cooks that quite satisfactory versions of pancetta have become broadly available, because bacon cannot be substituted for it, nor can it always be replaced by salt pork.

I had this sauce, in which pancetta is featured, many years ago at a trattoria near the Chiantigiana, the picturesque road that bisects the Chianti Classico zone between Florence and Siena. Their name for pancetta was *rigatino*, after *righe*, the word for stripes, because then it was made from free-range pigs whose bellies had discernible layers of lean meat alternating with narrower ones of fat.

It is the pancetta in this sauce that is responsible for the more forward show of flavor, but it benefits in balance from the submissively sweet foil of the onion. To achieve that balance, don't caramelize the onion; it must be cooked down slowly until it is very soft but not at all colored.

SUGGESTED PASTA: Boxed dry pasta such as *bucatini* or spaghetti or a short tubular shape such as penne.

1. Put the pancetta and the olive oil in a medium skillet and turn on the heat to medium. Cook for 2 or 3 minutes, occasionally turning the pancetta, until it becomes lightly browned but not crisp.

2. Add the onions, salt, and several grindings of pepper; turn over all ingredients a few times; then cover the pan and turn the heat down to low. Cook for about 40 minutes, turning the onion over from time to time, until it becomes very soft, but not colored. It should still be nearly white.

3. Taste and correct for salt, stir in the parsley, and turn off the heat.

4. Cook and drain the pasta and toss it immediately and thoroughly with the sauce, swirling into it the grated Parmesan.

AHEAD-OF-TIME NOTE: The sauce may be prepared several days in advance through step 2. When you are ready to cook and serve the pasta, reheat the sauce thoroughly, then taste and correct for salt and stir in the parsley.

Simple Veal Pasta Sauce

PICCOLO RAGÙ DI VITELLO

¾ pound fresh, ripe tomatoes OR 1 cup canned imported Italian plum tomatoes, cut up, and drained of juice

3 tablespoons butter

1 tablespoon vegetable oil

¼ cup chopped onion

½ pound ground veal

Salt

Black pepper ground fresh

¼ cup freshly grated Parmigiano-Reggiano cheese

Enough sauce for 1 pound of pasta, making 4 large or 6 small servings

It seems that almost every interview has to end with what I have come to call a media question, "What is your favorite dish, Marcella?" or in a gruesome vein, "If you were about to be executed, what would you order for your last meal?" Really! I couldn't eat a pea if there was a hangman waiting for me to finish, and I adore peas.

There are dishes, of course, that, depending on my mood, I find more irresistible than others. An example is a properly made Bolognese meat sauce over handmade—not just made at home, but made by *hand*—tagliatelle. I have tasted all manner of food, but I know of no single dish more perfectly conceived or better able to saturate the taste buds with pleasure. But that doesn't mean that I would want to have it always. There are moments when it might be more than I could handle.

For some time I had been thinking: How can I pare down a classic meat sauce for those occasions when I have neither the time to make nor the voracity to consume a full-scale *ragù*? The sauce below is the answer I came up with. I replaced beef with veal; eliminated the milk, the wine, the carrot, and the celery; and reduced the cooking time from several hours to half of one. It is as easy to take as it is to do. Is it a favorite dish? Sure—it is my favorite simple meat sauce.

SUGGESTED PASTA: The ideal carrier for this simple meat sauce is a homemade noodle, in particular the one scented with rosemary and sage described on page 191, cut into fettuccine or *tonnarelli*. Boxed dry pasta in a short tubular shape such as penne or *maccheroncini* can be a satisfactory alternative.

1. If you are using fresh tomatoes, peel them by dipping them in boiling water for 1 minute, then squeeze off their skin. (Any of the other peeling techniques described on pages 135–36 would also be satisfactory for this dish.) Halve the tomatoes, scoop out their seeds without squeezing, and chop up coarsely.

2. Put 2 tablespoons of butter and the vegetable oil in a small saucepan and turn on the heat to medium high. Cook the onion, stirring from time to time, until it becomes colored a pale gold.

3. Add the ground veal, and turn it over several times, using a wooden spoon, to brown it all over.

4. Add the cut-up tomato, salt, and several grindings of pepper, and with your wooden spoon turn over all ingredients two or three times. Cook at a steady but gentle simmer for 15 to 20 minutes.

5. Cook and drain the pasta and toss it immediately and thoroughly with the sauce, swirling into it the remaining tablespoon of butter and the grated Parmesan.

AHEAD-OF-TIME NOTE: The sauce may be cooked a day in advance and refrigerated in a tightly sealed container or in a bowl under plastic wrap. When reheating, add a tablespoon of water, bring to a gentle simmer, stir occasionally, and cook until hot through and through.

Lamb Sauce for Pasta, Abruzzi-Style

RAGÙ D'AGNELLO ALL'ABRUZZESE

½ pound boneless lamb, any cut that is not too lean

1 tablespoon extra virgin olive oil

¼ cup chopped onion

2 ounces pancetta, chopped very fine

1 tablespoon chopped rosemary leaves

Salt

Black pepper ground fresh

½ cup dry white wine

2 cups canned imported Italian plum tomatoes, cut up, with their juice

⅓ cup grated Romano or other sheep's milk cheese

Enough sauce for 1 pound of pasta, making 4 large or 6 small servings

It is said in France that the goat is the cow of the poor; in Italy one might say that the cow of the lower central and southern regions, for both rich and poor, is lamb. The cheeses are made from sheep's milk and the meats that you are likely to find in the cooking are those of both young lamb and *castrato*, an older gelded animal. In Abruzzi, it is the latter that would be used, making this a sauce for which the larger, older lamb of American markets is a natural choice.

The deep, intense flavor of lamb sets this apart from other classic meat sauces, and so does the fact that the meat is not ground up but cut into small pieces and cooked as though it were a stew. It leads to an earthier, more substantial pasta dish than most, an ample serving of which could well constitute a one-course meal.

SUGGESTED PASTA: In Abruzzi they toss lamb ragù with the square homemade noodle known as *maccheroni alla chitarra*, cut on the steel strings of a tool that looks like a guitar. You can duplicate it at home by following the instructions for *tonnarelli* on page 203. *Maccheroni alla chitarra* are sometimes found in boxed dry form, but other boxed dry pastas, such as *penne* or *maccheroncini*, are also quite delicious with this sauce.

1. Trim away any gristle, but none of the fat, from the lamb. Cut the meat into very, very fine dice.

2. Put the oil and the onion in a 10-inch skillet and turn on the heat to medium high. Cook, stirring frequently, until the onion becomes colored a pale gold.

3. Add the pancetta and rosemary, turning them over with a wooden spoon to coat them well. Cook, stirring from time to time, until the pancetta's fat has melted completely, but do not let the pancetta cook until crisp.

4. Put in the lamb dice, turning them over and cooking until the meat has been browned on all sides; add salt and liberal grindings of black pepper, turning the contents of the pan over again two or three times with a wooden spoon.

5. Add the wine and let it simmer until it has completely evaporated.

6. Add the tomatoes and cook at a steady but gentle simmer, stirring from time to time, until the fat begins to separate from the sauce as described in the Note on page 133, about 15 minutes.

7. Cook and drain the pasta and toss it immediately and thoroughly in a warm platter with the sauce. (If necessary reheat the sauce while the pasta is cooking.) Stir in half the grated cheese, and bring to the table with the remaining cheese available on the side.

AHEAD-OF-TIME NOTE: You can prepare the sauce a day or two in advance, reheating it thoroughly before tossing with the pasta.

Savoy Cabbage and Sausage Pasta Sauce

SUGO DI VERZA E SALSICCIA

---

1 pound Savoy cabbage

Salt

2 tablespoons vegetable oil

2 tablespoons chopped
   onion

1 teaspoon chopped garlic

½ cup plain sausage meat
   with no seasonings other
   than salt and pepper

Black pepper ground fresh

¼ cup heavy cream

1 tablespoon chopped
   Italian flat-leaf parsley

⅔ cup freshly grated
   Parmigiano-Reggiano
   cheese

---

*Enough sauce for 1 pound of
pasta, making 4 large or 6 small
servings*

Two regional traditions have inspired this sauce: those of Treviso, in the Veneto, and of Bologna, in Emilia-Romagna. Treviso stews Savoy cabbage with sausage for a dish called *verze e luganeghe* while Bologna has a pasta known as *gramigna con la salsiccia*, short, curved homemade macaroni tossed with sausages and cream. I had just had both of them in their respective habitats within an interval brief enough that the taste of one was still fresh in the mind when I was sitting down to the other. It was a gray, clammy February shortly thereafter that I felt strongly the need to make something cheering for lunch. It occurred to me that by borrowing something from each of those two dishes I might come up with a powerful chill chaser of a pasta sauce. And I did. So heartwarming is the dish that it all but makes me look forward to winter.

SUGGESTED PASTA: A boxed dry pasta with flanges, such as fusilli, or crevices, such as *conchiglie* (shells), would suit this sauce best.

1. Detach the leaves of the cabbage, discarding any that may be bruised or discolored. Trim a thin slice away from the root end and cut it into four pieces. Wash in cold water. Bring water to a boil, add salt, and as it resumes boiling, drop in the cabbage leaves and root. Cook at a moderate boil for about 25 minutes, until tender. Drain thoroughly and chop rather fine.

2. Put the oil and onion in a 10-inch skillet or sauté pan, and turn on the heat to medium. Cook the onion, stirring from time to time, until it becomes translucent.

3. Add the garlic and the sausage meat. If you are using sausage instead of loosely packed meat, skin the sausage first and crumble it in the pan. Turn over the meat a few times, and when it is browned all over add the chopped cabbage. Turn the cabbage over several times to coat it well. When it becomes lightly colored, cover the pan and cook

at medium low heat for about 10 minutes, occasionally stirring the contents of the pan.

4. Uncover, add salt and pepper, turn over the ingredients using a wooden spoon, then add the cream. Stir well and cook just long enough for the cream to bind the other ingredients softly. Off heat, stir in the chopped parsley.

5. Toss with the pasta, swirling in the grated Parmesan. Serve at once.

AHEAD-OF-TIME NOTE: The sauce can be cooked through to the end of step 3 several hours, or even a day, in advance. Reheat gently but thoroughly before adding the cream.

Quail Sauce for Fresh Pasta

SUGO DI QUAGLIE PER I TAJARIN

---

4 quail

¼ cup extra virgin olive oil

2 teaspoons very finely chopped onion

2 teaspoons very finely chopped celery

2 teaspoons finely chopped carrot

1 fresh sage leaf and 6 or 7 rosemary leaves, chopped very fine together

Salt

Black pepper ground fresh

½ cup dry white wine

1 fresh, ripe tomato, peeled, OR 1 canned Italian plum tomato, cut in large dice

Freshly grated Parmigiano-Reggiano cheese

Enough sauce for 1 pound of pasta, serving 4 persons

In the kitchen of Piedmont's splendid country restaurants it is usually a woman who rules. Invariably, she has been schooled not by chefs, but by her mother, and her professional accomplishments are founded on the region's home cooking, a cuisine that, for finesse and variety, is unsurpassed in Italy, or even in Europe.

One of the most gifted of these women is Ilvia Boggione of the restaurant Vicoletto in Alba. Among her specialties is this deft rendition of a classic game bird sauce that is sometimes served with *tajarin*—thin homemade noodles. To call it sauce may be misleading, however, particularly if one's idea of a pasta sauce is something juicy and all-enveloping. There is nothing runny or sauce-like about this one. Quail is cooked until its meat slips succulently off the bone, and small bite-size pieces of it are nestled among the pasta strands. A more accurate description of the dish would be pasta *with* quail.

SUGGESTED PASTA: Homemade noodles make the only satisfactory pairing for this sauce, particularly thick, square shaped *tonnarelli*, page 203; or the broad *pappardelle*, page 119; or fettuccine, page 118. In Piedmont (as noted above) they use *tajarin*, a thin noodle that in restaurants is made almost exclusively from a large number of egg yolks.

1. Wash the quail inside and out under cold running water, then pat thoroughly dry with kitchen towels.

2. Choose a sauté pan that can contain all the quail in one layer. Put in the oil and turn on the heat to medium high. When the oil is hot, add the quail. Brown the birds on all sides, then remove them from the pan. Leave the heat turned on.

3. Add the chopped onion, celery, carrot, sage, and rosemary, and cook for a minute or two, stirring frequently. When the vegetables have become lightly colored, return the quail to the pan, adding salt and pepper.

4. Turn the birds over a few times, and after 2 or 3 minutes, add the wine. Let the wine bubble for a minute or less, then turn the heat down to medium low and put a lid on the pan.

5. When the quail have cooked for 20 minutes, add the cut-up tomato; turn the birds over two or three times; put the lid on the pan, setting it slightly ajar; and cook until the quail meat comes easily off the bone, another 25 minutes or so. Check the pan from time to time, and whenever you find that the cooking juices are drying up, add 2 to 3 tablespoons of water.

6. Using a slotted spoon, remove the quail from the pan, and as soon as they are cool enough for you to handle, remove the skin and take the meat off the bone. Look out for and pick out any tiny bones.

7. Return the meat to the pan, and turn it in the pan juices for a minute or two over low heat. Toss the pasta with the entire contents of the pan, adding freshly grated Parmigiano-Reggiano cheese.

PRESENTATION NOTE: If you leave the tiny quail drumsticks with the bone in and hold them back when tossing the pasta, you can place them decoratively over each individual plate of pasta.

Mara's Broccoli and Scallop Pasta Sauce

IL SUGO DI CAPPE SANTE E BROCCOLI DI MARA MARTIN

---

1 pound broccoli

Salt

½ pound scallops,
    preferably bay

½ cup butter

⅓ cup finely chopped onion

2 teaspoons fresh thyme

Chopped hot chili pepper,
    ⅛ teaspoon or to taste

½ cup freshly grated
    Parmigiano-Reggiano
    cheese

---

*Enough sauce for 1 pound of
pasta, making 6 satisfactory
servings*

Mara Martin is one of the most precious friends I have gained through cooking. When she and her husband Maurizio were teenagers, they borrowed money to buy Da Fiore, an old wine bar in Venice, and proceeded to transform it into one of Italy's most sought-after seafood restaurants. They had no professional experience of food or of any other kind, but they had taste, cooking's principal root from which all other qualities germinate.

Mara's dishes are rigorously based on the superb seafood caught in Venice's portion of the Adriatic, and the preparations are by and large those of the understated, light-handed Venetian tradition. She doesn't shrink from updating them, however, when she finds a promising new union of ingredients, as in this combination of scallops, which are local, and broccoli, which originates in the south of Italy. A small migration to Venice of families from Abruzzi and Apulia in central and southern Italy has supplied customers at the Rialto market for produce of their regions—produce such as broccoli, which has consequently found a place on Venetian tables.

Mara has a generous hand with butter, which may distress those who think olive oil is the only cooking medium for Italian seafood. But it is butter here that does what needs to be done, tenderly reconcile the reticent mildness of the thin scallop slices with the sourish, vegetal quality of broccoli. It is impossible to imagine a seafood sauce with a blend of flavors more smooth or so ravishing. I had the pleasure of letting Mara make this with Long Island bay scallops in my Watermill kitchen when she and Maurizio came to visit me in the Hamptons one summer. And I discovered that she was using something she had forgetfully omitted from the recipe she had written out for me, thyme. Ah, those great Italian cooks— never question their taste; just take a second look at their recipes.

SUGGESTED PASTA: Mara uses *pennini*, a thin version of boxed penne pasta. Any short, narrow tubular shape such as *maccheroncini* will work well.

1. Pare away from the broccoli's main stems, and from the florets' stems as well, the hard, dark green rind and any other tough stringy part.

2. Wash the stems under cold running water, and the florets in several changes of cold water.

3. Bring a pot of water to a boil and add 2 tablespoons salt and the thick main broccoli stems. Cook for 7 or 8 minutes, then add the florets. When the water returns to a boil, cook for another 12 minutes or so, then drain and set aside.

4. Wash and drain the scallops; trim away from each its thin, tough, white filament; then cut them across the grain into thin rounds. Pat dry with kitchen towels.

5. Separate the larger floret clusters of the broccoli into smaller pieces and slice the main stems into thin rounds.

6. Put 6 tablespoons of butter and the chopped onion into a 12-inch skillet and turn the heat on to medium high. Cook, stirring frequently, without letting the onion become colored. Add all the broccoli and turn it over with a wooden spoon to coat it well. Cook for 6 to 7 minutes, stirring occasionally.

7. Add the sliced scallops and the thyme, chili pepper, and salt and cook briefly, just until the color of the scallops changes from translucent to flat white. Take the pan off heat and swirl in the grated cheese.

8. When the pasta is nearly done, add the remaining 2 tablespoons of butter to the pan with the scallops and broccoli. Return the pan to medium heat, turn over all ingredients with a wooden spoon, then add the drained hot pasta. Toss it thoroughly but for not more than 20 seconds in the pan that is still over medium heat, empty the contents of the pan into a warm serving bowl, and serve at once.

AHEAD-OF-TIME NOTE: You can boil and drain the broccoli a few hours in advance, but do not refrigerate it.

Mussel and Basil Sauce for Pasta

SUGO DI COZZE E BASILICO

———————— ❧ ————————

4 pounds mussels in their
    shells

½ cup water

Salt

¼ cup extra virgin olive oil

½ pound fresh, ripe
    tomatoes

½ cup chopped onion

1 tablespoon chopped garlic

½ cup chopped fresh basil

Chopped chili pepper,
    ⅛ teaspoon or to taste

½ cup dry white wine

2 tablespoons chopped
    Italian flat-leaf parsley

———————————————

*Enough sauce for 1 pound of
pasta, making 4 large or 6 small
servings*

Bruno Paolato is the cooking partner in Ai Mercanti, one of the Venetian restaurants where I feel most at home. I prefer to think of Bruno as a cook rather than a chef, a distinction that he, and his colleagues, may not find as flattering as I do. Never mind. The most satisfying source of Italian cooking is the home, rather than a professional academy, and I prize those restaurants whose food, however accomplished it may be, still tastes of cooks at home preparing it for their family. An example is this mussel sauce of Bruno's.

It has become my favorite mussel sauce by far. Its secret lies in lightly coloring chopped garlic together with chopped basil and chili pepper over a foundation of onion briefly sautéed in olive oil. In that simple, homey step an airy fragrance is established that eventually saturates the mussels, bestowing on them a sense of lightness and freshness that no other sauce using mussels shares.

You can easily convert this into a lovely soup by using all of the juices shed by the mussels when you open them. If served as soup, accompany it with a slice of grilled bread over which you have dribbled some olive oil.

SUGGESTED PASTA: Thin spaghetti—spaghettini—is the best carrier for this sauce, as it usually is for olive-oil based seafood sauces. The thicker regular spaghetti is a satisfactory second choice.

1. Soak the mussels in several changes of cold water and scrub clean as described on page 104.

2. Put the cleaned mussels in a 12-inch skillet or sauté pan together with the ½ cup water, salt, and 1 tablespoon of olive oil. Turn the heat on to high and cover the pan. As soon as the shells gape open, transfer the mussels to a bowl and set aside, pouring over them the liquid from the pan.

3. When they are cool enough to handle, detach the mussel meat from the shell and put it in a smaller bowl. Carefully spoon the juices from the larger bowl over the mussel meat, watching out for the sand that will have settled at the bottom of the bowl. Let the mussels steep in their juices for at least 20 minutes without moving them so that any sand remaining on the meat can sink to the bottom.

4. Cut the tomatoes in half, scoop out their seeds without squeezing them, then cut into small dice and set aside.

5. Put the chopped onion and the remaining olive oil in a medium skillet and turn on the heat to medium high. Cook the onion, stirring from time to time, just until it becomes translucent. Add the garlic, chopped basil, and chili pepper and cook, stirring frequently, until the garlic becomes colored a very pale gold. Take the pan off heat.

6. Using a slotted spoon, gently retrieve the mussel meat from the bowl without stirring up the juices. Choose the 16 loveliest mussels and set them aside. Chop the remainder not too fine. Filter the juices through a strainer lined with a paper towel, collecting them in a small bowl. You may be using these juices subsequently if you need to make the sauce runnier.

7. Return the pan with the onion, garlic, and basil to the stove, turn on the heat to medium high, and put in the chopped mussels and the white wine. Let the wine simmer until half of it has evaporated, then add the whole mussels, the tomato dice, and the parsley. If the sauce appears to be too dry, add some of the filtered mussel juice. Cook, stirring frequently, for about 3 minutes.

8. Thoroughly toss the sauce in a warm platter with just-cooked and -drained pasta and serve at once.

Lobster Pasta Sauce Busara-Style

PASTA ALLA BUSARA

Two 1¼-pound live lobsters

⅓ cup extra virgin olive oil plus some more for tossing the pasta

2 cups finely chopped onion

Salt

3 tablespoons finely chopped garlic

⅓ cup Italian flat-leaf parsley, chopped fine

½ cup dry white wine

2 cups canned imported Italian plum tomatoes cut up with their juice OR fresh, ripe tomatoes, skinned raw with a vegetable peeler and cut up

Chopped fresh or dried chili pepper, ¼ teaspoon or to taste

Enough sauce for 1 pound of pasta, making 4 large or 6 small servings

The portion of the Italian coast that, in the northeast, curves over the uppermost tip of the Adriatic Sea, is part of a region known as Friuli–Venezia Giulia. The Venetian Republic ruled here once, and the stamp of Venetian dominion is still clearly discernible in the local dialects and in the structures of the old towns. Both architecturally and gastronomically, the most important of the historic coastal towns is Grado, which, like Venice itself, has based its cuisine on the submarine delicacies of the upper Adriatic.

Of the many superb varieties of seafood native to those waters—the crabs, shrimp, mussels, clams—the most famous is the crustacean called *scampi*. It is a large prawn with an orange shell whose features—two long pincer claws, a flat tail ending in a fan shape—resemble those of a miniature lobster. Everything can be done with *scampi*, boiling, frying, stewing, using it in soup, in *risotti*, in pasta sauces. The tastiest pasta sauce I know made from *scampi* is the one that originates in Grado and is called, in the dialect of the town, *alla busara*. *Busara* means something thrown quickly together, and essentially that describes the sauce, a base of onion, garlic, parsley, and wine cooked briefly in olive oil, to which the shellfish and tomatoes are added.

Fresh *scampi* does not swim in American waters, but marvelous lobster does. The flavors are similar, and I found it irresistible to profit from the easy availability of New England lobsters and give them this simple and delicious *busara* treatment.

SUGGESTED PASTA: First choice is imported, high-quality Italian boxed dry pasta, specifically spaghettini, thin spaghetti. The only homemade noodles that may give you comparable satisfaction are the square ones known as *tonnarelli*; see page 118.

Killing the Lobsters

The meat will have the sweetest flavor if you kill the lobster yourself just before cooking it. Turn it on its back, holding it down with an oven

mitt on your hand, and with the other hand plunge a knife between its eyes and deep into its head. Although the lobster dies immediately, its nervous system may continue to flex the claws for a few more seconds. A less traumatic method—for you, not the lobster—is to drop it into boiling water for 2 minutes. If you don't feel prepared to deal with a live lobster yourself, you can have the fishmonger kill it, but time it so you can get back to your kitchen and cook the lobster as soon as possible.

Making the Sauce

1. Detach the lobster's head from the tail. Using poultry shears or a sharp knife, slit the underside of the tail's shell all along its length, then cut the tail into three pieces. Separate both claws from the head and snap them in two. Crack the claws in several places using a nutcracker or a mallet. Look for and pick out any pieces of shell. Divide the head lengthwise into two pieces. Do not remove any tomalley or roe.

2. Choose a skillet or sauté pan that can later contain all the lobster pieces without overlapping. Put in the ⅓ cup of olive oil, the chopped onion, and a pinch of salt, and turn on the heat to medium.

3. Cook the onion until it becomes colored a pale gold, then add the garlic. Cook a few seconds until the garlic becomes colored a very pale gold and you begin to notice its aroma. Add the parsley, stir once or twice, and then add the wine, letting it simmer for a couple of minutes, until the scent of alcohol subsides.

4. Put in the tomato, the chili pepper, and a generous pinch of salt, and cook at a steady simmer, until the fat begins to separate from the sauce as described in the Note on page 133, about 15 or 20 minutes.

5. Drop the pasta into a pot of boiling, salted water.

6. Put the lobster pieces in the skillet with another pinch of salt, turning them over in the sauce for 2 or 3 minutes. If by then the lobster has shed some watery liquid, remove it from the pan using a slotted spoon, and briskly boil away that liquid. Then return the lobster to the pan and cook for another 2 minutes, turning all the pieces over once or twice.

7. Drain the spaghettini when it is still quite firm to the bite, transfer to a very warm serving bowl, pour the contents of the skillet into the bowl, and toss thoroughly. Drizzle in some raw olive oil, toss again until the pasta is well coated, then serve at once.

AHEAD-OF-TIME NOTE: You can prepare the sauce an hour or so in advance midway through step 6, up to the point where you have removed the lobster from the pan and boiled away any excess liquid. When reheating, bring the tomato to a steady simmer before putting the lobster pieces back in.

Pleated Ravioli Piedmontese-Style Stuffed with Meat and Savoy Cabbage

RAVIOLI AL PLIN

FOR THE PASTA

Homemade yellow dough made with 2 extra-large eggs, approximately 1¼ cups unbleached flour, and 1 tablespoon milk following directions on pages 117–18 if using a pasta machine, OR those on pages 121–23 for the hand-rolled method

FOR THE STUFFING

2 tablespoons extra virgin olive oil

4 peeled whole garlic cloves

A sprig of fresh rosemary OR about 1 dozen dried leaves, chopped very fine

½ pound veal, cut into strips

½ pound pork, cut into strips

Salt

Black pepper ground fresh

On one of Victor's several extended visits to wine producers of the Langhe, that small district in southwestern Piedmont that gives birth to what my husband declares are the world's noblest red wines and the finest cooking in Europe, we stayed for several days at Da Felicin, a restaurant with rooms in Monforte d'Alba, the handsomest of the Piedmontese wine towns. Monforte is the ideal base from which to explore the Serralunga valley, where the most robust and profound Barolos are made. While Victor spent his days in the district's cellars I spent mine in the kitchen with Giorgio Rocca, Da Felicin's proprietor and prodigiously accomplished cook.

I was amazed to see Giorgio make dough for *tajarin*, the thin Piedmontese noodle, using forty egg yolks to 2 pounds of flour, but amazement was not succeeded by conviction. I am still persuaded that the ideal noodle for homemade pasta is that achieved with the Bolognese proportions of two whole eggs to approximately 1 cup flour. On another morning, however, Giorgio made *ravioli al plin* and they won my unqualified admiration.

Before cutting the ravioli from a long pasta tube that bulges intermittently with stuffing, Giorgio pinches the pasta between each bulge to make a pleat, the *plin*. It is the simplest of procedures and has a delicious result: Every one of the ravioli acquires a tiny pocket for collecting a dollop of sauce and conveying it into one's mouth.

You can put a *plin* into any kind of ravioli you like to make, but always take into consideration the balance of flavors between stuffing and sauce. A very tasteful stuffing needs a delicately complementary sauce, of which the recipe below is an example. A savory sauce, on the other hand, ought not to have to compete with too rich a stuffing.

¼ cup dry white wine

1½ cups shredded Savoy
  cabbage

2 egg yolks

For Cooking and
  Saucing the Ravioli

1 tablespoon olive oil

¼ cup choice sweet butter

6 to 8 fresh sage leaves

¼ cup freshly grated
  Parmigiano-Reggiano
  cheese

_____

*About 120 ravioli, serving 4 to 6
persons*

A warm serving platter

Making the Meat and Cabbage Stuffing

1. Choose a sauté pan or skillet that can later accommodate all the meat in a single layer without overlapping; put in 1 tablespoon of oil and all the garlic; and turn on the heat to medium high. Briefly cook the garlic, stirring frequently, until it becomes colored a very, very pale gold; then add the rosemary, stir once or twice, and put in the veal and pork.

2. Brown the meat thoroughly on both sides, add salt and pepper, turn the meat over once or twice, then put in the white wine. Let the wine bubble completely away, occasionally scraping the bottom of the pan with a wooden spoon, then use a slotted spoon or spatula to transfer the meat to a bowl. Pick out and discard the garlic.

3. Add remaining tablespoon of oil to the pan and put in the shredded cabbage. Turn up the heat to high and, using a wooden spoon, turn over the cabbage for 2 minutes until it has become evenly coated. At this point, lower the heat to minimum, cover the pan, and cook the cabbage, turning it occasionally, until it achieves a very soft, nearly creamy consistency, about 20 to 30 minutes.

4. Empty the entire contents of the pan into the bowl with the meat to combine all ingredients. Chop the combined ingredients using either a knife and chopping block or the food processor. In the latter case, avoid overprocessing the mixture to a pulp. Return the mixture to the bowl and add the egg yolks, incorporating them into the stuffing with a wooden spoon.

Making the Ravioli

1. Roll out the dough by the machine or hand method, as you prefer. From the soft, freshly rolled-out dough cut off a long rectangle 3 inches wide. Keep the uncut dough covered by plastic wrap.

2. Dot the rectangle with pellets of stuffing about the size of a large chickpea, setting them down in a row 1½ inches apart and ¾ inch away from one of the long edges of the rectangle.

3. When you have distributed as many dots of the meat and cabbage mixture as will fit along the pasta strip, bring the edge farther from the

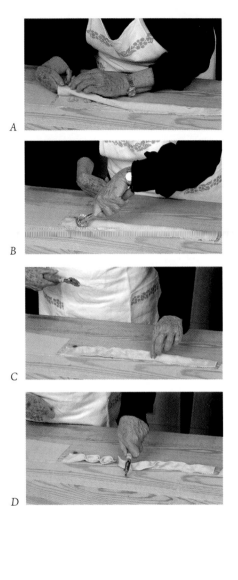

A

B

C

D

stuffing over them and join it to the other edge, pressing both edges together (*photo A*), creating a long tube that bulges with stuffing at regularly spaced intervals. Run a pastry wheel over the whole length of the cut side of the tube to trim it evenly and seal it securely (*photo B*).

4.   With your thumb and forefinger, firmly pinch the pasta tube together at each space in between the bulging mounds of stuffing (*photo C*). To finish forming the pleat, cut the pasta where you have pinched it, using the pastry wheel, running it from the rounded folded-over edge of the tube to the flat cut edge (*photo D*).

5.   Spread out the resulting "pinched" ravioli on clean, dry, cloth towels, making sure they do not touch. If they do they will stick to one another and tear when you pull them apart. If you are not cooking them right away, turn them over from time to time while they are drying.

Cooking and Saucing the Ravioli

1.   Bring 4 quarts of water to a boil, salt liberally, and drop in the ravioli with 1 tablespoon olive oil. Cook at a steady but moderate boil.

2.   While the pasta is cooking, put the butter in a small skillet and turn on the heat to medium. When the butter foam subsides, and just before the butter's color begins to turn from golden to brown, add the sage leaves. Cook for a few seconds, turning the sage leaves over once, and take the pan off heat.

3.   The pasta should be cooked by now. Taste it to make sure, then drain it and transfer it to a warm serving platter. Pour the contents of the pan over the pasta, toss thoroughly, add the grated Parmesan, toss again, and serve at once.

AHEAD-OF-TIME NOTE: You can make the ravioli as much as a day in advance, up to the point when they are ready to be cooked. When keeping them overnight, I don't refrigerate them, but if you prefer to do so make sure they have dried thoroughly at room temperature. You can also split the recipe into two parts, preparing the stuffing a day ahead. Bring the stuffing to room temperature before making the pasta.

Rosemary and Sage–Scented Homemade Pasta

PASTA FATTA IN CASA CON IL ROSMARINO E LA SALVIA

All-purpose flour and eggs
in the approximate
proportions given in the
basic homemade pasta
recipe on page 115. For
each whole egg use:

½ teaspoon fresh rosemary
leaves, chopped very,
very fine, to an almost
powder-like consistency

1 teaspoon fresh sage
leaves, chopped like the
rosemary, to a very fine
consistency

As a rule, I don't see the point of making pasta dough at home with anything but flour and eggs. Colored dough depends for its hues on coloring agents that either communicate no flavor, and therefore have no gastronomic interest, or else impart flavor that lacks freshness. The only desirable colored pasta is the splendid Bolognese kind with spinach. I have similar objections to pasta dough touched up with aromatic substances. They usually have nothing to express, unless it's staleness. Again there is an exception, and it is this delicately fragrant rosemary and sage pasta. The scent is not obtrusive, but it is perceptible and it stays fresh. Use sauces that do not have a rosemary and sage presence of their own to compete with that of the pasta.

1. Make a hollow in the mound of flour as described on page 115, break the eggs into it, and add the chopped herbs. Knead and roll out the dough as directed in the basic recipe.

2. Cut into fettuccine, page 118; or *tonnarelli*, page 203.

SUGGESTED SAUCE: The Simple Veal Pasta Sauce on page 172.

Homemade Ravioli with Asparagus and Scallops

RAVIOLI RIPIENI DI ASPARAGI E CAPPE SANTE

For the Pasta

Pasta dough made from 3 eggs and approximately 1½ cups unbleached flour (see page 115) and wrapped in plastic wrap

For the Stuffing

1 pound asparagus

Salt

2 tablespoons butter

2 tablespoons very finely chopped onion

1 pound fresh scallops, preferably bay

1 egg yolk

Black pepper ground fresh

⅓ cup freshly grated Parmigiano-Reggiano cheese

2 tablespoons fine, dry, unflavored bread crumbs

In recent years, scallops combined with vegetables have been appearing in many seafood pasta sauces in Italy and I felt that, together with asparagus, they would make a beautiful stuffing for ravioli. It took several tries to fine-tune both the stuffing and a suitable sauce to go with the pasta, but I am very pleased with the results. There is a classic balance of flavors at work here that lifts the dish above mere innovation and makes one want to have it again and again.

A word of advice: Scallops have a tendency to shed liquid that you certainly don't want in the stuffing because it would make the pasta wrappers soggy. The temptation is to save time by discarding the liquid, a temptation I succumbed to at first. Don't do it, but invest the few minutes required to cook down that liquid and you will be handsomely rewarded with a lively and flavorful concentrate.

Making the Asparagus and Scallop Stuffing

1. Slice off 1 inch or more from the dry, butt end of the asparagus to expose moister part of the stalk. The younger the asparagus, the less you need to trim away. The dark green fibers that surround the juicy, tender center of the stalk must be pared away. Hold the asparagus firmly with its tip pointing toward you, and using a sharp paring knife, peel away the stalk's very thin but very tough outer skin. Begin at the base, digging the knife blade into it to a depth of about ¹⁄₁₆ inch, gradually tapering toward the surface as you bring the blade up to the narrow portion of the stalk at the base of the bud. Give the stalk a slight turn and repeat the procedure until you have trimmed it all around. Then remove any small leaves sprouting below the spear's tip.

2. Soak the trimmed asparagus in a basin full of cold water for 10 minutes, then rinse in two or three changes of cold water. Cut the stalks in two, separating tips from bottoms.

3. Choose a broad pan that can later contain all the asparagus lying flat, fill it with water to a depth of 1½ to 2 inches, and bring to a boil. Add 2 tablespoons of salt and put in the bottoms of the stalks. Boil for 5 minutes, add the tips, and continue cooking for 5 more minutes. Drain thoroughly and set aside on a plate. Set a small object under one end of the plate so that any additional liquid will collect at the other end, to be discarded.

4. Put 1 tablespoon each of butter and chopped onion in a medium skillet, and turn on the heat to medium high. Cook the onion, stirring from time to time, until it becomes colored a light gold color. Add the asparagus and cook for about 10 minutes, turning them over frequently to color the stalks evenly on all sides. Transfer all the contents of the pan to a plate or small bowl, and wipe the pan clean with paper towels.

5. Look the scallops over and cut away any remaining bits of the tough tendon that once attached them to their shells. Wash the scallops in cold water, then pat them thoroughly dry with a cloth kitchen towel.

6. Put 1 tablespoon each of butter and chopped onion in the skillet where you cooked the asparagus, turn on the heat to medium high, and cook the onion, stirring from time to time, until it becomes colored a light gold. Add the scallops and some salt, and turn up the heat to very high. Cook the scallops for 1 or 2 minutes, turning them over frequently.

7. The scallops will shed some liquid. Using a slotted spoon or spatula, transfer the scallops to a strainer set over a bowl. Boil away the liquid in the pan over high heat, then turn the heat off.

8. When the scallops have rested for about 30 minutes, they will have shed more liquid. Pour that liquid from the bowl into the pan, return the pan to high heat, and boil away the scallop juices completely, scraping the bottom of the pan occasionally with a wooden spoon. When there is no more liquid left in the pan, put the scallops back in,

turn them over quickly once or twice over high heat, then combine them with the asparagus.

9. Put the scallops and asparagus into a food processor and chop them fine, using the pulse switch, but do not process into a creamy consistency. They should be chopped into pieces no larger than ¼ inch. If some of the pieces are larger, rather than continuing to run the processor, finish chopping by hand with a knife.

10. Put the scallops and asparagus into a bowl, add the egg yolk, a few grindings of black pepper, the ⅓ cup of grated Parmesan, and the bread crumbs, and mix thoroughly to obtain an evenly amalgamated consistency.

Making the Ravioli

Divide the pasta dough into several pieces and roll thin strips from it in the pasta machine, as described on pages 117–18. Following the directions for making ravioli on page 201, dot one half of each strip with 1 heaping teaspoon of the asparagus and scallop mixture, spacing it about 3 inches apart. Fold the strip over to enclose the mixture, and cut it into 1½-inch-wide ravioli. Press their edges down with your fingertip to make sure they are sealed tight. Spread the pasta out on a cloth towels laid flat on a work counter or table, taking care that the ravioli do not touch. Once they are all done, they can be cooked immediately or after several hours. If you are going to cook them later, turn them over every 15 minutes or so.

Cooking and Saucing the Ravioli

1. Cook the ravioli in a large pot of boiling, salted water with 1 tablespoon of olive oil. If you are cooking them some hours after making them, they will take a little longer than when very fresh. Taste one after 3 minutes; continue cooking, if necessary, until tender, but with some firmness to the bite. Retrieve them with a colander spoon or a Chinese wire strainer, transferring them to a pasta colander.

2. As soon as they are all done, place them on a warm serving platter, and toss with the butter, shredded basil, and grated Parmesan. Serve at once.

Homemade Ricotta and Mint Tortelloni

TORTELLONI DI RICOTTA E MENTA

For the Stuffing

½ pound whole-milk
    ricotta

⅛ teaspoon grated nutmeg

4 teaspoons chopped fresh
    mint leaves

1 egg yolk

Salt

Black pepper ground fresh

1 tablespoon butter

2 tablespoons chopped
    onion

½ teaspoon chopped garlic

These evolved from one of the classics of the Bolognese repertoire, *tortelloni di ricotta e prezzemolo*, large *tortelli* stuffed with ricotta and parsley. We have a lot of mint growing on our terrace that needs little encouragement to multiply, and in looking for ways to use it, I thought of substituting it for the parsley in the *tortelloni's* stuffing. We grow several varieties, from the sweet Roman *mentuccia* to spicy peppermint, *menta peperita*. Each has its distinctive aroma, but all of them work well here.

Mint has a more high-pitched fragrance than parsley, and to keep it from making too strident a solo I rounded it out with onion and garlic. I chose tomato for the sauce because mint gets on so well with it. The aromas of the sauce needed reinforcement at the bottom of their register, so I added the more profoundly scented bay leaves to do the job. This has the briskest, lightest flavor of any stuffed pasta I know, welcome at any time, but particularly in summer.

Making the Ricotta and Mint Stuffing

1. Unpack the ricotta and wrap it tightly in a layer of cheesecloth, making a knot at the top. Slip the handle of a long wooden spoon under the knot, and rest the spoon over a deep bowl so that the ricotta hangs free. Let the cheese drain for about 30 minutes or more.

2. Unwrap the cheese, discarding the cheesecloth. Put the ricotta in a clean bowl; add the nutmeg, mint, egg yolk, salt, and ground black pepper; and mix well to combine all ingredients homogeneously.

3. Put the butter and onion in a small skillet, turn on the heat to medium, and cook the onion, stirring occasionally, until it becomes colored a pale gold. Add the garlic and cook it, stirring frequently, until it becomes colored a shade of gold paler than that of the onion.

4. Empty the contents of the pan into the bowl with the ricotta mixture, and turn the mixture over several times with a wooden spoon to distribute the sautéed onion and garlic uniformly.

(continued)

For the Pasta

Homemade yellow dough made with 2 large eggs, approximately 1¼ cups unbleached flour, and 1 tablespoon milk, following directions on pages 117–18 if using a pasta machine, OR those on pages 121–25 for the hand-rolled method

Making the Tortelloni

1. Roll out the dough by the machine or hand method, as you prefer. From the soft, freshly rolled-out dough cut off a long rectangle 5 inches wide. Keep the uncut dough covered with plastic wrap.

2. Dot the rectangle with pellets of the ricotta and mint stuffing about the size of a cherry, setting them down in a row 2½ inches apart and 1¼ inches away from one of the long edges of the rectangle.

3. When you have distributed as many dots of the stuffing as will fit along the pasta strip, bring the edge farther from the stuffing over them and join it to the other edge. After forcing the air out with the palm of your hand, press both edges together gently but firmly, creating a long, sealed tube that bulges with stuffing at regularly spaced intervals. Run a pastry wheel over the whole length of the cut side of the tube to trim it evenly and seal it securely.

4. Using a pastry wheel, cut the tube straight across midway between each bulge to make 2½-inch-wide *tortelloni*. Press the cut edges down with your fingertip to make sure they are sealed tight. Spread the pasta out on cloth towels laid flat on a work counter or table, taking care that the *tortelloni* do not touch. Once they are all done, they can be cooked immediately or after several hours. If you are going to cook them later, turn them over every 15 minutes or so.

Making the Sauce

1. Wash the tomatoes in cold water, skin them raw with a swiveling-blade peeler, split them in half, scoop out the seeds without squeezing the tomato, and cut them up in small pieces.

2. Put 2 tablespoons of butter, 1½ tablespoons of oil, and ¼ cup chopped onion in a 10-inch skillet and turn on the heat to medium high. Cook the onion, stirring from time to time, until it becomes colored a medium gold.

3. Add the bay leaves and cook them for a few seconds, turning them over several times; then add the tomatoes, salt, and black pepper. Cook

For Cooking and
    Saucing the
    Tortelloni

¾ pound ripe, firm
    tomatoes

2 tablespoons butter plus
    1 tablespoon for tossing

1½ tablespoons extra virgin
    olive oil for the sauce
    plus 1 tablespoon for
    cooking the pasta

¼ cup chopped onion

4 bay leaves

Salt

Black pepper ground fresh

⅓ cup freshly grated
    Parmigiano-Reggiano
    cheese

---

*Approximately thirty-six 2-inch
tortelloni, making 6 appetizer
portions of pasta or a full course
for 4*

A warm serving platter

at a steady but gentle simmer, stirring periodically, for about 15 to 20 minutes, until the fat begins to separate from the sauce, as described in the Note on page 133. Retrieve and discard the bay leaves.

Cooking and Saucing the Tortelloni

1. Cook the *tortelloni* in a large pot of boiling, salted water, adding 1 tablespoon of olive oil. If you are cooking them some hours after making them, they will take a little longer than when very fresh. Taste one after about 3 minutes, and continue cooking, if necessary, until they are tender, but with some firmness to the bite. Transfer them from the pot to a pasta colander with a colander spoon or a Chinese wire strainer.

2. As soon as they are all done, place them on a warm serving platter, and gently toss with the sauce, 1 tablespoon of butter, and the grated Parmesan. Serve at once.

AHEAD-OF-TIME NOTE: The sauce can be cooked 1 or 2 days in advance and reheated at a gentle simmer before being tossed with the pasta. The *tortelloni* can be made as far ahead as early in the morning, if you are serving them for dinner.

Green Ravioli Pesaro-Style Stuffed with Lamb and Sauced with Yellow Peppers

RAVIOLI VERDI D'AGNELLO ALLA PESARESE COL SUGO DI PEPERONI GIALLI

For the Stuffing

1 tablespoon extra virgin olive oil

1⅔ pounds lamb with the bone in, any cut except the leg, cut into 3- to 4-inch pieces

4 or 5 garlic cloves, lightly mashed with a knife handle and peeled

1 tablespoon fresh rosemary leaves, chopped very fine

Salt

Black pepper ground fresh

½ cup dry white wine

1 medium boiling potato

½ cup freshly grated Parmigiano-Reggiano cheese

⅛ teaspoon ground nutmeg

2 tablespoons milk

For the Sauce

3 large, meaty yellow bell peppers

2 tablespoons extra virgin olive oil

If there is an Italian region that has largely been spared the jarring presence of mass tourism, or the scars of industrialization and other forms of exploitation, or the languor of economic stagnation, it is the Marches in central Italy, on the Adriatic. It is a land of fertile, peaceful hills, often capped by walled hamlets, many of them intact, with structures of earth-colored brick that make them seem so much warmer and accessible than say, the aloof and stone-faced hill towns of Tuscany. The pretty villages, the gentle, swelling hills, the luxuriant orchards and grainfields, the passage of a shepherd with his sheep, may persuade a visitor that the happy, pastoral Italy of one's romantic dreams still exists.

The food of the upper portion of the Marches shares with that of its neighbor to the north, Romagna, an emphasis on homemade egg pasta. On an Easter visit to friends in the country inland from the sea town of Pesaro, I was served an immensely satisfying dish of ravioli made of spinach pasta and stuffed with lamb. The pasta dough is identical to what they make in Romagna, but no *romagnolo* cook would have thought of stuffing it with lamb. That was as clear a sign that I had left northern Italy behind me and entered the center as though I'd been stopped at a border to have my passport stamped.

I marveled to find that for softness and cohesion the filling contained no béchamel or eggs, as it might have in Emilia-Romagna, but simply a mashed boiled potato. Thus, while it is a very savory stuffing indeed, it feels very light. The yellow peppers contribute sweetness, aroma, and—not to be disdained—a sauce lovely to see over the green pasta.

Making the Stuffing

1. Put the olive oil in a 10-inch skillet and turn on the heat to medium high. When the oil is hot put in the lamb pieces along with the mashed garlic cloves and chopped rosemary.

½ cup finely chopped onion

Salt

Black pepper ground fresh

FOR THE PASTA

Spinach, ¼ pound if small,
    a little more if leaves and
    stems are large

Salt

1½ cups flour,
    approximately

2 eggs

FOR TOSSING THE
    RAVIOLI

2 tablespoons butter

½ cup freshly grated
    Parmigiano-Reggiano
    cheese

---

*Approximately 76 ravioli,
making 4 regular or 6 appetizer
servings*

Cheesecloth

A colander spoon or a Chinese
wire strainer

A warm serving platter

2. Brown the pieces well on all sides, add salt and several grindings
of black pepper, turn them over once, then add the white wine.

3. When the wine has bubbled away, put a lid on the pan, turn the
heat down to very low, and cook until the meat feels very, very tender
when prodded with a fork. Turn the lamb over from time to time, and
whenever it should prove necessary, add 2 or 3 tablespoons of water to
keep the meat from sticking to the bottom of the pan.

4. While the meat is cooking, wash a potato and put it unpeeled in a
saucepan with enough water to cover amply. Bring to a boil. When
done, peel it while it is still hot and mash it in the food processor or
with any potato-mashing tool you like to use. Transfer it to a mixing
bowl.   *(continued)*

5. When the meat is done, remove it from the pan using a slotted spoon or spatula. With a small, sharp knife, carefully remove the bone from every piece.

6. Put the boned lamb in a food processor—better if it is still slightly warm—and chop it fine, but not to a creamy consistency. Transfer it to the mixing bowl.

7. Put 2 or 3 tablespoons of water in the skillet in which you browned the meat, turn on the heat to medium high, and while the water bubbles away scrape loose any browning residues from the bottom of the pan. Add these cooking juices to the bowl with the potato and ground meat. Mix thoroughly with a fork to achieve a homogeneous mixture.

8. Add the grated Parmesan, nutmeg, and milk to the bowl, and mix again until all ingredients are thoroughly combined. Taste and correct for salt and pepper.

Making the Sauce

1. Wash the peppers, and skin them with a swivel-bladed peeler. Split them, peel away any remaining bits of skin, remove the core and all seeds, and cut the peppers' flesh lengthwise into strips about ½ inch wide.

2. Put the oil and chopped onion in a 10-inch skillet and turn on the heat to medium. Cook the onion, stirring from time to time, until it becomes colored a pale gold.

3. Add the strips of yellow pepper, salt, and several grindings of black pepper, and turn over a few times to coat well. Turn the heat down and put a lid on the pan. Cook the peppers, turning them over occasionally, until they are thoroughly soft, but don't let them brown.

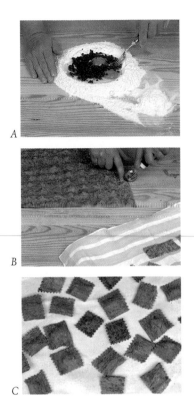

A

B

C

Making the Ravioli

1. Detach the stems from the spinach and discard any bruised or wilted leaves. Wash in a large basin or in the sink filled with water, changing the water repeatedly until no soil shows at the bottom.

2. Put some water in a saucepan and bring to a boil. Add 2 or 3 large pinches of salt, which will keep the spinach green, and drop in the spinach. When it is very tender, drain it.

3. As soon as it is cool enough to handle, collect the spinach in cheesecloth and twist tightly to force out as much water as possible.

4. Open the cheesecloth and take as much spinach as will form a ball the size of a large egg. Chop it very fine on a cutting surface with a knife. Do not use the food processor, because that will puree it.

5. Pour the flour onto a work surface, shape it into a mound, and scoop out a deep hollow in its center. Break the eggs into the hollow and add the chopped spinach. Incorporate the eggs, spinach, and flour (*photo A*) and then knead into a smooth, firm ball of dough, following the directions for both steps that appear on pages 115–16. Divide the pasta dough into several pieces and roll thin strips from it in the pasta machine, as described on pages 117–18. Do one strip at a time, and keep the remaining mass of dough wrapped in plastic wrap.

Stuffing and Cutting the Ravioli

1. When you have rolled out one strip of pasta, cut it into a long rectangle that is 4 inches wide. Dot the pasta with small nuggets of the lamb mixture, keeping the dots 2 inches apart and laying the row of dots parallel to the edges of the rectangle and set 1 inch back from one of those edges. Fold the strip over to enclose the mixture, and use a fluted pastry wheel to cut it into 2-inch-wide squares (*photo B*). Press the edges down with your fingertip to make sure they are sealed tight.

2. Spread the stuffed pasta out on cloth towels (*photo C*) laid flat on a work counter or table, taking care that the ravioli do not touch, or they will become glued to each other and tear open when separated.

(continued)

Cooking and Saucing the Ravioli

1. Have ready a very warm serving platter and make sure the sauce is hot. Cook the ravioli in a large pot of boiling, salted water with 1 tablespoon olive oil. If you are cooking them some hours after making them, they will take a little longer than when very fresh. Taste one after about 3 minutes, and continue cooking, if necessary, until they are tender, but with some firmness to the bite. Retrieve them from the pot with a colander spoon or a Chinese wire strainer, transferring them to the warm serving platter.

2. As soon as all the ravioli are done, toss with the pepper sauce. Add 3 tablespoons of butter and the grated Parmesan, turn the pasta over four or five times, then serve at once.

AHEAD-OF-TIME NOTE: You can finish making the stuffing the day before you plan to fill the ravioli. Refrigerate tightly covered, but bring to full room temperature before using it.

You can make the sauce a day or two in advance of serving the pasta. Refrigerate tightly covered, but bring to full room temperature before reheating and proceeding with the recipe.

Although you can cook the ravioli as soon as they are done, you will probably want to do so later. You can complete stuffing and cutting them several hours in advance, even in the morning, if you are serving them for dinner. If you are not cooking them right away, turn them over every 15 minutes or so.

Spinach Tonnarelli Sauced with Yellow Peppers and Tomato Dice

TONNARELLI VERDI CON PEPERONI GIALLI E POMODORO A DADINI

FOR THE PASTA

¼ pound spinach

Salt

2 eggs

1½ cups flour

FOR THE SAUCE

2 large, yellow bell peppers

½ cup chopped onion

2 tablespoons extra virgin olive oil

Salt

1¼ cups fresh, firm, ripe tomatoes, cut into ½-inch dice with their skins on, all seeds scooped away

Chopped hot chili pepper, ⅛ teaspoon or to taste

FOR TOSSING THE TONNARELLI

2 tablespoons butter

⅓ cup freshly grated Parmigiano-Reggiano cheese

For 4 persons

Cheesecloth

A shallow, warm serving platter

In my pantheon of illustrious homemade pastas there is a special niche for the *tonnarelli* noodle. If you cut across it you will find that it is square, as broad as it is high. It has the buoyancy and sauce-absorption capacity of other homemade pastas, because that is what it is made of, but *tonnarelli*'s chunkier profile also endows it with a firm bite comparable to that of factory-made, dried, boxed pasta. *Tonnarelli* is a specialty of Latium, the region where Rome is located, and its neighbor to the east, Abruzzi. In Abruzzi it is known as *maccheroni alla chitarra* because the dough for it is cut on the steel strings of a guitar-like tool. With a hand-cranked pasta machine, the making of *tonnarelli*, as described below, becomes extraordinarily simple.

The *tonnarelli* noodles for this recipe are green because they are made of spinach dough, an attractive background for the yellow peppers and tomato dice of the sauce. Please note that the tomatoes are just scalded, not cooked. They must retain their dice-like shape and the liveliness of their fresh ripe taste and the firmness of a nearly raw consistency.

Making Green Tonnarelli

1. Trim, wash, and cook the spinach with some salt, incorporate it with eggs and flour, knead the mass to produce a ball of spinach pasta dough, and roll out the dough in a pasta machine as described in Making the Pasta, steps 1 through 5, of the spinach ravioli recipe on page 201. Before you roll the dough out, however, carefully go over the instructions in the step that follows.

2. Because you are making *tonnarelli*, the strips of pasta that you are stretching out through the machine's adjustable rollers need to be rolled out thicker than those for fettuccine and other noodles. *Tonnarelli* owe their marvelous chewy consistency to their shape—the four sides being

of equal length when looked at in cross-section. To obtain that square shape, you must roll out the pasta strip to a thickness equal to the width of the grooves in the narrower of the machine's two noodle cutters. On most machines' thinning rollers, the setting most suitable for rolling out pasta dough that you can then cut for *tonnarelli* is either the second or third before the last. To make sure, run some dough through one of those settings and see whether it is as thick as the grooves of the narrower cutter are wide.

3. Spread each pasta strip, as you roll it out of the final thinning setting you've chosen, onto clean cloth towels laid flat on a counter. The strips must dry for 10 minutes or more, depending on the temperature and ventilation of your kitchen. From time to time, turn the strips over. The pasta is ready for cutting when it is still supple enough that it won't crack when cut, but not so soft and moist that the strands will stick to each other.

4. Install the narrower of the machine's two pairs of cutters. When the pasta strips are dry enough not to stick, but still pliant enough not to crack, run them, one at a time, through the cutter. As the ribbons of *tonnarelli* emerge, separate them and spread them out on the cloth towels.

AHEAD-OF-TIME NOTE: Homemade noodles can be stored for weeks in a cupboard, just like a box of store-bought macaroni. If you plan to use the *tonnarelli* at a much later date, proceed thus: As the noodles are cut, curl several strands at a time into circular nest shapes. Lay them on the towels, making sure the nests don't touch each other. Allow them to dry totally before storing them, because if any moisture remains when they are put away, mold will develop. To be safe, let the nests dry on towels for at least 24 hours, turning them over occasionally. When dry, place them in a large box or tin, interleaving each layer of nests with paper towels. Handle carefully because they are brittle. Store in a dry cupboard, not in the refrigerator. Allow more cooking time for dried homemade pasta than for the freshly made.

Making the Sauce

1. Wash the peppers, and skin them with a swivel-bladed peeler. Split them, peel away any remaining bits of skin, remove the core and all seeds, and cut the peppers' flesh lengthwise into strips about ¼ inch wide, or thinner if you can.

2. Put the chopped onion and oil in a 10-inch skillet and turn on the heat to medium high. Cook the onion, stirring from time to time, until it becomes colored a pale gold.

3. Add the strips of yellow pepper and the salt, and turn over a few times to coat well. Turn the heat down and put a lid on the pan. Cook the peppers, turning them over occasionally, until they are thoroughly soft, but don't let them brown.

AHEAD-OF-TIME NOTE: You can cook the sauce up to this point a day or two in advance. Refrigerate under plastic wrap, bring to full room temperature before resuming cooking, and reheat thoroughly before proceeding with the next step.

4. When the peppers are completely limp, add the diced tomato and the chili pepper, turn over all ingredients to coat them, but cook for less than a minute, taking the pan off heat. Try to time this concluding step so that it is completed just as the pasta is done and about to be drained. The tomato in the sauce should still be almost raw.

Cooking and Saucing the Tonnarelli

1. To a large pot of boiling water, add a small fistful of salt. Gather all the *tonnarelli* in a dish towel, tightly hold one end of the towel high above the boiling water, loosen the bottom end, and let the pasta slide into the pot.

2. As soon as the *tonnarelli* are tender, but still firm to the bite, drain thoroughly, transfer to a shallow, warm serving platter, pour the sauce from the pan over them, and toss a few times to distribute the sauce well. Add the 2 tablespoons of butter and the grated Parmesan, toss once or twice again, then serve at once.

Sardinian Sheet Music Bread with Lamb Sauce

PANE FRATTAU COL SUGO DI AGNELLO

For the Sauce

¼ cup extra virgin olive oil

½ cup chopped onion

1 medium carrot, chopped fine

⅔ cup chopped celery

½ teaspoon chopped garlic

1 tablespoon chopped Italian flat-leaf parsley

½ pound ground beef chuck

½ pound boned lamb shoulder, cut into fine dice

1 cup dry white wine

2 cups canned imported Italian plum tomatoes, cut up, with their juice

Salt

Black pepper ground fresh

For the Frattau

Salt

12 disks Sardinian Sheet Music Bread, made as described on page 39

1½ cups freshly grated mellow Sardinian or

I had come to the mountainous Barbagia district in eastern Sardinia to observe the making of *pane carasau*, the celebrated wafer-thin bread. We stopped for the night at Su Gologone, a handsome resort whose restaurant serves a broad variety of Sardinian specialties. I was puzzled at dinner to find among the first courses a dish called *pane frattau.* "Is this yet another kind of bread?" I asked our waiter. "No," he said. "It is always *pane carasau*—sheet music bread—but it is called *frattau* when cooked like pasta and served with lamb sauce."

Once I had discovered how to make my own *carasau* at home, I was eager to try it as *frattau.* When served, it resembles the loose, soft lasagne-like dish called *piccagge* that is made on the Riviera. The cooked bread has excellent, sturdy flavor that is a perfect match for the lamb sauce. It takes less than a minute for it to cook, so you must stay right on top of it to make sure it isn't overdone.

Making the Sauce

1. Put the oil and chopped onion in a heavy-bottomed medium saucepan and turn on the heat to medium high. Cook the onion, stirring from time to time, until it becomes colored a very pale gold.

2. Add the carrot, celery, garlic, and parsley. Stir with a wooden spoon for about 1 minute to coat all ingredients well, then add the ground beef and the diced lamb. Turn the meat over for a minute or two to brown it on all sides.

3. Add the wine and let it bubble gently for a couple of minutes, while scraping loose with the wooden spoon any browning residues from the bottom of the pan. Add the tomatoes, salt, and generous grindings of pepper; turn over all ingredients; then adjust the heat so that the sauce put-puts sporadically at the gentlest of simmers. Cook for 1 hour, stirring from time to time. If you are ready to cook the *pane frattau,* keep the sauce simmering slowly.

Tuscan pecorino sheep's milk cheese OR ½ cup grated Romano cheese mixed with 1 cup Parmigiano-Reggiano cheese

---

For 6 persons

A warm, deep serving platter

A colander spoon

Cooking and Saucing Pane Frattau

Bring a large pot of water to a boil; add salt; and, as the water resumes boiling, drop in six disks of sheet music bread. After no more than 1 minute, retrieve the bread with a slotted spoon or skimmer, and spread it out on the warm serving platter. Cover with part of the sauce and sprinkle with grated cheese. Cook the other six disks in the same manner, laying them out in the platter, covering with the remaining sauce, and sprinkling with the rest of the grated cheese. Serve at once.

AHEAD-OF-TIME NOTE: You can cook the sauce 2 or 3 days in advance, keeping it refrigerated in a tightly sealed container. Reheat thoroughly and keep at a slow simmer while cooking the *pane frattau*.

Baked Crêpes Pie with Eggplant and Peppers

TORTINO DI CRESPELLE CON MELANZANE E PEPERONI

For 5 Crespelle

½ heaping cup flour

¾ cup milk

1 whole egg plus 1 yolk

Salt

½ tablespoon cold, hard butter

For the Pie

¾ pound eggplant, the white variety if available, otherwise the long, thin kind

Salt

Vegetable oil, enough to come at least ¾ inch up the sides of a skillet plus a little for smearing the baking pan

2 medium red bell peppers

1 cup freshly grated Parmigiano-Reggiano cheese

2 tablespoons butter

For 6 persons

A nonstick 10-inch skillet

A large platter lined with a double layer of paper towels

A 10-inch round cake pan

When I had a cooking school in Bologna, we welcomed our students on the evening of their arrival with a banquet at that city's imperishable gastronomic institution, the restaurant Diana. There were many courses that displayed the kitchen's skill with handmade pasta, game birds, and other Bolognese specialties. All of them were well received, I think, but the one course that invariably excited the most wonder and delighted surprise was a pie-like affair made with *crespelle*—Bolognese crêpes. In that specific instance it was layered with fresh porcini mushrooms, but it can be made with a wide variety of vegetables or meat and cheese, as described in my earlier books. The combination of pepper and eggplant that is given below has a full-blown taste of summer that makes it one of my favorites.

In Bologna, crêpes are used like pasta dough either to produce lasagne-like, layered assemblages or as cannelloni. They are not a replacement for homemade pasta but an easy-to-make alternative with great finesse and a distinctive, immensely appealing texture.

I like the practicality of this dish. As you will see when reading through the recipe, you can stop at several points along the way and resume any time later that is convenient. Bear in mind that you can make it not only in layered pie form but, with exactly the same vegetable filling, as cannelloni, rolling up a single *crespella* around the filling to make a large cannellone out of each.

Making the Crespelle

1. Put the flour in a small and not too shallow a bowl. Add the milk in a very thin stream, beating steadily with a whisk, taking care that lumps do not form.

2. When all the milk has been incorporated, add the whole egg, the egg yolk, and a pinch of salt. Mix steadily for about 2 minutes, then transfer the batter through a strainer into another small, deep bowl.

3. Turn the heat on under the nonstick skillet to very low. When the skillet is hot, spear the hard pat of butter with a fork and, with a rapid motion, very lightly swipe the bottom of the pan with it.

4. Scoop up ¼ cup of the *crespelle* batter and pour it into the pan, spreading it as much as possible. Lift up the pan by its handle, quickly tilt and rotate it with a seesawing up-and-down motion to distribute the batter evenly, and return it to the burner. As soon as the batter sets and becomes colored a light gold, slip a spatula underneath it and flip it over to do the other side. Cook it briefly, then transfer it to a plate.

5. Repeat the operation four more times, each time filming the bottom of the pan with butter, and stacking the *crespelle* one above the other on a plate.

AHEAD-OF-TIME NOTE: You can make the *crespelle* 3 or 4 days ahead of time. As soon as they have cooled off completely, cover the plate on which they are stacked with plastic wrap or aluminum foil and refrigerate.

Preparing the Eggplant for the Pie's Filling

1. Cut off the eggplants' spiky green tops. Cut the eggplants lengthwise into slices about ½ inch thick. If you are using purple eggplant, remove their tough skin.

2. Set a colander over a bowl or deep dish. Line the colander with one layer of eggplant slices, placing them vertically; sprinkle lightly with salt; place another layer of eggplant over the first; sprinkle a tiny bit more salt over it; and proceed thus until you have used up all the slices. Let stand for at least 30 minutes to allow the eggplant to shed some of its astringent liquid.

3. Remove the eggplant slices from the colander and pat them dry with paper towels.

4. Pour enough vegetable oil into a 12-inch skillet to come at least ¾ inch up the sides of the pan, and turn the heat on to high. When the oil is hot enough to sizzle if tested by dipping one end of an eggplant

slice into it, slip in as many slices as will fit very loosely, without crowding. Fry the eggplant to a rich golden brown, and use a slotted spatula to transfer to a platter lined with a double thickness of paper towels. Lay the slices flat without overlapping too much. Add more slices to the pan. When they are done transfer them to the platter, after having covered the previous layer with a double thickness of paper towels, and proceed thus until all the eggplant is done. Let cool completely.

5. Cut the eggplant into 1-inch nuggets or into strips about ½ inch wide.

Preparing the Peppers for the Pie's Filling

1. Wash the peppers and, if you have gas, put them directly on the lit burner; otherwise put them under a hot electric broiler. Turn them periodically to char the skin on all sides, then put them in a plastic bag and knot it tightly closed. Let them cool off completely.

2. When the peppers are cool enough to handle comfortably, remove them from the bag and pull off all their skin. Split them open and remove their core and all the seeds. Do not wash the peppers. If necessary, you can wipe off bits of charred skin clinging to them using a paper towel. Cut the peeled pepper flesh into strips or pieces that more or less match the eggplant's, and sprinkle with salt.

AHEAD-OF-TIME NOTE: You can prepare the vegetables up to this point several hours in advance. If refrigerating them, cover with plastic wrap and bring to room temperature before proceeding with the recipe.

Assembling and Baking the Pie

1. Turn on the oven to 450°.

2. Combine the eggplant and peppers, mixing them with all but 3 tablespoons of the grated Parmesan.

3. Lightly smear the inside of the baking pan with vegetable oil.

4. Lay one of the *crespelle* on the bottom of the pan.

5. Divide the eggplant and peppers mixture into four equal parts. Evenly spread one of the parts over the *crespella* in the pan. Top with another *crespella*, then another portion of the eggplant and peppers mixture, and proceed thus until you have topped off the pie with the fifth *crespella*.

6. Sprinkle the 3 tablespoons of Parmesan over the pie and dot with the 2 tablespoons of butter.

7. Bake in the uppermost level of the preheated oven for 25 minutes, until the top of the pie becomes colored a rich gold. Let the pie settle for 5 to 8 minutes, then use a metal spatula to lift it out of the pan, and without turning it over, transfer to a platter and serve.

Risotto and Polenta

Risotto and Polenta
Il Risotto e la Polenta

Risotto

Risotto Sondrio-Style with Spinach and
Other Vegetables

Risotto with Sausages and Cranberry Beans

Risotto with Red Cabbage and Pancetta

Risotto Friuli-Style, with Rosemary and
White Wine

Onion Risotto Beaten with Butter and Sage

Risotto with Green Beans and Yellow Bell
Pepper

Risotto with Mushrooms and Almonds

Polenta

Cornmeal and Buckwheat Flour Polenta

Trento-Style Buckwheat and Cornmeal
Polenta with Melted Butter and
Anchovies

Buckwheat and Cornmeal Polenta Baked
Marcella's Way

Venetian-Style Milk Polenta

Risotto
Il Risotto

Other nations can claim pasta as part of their cuisine, and in much of the world cooks use rice in one way or another, but risotto is unique to Italy, made by a unique cooking method, with varieties of rice that are uniquely Italian. Risotto is the product of a single, immutable technique, a technique, however, that allows you to make as many different *risotti* as there are days in the year. What changes is the base over which you scald the rice, and the key flavor components with which you cook it.

THE FLAVOR BASE

AT THE BASE OF THE BASE   The foundation that supports the succeeding layers of flavor of a risotto is what Italian cooks call a *soffritto*: onion, and occasionally garlic, sautéed more often than not in butter, or alternatively in olive oil. The sautéing procedure must liberate a judicious measure of taste from the onion and, if present, the garlic. Judicious because if it is executed timidly, you will have too flimsy an underpinning of flavor, but if too insistently, the flavor you have extracted will have a sharp and intrusive presence in the finished dish.

BUILDING UP THE BASE   What makes one risotto different from another is what you add to the *soffritto*, which includes almost everything that is good to eat:

- Any kind of fish, alone or variously combined, dark-fleshed oily fish excepted because of its strong taste; nearly all shellfish.
- Any fresh meat, if ground or diced fine, as well as meat sauce and such cured meats as sausages, ham, and pancetta.
- A wide variety of vegetables and legumes: artichokes, asparagus, bell peppers, broccoli, endive, green beans, mushrooms, peas, radicchio, red cabbage, Savoy cabbage, spinach, tomatoes, zucchini; *cannellini* beans, chickpeas, cranberry beans, lentils.
- Cheese: either one or several. Herbs: basil, mint, parsley, rosemary, sage, thyme. Spices: allspice, nutmeg, saffron. White or black truffles. Nuts.

Ingredients are put in the base from the start so that during a cooking process that takes 20 or more minutes, they can surrender their flavor to the risotto. Maintaining the separate character of their texture if of little importance.

There are ingredients such as clams or mussels that would be disagreeably altered by overcooking. In that instance, the juices of the bivalves must be extracted in advance and added to the risotto from the beginning, while the clam or mussel meat itself will be stirred into the risotto when the rice is nearly done.

Another ingredient that is bound into a risotto only in the final stage is grated Parmesan, which when blanketed with shaved white truffle makes a dish to curtsey to.

THE PRINCIPAL RISOTTO RICE VARIETIES

Rice for risotto must satisfy two complementary but separate requirements: On the kernel's surface it must have a soft starch, part of which will dissolve in the cooking to produce a clinging, creamy texture; and within the kernel it must have a different starch that will stay firm and give the cooked rice an *al dente* consistency. If you look at a single grain of rice against the light, you will see both starches—the firm one, chalky white in the center of the kernel, the soft one translucently surrounding it.

Even among the rice varieties grown specifically for risotto, the proportions of the two starches differ, and thus each kind of rice will cook somewhat differently and lead to the making of risottos that vary in style.

Arborio. A large, plump, beautiful grain that abounds in amylopectin, the starch that dissolves in cooking, while it is less rich in amylose, the firm, inner starch. It is the rice of preference to achieve the denser consistency that is popular with cooks in the regions of Lombardy, Piedmont, and Emilia-Romagna where they make risotto with saffron, or with Parmesan and white truffles, with meat sauce, or with game. This can be a fine all-purpose variety yielding a luscious risotto, but because of all the soft starch that envelops it, it must be followed with great care in the cooking. When inattentive cooks use arborio they are rewarded with gummy risottos.

Vialone Nano. A small, stubby, homely grain well endowed with amylose, the starch that does not soften easily in cooking, although it has enough of the softer starch to qualify it as a suitable variety for risotto. It is the nearly unanimous choice in the Veneto, where the preferred consistency is loose—rippling or *all'onda*, to use the Venetian expression—and where people are partial to a kernel that offers considerable resistance to the bite. It is an excellent variety to use for the delicately conceived Venetian-style risotto*s* with seafood or spring vegetables.

Carnaroli. A premium variety developed in 1945 by a Milanese rice grower who crossed *vialone* with a Japanese strain. It has become more easily available than it was when I first wrote about it several years ago, but it is still less abundant and costs more than either *arborio* or *vialone nano*. The *carnaroli* kernel is sheathed in enough soft starch to dissolve deliciously in cooking, but it also contains more of the tough starch than any other risotto variety so that it cooks to an exceptionally satisfying firm, beautifully balanced consistency.

THE COOKING LIQUID

WHEN TO USE BROTH The most desirable liquid for cooking all risottos, save those with seafood, is a homemade meat broth (see the simple directions on page 316). Broth is not stock. It is water in which a piece of fresh meat and a bone or two have been boiled slowly with salt and some vegetables. It is light-bodied and gentle, self-effacingly bringing savor to the dishes of which it is part. In anticipation of future use—and not just in risotto but in many soups—you can make broth several weeks ahead of time in substantial quantity, freeze it into cubes, and store it in the freezer in tightly sealed plastic bags. It takes little effort and no special skill to make, and becomes an invaluable aid to good cooking. The meat you use need not be a fancy cut at all; in fact, the least expensive ones are often the tastiest, but there should be real flesh for the broth, not just bones and sinew. Beef and veal together are what you want for good balance. Omit pork and lamb. I find the flavor of chicken has become distractingly pungent, and I no longer use it.

WHEN TO USE PLAIN WATER Water is the best choice for seafood risotto. Fish fumets, or French-inspired broths enriched with shellfish carcasses, become too emphatic as they cook down, thus undoing the delicacy and freshness that a carefully made fish risotto ought to have.

OTHER LIQUIDS Flavorful liquids shed by ingredients that will go into the flavor base should be kept aside and used when cooking the risotto. Examples are the juices released by clams or mussels, and the filtered water in which dried mushrooms have been soaked.

Vegetable broths alone are not a satisfactory replacement for homemade meat broth. The shorter time they take to cook is more than offset by the length of their preparation, and unlike meat broth, they cannot be made in advance. Nor can their thin, watery taste compete with a good broth's depth of flavor.

Wine may not be used as the sole liquid, but in certain risottos a cup of it may certainly be added.

All the flavors that the cooking liquid starts out with become more concentrated and intense as it evaporates. I often find, when ordering risotto in restaurants in Italy, that if the restaurant has just reopened after its weekly closing day, the risotto is fine, but as it approaches the end of the week, it becomes saltier and sharper. This is because the broth or fish stock professional cooks use has been cooking down day after day.

BOUILLON CUBES I wonder if there is a single kitchen in Italy that has not known the use of *il dado*, the bouillon cube. It is not—or should not be—employed to make quick broth for those dishes where the broth itself is a substantial component, as for example, *tortellini in brodo*, tortellini served in broth. The cube, in small quantity, gives a useful flavor boost to plain water that evaporates while something is cooked in it. Admittedly, good meat broth should be your first choice, but a tiny dose of the cube helps water pretend it's broth for a just a little while, and when it has vanished, the taste of the soup or risotto is a bit more rounded out for it.

THE TOOLS

A Pot to Cook In. The pot must efficiently transmit and evenly retain constant high heat so you can cook the rice at a very lively pace without scorching it. Do not use light ware such as aluminum. Sturdy, heavy-bottomed pots made of steel-jacketed alloys are a practical choice, but for me nothing does the job better than heavy cast iron with a thick enamel coat.

The Stirring Spatula. To stir, get a long-handled wooden spatula with a straight edge and sharp corners. The straight edge wipes the bottom of the pot clean every time you pass it, and its corners allow you to get into that hard to reach angle between the pot's sides and bottom to dislodge the rice that loves to stick there.

THE UNIQUE COOKING METHOD

1. When you have sautéed the base ingredients, turn up the heat to high, add the raw, unwashed rice, and scald it, stirring thoroughly to coat every grain.

2. Add a ladleful of cooking liquid to the pot, stirring the contents, scraping them away from the bottom and sides with your wooden spoon or spatula, until the liquid is

gone. Whenever you find that there is no more liquid in the pot, add less than a cup at a time, stirring constantly, wiping the sides and bottom of the pot clean as you stir. You must never stop stirring and you must be sure to frequently wipe the bottom of pot completely clean, or the rice will stick to it.

3. Taste the rice after it has been cooking for 20 minutes. It is done when it is tender, but firm to the bite. As it gets close to that stage, gradually reduce the amount of liquid you add, so that when the risotto is fully cooked, it is just slightly moist, but not runny.

4. The final step is called *mantecare*. The word is borrowed from the Spanish for butter, *mantequilla*. In Italian it means to work butter or cream into what you are cooking to give it a soft consistency. In making risotto you do it when the risotto is cooked but is still steaming in the pot. You add a tablespoon or two of butter and a half cupful or so of grated Parmesan, and swirl them in vigorously. It is the final and best touch, bestowing on your risotto a creamy consistency of great opulence. It is generally applied to risottos made over a base that contains butter. Sometimes you may feel justified in breaking the rule and you will *mantecare* with butter even if there was oil in the base. In most cases, however, if a risotto has been made with olive oil, before you remove it from the pot, stir into it a tablespoon or two of fine raw extra virgin olive oil.

HOW THE METHOD WORKS

The gradual addition of small quantities of liquid at steady high heat gradually dissolves the soft starch surrounding the kernel, which begins to swell. Constant stirring rubs away the dissolving starch and at the same time distributes it, binding it uniformly to every single grain of rice and to all the ingredients in the pot. It is only through that sustained stirring motion that you produce the marvelous amalgam, the creamy fusion of swollen rice and vegetables, or seafood, or meat that is risotto.

Risotto Sondrio-Style with Spinach and Other Vegetables

RISOTTO COI SPINACI COME LO FANNO A SONDRIO

1½ pounds fresh spinach

Salt

1 medium leek

8 cups homemade meat broth, prepared as on page 316 OR 1 cup canned beef broth diluted with 7 cups water

3 tablespoons butter

1 tablespoon vegetable oil

⅓ cup chopped onion

2 tablespoons very finely chopped carrot

2 tablespoons very finely chopped celery

Black pepper ground fresh

2½ cups *carnaroli, arborio,* or other imported Italian rice for risotto

FOR *MANTECARE* (SEE PAGE 219)

2 tablespoons butter

1½ cups freshly grated Parmigiano-Reggiano cheese

For 8 persons

Long ago, Victor and I were living in Milan. I was teaching biology and mathematics and he was working for the McCann-Erickson advertising agency, producing television commercials. On one occasion the crew was working near the Lombard town of Sondrio in Valtellina, the mountainous district backed up against the Alpine wall that separates Italy from Switzerland.

Valtellina is celebrated for robust red wine and robust cooking to go with it. I was fascinated to find so many dishes new to me then, pastas, polenta, and fritters made with buckwheat flour, *bresaola*—beef tenderloin cured in the mountain air and sliced like prosciutto—and dumplings and other dishes using spinach. Among them was an excellent risotto with spinach.

I tried and tried to reproduce it after we got back to Milan, but it lacked something of the mellowness and teasing fragrance of the original. I had put it completely out of mind when, a great many years later, it came up in conversation with a woman who happened to be from Sondrio and who said, "I'll tell you how I make it. Try it and see if it is the way you remember it." It was indeed, and I found I had been omitting the leeks and celery from the flavor base, which when sautéed all together with the spinach, produced that teasingly fragrant and mellow quality that I had long before sought.

1. Detach the stems from the spinach leaves and discard them. Soak the leaves in a basinful of cold water, drain, and repeat the step several times until the spinach is free of all soil and grit.

2. Pour enough water in a saucepan to come 3 inches up the sides, bring it to a boil, add 2 tablespoons of salt, put in the spinach, cook for 3 or 4 minutes, then drain.

3. When the spinach is cool enough to handle, squeeze as much water out of it as you can with your hands, then chop it very fine.

4. Wash the leek, trim away about 1 inch from the green tops and a thin slice from the root end, then slice it into thin rounds.

5. Pour the broth into a saucepan, bring it to a simmer.

6. Place the heavy-bottomed saucepan where you'll be making the risotto on the burner nearest to the broth; put in 3 tablespoons of butter, the vegetable oil, and the chopped onion; and turn on the heat to medium high. Cook the onion, stirring frequently, until it becomes colored a pale gold; add the sliced leek and cook it as you did the onion.

7. Add the carrot and celery and, turning them over several times, cook them for about 1 minute until they are well coated. Add the spinach, salt, several grindings of black pepper; turn over all ingredients several times using a wooden spoon; and cook for 1 more minute.

8. Add the rice and stir it vigorously with a wooden spoon or a spatula for about a minute until the grains are well coated. Add 1 cup of simmering broth, and cook the rice, stirring it and periodically adding liquid, as described in the basic risotto directions on page 218.

9. Finish cooking the rice, stirring always, until it is tender but firm to the bite, about 25 minutes. Although there ought to be no free liquid left in the pot, the risotto's consistency should be rather rippling, *all'onda*. Turn off the heat and perform the *mantecare* step, adding 2 tablespoons of butter and all the grated Parmesan, stirring vigorously, turning the risotto over four or five times. Taste and correct for salt. Serve at once.

AHEAD-OF-TIME NOTE: The vegetables may be sautéed up to the end of step 7 a few hours in advance. Do not refrigerate them or the spinach will acquire a grassy, metallic taste. Reheat the vegetables thoroughly before putting in the rice.

Risotto with Sausages and Cranberry Beans

RISOTTO CON SALSICCIE E FAGIOLI BORLOTTI

――――――― ❧ ―――――――

1 pound fresh unshelled
 cranberry beans OR ⅔
 cup dried, soaked and
 boiled; see page 401

1 tablespoon extra virgin
 olive oil

½ cup finely chopped onion

¾ cup crumbled, skinned
 pork sausage; please see
 headnote

5 cups homemade meat
 broth, prepared as
 described on page 316,
 OR ½ cup canned beef
 broth diluted with 4½
 cups water

1½ cups *carnaroli, arborio,* or
 other imported Italian
 rice for risotto

I love rice and beans even when the dish is not Italian, but for me, the tastiest expression of that combination is beans in risotto. What makes this particular risotto with beans even better than most is, first, that the beans are sautéed with pork sausage, itself another winning combination; and, second, that they are partly mashed to contribute to the quality that characterizes all successful risottos, creaminess.

You can substitute *cannellini* for cranberry beans if you must, but try hard for the latter because they are tastier. The pork sausage should be as plain as possible, without tomato, fennel seeds, sage, chili pepper, or other exotic flavorings. If you cannot find good, plain sausage, use fresh ground pork, not too lean, seasoning it liberally with salt and pepper.

If Using Fresh Beans:

1. Shell them, put them in a pot with enough cold unsalted water to cover by about 2 inches, bring the water to a gentle simmer, cover the pot, and cook at a slow, steady pace until tender, about 45 minutes to 1 hour. Let them steep in their liquid until ready to use.

If Using Dried Beans:

Soak them overnight or for at least 6 hours, drain, then boil them in a fresh change of water. Let them steep in their liquid until ready to use.

2. Put the oil and chopped onion in a medium skillet, turn on the heat to medium, and cook the onion, stirring frequently, until it becomes just translucent but not colored.

3. Add the crumbled sausage and cook it, turning it over with a wooden spoon, until it becomes colored a rich brown all over.

4. Retrieve the cooked beans from their pot using a colander spoon or another slotted spoon, and put them in the skillet. Add 1 or 2 tablespoons of water from the bean pot, and mash about half the beans, pressing them against the bottom of the skillet with the wooden

FOR *MANTECARE* (SEE PAGE 219)

2 tablespoons butter

1 cup freshly grated Parmigiano-Reggiano cheese

1 tablespoon chopped Italian flat-leaf parsley

Salt

Black pepper ground fresh

For 4 to 6 persons

spoon. Cook for about a minute, turning the contents of the pot over with the spoon from time to time.

5. Pour the broth into a saucepan, bringing it to and keeping it at a slow, sputtering simmer.

6. Place the heavy-bottomed saucepan where you'll be making the risotto on the burner nearest to the broth, empty the contents of the skillet into it, and turn the heat under the risotto pot to medium high. Stir and, when the beans and sausage are sizzling hot, add the rice. Stir quickly and thoroughly to coat the rice well.

7. Add 1 cup of simmering broth, and cook the rice, stirring it and periodically adding liquid, as described in the basic risotto directions on page 218. Finish cooking the rice, stirring always and adding broth when needed, until it is tender but firm to the bite, about 25 minutes.

8. Take the pot off heat and do the *mantecare* step, swirling in the butter and grated Parmesan, turning the risotto over four or five times. Add the chopped parsley, salt, and ground pepper to taste; stir once or twice more; transfer to a warm platter; and serve at once.

AHEAD-OF-TIME NOTE: You can sauté the sausage and beans through to the end of step 4 several hours ahead of time or even overnight. Reheat thoroughly in a skillet, adding a tablespoon of water.

Risotto with Red Cabbage and Pancetta

RISOTTO COL CAVOLO ROSSO E LA PANCETTA

1 pound red cabbage

2 tablespoons extra virgin olive oil

⅔ cup chopped onion

½ cup very finely chopped pancetta

2 medium garlic cloves, peeled and sliced very thin

Salt

Black pepper ground fresh

5 cups homemade meat broth, prepared as described on page 316, OR a bouillon cube dissolved in 5 cups simmering water OR ½ cup canned beef broth diluted with 4½ cups water

1½ cups *carnaroli, arborio,* or other imported Italian rice for risotto

For Mantecare (see page 219)

1 tablespoon butter

½ cup freshly grated Parmigiano-Reggiano cheese

For 4 to 6 persons

The base flavor of this heartwarming cold-weather risotto has its roots in the Venetian practice of cooking shredded Savoy and other cabbages very slowly in olive oil, garlic, and a bit of pork fat. When prepared in that manner they are called *sofegae* in Venetian dialect, which is to say smothered.

Although here we have an olive-oil base, I chose to complete the risotto with the *mantecare* technique described on page 219, swirling in at the end a little butter and grated Parmesan. It pulls the dish together and gives it a gracious finish.

1. Shred the cabbage very fine, obtaining about 4 cups.

2. Put the oil, chopped onion, and pancetta into the pot where you will be making the risotto, and turn on the heat to medium high. Cook, stirring from time to time, until the onion becomes colored a very pale gold. Add the sliced garlic and cook, stirring frequently, until its scent begins to rise, but without letting it become colored.

3. Add the shredded cabbage and cook for 2 or 3 minutes, turning it over and over with a wooden spoon to coat it well. Add ½ cup water, salt, and generous grindings of pepper; turn the cabbage over once again; put a lid on the pot; and turn the heat down to medium low. Cook until the cabbage has softened completely and all but dissolved to a creamy consistency, about 1 hour. If, during the cooking, you find that there is not sufficient moisture in the pot to keep the cabbage from sticking to the bottom, add 2 to 3 tablespoons of water whenever necessary.

4. When the cabbage is just about done, pour the broth into a saucepan and bring it to and keep it at a slow, sputtering simmer on a burner close to the pot with the cabbage.

5. Uncover the pot with the cabbage, turn the heat up to medium high, and add the rice. Turn it over thoroughly and continuously for about 1 minute to coat it well. Add 1 cup of simmering broth, and cook the rice, stirring it and periodically adding liquid, as described in the basic risotto directions on page 218. Finish cooking the rice, stirring always and adding broth when needed, until it is tender but firm to the bite, about 25 minutes.

6. Off heat, perform the *mantecare* step, swirling in the butter and grated Parmesan, turning the risotto over four or five times with your wooden spoon. Transfer to a warm platter and serve at once.

AHEAD-OF-TIME NOTE: You can cook the cabbage as far in advance as early in the morning of the day you will be making the risotto. Before proceeding with the recipe, reheat gently but thoroughly, adding a little bit of water if necessary.

Risotto Friuli-Style, with Rosemary and White Wine

RISOTTO ALLA FRIULANA COL ROSMARINO E VINO BIANCO

6 cups homemade meat broth, prepared as described on page 316, OR a bouillon cube dissolved in 6 cups simmering water OR ½ cup canned beef broth diluted in 5½ cups water

1½ tablespoons butter

1½ teaspoons chopped garlic

1 tablespoon chopped fresh rosemary leaves

2½ cups *carnaroli, arborio,* or other imported Italian rice for risotto

1 cup dry, full white wine

FOR MANTECARE (SEE PAGE 219)

1 to 2 tablespoons butter

1 cup freshly grated Parmigiano-Reggiano cheese

1 teaspoon chopped fresh rosemary leaves

Black pepper ground fresh

Salt

For 4 to 6 persons

The flavor base here rests squarely on the aromatic properties of rosemary, which are exploited two ways. Most of the herb is sautéed along with the garlic, which produces a heady, earthy aroma recalling the background fragrance of an Italian roast. When the risotto is fully cooked, I add the remainder of the rosemary off heat, during the *mantecare* process. At this stage, when the herb is raw, its scent is fresher and more ethereal.

The risotto comes from Friuli, the region in the northeastern corner of Italy that is celebrated for its white wines. According to my husband, the in-house wine adviser, an ideal choice for the wine you add to the cooking liquid would be a full Friuli white such as Tocai.

1. Bring the meat broth or its substitute to a slow, sputtering simmer on a burner next to the pot where you'll be cooking the risotto.

2. Put 1½ tablespoons of butter and the garlic into the pot where you will be making the risotto, and turn on the heat to medium. Cook the garlic, stirring often, just until it becomes colored a very, very pale gold. Add 1 tablespoon chopped rosemary leaves, stir for a few seconds, then add the rice.

3. Turn the heat up to high and quickly stir the rice with a wooden spoon to coat it all over. Add the wine, and when it has completely bubbled away, add 1 cup of simmering broth. Cook the rice, stirring it and periodically adding liquid, as described in the basic risotto directions on page 218. Finish cooking the rice, stirring always and adding broth when needed, until it is tender but firm, about 25 minutes.

4. Off heat, perform the *mantecare* step, swirling in the butter, the grated Parmesan, 1 teaspoon of chopped rosemary, and black pepper, and turning the risotto over four or five times with your wooden spoon. Taste and correct for salt. Transfer to a warm platter and serve.

Onion Risotto Beaten with Butter and Sage

RISOTTO CON LE CIPOLLE MANTECATO ALLA SALVIA

1½ cups very thinly sliced onion

1 tablespoon vegetable oil

1 tablespoon butter

Salt

5 cups homemade meat broth, prepared as described on page 316 OR a bouillon cube dissolved in 5 cups simmering water OR ½ cup canned beef broth diluted with 4 ½ cups water

1½ cups *carnaroli, arborio,* or other imported Italian rice for risotto

FOR MANTECARE (SEE PAGE 219)

2 tablespoons butter

16 to 20 fresh sage leaves cut into thin lengthwise strips

¾ cup freshly grated Parmigiano-Reggiano cheese

Black pepper ground fresh

For 4 to 6 persons

I have put *mantecato* into the Italian title because here that process carries 50 percent of the responsibility for the risotto's taste. The base is rigorously simple and pure, endowing the risotto with a lovely, sweet foundation of flavor. All of the sage is added off the heat, its fragrance coaxed free by the warmth of the steaming risotto.

1. Put the sliced onions, 1 tablespoon vegetable oil, 1 tablespoon butter, and a sprinkling of salt into the pot where you will be making the risotto, and turn on the heat to medium. Cook the onion, stirring it from time to time, until it is very soft, first letting it wilt completely, then continuing to cook it until it becomes colored a tawny gold.

2. When the onion is just about done, pour the broth into a saucepan, bring it to and keep it at a slow, sputtering simmer on a burner close to the risotto pot.

3. Turn up the heat under the onion to medium high, and add the rice. Turn it over thoroughly and continuously for at least 1 minute to coat it well, so that its white color takes on some of the onions' warmer hue. Add 1 cup of simmering broth, and cook the rice, stirring it and periodically adding liquid, as described in the basic risotto directions on page 218. Finish cooking the rice, stirring always and adding broth when needed, until it is tender but firm to the bite, about 25 minutes.

4. Off heat, do the *mantecare* step, whisking in 2 tablespoons of butter, the shredded sage leaves, the grated Parmesan, and liberal grindings of black pepper. Turn the risotto over four or five times with your wooden spoon. Taste and correct for salt, transfer to a warm platter, and serve at once.

AHEAD-OF-TIME NOTE: You can cook the onions a couple of hours in advance. Reheat them thoroughly and have the heat going strong when you put in the rice.

Risotto with Green Beans and Yellow Bell Pepper

RISOTTO COI FAGIOLINI VERDI E IL PEPERONE GIALLO

———— 🌿 ————

A yellow bell pepper

½ pound green beans

Salt

1½ tablespoons butter

1 tablespoon vegetable oil

½ cup finely chopped onion

6 cups homemade meat broth, prepared as described on page 316 OR a bouillon cube dissolved in 6 cups simmering water OR ½ cup canned beef broth diluted with 5 ½ cups water

1⅔ cups *carnaroli, arborio,* or other imported Italian rice for risotto

FOR *MANTECARE* (SEE PAGE 219)

1½ tablespoons butter

⅔ cup freshly grated Parmigiano-Reggiano cheese

Black pepper ground fresh

———————————

For 4 to 6 persons

If the Italian word for summer were not *estate*, which in English has meanings wholly unrelated to the season, it would have become part of the title of this risotto, a warm-weather companion to the well-known *primavera*, the risotto with spring vegetables. Title aside, it is very much a summer dish, whether or not your market has yellow peppers and green beans all year round. It tastes and looks like summer, the appropriate time for enjoying it.

I give the beans a preliminary blanching so that, when sautéed with the onion, they can absorb more flavor than they would if they were completely raw. The pepper is quicker to draw flavor so I don't precook it. Although their most important contribution is the flavor they release while the rice is stirred, I am happy to see the bits of green bean and yellow pepper around at the end, when they give the finished risotto a cheery, summery look.

1. Split the pepper, remove the pulpy core and seeds, and cut enough of the pepper flesh into ½-inch squares to produce 1 cup. (If there is pepper left over, shred it and add it to a mixed salad.)

2. Snap both ends off the beans, and wash the beans in cold water. Bring water to a boil in a medium saucepan; add a liberal amount of salt, which will keep the beans green; and as the water resumes boiling, drop in the beans. When the water returns to a boil, cook the beans another minute and a half, then drain. Cut the partly cooked beans into lengths of 1 inch.

3. Put 1½ tablespoons butter, 1 tablespoon vegetable oil, and the chopped onion into the pot where you will be making the risotto, and turn on the heat to medium high. Cook the onion, stirring it frequently, until it becomes colored a pale gold.

4. Add the pepper squares, turn up the heat, and cook the pepper for about half a minute, turning it to coat it well. Add the green beans, turn them several times to coat them well, and cook, always at high heat, for 3 or 4 minutes.

5. While the beans are cooking, pour the broth into a saucepan; bring it to and keep it at a slow, sputtering simmer on a burner close to the risotto pot.

6. Add the rice to the beans and pepper, turning it over thoroughly and continuously for about half a minute to coat it well and combine it with the vegetables. Add 1 cup of simmering broth, and cook the rice, stirring it and periodically adding liquid, as described in the basic risotto directions on page 218. Finish cooking the rice, stirring always and adding broth when needed, until it is tender but firm to the bite, about 25 minutes.

7. Off heat, perform the *mantecare* step, whisking in 1½ tablespoons of butter, the grated Parmesan, and liberal grindings of black pepper. Turn the risotto over four or five times with your wooden spoon. Taste and correct for salt, transfer to a warm platter, and serve at once.

AHEAD-OF-TIME NOTE: You can cook the pepper and beans through to the end of step 4 several hours ahead of time. Reheat them thoroughly and have the heat going strong when you put in the rice.

Risotto with Mushrooms and Almonds

RISOTTO COI FUNGHI E LE MANDORLE

6 ounces fresh white button
   mushrooms

2 tablespoons butter

½ cup finely chopped onion

Salt

Black pepper ground fresh

2 medium fresh, ripe
   tomatoes, peeled, seeds
   scooped out, and cut up,
   about ⅔ cup, OR ⅔ cup
   canned, imported, Italian
   plum tomatoes, drained
   and cut up

5 cups homemade meat
   broth, prepared as
   described on page 316 OR
   ½ cup canned beef broth
   diluted with 4½ cups
   water

1½ cups *carnaroli*, *arborio*, or
   other imported Italian
   rice for risotto

For MANTECARE (SEE
   PAGE 219)

1 tablespoon butter

½ cup freshly grated
   Parmigiano-Reggiano
   cheese

16 shelled almonds

For 4 persons

The Piedmontese town of Gavi, today at the center of a district in the southeastern corner of the region that produces a charming white wine by the same name, was not Piedmontese at all until the middle of the nineteenth century, but owed allegiance to Genoa, the capital of the modern region of Liguria, whose coast constitutes the Italian Riviera. I am not all that interested in historical vicissitudes, but I was intrigued when I was served this risotto in Piedmont's Gavi to find echoes in it of the light and aromatic cooking of Liguria.

What I find interesting in the dish is how a feature of mushroom flavor becomes submerged in the cooking and then is rescued and hauled up at the end, when the risotto is *mantecato*. Very good fresh mushrooms, particularly porcini mushrooms, have a faint taste of almonds when raw. When cooked with tomatoes, that almond-like note disappears. For this recipe, chopped almonds are stirred into the finished risotto, which at that moment acquires the flavor not just of almonds but of mushrooms that taste of almonds. How lovely.

I am satisfied with cultivated button mushrooms in this recipe, but of course if you should have nice, fresh, firm porcini on hand, use them.

1. Wash the mushrooms rapidly under running water. Pat thoroughly dry with kitchen towels, then cut them lengthwise, from cap to bottom of the stem, into the thinnest slices you can.

2. Put the butter and the chopped onion into the pot where you will be making the risotto, and turn on the heat to medium high. Cook, stirring from time to time, until the onion becomes colored a very pale gold.

3. Add the mushrooms, salt, and liberal grindings of pepper. Toss the mushrooms or turn them with a long spoon to coat them well. Cook, stirring from time to time, for another 5 to 6 minutes.

4. Add the tomatoes, turn the contents of the pot over two or three times to coat them well, then turn the heat down to medium. Cook, stirring from time to time, until the fat begins to separate from the sauce, as described in the Note on page 133.

5. If the almonds have their skin on, plunge them into boiling water for about 1 minute, then drain, and rub them vigorously in a towel to remove the skins. Chop them to a coarse consistency, with the largest piece no bigger than ¼ inch.

6. Bring the broth to a slow, sputtering simmer on a burner next to the pot where you'll be cooking the risotto.

7. Turn the heat under the mushrooms and tomatoes up to high, add the rice, and stir quickly with a wooden spoon or spatula to coat it all over. Add 1 cup of simmering broth, and cook the rice, stirring it and periodically adding liquid, as described in the basic risotto directions on page 218.

8. Finish cooking the rice, stirring always, until it is tender but firm to the bite, about 25 minutes.

9. Off heat, do the *mantecare* step, whisking in 1 tablespoon of butter, the chopped almonds, and the grated Parmesan. Turn the risotto over four or five times with your wooden spoon or spatula. Taste and correct for salt and pepper, transfer to a warm platter, and serve at once.

AHEAD-OF-TIME NOTE: You can cook the mushrooms and tomatoes and blanch and chop the almonds several hours in advance. Reheat the mushrooms and tomatoes gently but thoroughly before proceeding.

POLENTA
La Polenta

Polentoni, "polenta eaters," Italians of the south call the dwellers of the north. It's a well-deserved description. If you stay long enough in the regions of the north and the north-east, in northern Lombardy, in Trentino, in the Veneto, or in Friuli, you become aware that rarely do you sat down at a table, whether in the house of friends or in a restaurant, where polenta in some form does not appear. Polenta sprang from the hunger of these once poor regions. Now that they are among the wealthiest in the world, it is the people's souls that continue to yearn for polenta; and polenta has stayed on, a witness of their self-sacrifice and industriousness, to comfort them.

Polenta can be stretched further to do more things than anything else you cook. It can be fried, grilled, and baked. You can eat it steaming soft or cold and firm; you can have it alone with butter or ripe cheese spreading loose within its warm folds, as a snack with prosciutto or salami, or as a full course with seafood, game, sausages, stew, roast birds, liver smothered in onions; you can serve it for breakfast, or make bread, cookies, and cakes with it, or use it for the crispest of frying batter.

I adore polenta and have written about it at length. Certainly the subject justifies a whole book, but I am not going to do that. Here I'll tell you about just a few things I have recently been doing with polenta that I was pleased with, and later, in the dessert chapter, you'll also find a recipe for Venetian polenta cookies.

Cornmeal and Buckwheat Flour Polenta

POLENTA TARAGNA

10 cups water

1¾ cups coarse-grained
   yellow cornmeal

1¾ cups buckwheat flour

1½ tablespoons salt

1 cup dry white wine

1 tablespoon extra virgin
   olive oil

---

*A mound of gray polenta about
16 inches in diameter and 1¾ to
2 inches high, serving 6 to 8
persons*

I encountered dark polenta a great many years ago when my husband, who was then an advertising whiz, invited me to join him in Valtellina, in northern Lombardy, where he was shooting a television commercial. It is not a popular polenta in Venice, where we have long lived, and it had slipped out of mind until I became acquainted with a woman—the same one who gave me the correct procedure for making the risotto with spinach on page 220—who was from Sondrio, in Valtellina. As we chatted about the cooking of her region, she rekindled my recollections of *polenta taragna's* deep and distinctive flavor.

1. Put the water in a large, heavy pot and bring to a boil over medium high heat.

2. Mix the cornmeal and the buckwheat flour in a bowl.

3. Pour a fistful of the cornmeal and flour mixture into the pot in a very thin stream, letting it trickle through nearly closed fingers. You should be able to see some of the cornmeal's individual grains spilling into the pot. While you pour the mixture, stir it with a whisk, keeping the water always at a boil.

4. When all the meal and flour mixture is in the pot, begin to stir with a long-handled wooden spoon, stirring continuously and with thoroughness, bringing the mixture up from the bottom and loosening it from the sides of the pot. Continue to stir for 40 to 45 minutes. The meal and flour mush is fully transformed into polenta when it becomes a mass that, when you stir it, pulls cleanly away from the sides of the pot.

No-Standing-and-Stirring Alternative:

If you are willing to stand at the stove and stir the polenta the entire time it cooks, you will obtain the best result in terms of texture, fragrance, and overall flavor. It is nonetheless possible to make very good polenta with hardly any stirring. It will take no less time, but it will free you from the stove for the better part of an hour. Proceed as follows:

1. When all the cornmeal and flour mixture is in the pot, stir with a long-handled wooden spoon for 2 minutes, then cover the pot. Adjust heat so that the water bubbles at a steady, sustained simmer, but not at a full boil.

2. After 10 minutes, uncover and stir for 1 full minute, then cover again. Step away for 10 minutes, return to stir for 1 minute, then cover, and repeat the procedure twice.

3. When 40 minutes have elapsed from the time you first poured in the cornmeal and flour, the polenta will need approximately another 5 minutes to shed its grainy texture completely and come together into a single soft, creamy mass. Before you turn off the heat, stir vigorously for about 1 minute, loosening the mass from the sides and bottom of the pot.

5. Serve the polenta immediately if you want it soft and hot to accompany a runny cheese or a roast or sausages or grilled shrimp or any other dish with which you enjoy loose, warm polenta. If you will use it later grilled, baked, or fried, or in other ways, moisten with cold water a wooden board or steel, marble, or Formica countertop that is at least 24 inches wide and pour the hot polenta over it, spreading it out to a thickness of about 3 inches. Let it cool down until it is firm.

AHEAD-OF-TIME NOTE: When the polenta is cold and firm, wrap it in plastic wrap, then with aluminum foil, and refrigerate for 4 to 5 days in advance of using.

CLEANING THE POT: A pot in which you have just made polenta looks as though cornmeal has been permanently baked to its sides and bottom. Fill it with cold water and soak overnight. In the morning, the polenta crusts lift off with hardly any effort. If you are using a *paiolo*, the traditional polenta pot made of unlined copper, after you have scraped away all the crusts, clean it with ¼ cup of vinegar and some salt. Rinse with two or three changes of plain water, using no detergent, and wipe.

Trento-Style Buckwheat and Cornmeal Polenta with Melted Butter and Anchovies

POLENTA SMALZADA

Butter for smearing a serving dish plus 4 tablespoons

Half the polenta from the Cornmeal and Buckwheat Flour Polenta recipe on page 233; please see Note at right before proceeding

⅔ cup freshly grated Parmigiano-Reggiano cheese

6 anchovy fillets, preferably the ones prepared at home as described on page 148, chopped very fine

For 8 persons as an appetizer, for 4 to 6 as a principal course

Hot melted butter saturated with anchovies that have been reduced to a pulp can rouse the taste buds as powerfully as any fusion of flavors I know. In this specialty of the Trentino region, *polenta taragna*—buckwheat and cornmeal polenta—is the softly sprung vehicle that gives that explosively tasty cargo a very smooth ride.

You can serve it as an appetizer preceding a meal that would include earthy dishes such as a stout bean soup followed by a garlicky roast or stew. Or serve it with a salad of radicchio and other greens for a winter lunch or supper by the fire. In Italy, where one's appetite lies dormant long after the large midday meal, we would enjoy a serving of *polenta smalzada* as a bracing very late-night snack.

NOTE: This recipe calls for warm polenta. If it is inconvenient to make it just before assembling the dish, you can make it in advance, and warm it up for about 15 minutes in a 350° oven.

1. Choose a deep serving dish about 7 by 9 inches and 2 inches high or any other dimensions of comparable capacity, such as one you would use for oven-to-table service. Lightly rub the bottom with butter.

2. Cut the warm polenta into 1-inch squares and place them in the buttered dish slightly overlapping each other.

3. Sprinkle all the Parmesan over the polenta.

4. Put the 4 tablespoons butter in a small skillet or saucepan and turn on the heat to low. When the butter has melted completely, put in the chopped anchovies and mash them to a puree, pressing against the bottom of the pan with a wooden spoon. You may want to take the pan on and off heat as you do this to keep the anchovies from hardening.

5. Stir the contents of the pan and pour it over the polenta, distributing it evenly, and serve at once.

Buckwheat and Cornmeal Polenta Baked Marcella's Way

LA POLENTA TARAGNA AL FORNO ALLA MIA MANIERA

1 medium onion, peeled

2 pounds fresh, ripe tomatoes, peeled, seeds scooped out, and cut up, OR 2 cups canned imported Italian plum tomatoes, cut up, with their juice

4 tablespoons butter plus more to smear the baking dish

Salt

Cold polenta, half the recipe on page 233

⅔ cup freshly grated Parmigiano-Reggiano cheese

For 6 persons

An oven-to-table baking dish

The first tomato sauce I ever cooked in my life is, to this day, one of my family's favorites and, I am told, one of the most popular with my students and with many of my readers. Perhaps because it is so simple: It is just tomato, butter, and a whole onion. No chopping, no sautéing; it practically cooks itself, and to me, it has the clearest, sweetest taste of any tomato sauce.

I often have some in the refrigerator to satisfy any sudden yearnings for it that may manifest themselves. On a day that I had made a lot of *polenta taragna*, I had the sauce in the refrigerator and I thought to bake some polenta with it. If you enjoy the pure taste of a simple tomato sauce, and appreciate the distinctive flavor of this particular polenta, you will find that the two do very nice things for each other.

1. Turn on the oven to 400°.

2. Put the onion, tomatoes, and 4 tablespoons of butter in a saucepan, add salt, and bring to a slow simmer. Cook at that slow simmer, with bubbles gently breaking through the surface of the sauce, for 45 minutes, or until the fat begins to separate from the sauce, as described in the Note on page 133. Stir once every while, mashing any large piece of tomato in the pan with the back of a wooden spoon. Taste and correct for salt. Discard the onion.

3. Cut the polenta into narrow rectangles, about 1 by 3 inches.

4. Lightly smear an oven-to-table baking dish with butter and lay down the polenta pieces it, slightly overlapping them, shingle-fashion.

5. Spread the tomato sauce over the polenta, sprinkle with the grated Parmesan, and bake in the preheated oven for 15 minutes. Allow to settle briefly, about a minute or two, before serving.

Venetian-Style Milk Polenta

POLENTA ALLA VENEZIANA CON IL LATTE

2½ cups water

3 cups whole milk

3 teaspoons salt

1 pound coarse-grained
    yellow cornmeal

4 liberal or 6 small servings

The cooking of Venice is Italy's most light-handed, and it is reflected in this delicate, less rustic-tasting polenta. I first tasted this dish after settling in Venice, when I began to eat in people's houses both in the city and in the farms just beyond the bridge connecting the city of canals to the mainland.

1. Put the water, milk, and salt in a copper polenta pot or a heavy-bottomed large saucepan, turn the heat on to medium, and bring to a steady but moderate boil.

2. Pour a fistful of the cornmeal into the pot in a very thin stream, letting it trickle through nearly closed fingers. You should be able to see some of the cornmeal's individual grains spilling into the pot. While you pour the cornmeal, stir it with a whisk, keeping the water and milk always at a steady, but moderate boil.

3. When all the cornmeal is in the pot, begin to stir with a long-handled wooden spoon, stirring continuously and with thoroughness, bringing the mixture up from the bottom, and loosening it from the sides of the pot. Continue to stir for 40 to 45 minutes. The meal and milk mush is fully transformed into polenta when it becomes a mass that, when you stir it, pulls cleanly away from the sides of the pot. Serve while still soft and hot.

NOTE: You can also make this milk polenta by the reduced-stirring method described above, page 233.

Fish

FISH
Il Pesce

Fish in Crazy Water

Steamed Salmon Steaks with Radicchio and Balsamic Vinegar

Scallops with Tomato, Garlic, and Rosemary

Sautéed Scallops with Cime di Rapa, Garlic, and Chili Pepper

Scallops and Fish Steaks or Fillets with Tomatoes and Peas

Baked Artichokes, Shrimp, and Mozzarella

Swordfish Sardinian-Style with Mint and Saffron

Pan-Grilled Swordfish Steaks with Warm Salmoriglio and Capers

Baking Bluefish

Bluefish with Baked Onions, Peppers, and Potatoes

Baked Bluefish with Leeks and Potatoes

Sautéed Fresh Tuna Cubes with Smothered Onion, Tomato, and Chili Pepper

Squid Braised in Olive Oil and White Wine with Spinach, Fresh Tomato, and Chili Pepper

Stuffed Whole Squid Braised with Onions, Tomatoes, Chili Pepper, and White Wine

Bacaro-Style Frying Batter

PHOTO KEY FOR PAGES 238–39

Salmon (*Salmone*)

Monkfish

Bass (*Brongino*)

Red Snapper (*Dentice*)

Scallops (*Cappe Sante*)

Mussels (*Cozze*)

have been a wandering cook. I have stood over stoves in Cesenatico, my native town in Romagna, in Florence, in Milan, in Bologna, in Rome, in Palermo, in Venice, in Sori, a village on the Riviera coast. I have cooked in New York and in more cities and towns throughout America than I could now enumerate. I have cooked in Canada, in Mexico, in St. Barts, in Ireland, England, South Africa, Hong Kong, Australia. Surprises of every kind came with every change of scenery, some welcome, some less so. Among the most welcome ones were those of a culinary kind, as I discovered that even the humblest ingredient—a radish, a tomato, an onion—can have a distinct territorial identity of its own. No other category of ingredients, however, displays even remotely the wide variety of flavors and texture that exists among fish.

In the town where I grew up, fish was plentiful, good, and cheap. It was what we ate most often. The taste of mullet, of sole, of mackerel, of hake, of every variety that my father brought home and cooked, became a familiar feature of everyday life. Only much later did I become aware of what remarkable character traits these tastes were, traits formed by, and specific to, the very sea where I used to swim and sail with my friends.

It is wonderful to discover how closely the taste of fresh fish is related to the waters it inhabits. My native Cesenatico and my adoptive home, Venice, both face the Adriatic, with just 100 miles of quiet, shallow sea between them. Yet the small soles of Cesenatico, although they appear to be identical to those of Venice, are infinitely superior: They are nuttier, sweeter, substantially firmer. If fish can change so markedly within one short stretch of the same sea, imagine what differences exist between varieties that are separated by an ocean.

When working with Italian recipes to determine which preparations can be most successful with the ingredients that are available elsewhere, the dishes that give me most to think about are those with fish. None of the smaller Adriatic fish that have such extraordinary flavor—*branzini, orate, rombi, mormore, triglie*, or Venice's priceless *seppie*, cuttlefish—appear on the far side of the Atlantic.

There is, however, much North American seafood that, although its flesh and structure may be differently constituted, slips comfortably into Italian garb. Sea bass, for example, or porgy, red snapper, tuna, monkfish, young halibut, swordfish. Clams, even if they fall short of the tenderness and savory quality of those in Italy, give satisfactory results; the mussels and shrimp are excellent, the bay scallops exquisite, and the northeastern lobsters magnificent. Squid, specifically that of medium size, tastes and handles almost exactly like the kind I buy in the Rialto market.

In developing the recipes for this chapter, as well for the soups, pastas, and salads with seafood, I worked with two objectives in mind: first, to compile a small but representative sampling of one of the most resourceful and lively of all maritime cuisines, a sampling whose Italian accents would be unmistakable; second, to make as certain as I could that those accents will come through undistorted when the dishes are, so to speak, played back with components available in America. To achieve the latter end, I left Venice for two consecutive summers to work on the southeastern shore of Long Island, where I had some of the best fish that has ever landed in my kitchen.

There are dishes in this collection—the Fish in Crazy Water (*photo below*), the two swordfish recipes, the stuffed squid, the tuna with onions—taken directly from their regional sources in Naples, the Marches, Sardinia, Sicily. Other dishes here, such as the bluefish and scallops recipes, take their cue from seafood whose attributes are specifically and indigenously American, and I hope they show how flattering to those attributes the Italian style of cooking can be.

Fish in Crazy Water

PESCE ALL'ACQUA PAZZA

1½ pounds fresh, ripe
tomatoes

4 cups water

3 large garlic cloves, peeled
and sliced very thin

2 tablespoons very finely
chopped parsley

Chopped red chili pepper,
⅛ teaspoon or to taste

¼ cup extra virgin olive oil

Salt

A 1½- to 2-pound red
snapper, filleted with its
skin left on

Optional: 4 slices of day-old
or grilled sourdough
bread

For 4 persons

One of the most frequently recurring conversational expressions in the dialect of my native Romagna is *anicreid*, "I don't believe it." That skepticism is a characteristic I share with the people of my region. When a dish has a fanciful name, I resist trying it, feeling that it has been dressed up to cover up a lack of substance.

Had it been up to me, I never would have sampled that Neapolitan creation, fish in crazy water. "What's crazy water got to do with cooking and anyway, who wants to eat fish in water?" Such were my thoughts, until my friend from Amalfi, Pierino Jovine, one day simply brought the dish to the table without asking or telling. Now, I am the one who goes crazy over it.

Water is what brings together all the seasoning ingredients, the tomatoes, garlic, parsley, chili pepper, salt, and olive oil. They simmer in it for a full 45 minutes, exchanging and compounding their flavors, producing a substance that is denser than a broth, looser, more vivacious, and fresher in taste than any sauce, in which you then cook the fish.

1. Peel the tomatoes raw using a swiveling-blade vegetable peeler, and chop them roughly with all their juice and seeds. The yield should be about 2 cups.

2. Choose a sauté pan in which the fish fillets can subsequently fit flat without overlapping. Put in the water, garlic, chopped tomatoes, parsley, chili pepper, olive oil, and salt. Cover the pan, turn the heat to medium, for 45 minutes.

3. Uncover the pan, turn up the heat, and boil the liquid until it has been reduced to half its original volume.

4. Add the fish, skin facing up. Cook for 2 minutes, then gently turn it over, using two spatulas. Add a little more salt and cook for another 12 minutes or so.

5. Serve promptly over the optional bread slices.

Steamed Salmon Steaks with Radicchio and Balsamic Vinegar

SALMONE A VAPORE CON RADICCHIO E ACETO BALSAMICO

FOR EACH 1-INCH-THICK SALMON STEAK

4 leaves red radicchio

Salt

~~Black pepper ground fresh~~

1 teaspoon extra virgin olive oil

½ to 1 teaspoon balsamic vinegar (the finer the vinegar, the less is required)

For 6 persons

A fish poacher OR see the suggestion in the headnote for rigging one up

Several years ago in Venice our downstairs neighbor invited us to dinner. Venetian neighbors just don't do that. What was equally gratifying was that I walked back upstairs with a recipe for the excellent fish we'd had for dinner.

I admire the delicate play of flavors in this salmon. There is the luxurious, pure taste of the steamed fish set off by the bracing astringency of radicchio, which in turn is tempered by the sweet-and-sour balsamic vinegar.

I have a long, horizontal poacher with an insert on which the fish rests that lifts straight out. It is very practical to use if you poach a whole fish often or, as we do, if you cook *cotechino*, the long, creamy pork sausage. My neighbor had no steamer of any kind but had rigged up an efficient substitute by placing a rectangular cake-drying rack in a lasagne pan and improvising a lid with a large metal tray.

1. Remove the skin circling the salmon. Look for and pick out any bones. Curl the ends of the steak inward to give it a round, tight shape.

2. Detach the required number of leaves from the head of radicchio, and drop them in boiling water for 2 minutes. Drain and let cool.

3. Sprinkle the salmon with salt and liberal grindings of black pepper, then wrap each steak in 4 radicchio leaves.

4. Bring water in a steamer to a simmer, put in the wrapped salmon steaks, and cook for 13 to 15 minutes, depending on their size.

5. Transfer to a platter, dress each steak with 1 teaspoon olive oil and ½ to 1 teaspoon balsamic vinegar, and serve at once.

AHEAD-OF-TIME NOTE: It wouldn't save you very much time, but if you wish you can prepare the steaks, making them ready to go in the steamer, several hours in advance. Store in the refrigerator.

Scallops with Tomato, Garlic, and Rosemary

CAPPE SANTE CON POMODORO, AGLIO, E ROSMARINO

2 pounds fresh scallops

¼ cup olive oil

4 teaspoons finely chopped garlic

1½ tablespoons chopped fresh rosemary

⅔ cup cut-up canned Italian plum tomatoes with their juice OR fresh, ripe tomatoes, peeled and cut up

Chopped fresh or dried chili pepper, to taste

Salt

For 4 persons

Rosemary has a sultry scent which, on scallops and fish, I like to quicken through the intervention of something acidulous. In an earlier version it was lemon, but here I have chosen the milder tartness of tomatoes.

In its rather liberal use of rosemary, the recipe is an exception to the restraint that most Italian cooks exercise when working with fragrant ingredients, but here the taste impressions rely heavily on the herb's contribution and you don't want to be too tightfisted with it.

1. With a sharp paring knife, cut away the tough, white strip of connective tissue you'll find on most scallops. Wash the scallops in cold water and pat thoroughly dry with a kitchen towel.

2. Choose a skillet large enough to contain all the scallops without overlapping, put in the oil and garlic, and turn on the heat to medium high. Sauté the garlic, stirring it once or twice, until it becomes colored a pale gold; then add the chopped rosemary, stir just once or twice, and add the cut-up tomatoes and the chili pepper, turning the heat down to medium.

3. Cook, stirring occasionally, until the until the fat begins to separate from the sauce, as described in the Note on page 133, about 15 or 20 minutes.

4. Turn the heat up to high and put in all the scallops. In 1 or 2 minutes, when the scallops will have shed some watery liquid, remove them from the pan with a slotted spoon and continue cooking at high heat to evaporate that liquid. When the pan juices are no longer watery, return the scallops to the pan, add salt, and cook for another minute.

AHEAD-OF-TIME NOTE: You can prepare the scallops an hour or two in advance up to the moment when you have evaporated the excess liquid from the pan. When ready to serve, reheat the pan juices over high heat, return the scallops to the pan, add salt, and cook for a full minute.

Sautéed Scallops with Cime di Rapa, Garlic, and Chili Pepper

CAPPE SANTE SALTATE CON LE CIME DI RAPA

1½ pounds *cime di rapa*, also known as *rapini* or *broccoletti di rape*

Salt

1 pound scallops, preferably bay

8 anchovy fillets, preferably the ones prepared at home as described on page 148

4 tablespoons extra virgin olive oil

1 tablespoon very finely chopped garlic

Chopped chili pepper, ⅛ teaspoon or to taste

For 4 persons

Scallops have the sweetest taste of any seafood, a most companionable taste that makes possible a wide, and sometimes surprising, variety of flavor harmonies. The recipe below is one of the best examples I have ever found of that delicious versatility.

We are accustomed to enjoy, in the cooking of Apulia, by whose flavors this recipe is inspired, the rustic, teasing bitterness of *cime di rapa*, the intensity of anchovies, the provocative call of chili pepper, but they are never more appealing than when they are presided over by the endearingly gentle taste of scallops.

1. After detaching and discarding the thickest, toughest stalks of the *cime di rapa*, use a paring knife or a peeler to trim away the tough outer skin of the others. Wash the vegetable in several changes of cold water.

2. Bring a pot of water to a boil, add at least 1½ tablespoons of salt—which will not make the vegetable salty but will keep it green— and put in the *cime di rapa*. Cook at a steady but gentle boil until the thickest portions feel tender when prodded with a fork, about 7 minutes. Drain and let the vegetable cool down for subsequent handling.

3. While the *cime di rapa* is cooking, trim away the tough white tendon attached to one side of the scallops. If the scallops are of the large sea variety, cut them into two or three pieces. Wash them in cold water, drain, and pat dry with a clean dish towel.

4. Chop the anchovies very, very fine to a pulp.

5. When the *cime di rapa* is cool enough to handle, chop it up coarsely.

6. Put the olive oil and garlic in a 12-inch skillet and turn on the heat to medium high. Cook the garlic, stirring it frequently, until it loses its

translucency and becomes colored a warm white. Turn the heat down and add the anchovies, stirring them constantly with a wooden spoon until they dissolve into a paste.

7.   Add the *cime di rapa*, turn the heat up again, and with the wooden spoon turn the vegetable over several times to coat it well. Cook for 2 or 3 minutes, then add the chili pepper, turning the *cime di rapa* once or twice.

8.   Add the scallops, turn them over a few times, and cook just until they become colored a flat white, about 2 minutes. Add salt, stir, taste and correct for seasoning, then pour the entire contents of the skillet into a warm platter and serve at once. It would be nice to have good crusty bread on hand to sop up the delicious juices.

AHEAD-OF-TIME NOTE: It is desirable to make the whole dish only when ready to serve it, but if you must prepare some of it a few hours in advance (though not overnight), you can cook it through to the end of step 7, up to the point when you would be putting in the scallops. When resuming cooking, warm up the vegetable thoroughly before adding the scallops.

Scallops and Fish Steaks or Fillets with Tomatoes and Peas

UMIDO DI CAPPE SANTE E PESCE CON POMODORI E PISELLI

1 pound fresh ripe
   tomatoes OR 1 cup
   canned imported Italian
   plum tomatoes, drained
   and cut up

1¾ pounds fresh young
   peas in the pod OR a 10-
   ounce package small
   frozen peas

4 tablespoons extra virgin
   olive oil

3 tablespoons chopped
   onion

Chopped chili pepper, ⅛
   teaspoon or to taste

Salt

1 pound scallops

1 pound firm fish fillets
   with skin on OR fish
   steaks

For 4 persons

Here is an example of how I let the market manage my cooking decisions. While staying in the Hamptons, I had gone to see my friend John of the Wainscott Seafood Shop about a nice piece of fish to grill or sauté and, finding a portly red snapper, I let him slice it into lovely fat fillets. As he was wrapping it, he said, "If you can use some bay scallops, these just came in an hour ago." How I was going to use them I didn't know yet, but I act on the principle that if you are buying fish and happen to find some that wriggles or nearly so, you get it and later figure out what to do with it.

On the way home I spotted peas at one of the farmstands. I snapped a pod open, and tasted the peas that popped in my mouth like bubbles of sugar. I now had three superfresh ingredients without any apparent relation to one other, but I resolved to use them all that same day before a single one of them could lose its bloom.

I was reminded of a dish from one of my earlier books—squid, tomatoes, and peas—which Victor and I adore. From squid and peas my thoughts turned to the stew I make with squid and fish steaks. I had the fish and the peas. I didn't have the squid but, even better perhaps, I had those superb scallops. *Ecco!* The scallops replaced the squid and out of two recipes, I made one.

In a perfect world, you would use only freshly picked young sweet peas and freshly landed bay scallops. In this world, however, you can still achieve rather delicious results with frozen peas, which are to be preferred to old, starchy fresh peas, and good-quality sea scallops, if the bay are not available. There can be no compromise on the fish steaks; they must be absolutely fresh.

1. If you are using fresh tomatoes, peel them by dipping them in boiling water for 1 minute, then squeeze off their skin. For this dish,

any tomato-peeling technique you find practical is satisfactory (see Working with Tomatoes, pages 135–37). Halve the tomatoes, scoop out their seeds without squeezing, and chop up coarsely.

2. If using fresh peas, shell them.

3. Put the olive oil and chopped onion in a 12-inch sauté pan or skillet, turn on the heat to medium, and cook the onion, stirring it from time to time, until it becomes colored a pale gold.

4. Add the tomatoes and chili pepper. Cook, stirring occasionally, until the fat begins to separate from the sauce, as described in the Note on page 133, about 15 to 20 minutes.

5. Add the peas and a pinch of salt. If you are using fresh peas, add ½ cup water and cook until tender, about 15 to 20 minutes, depending on the peas. If you are using frozen peas, no water is required and 5 minutes' cooking is sufficient.

6. While the tomatoes and peas are cooking, wash the fish fillets or steaks, wash the scallops, remove their white filament, cut them in half if they are large sea scallops, and pat both fish and scallops dry with kitchen towels.

7. When the peas are done, make room for the fish by pushing the peas and tomatoes to one side of the pan with a wooden spoon. Put the fish in the pan, skin up if they are fillets; cook for 5 minutes; add a little salt; then turn the fish over gently, cover the pan, and cook for 3 more minutes.

8. Uncover, add the scallops, and cook briefly just until their translucent color becomes a flat white. Taste and correct for salt and chili pepper, and serve promptly.

AHEAD-OF-TIME NOTE: You can do everything several hours in advance up to the end of step 5. Reheat the tomatoes and peas gently but thoroughly before proceeding.

Baked Artichokes, Shrimp, and Mozzarella

TEGLIA DI CARCIOFI, MAZZANCOLLE, E MOZZARELLA

½ lemon

5 medium artichokes

2 tablespoons extra virgin olive oil

4 whole, peeled garlic cloves

Salt

Black pepper ground fresh

1 pound medium shrimp in their shells

¾ pound mozzarella, preferably imported Italian buffalo milk mozzarella

2 tablespoons butter including some for smearing the baking dish

2 tablespoons freshly grated Parmigiano-Reggiano cheese

For 6 persons

A 2-inch-high oven-to-table baking dish, 11 inches long and 7 inches wide, or one of approximately equivalent capacity

In cooking, as in other imaginative activities, it isn't always possible to explain exactly why some things work. This is one of its mysteries that keeps you from being self-satisfied, that causes you always to think about what you are doing, that prevents you, no matter how long you have been at it, from putting your curiosity away.

We were in Rome at a crowded time, we had failed to make timely plans for dinner, and had to settle for a table at an unfamiliar trattoria. All of the dishes on the menu were standards but for this one. It seemed peculiar within the unadventurous context of the other offerings, and as I briefly thought about it—*mazzancolle*, a variety of shrimp popular in Rome, baked with artichokes and mozzarella—I couldn't imagine how it could be any good. But I was intrigued, as well as bored by the alternatives, so I ordered it.

At the first taste I couldn't believe my luck. It was sublime. If I hadn't been ashamed to appear so gluttonous, I would have ordered another portion.

1. Squeeze the juice of ½ lemon into a bowl of cold water.

2. Prepare the artichokes as described on page 362, trimming away all the tough, inedible portions. Cut off but do not discard the stems, paring them down to their pale core. Cut the trimmed artichokes lengthwise into the thinnest possible slices. Drop each slice and stem into a bowl containing water and lemon juice. When all the artichokes are done, drain and rinse them in two changes of cold water.

3. Put the oil and whole garlic cloves into a 10- to 12-inch skillet, preferably nonstick, and turn the heat on to high. Cook the garlic, turning it frequently, until it becomes colored nut brown, then remove it from the pan and discard it.

4. Add the artichoke slices and stems, sprinkle with salt and generous grindings of pepper, turn them three or four times to coat them

well, then put a lid on the pan and turn the heat down to low. Cook for about 5 minutes, then add ¼ cup water, turn the artichokes over, put the lid back on, and continue cooking over slow heat. Turn them every 5 minutes or so, cooking them, without adding any more water if possible, until they feel tender when prodded with a fork and have turned slightly brown around the edges. Depending on their youth and freshness it may take 30 to 45 minutes. Remove from heat when done.

5. Turn on the oven to 450°.

6. While the artichokes are cooking, shell the shrimp, remove the dark central vein in their back, wash them in cold water, and pat dry with kitchen towels.

7. Cut the mozzarella into very thin slices, ¼ inch thick or less.

8. Lightly smear the bottom of the pan with butter, and put in the artichokes with all their cooking juices and oil. Spread them out over the bottom of the dish.

9. Place the shrimp over the artichokes, spreading them out as much as possible. Sprinkle salt and 1 tablespoon of grated Parmesan over them. Top with the mozzarella slices, slightly overlapping them if you need to. If you are not using imported buffalo-milk mozzarella, which already contains some salt, sprinkle salt over it. Top with the remaining tablespoon of Parmesan. Cut the butter left over from smearing the dish into tiny dots and scatter these on top.

10. Place the dish in the upper third of the preheated oven and bake for 20 minutes, until the mozzarella melts and begins to be flecked with brown. Allow to settle for a few minutes, bringing the dish to the table while its contents are still warm, but no longer scalding. Some liquid may have collected at the bottom; do not discard it because it is quite tasty and only needs a good crusty piece of bread to sop it up.

AHEAD-OF-TIME NOTE: You can assemble all the ingredients in the baking dish several hours in advance and refrigerate under plastic wrap. Bring to room temperature before baking.

Swordfish Sardinian-Style with Mint and Saffron

PESCE SPADA COME LO FA LA RITA

⅓ cup extra virgin olive oil

2½ tablespoons finely chopped garlic

About 35 small fresh mint leaves, torn into bits

1 cup dry white wine

A large pinch of saffron

1 cup canned Italian plum tomatoes OR peeled, fresh, ripe tomatoes, chopped up

Salt

Chopped fresh or dried red chili pepper, to taste

2½ pounds fresh swordfish steaks, about 1 inch thick

For 4 to 6 persons

Not least among the pleasures of the south shore of Long Island is the native swordfish. The fine, pale pink, creamy flesh cannot be surpassed by that of any other example of the species. When we took a small summer place in Watermill, I hastened to duplicate the pasta with swordfish I'd had in Sardinia at Rita D'Enza's restaurant Gallura in Olbia.

When I first served it, we found ourselves scraping the bowl not for more pasta, but for the sauce. And so we agreed, Victor and I: Next time we make it let us, for once, forget the pasta and just have the sauce. And that is how Rita's swordfish pasta became Rita's swordfish, period.

1. Choose a sauté pan or skillet that can later contain all the fish without overlapping, put in the olive oil and garlic, and turn on the heat to medium. Cook the garlic, stirring once or twice, until it becomes colored a very pale gold.

2. Add the mint, stir quickly three or four times, then add the white wine and the saffron. When the wine has simmered a minute or so and the scent of alcohol has subsided, add the chopped tomato, salt, and chili pepper. Cook at a lively simmer, stirring occasionally, until the fat begins to separate from the sauce, as described in the Note on page 133, about 15 or 20 minutes.

3. Strip away the skin that circles the fish steaks and, if they are very large, cut them into pieces no longer than 4 inches. Put the fish in the pan, sprinkling it with salt and turning it over a couple of times in the sauce. Cook, at lively heat, for 3 minutes on one side and 2 to 3 minutes on the other. Transfer the entire contents of the pan to a warm serving platter and bring to the table at once.

AHEAD-OF-TIME NOTE: You can prepare everything through step 2 several hours in advance. When ready to serve, reheat the sauce at a gentle simmer, then turn up the heat and put in the fish.

Pan-Grilled Swordfish Steaks with Warm Salmoriglio and Capers

PESCE SPADA AL SALMORIGLIO CALDO

3 tablespoons lemon juice, squeezed fresh

4 garlic cloves, lightly mashed with the handle of a knife and peeled

Salt

Black pepper ground fresh

Oregano, 2 teaspoons if fresh, 1 teaspoon if dried

¼ cup extra virgin olive oil

2 pounds swordfish, cut into 1- to 1¼-inch-thick steaks

1 tablespoon chopped capers

For 4 to 6 persons

A cast-iron griddle or skillet

A warm serving platter

*S*almoriglio is a blend of olive oil, lemon juice, and oregano that, in Sicily, you brush on hot, thin, grilled swordfish steaks. The recipe appears in an earlier book of mine, and it is one that I have known readers and friends to be very fond of. The more familiar *salmoriglio* is poured cold, like a dressing, but there is also the version that you find below, in which heat is applied briefly to bring the fish and its dressing together. An additional ingredient here is the capers, added off heat.

Do not exceed the recommended thickness of the swordfish steak. You are pan-searing it and to keep the fish juicy you need to do it quickly, but at the same time you don't want to serve it partly raw inside, which might happen if the slice is too thick.

1. Into a small bowl put the lemon juice, garlic, salt, liberal grindings of black pepper, and oregano and beat with a fork until the salt has completely dissolved.

2. Add the olive oil in a thin trickle, beating it in with a fork as though you were making mayonnaise by hand.

3. Heat up the cast-iron griddle or skillet. It should sizzle instantly on contact with the fish. Slip in the swordfish steaks. As soon as they have formed a thin but dark crust on the side next to the griddle, use a broad spatula to turn them over. As soon as the steaks have a crust on both sides, transfer them to a warm platter.

4. Choose a regular skillet that can accommodate the swordfish steaks on a single level without overlapping, put in the fish, pour the lemon juice and oregano mixture over them, and turn on the heat to high. Cook for about a minute, turning the steaks once. Off heat, add the capers. Transfer the full contents of the pan to a very warm platter and serve at once.

BAKING BLUEFISH

PESCE AZZURRO AL FORNO

Azzurro—"blue"—is what in Italy we call all such dark-fleshed fish as tuna, mackerel, sardines, and anchovies. These species, and several of their related varieties, are dense in the Italian seas, yet among them there is nothing to surpass a freshly caught Atlantic bluefish. Freshly caught is the necessary distinction, because the oils that make the flesh of this fish sweet and succulent begin to turn rancid and sharp within 36 to 48 hours after it's landed.

Start with bluefish as fresh as the kind I get on the south shore of Long Island from my favorite fishmonger, John Haessler of Wainscott; prepare it as a cook on the Riviera or the Adriatic shore might if she or he could come by

such a specimen; and you may find yourself contracting the craving that Italians have for the dark flesh of all kinds of *pesce azzurro*.

Potatoes and bluefish baked together make an ideal match and they set the theme which the two following recipes pick up and develop in divergent directions. In the first of the recipes, in addition to potatoes you'll find leeks—in the other recipe, peppers. Leeks prompt the use of butter and Parmesan in emulation of the suave style that some Venetian cooks are partial to, while the one with peppers, made with olive oil, onion, and garlic, resonates with the forthright accents of the Riviera.

Bluefish with Baked Onions, Peppers, and Potatoes

PESCE AZZURRO CON VERDURE E PATATE AL FORNO

2 large red meaty bell
    peppers

1½ pounds new potatoes

¼ cup extra virgin olive oil

3 medium onions sliced
    very thin, about 3 cups

1 large garlic clove OR
    2 small cloves, peeled
    and sliced very thin

Salt

Black pepper ground fresh

2 pounds bluefish fillets
    with the skin on

1 tablespoon fine, dry,
    unflavored bread crumbs

For 4 to 6 persons

An ovenproof serving dish

1. Turn on the oven to 450°.

2. Split the peppers lengthwise in two, remove the white pulpy core with all its seeds, then use a vegetable peeler with a swiveling blade to skin the peppers. Cut the pepper flesh lengthwise into ½-inch-wide strips. You should have approximately 4 cups.

3. Peel the potatoes, slice them very thin, wash in cold water, and pat dry with kitchen toweling.

4. Choose a rectangular ovenproof serving dish or pan that can contain the fish and all the vegetables. Put in 3 tablespoons of olive oil; the peppers, potatoes, onions, garlic, and salt; and liberal grindings of black pepper. Toss several times to coat the vegetables well and place in the uppermost level of the preheated oven. Bake until all the vegetables feel tender when prodded with a fork, about 45 minutes, turning the vegetables over every 15 minutes.

5. Remove the pan from the oven and turn on the broiler.

6. Gather the vegetables in the center of the pan, making room at the sides for the fish fillets. Put in the fish; sprinkle with salt, black pepper, and bread crumbs; and trickle over it the remaining tablespoon of olive oil.

7. Slip the pan under the broiler. (Do not let the flame or heating element touch or even come close to the dish unless it's flameproof.) After 8 minutes, turn the vegetables over. After another 7 to 8 minutes, the fish should be done. Before serving, draw some of the vegetables over the fish. Allow to settle for a few minutes before bringing to the table.

AHEAD-OF-TIME NOTE: The fish has to be cooked only when you are ready to serve it, but the vegetables may be baked a few hours in advance. When ready to resume cooking, reheat them in a 400° oven.

Baked Bluefish with Leeks and Potatoes

PESCE AZZURRO AL FORNO CON PORRI E PATATE

6 medium leeks

2 tablespoons extra virgin
   olive oil

Salt

3 tablespoons butter

2 pounds new potatoes

Black pepper ground fresh

¼ cup freshly grated
   Parmigiano-Reggiano

2 tablespoons fine, dry,
   unflavored bread crumbs

2 pounds bluefish fillets
   with the skin on

For 4 persons

An ovenproof baking-serving
dish

1. Detach and discard the leeks' green tops. Slice the lower white parts of the stalks into very thin rounds. The yield should be about 4 cups.

2. Put the sliced leeks into a medium sauté pan or skillet, add the olive oil, sprinkle with salt, and put in ⅓ cup of water. Cover the pan, turn on the heat to low, and cook, stirring from time to time, until the leeks are reduced to a soft pulp. When done, with the heat turned off, put 2 tablespoons of butter into the pan, stirring it into the warm leeks to melt it.

3. Turn on the oven to 450°.

4. Peel the potatoes, slice them very thin, wash in cold water, and pat dry with kitchen toweling.

5. Choose a baking dish that can later accommodate the bluefish fillets laid out flat without overlapping, and lightly smear the bottom with about ½ tablespoon of butter.

6. Put the potato slices and all the leeks and juices from their pan into the baking dish and sprinkle with salt and pepper. Mix thoroughly and spread evenly over the bottom of the dish. Place the dish in the preheated oven and bake for 35 minutes until the potatoes are tender and a light crust has formed on their edges.

7. Combine the grated Parmesan and bread crumbs, sprinkle about 2 to 3 tablespoons of the mixture over the potatoes and leeks in the baking dish, and continue baking for another 5 to 7 minutes.

8. Lay the fish fillets, skin side down, flat over the potatoes and leeks, sprinkle the remaining Parmesan and bread crumb mixture over them, and dot with the remaining butter. Return the dish to the oven and bake for about 10 minutes, or slightly longer if the fillets are thicker than ½ inch.

9. Turn on the broiler and place the dish under it (do not let the flame or heating element touch or even come close to the dish unless it's flameproof) for about 3 minutes until a light crust has formed over the fish. Before serving, let the heat subside for 2 or 3 minutes.

AHEAD-OF-TIME NOTE: You can cook the leeks through to the end of step 2 several hours in advance, but always on the same day that you are serving the dish. Before mixing the leeks with the sliced potatoes, reheat them briefly so that they will combine more smoothly.

Keeping Fish

Except for bluefish, which should be eaten as quickly as possible after it is caught, whole gutted fish with its skin on, such as this red snapper, whole squid, or unshelled shrimp can be kept in good condition for two or three days in the refrigerator. Cover with ice and put the fish on a rack to let the melting ice drain. Shrimp and squid will fit into a footed pasta colander set over a bowl.

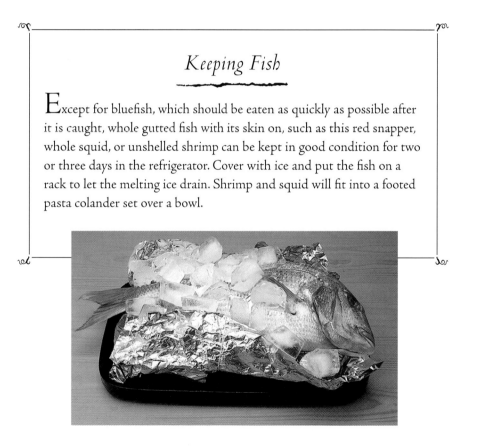

Sautéed Fresh Tuna Cubes with Smothered Onion, Tomato, and Chili Pepper

TOCCHI DI TONNO SALTATI CON CIPOLLA, POMODORO, E PEPERONCINO

4 cups very, very thinly sliced onions

4 tablespoons extra virgin olive oil

Salt

1¾ pounds fresh, ripe tomatoes OR 3 cups canned imported Italian plum tomatoes, cut up with their juice

3 tablespoons chopped Italian flat-leaf parsley

Chopped hot chili pepper, ⅛ teaspoon or to taste

1½ pounds fresh yellowfin tuna, cut into 1-inch cubes

For 6 persons

The taste and appearance of this dish are those of a stew. The tuna is cut into cubes and it is served with some of the things that are kindest to it, slowly cooked onion combined with tomato and chili pepper. We know, however, that we cannot subject tuna to the unhurried cooking stews require because its meat stays tender until it just begins to feel the heat, and then starts to turn irreparably tough and dry. The solution is to cook the onion and tomato for as much time as necessary, but separately from the fish. When they are done, the tuna is browned in hot olive oil, a step lasting barely long enough to give its surface some crispness, yet sufficiently brief to keep the interior of the cube juicy. The savory bond that pulls the tuna and the onion and tomatoes together is then fastened by the lively heat of a skillet where they are all tossed rapidly just before serving.

1. Put all the sliced onions and half the olive oil in a 10-inch skillet with a pinch of salt and turn on the heat to medium low. Cook, turning the onions over from time to time. At first they will shed juice, then wilt. They are done when they are reduced to one-third their original volume and have become lightly colored. If and when it becomes necessary, add 2 tablespoons of water to keep the onions from drying out and sticking while they cook.

2. While the onions are cooking, if you are using fresh tomatoes, peel them by dipping them in boiling water for 1 minute, then squeezing off their skin. For this dish, any tomato-peeling technique you find practical is satisfactory; please see Working with Tomatoes, pages 135–37. Chop up the tomatoes coarsely, keeping all their juice and seeds.

3. When the onions are done, add the tomatoes, 2 tablespoons of chopped parsley, the chili pepper, and salt. Turn the heat up to

medium high and cook, turning over all ingredients with a wooden spoon from time to time, until the sauce acquires density and the fat begins to separate from the sauce, as described in the Note on page 133, about 15 or 20 minutes.

4. Put the remaining 2 tablespoons of olive oil in a 12-inch skillet and turn up the heat to high. When the oil is hot enough to sizzle when slipping in a piece of fish, put in the tuna, turning it to brown it on all sides. The moment the tuna has been browned, pour all the contents of the smaller pan over it, turn the ingredients over with a wooden spoon for about half a minute, taste and correct for salt and chili pepper, and serve at once.

AHEAD-OF-TIME NOTE: You can prepare the dish up to a day in advance to the end of step 3, when the onion and tomato are done. Reheat gently but thoroughly before proceeding with sautéing the tuna. On a summer day, this tuna can be quite agreeable at room temperature, but please don't refrigerate it first.

Squid Braised in Olive Oil and White Wine with Spinach, Fresh Tomato, and Chili Pepper

CALAMARI STUFATI CON SPINACI E PEPERONCINO

---

2 pounds whole, medium squid OR 1½ pounds presliced large squid rings

⅓ cup extra virgin olive oil

1 cup thinly sliced onion

1 cup dry white wine

1 pound fresh spinach

½ pound fresh, ripe tomatoes

2 tablespoons capers

Salt

Chili pepper, ¼ teaspoon or to taste

For 4 persons

As anyone who has had it raw in Japanese restaurants already knows, squid is naturally tender. It becomes rubbery when cooked either not quickly or not long enough. It maintains its natural tenderness when floated briefly in a large amount of very hot oil, or when dipped in boiling water to blanch it for a seafood salad. And it can become exquisitely tender when braised slowly for close to an hour. The latter is my favorite way of doing squid, and it is the one used to produce this superb pairing of squid and fresh spinach.

It is a pairing, liberally adapted in the recipe that follows, that I owe to an economist. Or rather to a would-be economist, for such was Stefano Bartolini before he opened La Buca, a restaurant in my hometown with a dozen much-sought-after tables. It was a change of careers that no one can regret. We can struggle on with one less economist, but there are never enough good places to eat.

1. If you are using whole squid, clean it as directed on page 262. Separate the sacs from the tentacles and divide the tentacles into two parts. Slit the sacs lengthwise, opening them up flat. Remove any inner membranes, and cut the sacs into squares of more or less 1½ inches. If you are using presliced large squid rings, cut them to open them flat. Wash the squid in cold water and place in a colander to drain.

2. Put the olive oil and sliced onion in a 12-inch skillet or sauté pan and turn on the heat to medium low. Cook the onion, turning it over from time to time with a wooden spoon, until it becomes very lightly colored, about 6 or 7 minutes.

3. Add the squid, turning it over two or three times to coat it well, and cook for 3 to 4 minutes until it turns from translucent to flat white.

4. Add the wine, let it simmer briefly, then cover the pan and turn the heat down to low. Cook for approximately 45 minutes until the squid feels very tender when pricked with a fork. Turn it over occasionally, and whenever the cooking liquid needs to be replenished, add ⅓ cup water each time.

5. While the squid is cooking you can clean the spinach. Detach the thicker stems and soak in several changes of water until there is no trace of soil left in the water. Drain and shake dry in a towel or a salad spinner, then chop into large pieces.

6. Peel the tomatoes raw, using a swiveling-blade vegetable peeler. Scoop out the seeds without squeezing the tomatoes. Cut the peeled tomatoes into small dice.

7. Drain the capers if packed in vinegar; soak, rinse, and drain if packed in salt. Then chop them fine.

8. When the squid is tender, add the capers, mix once or twice, then add the spinach. If all the spinach won't fit at one time, put in as much

as will fit comfortably, cover the pan, cook until the first batch wilts and diminishes in volume, then put in the rest. Add salt and turn the spinach over several times with a wooden spoon to coat it well.

9. When the spinach is cooked, in 5 to 6 minutes, add the tomatoes and chili pepper, turning over all the contents of the pan two or three times. Cook, uncovered, for just another 5 to 6 minutes. Serve piping hot.

AHEAD-OF-TIME NOTE: You can cook this a day in advance up to the end of step 4, when the squid has become fully tender. Reheat very, very gently; otherwise the squid may toughen. Add a little bit of water if necessary. Wash and chop the spinach only when you resume cooking. When the squid is hot add the spinach and complete the recipe.

Stuffed Whole Squid Braised with Onions, Tomatoes, Chili Pepper, and White Wine

CALAMARI RIPIENI

6 whole squid with 6- to 8-inch-long sacs

¼ cup extra virgin olive oil

2 teaspoons chopped garlic

2 tablespoons chopped Italian flat-leaf parsley

½ cup fresh, ripe tomatoes, skinned, seeded, and cut up, OR canned, imported Italian plum tomatoes, cut up, with their juice

Salt

Chopped red chili pepper, ⅛ teaspoon or to taste

1 egg yolk

¼ cup fine, dry, unflavored bread crumbs

1½ cups very, very thinly sliced onions

½ cup dry white wine

For 6 persons

Fine needle and cotton thread OR strong, round wooden toothpicks

It is only recently that I discovered that what I mean by *calamari* isn't necessarily the same as what an American guest has in mind. Good friends from the States were visiting in Venice and we had gone together to the city's best fish restaurant. I asked if I could help decipher the menu, but one of them replied, "It isn't necessary. I see from it they have *calamari* and that is what I am going to have." When a platter with whole, roasted squid was brought to him he was indignant. "What is that!" "Didn't you order *calamari?*" I asked. "Sure, but that isn't *calamari*; *calamari* comes in rings and it is fried."

I yield to no one in fondness for what my friend refers to as *calamari*, but slicing it up into rings is not the only wonderful thing you can do with a squid's sac. You can use it whole as a remarkable, ready-made, tender container of tasty stuffings.

I have always marveled at the goodness of things stuffed. I don't know entirely how to account for it. A mysterious interpenetration of flavors takes place and stuffed squid—or stuffed cabbage leaves, stuffed zucchini, a stuffed bird—exceeds in its capacity to please the separate endowment of both the wrapper and what it contains. Could it be too that there is a childlike joy in retrieving, as though it were treasure, something that has been concealed within something else?

Preparing the Squid for Stuffing

1. Put the squid in a bowl filled with cold water, and soak them for 30 to 45 minutes.

2. Hold a squid sac in one hand, and with the other, grasp and firmly pull off the tentacles. They will come away easily, taking with them the squid's pulpy insides.

3. Cut the tentacles straight across just above the eyes, and discard everything below them. Squeeze off the small, bony beak at the base of

the tentacles. Wash the tentacles in cold water and pat thoroughly dry with kitchen towels.

4. Look for the end of the cellophane-thin, quill-like bone protruding from the sac, grasp it, and pull the quill away.

5. Peel off all the skin enveloping the sac. Cut a tiny opening—absolutely no larger than ¼ inch—at the tip of the sac, hold the large open end of the sac under a faucet, and run cold water through it.

6. Cut off the fleshy fins at the sides of the sac, taking care not to perforate the sac itself. Chop the fins and tentacles together. If using the food processor, do not chop too fine, to a pulp.

Making the Stuffing

1. Put 1½ tablespoons of olive oil and the chopped garlic in a small skillet, turn the heat on to medium, and cook the garlic, stirring frequently, until it becomes colored a pale gold.

2. Add the parsley, stir two or three times, then add the chopped tentacles and squid fins. Turn over a few times during 1 minute, then add the tomatoes, salt, and chili; turn over two or three times to coat all ingredients well; and cook at a steady but gentle simmer until the tomatoes are no longer watery but dense, about 30 minutes. Pour the contents of the skillet into a bowl, letting them cool completely.

3. When the tentacles and tomatoes are cold, add the egg yolk and bread crumbs, turning over all ingredients several times to produce a smooth, homogeneous mixture.

Making the Onion Base and Stuffing and Cooking the Squid

1. While the tentacles and tomatoes are cooling off, you can begin to cook the onions. Choose a sauté pan or skillet large enough to contain all the squid sacs later in a single, uncrowded layer, without overlapping. Put in 1½ tablespoons of olive oil and the sliced onions, and turn on the heat to medium low. Cook the onions, turning them over from time to time, until they become colored a rich golden caramel and are considerably reduced in bulk.

(continued)

2. When you have combined the tentacles, tomatoes, egg yolk, and bread crumbs, divide the mixture into six parts and spoon it into the squid sacs. Do not fill the sacs too tightly or they may burst while cooking when they begin to shrink. Sew up the opening of each sac with needle and thread or fasten it securely shut with a toothpick. If using needle and thread, remove the needle from the kitchen as soon as you have completed the procedure.

3. Add the remaining tablespoon of olive oil to the cooked onions, turn the heat up to medium high, and put in the stuffed squid. Cook the sacs, turning them over, until they have been browned on all sides.

4. Add the white wine, let it bubble away completely, then turn the heat down to low and put a lid on the pan. Cook at the gentlest of simmers for at least 45 minutes. Longer will do no harm. Should you find during this time that the juices in the pan are insufficient to keep the squid from sticking, add 2 to 3 tablespoons of water when necessary.

5. When done transfer the squid to a cutting board, cut the sacs into ½-inch-thick slices, and return the slices to the pan. Over low heat, for about half a minute, turn the slices over to coat them well. Serve from a warm platter, pouring the full contents of the pan over the sliced squid.

AHEAD-OF-TIME NOTE: If you can manage it, try to time this dish so you can serve the squid when just freshly cooked. Otherwise, you can cook the dish all the way through, including the slicing of the sacs, several hours in advance or even overnight. If refrigerating it overnight, bring it to room temperature before reheating. Reheat at a gentle simmer in a covered pan, adding a tablespoon or two of water, and turning the slices over occasionally, until thoroughly warmed through.

Bacaro-Style Frying Batter

LA PASTELLA DEI BACARI

2 eggs

1⅓ cups whole milk

Salt

Black pepper ground fresh

1 teaspoon baking powder

1½ cups flour

It's possible to argue that the best cooking technique is that which alters as little as possible the natural character of food, and if one accepts that proposition, one must conclude that frying, when properly executed, is the ideal way to cook. It seals in the juices of vegetables, meats, and fish; it protects their texture; and it enhances their surfaces with a crisp, light crust.

In the wine bars of Venice they fry with a lovely batter that tastes good and stays crisp for hours. Particularly good with this batter is eggplant, the large kind, cut into ½-inch-thick round slices; or artichoke, trimmed down to the heart and cut into wedges; or firm-fleshed fish fillets. For the latter, in Venice, they use cod a lot, but if I am somewhere in the States where I can get fresh grouper, I prefer that. Wash the grouper fillets and cut them into boxy pieces about 2 inches long and 1 inch wide. Dip in the batter and fry in very hot vegetable oil that comes at least ¾ of an inch up the sides of a large skillet.

1. Break the eggs into a deep dish and beat them with a fork or whisk, adding the milk a very little bit at a time.

2. Stir in salt and liberal grindings of black pepper.

3. Separately, mix the baking powder into the flour. Add the flour and baking powder mixture to the eggs a little bit at a time, beating constantly with the fork or whisk.

4. Let the batter rest for at least 40 minutes but no more than 2 or 3 hours before using it. After that time, leftover batter must be discarded.

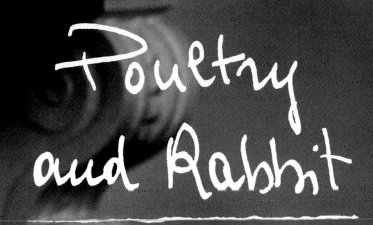

Poultry and Rabbit

POULTRY AND RABBIT
Pollo e Coniglio

Fricasseed Chicken with Dried Porcini
Mushrooms and Marsala Wine

Fricasseed Chicken Abruzzi-Style with
Rosemary, White Wine, Cherry
Tomatoes, and Olives

Fricasseed Chicken with Bay Leaves

Fricasseed Chicken with Garlic, Capers,
White Wine, and Jerusalem Artichokes

Roast Boned Chicken with Liver
and Sausage Stuffing

Chicken or Turkey Breast Marinated in
Herbs and Spices and Layered with
Zucchini

Fricasseed Rabbit with Yellow or Red
Peppers

Fricasseed Rabbit with Herbs, Tomato,
and White Wine

Pan-Roasted Rabbit Riviera-Style with
Herbs, Walnuts, and Olives

*Preceding photograph (left to right): Roast Boned
Chicken, Fricasseed Rabbit with Yellow or Red Peppers,
and Chicken Breast Marinated in Herbs.*

Chicken and rabbit were the meats that we ate most frequently at home when I was growing up. My father had a farm not far from the town where we lived and it was run, according to the practice that prevailed in Italy until well after the end of the Second World War, by a tenant farmer. He lived on the land with his family in the house my father had provided, unencumbered by such contrivances as running water, electricity, and indoor plumbing, sharing a roof with the cows and a few other domestic animals. He planted, grew, and harvested the crops, and was expected to turn over a little more than half of the proceeds of any sale to my father. I remember the periodic reckonings well, my father and his farmer hunched over the numbers on the scraps of paper that were spread on the dining table, each exercising his natural right, the one to determine the true extent of his legitimate share, the other to disclose as little of it as he could get away with.

Twice a year, at Easter and Christmas, tradition required that the farmer express his respect for the landowner by bringing gifts from the land he worked for him, baskets of vegetables and fruit and live chickens and rabbits. The rabbits were brought in a large wicker cage, while the chickens, tied in pairs by the leg, were dropped on the floor of the kitchen where they fluttered convulsively in a frantic attempt to escape bondage.

We killed the birds we needed for the holiday dinners, and fattened the others for subsequent occasions, letting them run free in a fenced-in corner of the garden that circled the house, where there was also a separate pen for the rabbits. Twice a day we would hear my grandmother call the chickens when she brought their feed, "Bee-shoo, bee-shoo, bee-shoo." It was a cry the chickens clearly understood, but they also understood when we entered their enclosure to take one, and it took three or four of us to maneuver the one we had chosen into a corner.

Some years later I was married and beginning to set up house in New York. I spoke no English then, so my husband Victor suggested I do my shopping at a supermarket where I didn't need to talk to anyone. This was more than forty years ago, long before supermarkets appeared in Italy, and I had never before seen anyplace like it. I walked up and down the aisles as though I had been dropped onto a different planet. My greatest shock came when I saw the chickens, plucked, without feet, head, or neck, and wrapped in shiny plastic. I wasn't even sure they were meant to be eaten.

Startling though the packaging was, I was persuaded that they really were chickens and—grateful at least that I didn't have to catch them, wring their necks, and pluck them—I began to cook them as I had seen my mother and grandmothers do. I cut them into pieces; sautéed them with garlic or onion, or both, in olive oil, or in butter combined with vegetable oil; added wine and tomato or another vegetable, or no tomato or vegetable at all; and cooked them through to the end over the stove. The first chicken I ever made in that New York kitchen was done with garlic, rosemary, and white wine, and it became, nearly twenty years later, when I was asked to write the cookbook that changed my career, the first chicken recipe I set down.

All the cooking I had ever seen at home when I was young was done over the stove, inasmuch as we had no oven. Any dish that needed to be baked, such as lasagne, had to be bicycled over to a bread bakery in town, a task that usually fell to me to perform. I have since become intimately acquainted with ovens and their workings, but if I am cooking any bird or rabbit I still, with rare exceptions, prefer the cooktop to the oven.

For one thing, the oven keeps me at a distance from the act of cooking. My emotions are deeply rooted in that act: I need to smell its smells, to hear its sounds, to see food in a pot that simmers, bubbles, sizzles. I enjoy the physical involvement of stirring, turning, poking, mashing, scraping. I get no thrills from turning thermostats and timer clocks, from cooking by remote control. Just on that account alone I turn on the oven only if there is no other choice. But there is an even more objective reason. Fricasseeing, cooking over the stove as I do, bestows on a bird or rabbit the supremely comforting flavor that I associate with stews—a density, a richness that, for me, no other method produces. Virtually all of the recipes in this chapter are examples of that method and that flavor.

Fricasseed Chicken with Dried Porcini Mushrooms and Marsala Wine

POLLO IN PADELLA CON FUNGHI SECCHI E MARSALA

1 ounce imported dried porcini (*Boletus edulis*) mushrooms OR if in packets, a ¾ ounce packet

A 3½-pound chicken, cut into 8 pieces

Flour for coating the chicken, about ½ cup

2 tablespoons vegetable oil

1 tablespoon butter

Salt

Black pepper ground fresh

3 tablespoons chopped onion

⅓ cup dry Marsala wine; see headnote

For 4 persons

There are two ingredients at work in this dish, the dried porcini mushrooms and the Marsala wine, that invest the chicken with complex flavors and aromas of exceptional depth and earthiness.

In dried porcini we have not just a conveniently packaged alternative to the fresh mushroom, but an inimitable ingredient with its own separate repertory of applications. You are no longer using it as a mushroom, but as the aromatic forest essence of that mushroom. The difference between fresh and dried porcini may be compared to the difference between a bouquet of fresh flowers and the potent concentrate of their fragrance in a vial of perfume.

Marsala too is a product of a special process through which certain properties of the wine are concentrated and altered by aging and blending. Vanilla, spice, smoke, and caramel are some of the scents it can manifest. There are many classifications for Marsala, depending on the specific production method that was used. For all cooking purposes, look for the word *secco*, which means dry, although it is still slightly sweet. It will be even better if you find the additional qualifying words *superiore* and *ambra*.

1. Soak the mushrooms in 2 cups barely warm water for at least 30 minutes. Lift out the mushrooms by hand, squeezing as much water as possible from them, letting it flow back into the container where they soaked. Rinse the reconstituted mushrooms in several changes of fresh water. With the tip of a small paring knife scrape clean any place where soil appears to be still embedded. Pat dry with paper towels and chop them very fine. The water in which the mushrooms soaked is richly infused with porcini flavor. To clear it of the soil that has become deposited in it, filter it through a strainer lined with single-ply paper toweling, collecting it in a bowl or a pouring cup. Set aside.

(continued)

2. Wash the chicken pieces thoroughly, and pat them as dry as you can with paper or cloth towels. Spread the flour on a plate and turn the chicken in it.

3. Choose a skillet or sauté pan that can accommodate all the chicken pieces in a single layer without overlapping, put in the oil and butter, and turn on the heat to medium high. When the butter foam begins to subside, slip in the chicken. When all the pieces have become well browned on one side, add salt, black pepper, and the chopped onion, and turn the pieces over.

4. When the chicken has become browned all over and the onion has become colored a rich gold, add the Marsala wine. Let it bubble briskly for just a few seconds, add the chopped *porcini* mushrooms, turn the ingredients over with a wooden spoon, then cover the pan and turn the heat down to medium low.

5. Cook the chicken at a slow but regular simmer, replenishing the cooking juices when they begin to dry out with 2 or 3 tablespoons of the filtered water from the mushroom soak. Turn the chicken pieces over every once in a while and continue cooking until they feel very tender when prodded with a fork and the meat looks as though it would easily fall off the bone, about 50 minutes to 1 hour. The cooking juices should have condensed into a small amount of creamy sauce. If there is too much fat floating free, tip the pan and spoon it off. Transfer the entire contents of the pan to a warm platter and serve at once.

AHEAD-OF-TIME NOTE: This is a dish you can cook all the way through, but without spooning off any fat, several hours or even a day in advance. When making it ready to serve, warm the chicken in a covered skillet over slow heat, adding a little water if it seems necessary. Spoon off any free excess fat from the pan when the chicken is hot, just before serving.

Fricasseed Chicken Abruzzi-Style with Rosemary, White Wine, Cherry Tomatoes, and Olives

POLLO ALL'ABRUZZESE COI POMODORINI E LE OLIVE

A 3½-pound chicken, cut
 into 8 pieces

1 tablespoon extra virgin
 olive oil

4 or 5 whole peeled garlic
 cloves

2 teaspoons rosemary
 leaves, chopped very fine

Salt

Chopped hot chili pepper,
 ¼ teaspoon or to taste

½ cup dry white wine

Two dozen cherry tomatoes
 if no larger than 1 inch
 or proportionately fewer
 if larger

A dozen small black olives
 in brine such as Italian
 Riviera or French niçoise
 olives; see headnote

For 4 persons

Small, ripe, thin-skinned, very savory cherry tomatoes have become extremely popular and widely available in Italy in recent years. They are destined for the salad bowl, but one can certainly cook with them, if one is careful about choosing a preparation where they will show to best advantage. If you are making a sauce in which you need a lot of tomato, it would be more efficient and economical to use the plum or round varieties grown for the purpose. But when I had this particular chicken, I thought I saw in it a good opportunity for the miniature tomato.

In the original dish there was tomato of conventional size cooked the necessary 20 minutes or more, and the taste was close to the familiar one of chicken *cacciatora*. It seemed to me that I could capitalize on the brief cooking time cherry tomatoes require to achieve flavor that was fresh and sprightly. Thus you will see that the tomatoes are put into the pan when the chicken is already done, and they stay no longer than is necessary for their skin to begin to crack. The resulting sweet and juicy taste is just what I was hoping for.

With that taste, olives similar to the strong-flavored ones of Abruzzi no longer seemed to be the most congenial ones to use, so I chose *taggiasche* olives, the small, mellow ones of the Italian Riviera. If you cannot find them, you can substitute French niçoise olives, which are similar.

I rarely have an occasion to mention how attractive an Italian dish is because presentation doesn't get much attention from this cuisine. This chicken, however, whose nut-brown color is a rich foil to the red of the nearly intact whole tomatoes and the black of the olives, appeals no less to the eye than it does to the palate.

1. Wash all the chicken pieces in cold water and pat dry with kitchen towels.

(continued)

1 egg

1 ½ cups unflavored bread crumbs lightly toasted in a skillet or in the oven and spread on a plate

---

For 6 persons or up to 10 portions if served as an appetizer

A deep rectangular serving dish about 13 by 9 inches, or one of comparable size

3. Put the olive oil, onion, celery, and some salt into a medium skillet and turn on the heat to low. Cook, stirring occasionally, until the onion is very tender, but without letting it become colored.

4. Add the garlic, bay leaves, sage, vinegar, wine, water, sugar, cloves, and cinnamon and liberal grindings of black pepper, and cook for 10 to 15 minutes, turning the ingredients over from time to time.

5. Pour enough vegetable oil into a frying pan to come at least ½ inch up its sides, and turn on the heat to medium high. When the oil is hot enough to sizzle as a zucchini round is dropped into it, slip in as many zucchini as will fit without being crowded. Cook them just until they have become colored a medium brown, transfer them to a bowl using a slotted spoon or spatula, and sprinkle lightly with salt. Repeat the procedure until you have fried all the zucchini. Do not empty out the oil in the pan.

6. Beat the egg in a small bowl or deep plate. Dip each piece of chicken or turkey in the beaten egg, letting the excess flow back into the bowl or plate, then turn it in the bread crumbs, coating both sides. Lay each piece down in a platter, and pat both sides lightly with the palm of your hand to cause the coating to adhere securely and evenly.

7. Place the pan in which you fried the zucchini back on the burner and turn on the heat to medium high. As soon as the oil is hot slip in as many pieces of chicken or turkey as will fit loosely. Cook until a fine brown crust has formed on both sides, then, using a slotted spoon or spatula, transfer them to a platter lined with paper towels and sprinkle with salt. Repeat the procedure until you have done all the chicken or turkey.

8. Cover the bottom of the serving dish with a single layer of chicken or turkey, distribute some of the zucchini over it, then top with some of the onion, vinegar, and herb marinade. Proceed thus, continuing to build up layers of meat, zucchini, and marinade until you have used up all the ingredients. Top off with a layer of marinade. Cover with plastic wrap and refrigerate for at least 24 hours, or up to 4 or 5 days. Discard bay leaves; allow to return to room temperature before serving.

Fricasseed Rabbit with Yellow or Red Peppers

CONIGLIO IN UMIDO COI PEPERONI

───────�֍───────

A 3- to 4-pound rabbit, cut into 7 or 8 pieces

1 cup wine vinegar, preferably white

3 tablespoons coarse salt

3 tablespoons extra virgin olive oil

1 medium onion, sliced thin

1 garlic clove, peeled and sliced very thin

½ cup dry white wine

3 yellow or red peppers, skinned raw with a peeler, cores and seeds removed, and sliced into thin strips

Chopped hot chili pepper, ⅛ teaspoon or to taste

1 tablespoon chopped Italian flat-leaf parsley

──────────────

For 4 persons

Italians market not as a chore, but for the pleasure of it, and like all social pleasures, it establishes an immediate relationship between those engaged in a similar pursuit. I was traveling in Piedmont, browsing in one of Alba's marvelous food shops, and soon I was having a warm conversation about cooking with a woman who was there to decide what to make for dinner. When she decided on a rabbit, of course I had to know how she was going to use it.

After she good-naturedly explained the procedure in that shorthand that Italian cooks use, ignoring measurements and taking the basics for granted, she added, "I doubt you'll find rabbit done this way in any of the restaurants you are going to. My mother was the only one I knew who made it and she got it from her mother." It's a lovely, homey dish; the meat stays very juicy; and the peppers practically dissolve, turning into sauce for the rabbit.

1. Put the rabbit pieces in a bowl where they will fit snugly, and add the vinegar, coarse salt, and enough water to cover. Let steep for 6 to 7 hours at cool room temperature, or overnight in the refrigerator. Turn the pieces occasionally.

2. When ready to cook the rabbit, drain the bowl and wash the pieces in cold water. Look for any loose small bones and pick them out. Pat the meat dry with a kitchen towel.

3. In a sauté pan able to contain all the rabbit pieces in a single layer, put the olive oil, and turn the heat on to high. When the oil is hot, put in the rabbit and brown it on all sides.

4. Take the meat out of the pan, lower the heat to medium, and put in the sliced onion. Turn it occasionally and when it becomes lightly colored, add the sliced garlic. Cook for a minute or two, stirring occasionally, then return the rabbit pieces to the pan.

5. Turn the meat over once or twice, then add the wine. Scrape the bottom of the pan with a wooden spoon to loosen any browning residues.

6. Add the peppers, salt, and chopped hot chili pepper to taste. Turn over all the ingredients once or twice, put a lid on the pan, and turn the heat down to low. Cook for 1 hour to 1½ hours until the meat is tender and comes off the bone and the peppers have dissolved almost entirely into a sauce. Check the pan from time to time during the cooking, turning over its contents, and if you find that the cooking juices have dried up, add 3 to 4 tablespoons of water when needed. On the other hand, if, when the rabbit is done, the pan juices are too runny, remove the meat from the pan and turn up the heat to high, stirring and reducing the juices to a desirable density.

AHEAD-OF-TIME NOTE: You can finish the dish a day in advance and serve it the following day, after reheating it gently.

Fricasseed Rabbit with Herbs, Tomato, and White Wine

CONIGLIO IN FRICASSEA CON POMODORI, GLI ODORI, E VINO BIANCO

1 cup wine vinegar

Salt

A 3- to 4-pound rabbit, cut into 7 or 8 pieces

¼ cup extra virgin olive oil

¼ pound pancetta cut into ¼-inch dice

½ cup chopped onion

½ cup carrot, cut into ¼-inch dice

½ cup celery, cut into ¼-inch dice

½ cup dry white wine

½ cup fresh, ripe tomatoes, peeled, seeded, and chopped, OR canned Italian plum tomatoes, cut up with their juice

Chopped sage leaves, 1½ teaspoons if fresh, 1 teaspoon if dried

A small sprig of fresh rosemary OR 2 teaspoons chopped dried leaves

1 teaspoon chopped fresh basil

Black pepper ground fresh

For 4 persons

In most of Italy's regional cuisines, herbs have a limited role. They are a little like the cymbals player in an orchestra, called upon to supply punctuation but not to carry the melody. The most prominent exception to this austerely restrained style is the cooking of the Italian Riviera. This rabbit with sage, rosemary, and basil is a good example of the unbuttoned use of herbs that gives the cooking of the Riviera a provocatively fragrant appeal that has no equivalent among the food of other Italian regions.

1. In a bowl that can contain all the rabbit pieces, put the vinegar and 3 tablespoons of salt, stirring to dissolve the salt.

2. Wash the rabbit in cold water and put it in the bowl. Pour in enough water to cover, and let the rabbit steep thus in a cool place for 3 to 4 hours. If you want to start this procedure the previous day, refrigerate the rabbit overnight.

3. Drain the rabbit and pat all the pieces thoroughly dry with kitchen towels. Choose a lidded skillet or sauté pan large enough to accommodate later all the rabbit pieces without overlapping. Put in all the olive oil and turn on the heat to high. When the oil is hot slip in the rabbit. Turn the pieces over until you have browned them all on every side. Using a slotted spoon or spatula, transfer the rabbit to a platter or bowl.

4. Turn the heat down to medium high and put the diced pancetta in the pan. Stir to brown it lightly all over, then put in the chopped onion. Stir two or three times and when the onion has become colored a light gold, put in the carrot and celery. Cook, stirring from time to time, until they too become lightly colored.

5. Return the rabbit pieces to the pan together with any juices they may have shed. Add the wine, and scrape loose any cooking residues from the bottom of the pan, using a wooden spoon. Add the chopped tomato, sage, rosemary, and basil, and sprinkle salt all over together with liberal grindings of black pepper. Turn all ingredients over once or twice, cover the pan, turn the heat down to low, and cook for about 1½ hours, until the rabbit feels tender when prodded with a fork. Should it become necessary to replenish the cooking juices during the cooking, add up to ⅓ cup water. By the time the rabbit is done, however, there should be no runny liquid in the pan, just a little bit of dense juice.

AHEAD-OF-TIME NOTE: You can cook the rabbit through to the end as long in advance as the morning of the day on which you plan to serve it. Reheat it gently but thoroughly, adding a tablespoon or two of water if necessary.

Pan-Roasted Rabbit Riviera-Style with Herbs, Walnuts, and Olives

CONIGLIO IN TEGAME ALLA RIVIERASCA

A 3- to 4-pound rabbit

½ cup red wine vinegar

¼ cup extra virgin olive oil

A large yellow onion, cut into thin slices, about 1½ cups

2 whole bay leaves

Coarsely chopped rosemary leaves, 1 tablespoon if fresh, 2 teaspoons if dried

½ cup chopped celery

Thyme, 1 teaspoon if fresh, ½ teaspoon if dried

1½ cups dry red wine

⅓ cup shelled walnuts, mashed in a mortar or ground fine

Salt

Black pepper ground fresh

The rabbit's liver OR 3 fresh chicken livers

20 unpitted Italian Riviera OR niçoise olives

For 6 persons

When we yearn for aromatic cooking we turn to the Riviera, and it never lets us down. I had this rabbit in the town of Chiavari, after having spent the latter part of the morning at the small but splendid outdoor market it holds daily in a handsome piazza. The bay leaves, rosemary, and thyme; the walnuts; the olives—as I list the ingredients I can hear the singsong cadences of the musical Genoese dialect.

The liver enriches the taste of this rabbit—which has moved to the front rank of my favorites—to a significant degree. If you can buy rabbit with its own liver, that will give you exactly the flavor accent you need. If not, you can come close by using chicken livers.

On the Night Before

Cut the rabbit into 8 pieces, and put the pieces in a bowl with enough water to cover and ½ cup red wine vinegar. Refrigerate overnight.

Cooking the Rabbit

1. When ready to cook the rabbit, retrieve it from its marinade, wash every piece thoroughly in cold water, and pat dry with kitchen towels.

2. Choose a sauté pan or skillet that can subsequently contain all the rabbit pieces in a single layer without overlapping. Put in the olive oil and turn on the heat to medium high. When the oil is hot enough to sizzle the moment the meat is put in, slip all the rabbit pieces into the pan. Brown them well on one side, then turn them to brown the other side. When they have been nicely browned all over, use a slotted spoon or spatula to transfer them to a deep platter or bowl.

3. Put the onion in the pan and cook it, stirring frequently, until it becomes colored a pale gold. Lower the heat just slightly, and add the bay leaves, rosemary, celery, and thyme, turning them over for about a minute.

4. Return the rabbit pieces to the pan, turn them over three or four times during 1 minute, then add the wine. Let the wine bubble away completely while using the wooden spoon to scrape loose the browning residues from the bottom of the pan.

5. Add the walnuts, sprinkle with salt and grindings of pepper, turn over the contents of the pan once or twice to coat them well, then turn the heat down to low and cover the pan. Cook at a gentle pace, occasionally turning the rabbit pieces over.

6. Bring water to a boil in a saucepan and put in the liver or livers. Cook less than 5 minutes, draining the liver while it is still slightly pink. Chop it very fine, using either a knife or the food processor.

7. When the rabbit has cooked for about 30 minutes, add the chopped liver to the pan, turning over the pan's contents once or twice. Continue cooking, always at low heat and with a lid on the pan, for 45 minutes or more, until the meat feels very tender when poked with a fork.

8. When the rabbit is done, put in the whole olives, turn the contents of the pan over for about 1 minute, then serve at once from a warm platter.

AHEAD-OF-TIME NOTE: Rabbit is never so succulent as it is the moment it finishes cooking, but if you reheat it very gently but thoroughly, adding 2 tablespoons of water if necessary, you can make it several hours in advance, such as early in the morning of the day you will serve it. Add the olives only when reheating it.

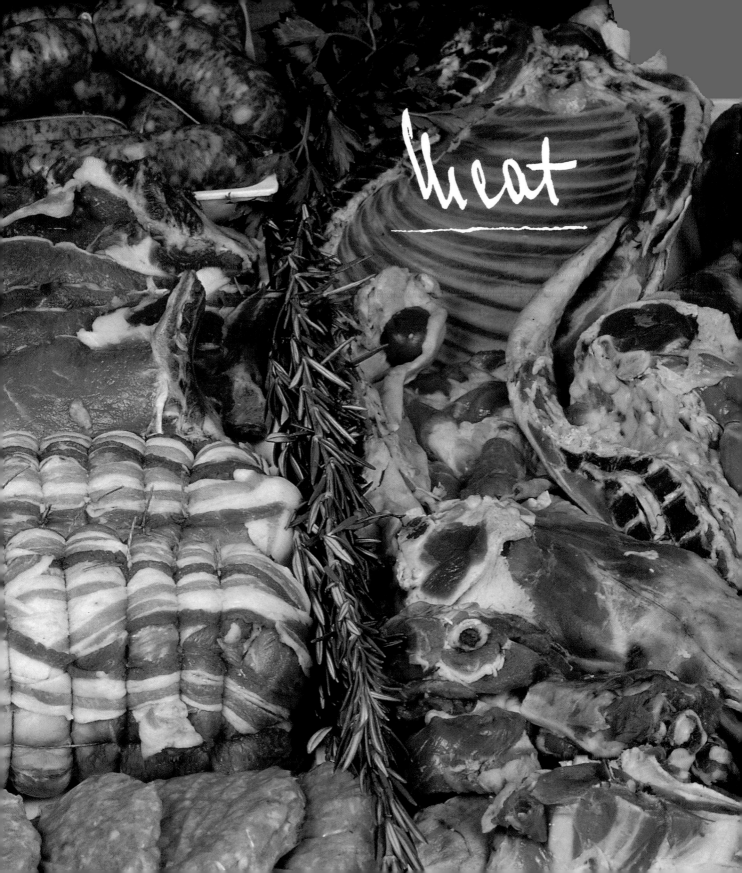

MEAT
Le Carni

VEAL
Il Vitello

Pan-Roasted Veal with Radicchio

Stewed Shoulder of Veal with White Wine,
    Artichokes, and Cream

The Scaloppine Cut

Involtini

    Veal Rolls Stuffed with Tomato,
        Capers, Anchovies, and Parmesan

    Veal Rolls with Leeks and White Wine

Veal Patties

    Breaded Veal Patties with Bell Pepper,
        Scallions, and Tomato

    Simple Breaded Veal Patties
        with Capers

BEEF
Il Manzo

Two Beef Stews

    Beef Stew with Peppers, Potatoes,
        and Milk

    Stewed Beef Cubes with Pickles,
        Capers, and Red Wine

Seasoned Sliced Grilled Beefsteaks

    Over-the-Stove Version

    Outdoor Version

Boiled Beef and Its Broth

LAMB
L'Agnello

Roast Boned Leg of Lamb Abruzzi-Style
    with Potatoes

Lamb Stews

    Rita D'Enza's Fricasseed Lamb
        Shoulder with Cauliflower

    Stewed Shoulder of Lamb Marches-
        Style with Potatoes, Rosemary, and
        Chili Pepper

    Pan-Roasted Lamb Apulian-Style with
        Onions and Potatoes

PORK
Il Maiale

Pan-Roasted Pork Tenderloin Wild
    Boar–Style with Shiitake Mushrooms

Pork Strips with Broccoli and Carrots

Stuffed Pork Rolls with Pickles and Sage
    Braised in Tomatoes and White Wine

Pork Balls with Beans and Tomato

Sautéed Pork Scallops with Scallions
    and Capers

Two Condiments for Meat

    Apple and Basil Condiment for Meats

    Raw Savory Condiment for Warm
        or Cold Meats

I have two 5-foot-tall maps of Italy that I refer to from time to time when I give a cooking class. One of the maps is organized politically to show the regions into which the nation is divided, while the other is topographical, using color to illustrate the height of the mountains and the varying depths of the seas. Pointing to the topographical map I tell my students, "See the large, triangular, bright green area that covers much of the north? This is Italy's only large plain. Here we can have cows, and with them the milk for butter and Parmesan. Here people eat beef, veal, and pork that has been raised on the residual whey from cheese making. See how the colors of the rest of the country range from yellow to ocher to dark brown? Those are hills and mountains. There are few cows there and most of the meat that people eat, aside from chicken and rabbit, is lamb, and their cheese is pecorino, made from ewe's milk."

Within these areas there are local specialties. Piedmont, in the northwest, has a prized local breed of beef, the *razza Piemontese*, whose calves yield the most tender and juicy veal anyone has ever taken knife and fork to. An older male calf is often gelded, *sanato*, and the succulence of its deep pink flesh has few peers.

In the Veneto, grass-fed cows are butchered when they begin to ovulate, but before they have been mounted and given birth. They are known as *sorana*, and their meat is distinguished by a unique delicacy of flavor and texture. A *sorana*'s liver, when prepared in the Venetian style with smothered onions, is the sweetest I have known.

For great loins that produce the celebrated *fiorentina* T-bone steaks, one turns either to the Chianina cattle of western Tuscany or to the *razza romagnola* from Lugo, in Romagna, on the country's opposite coast.

Rome's specialty is *abbacchio*, milk-fed lamb that, dressed, weighs little more than 14 pounds from head to tail. Elsewhere in the hillier zones they use older lamb, sometimes gelded and then known as *castrato*. On the island of Sardinia, the national meat dish is *porcetto*, a whole suckling pig that is skewered and roasted for several hours near a slow wood fire.

For most families in Italy, meat has been a luxury, and today even affluent Italians feel uncomfortable sitting down to large portions of it. To the people it isn't just meat; it is what you eat with bread. The language has a word for it, *companatico*, from the Latin *cum panis*, which means precisely that, "with bread."

What has bread got to do with meat dishes? In the Italian tradition it is the implicit accompaniment, and the regional styles of Italy's meat cookery were conceived on the basis of that assumption. Whatever importance may or may not be attached to bread outside Italy, the flavors Italian meats are expected to deliver are related to the supporting part played by bread, a relationship that those attracted to Italian cooking might find illuminating to understand.

On American and English tables bread has a different role. It is an introduction to the meal and it could well be considered the preliminary course. It sometimes contains nuts, raisins, spices, or other components that make it unsuitable to eat with sauced meat. As though it were an extension of breakfast, one slathers it with butter or, in the current lamentable fashion, dunks it in olive oil. If soup is served one has a piece of bread with it, and I have seen people have bread with pasta. From that point on it is largely ignored, and in provincial English restaurants I have even had to struggle with waiters who wanted to remove it from the table before the meat course arrived.

In Italy the order of bread consumption is inverted. Save for establishments that cater to English-speaking visitors, there is no butter on the table to spread on bread before the meal is served. And we would find it grotesque to waste good olive oil by pouring it into saucers for dipping bread. Italians will eat bread with soup, if it has been placed in the dish and the soup poured over it, but they do not have it with pasta or risotto. Except when it is served with an antipasto of prosciutto and other cold meats, or as an appetizer of its own, in the form of *bruschetta*, at an Italian table bread begins to participate actively in the meal only when the meat course is served.

In the past, in Italy, meat was always too expensive for most people to appease their hunger with it. That task was satisfied by pasta, or soup, or risotto, which therefore became the protagonists of Italian menus. Yet the meal was incomplete if it didn't continue with a meat dish, however small. Even those who lived by the sea, such as my own family, alternated fish with meat.

On an Italian plate, the portion of meat may be frugal, but if quantity is short the length of flavors, with bread to extend them, makes up for it. Italian meat cookery has many stews and fricassees, which are the methods that extract most savor and which can be executed with economical cuts. Often there are vegetables that cook along with the meat, so that they enrich it with their own flavor while they help to fill the plate. There are ingenious ways of using ground meat, and of rolling meat slices around taste-enhancing ingredients.

All these are preparations whose flavors, to an Italian palate, call for bread. About serving the bread itself, you can choose to do as you please, but if you are after Italian flavor you should ask yourself, "How would this stew, this roast, this meat roll be with a thick slice of crusty bread? Is it juicy enough? Is its taste full enough?"

Veal

Pan-Roasted Veal with Radicchio

VITELLO IN TEGAME COL RADICCHIO

½ pound long-leaf Treviso radicchio OR Belgian endive

2 tablespoons extra virgin olive oil

1½ pounds veal tenderloin OR boned shoulder; see headnote

2 garlic cloves, peeled and lightly mashed with the handle of a knife

1½ tablespoons very finely chopped pancetta

Salt

⅓ cup dry white wine

Black pepper ground fresh

For 4 persons, or for 6 if preceded by a substantial first course

The succulence and tastiness of this roast derive in part from the cooking method and in part from the specific combination of meat and vegetable. The method is the characteristically Italian one of cooking meat on top of the stove rather than in the oven, a procedure that, as I have mentioned elsewhere in these pages, produces very satisfying depth of flavor.

You should also note that once the veal is cooked and sliced, you return it to the pot and turn the slices over at low heat in the combined cooking juices and vegetables. This is a brief step, taking less than a minute, which does wonders for the finished dish because every surface of the meat becomes impregnated by the flavors of the roast, and at the same time the meat recovers some of the heat lost during the slicing. I follow this step any time that I am roasting a whole piece of meat, whether it is veal, beef, or pork.

The radicchio helps the naturally mild-flavored veal achieve a greater intensity and richness of taste than it would otherwise be capable of. If the long-leafed Treviso radicchio is available to you, it should be your first choice, but failing that you can obtain equally satisfactory results with that closely related member of the chicory family, Belgian endive.

Tenderloin yields the most tender and juicy results with this recipe, but a nice boned shoulder will certainly not disappoint. If you are using shoulder, do not have the butcher roll it up and truss it, because you would then not be able to brown all its parts.

1. If you are using Treviso radicchio with its long root still attached, pare the root down to a short nub. If the root has been cut off, as it is in endive, trim away a thin slice from the butt end and detach the leaves from the radicchio or endive, discarding any blemished ones. Shred the leaves lengthwise into narrow strips about ¼ inch wide, soak briefly in cold water, and drain.

2. Choose a sauté pan or skillet into which the meat can fit cozily, put in the olive oil, and turn the heat on to medium high. When the oil is hot enough that it sizzles instantly on contact with the meat, put in the veal. Brown it thoroughly on one side, then turn it, adding the mashed garlic cloves.

3. When the meat has been browned on all sides, transfer it to a plate and add the pancetta to the pan. Turn the pancetta over three or four times during 1 minute of cooking, then put in the shredded radicchio or endive, sprinkling it lightly with salt. Turn the vegetable over a few times to coat it well, and cook it until it becomes limp and colored a light brown.

4. Return the meat to the pan, and add the wine. While you let the wine bubble completely away, use a wooden spoon to scrape loose any browning residues stuck to the bottom of the pan. Sprinkle the meat with salt and several grindings of pepper, turn it a few times, then lower the heat and put a lid on the pan. Cook at a slowly sputtering simmer, turning the meat over occasionally. Whenever you find that the juices in the pan are insufficient to keep the meat from sticking, add 2 to 3 tablespoons of water. Cook until the meat feels very tender when poked with a sharp fork, about 1 hour or more.

5. When done, transfer the piece of veal to a cutting board, slice it thin, and return the slices to the pan. Over low heat, for about half a minute, turn the slices over to coat them well. Serve from a warm platter, pouring the full contents of the pan over the meat.

AHEAD-OF-TIME NOTE: You can prepare the dish, including the slicing of the meat, several hours in advance, but preferably not overnight . Reheat gently but thoroughly, adding 2 tablespoons of water.

Stewed Shoulder of Veal with White Wine, Artichokes, and Cream

SPEZZATINO DI VITELLO CON CARCIOFI

———— ❧ ————

1 tablespoon vegetable oil

1 tablespoon butter

¼ pound pancetta, cut into very fine dice

2 pounds veal shoulder, cut into 2- to 2½-inch cubes

⅓ cup very thinly sliced onion

Salt

Black pepper ground fresh

½ cup dry white wine

6 medium artichokes, preferably with their stems on

A lemon cut in half

For Cooking the Artichokes

2 tablespoons extra virgin olive oil

½ cup chopped onion

2 tablespoons chopped garlic

2 tablespoons chopped Italian flat-leaf parsley

Salt

Black pepper ground fresh

It is no secret that I am partial to stews. There is no way to cook meat that pulls flavors so closely together or that permits such an expressive variety of combinations with vegetables, spices, and other ingredients.

This stew with onion, artichokes, and cream capitalizes on the finesse and delicacy that are veal's attributes. The onion, sliced very thin, cooks right along with the meat without any preliminary sautéing, thus binding its sweet flavor to it from the beginning. The artichoke is sliced and cooked apart at first so that it is already tender when it is added to the meat. When the stew is finished neither onion nor artichoke has a separate identity.

1. Choose a sauté pan or skillet large enough to contain both the meat and the artichokes later. Put in the vegetable oil, the butter, and the diced pancetta and turn on the heat to high. Lightly brown the pancetta, stirring it two or three times.

2. Slip in as many pieces of veal as will fit loosely, brown them well on all sides, transfer them to a bowl using a slotted spoon or spatula, put in more meat, and proceed thus, browning the veal in as many batches are required to do all the pieces.

3. Put the sliced onion in the pan, turn it over once or twice, return all the meat to the pan, add salt and several grindings of pepper, and turn over all ingredients. Cook until the onion becomes colored a light gold, then add the wine, scraping the bottom of the pan with a wooden spoon. Let the wine bubble for a few moments, then cover the pan and turn the heat down to minimum low.

4. If your artichokes have stems, cut them off and, with a small knife, pare away their hard, dark, outer skin, exposing the paler, tender core. If the stems are thick and long, cut them in half both lengthwise and

½ cup heavy cream

For 8 persons

crosswise. Put them in a bowl of cold water, squeezing lemon juice into it. From the artichokes themselves trim away the outer leaves and the tough, inedible tops as described on page 362. Cut the remaining hearts lengthwise in half, and slice these very, very fine. Add the slices to the bowl as you do them, squeezing a little more lemon juice over them.

Cooking the Artichokes

1. Choose another large skillet, put in the olive oil and the chopped onion, and turn on the heat to medium high. Cook, stirring frequently. When the onion begins to be colored a light gold, add the garlic, stirring as it cooks. As soon as you notice the garlic's aroma rising, add the parsley, stirring it once or twice.

2. Working very quickly, rinse the artichokes in fresh cold water, drain well, and add them to the pan together with salt and grindings of pepper. Cook, stirring frequently, until the artichokes begin to feel tender when tested with a fork. If the pan juices are not sufficient to keep the artichokes from sticking, add a few tablespoons of water, up to ½ cup.

3. Empty the contents of the artichoke pan into the pan with the meat, use a wooden spoon to turn over all ingredients, cover the pan, and continue cooking at very low heat until the meat feels very tender when prodded deeply with a fork. If the pan juices are not sufficient to keep the food from sticking, add a few tablespoons of water, up to ¼ cup at a time.

Finishing the Veal and Artichokes

By the time the veal is cooked, if you have sliced the artichokes fine enough you will find that they have nearly dissolved into a sauce-like consistency. Add the heavy cream, turn over the contents of the pan for about 1 minute with the wooden spoon, transfer to a warm platter, and serve at once.

AHEAD-OF-TIME NOTE: You can cook the whole dish, up to but not including the moment you add the cream, several hours in advance. Reheat gently, adding a little water if necessary. Swirl in the cream only when the meat has been warmed up through and through.

THE SCALOPPINE CUT

Veal *scaloppine* are the most useful cut of meat that a cook can work with. *Scaloppine* with Marsala, with lemon or orange, with mushrooms, *alla pizzaiola* (with tomato and capers), *saltimbocca* (*scaloppine* skewered with prosciutto and cheese), *involtini* (*scaloppine* rolled up as wrappers for cheese or vegetables), *uccelli scappati* (flown birds, *involtini* with sage, pancetta, and white wine)—these are some of the enticing combinations that win admirers wherever Italian food is served.

Cooking veal that has been cut into *scaloppine* is the fastest thing you can do in the kitchen, the flavor choices are broad, and a small quantity of meat goes a long way because there is absolutely no waste. It is all so simple and straightforward that one could say that *scaloppine* present no problems. Or rather they would present no problems if only more butchers would cut them correctly.

Scaloppine must be cut and pounded thin enough for you to cook them in a few bats of the eyelashes. But thinness is only half of the requirement. The sliced veal must lie perfectly flat on the bottom of the pan so that its surface can be browned uniformly and the meat cooked evenly throughout. Whether or not this happens depends on how the meat has been cut.

If it is understood that the piece from which *scaloppine* are sliced is a muscle, as indeed is all the meat we consume, the principle of the correct cut for *scaloppine* will become easy to grasp. Muscles are stacked in layers which, seen in cross section, form a finely hatched grain. The muscle layers, like so many bands of elastic, can stretch or contract. If one cuts through those layers or bands, severing them, the *scaloppine* will always lie flat. If, however, the butcher cuts the muscle along the same direction in which its layers are stacked, the moment the meat feels the heat of the pan of the pan it will tighten and contract. Instead of a flat slice you will bite into a wavy one; instead of a relaxed, tender piece of meat, you have a stringy, chewy one.

The packages of already sliced *scaloppine* that you find in your market's meat counter almost certainly contain meat cut the wrong way. A very good market, however, will usually have a good butcher; and a good butcher, like any good artisan, responds positively to a customer who knows. Get acquainted with your market's butcher. He will be happy for the opportunity to talk to someone on the other side of his enclosure. Explain to the man that you want *scaloppine* cut from the top round—the solid muscle from the upper part of the hind leg—and that you want them cut across, or perpendicular to, rather than along, or parallel to, the muscle's grain. Once the slices are cut correctly, the butcher can easily pound them thin, to an even thickness all around.

Marcella's shopping list with Victor's comments.

INVOLTINI

Involtini, also called *rollatini*, are thin slices of meat wound, jelly-roll fashion, around some other ingredient or ingredients. They have always been popular with my family, and I have grown fonder of them than any other way of using veal *scaloppine*. I enjoy putting them together, I like their look when they are on the plate, and I have not ever been bored with their taste—their ability to satisfy seems never to fail.

The two recipes that follow employ the same simple basic method of making *involtini* and illustrate the options that are available at distant ends of a remarkably broad range of flavors.

A quick look at the list of ingredients shows just how broad that range can be. In the first of the recipes there is tomato, garlic, capers, anchovy, and parsley, fundamental elements of an earthy, savory, fragrant, immediately gratifying style borrowed from the cooking of the south. The second *involtini* really contain just one soft-spoken ingredient, leeks, supported by slivers of Parmesan. The approach, less assertive yet not a bit less pleasing, is the sophisticated one of Piedmont.

In the south, it is probable that the first dish, whose name would change from *involtini* to *braciole*, would be made with beef, a less expensive meat. It's a choice available to you. But if you make it with veal, you may find, as I do, not only that it is juicier and sweeter, but that the total flavor of the meat roll has matchless freshness and lightness.

Veal Rolls Stuffed with Tomato, Capers, Anchovies, and Parmesan

INVOLTINI DI VITELLO FARCITI

2 or 3 fresh, ripe, firm plum tomatoes

2 medium garlic cloves, peeled

2 tablespoons capers

2 or 3 flat anchovy fillets, preferably the ones prepared at home as described on page 148

¼ cup chopped Italian flat-leaf parsley

1 pound veal *scaloppine*; please see "The Scaloppine Cut" (page 302) for introductory discussion

3 tablespoons freshly grated Parmigiano-Reggiano cheese

2 tablespoons vegetable oil

1 tablespoon butter

Flour, spread on a plate

Salt

Black pepper ground fresh

⅓ cup dry white wine

For 4 persons

Sturdy round wooden toothpicks

1. Peel the tomatoes raw using a vegetable peeler with a swiveling blade. Cut them lengthwise in half and scoop out the seeds without squeezing them. Cut them lengthwise into wedges ¼ inch wide.

2. Chop the garlic, capers, and anchovies together to a very fine consistency, reducing the anchovies to a pulp. Add the parsley and chop it briefly together with the other ingredients.

3. Lay the veal slices flat on a work surface, and coat them with the caper and anchovy mixture, distributing it thinly and uniformly. Sprinkle about ½ teaspoon Parmesan on top of each scallop and over it place one or two wedges of tomato. Roll up the scallop tightly and fasten with a toothpick or two.

4. Choose a skillet where all the *scalloppine* can subsequently fit in one uncrowded layer, without overlaps. Put in the oil and butter and turn on the heat to high. When the butter foam begins to subside, turn the scallops in the flour and slip them into the pan. Brown them on all sides, adding salt and pepper; then transfer them to a plate.

5. Add the wine to the pan, and any juices that may have run onto the plate with the veal. While the wine bubbles, scrape loose the browning residues from the bottom of the pan. When the wine has cooked down, forming a little dense sauce, return the scallops to the pan. Turn them for just a few seconds in the sauce, then transfer the entire contents of the pan to a warm platter and serve at once.

AHEAD-OF-TIME NOTE: You can cook the scallops an hour or two in advance up to the end of step 4, leaving the pan as it is. When reheating, before putting in the wine, warm up the pan with about 1 tablespoon of water, loosening the browning residues. When the water has evaporated, add the wine and proceed as described in the recipe.

Veal Rolls with Leeks and White Wine

INVOLTINI DI VITELLO CON I PORRI E IL VINO BIANCO

———————— 🍂 ————————

1 pound veal *scaloppine*;
please see the "The
Scaloppine Cut" (page
302) for introductory
discussion

2 large or 3 medium leeks

Salt

⅔ cup Parmigiano-
Reggiano cheese
whittled into slivers with
a peeler

Black pepper ground fresh

2 tablespoons butter

1 tablespoon vegetable oil

1 cup flour, spread on a
plate

½ cup dry white wine

————————————————

For 4 persons

Round wooden toothpicks

1. Trim the scaloppine into rectangles about 3 or 4 inches on one side and 5 to 6 inches on the other. If some of the slices don't yield quite those measurements, it won't affect the flavor of the *involtini*, but try to keep them reasonably similar in size.

2. Cut away all the green tops of the leeks, and slice the remainder lengthwise in half. Wash in a few changes of cold water.

3. Cook the leeks in boiling salted water until very soft when tested with a fork. The time depends on the youth and freshness of the leeks, but it will be in excess of 30 minutes. Drain thoroughly.

4. Lay the scaloppine flat on a work surface and cover each with a layer of leeks. Top with a few slivers of Parmesan and add salt and liberal grindings of black pepper. Roll up the *scaloppine* and fasten each one with a toothpick, inserting it lengthwise so that it lies parallel to the roll.

5. Choose a skillet large enough to accommodate the veal rolls later in a single layer without overlapping. Put in the butter and oil and turn on the heat to medium high. When the butter foam begins to subside, quickly turn the rolls over in the flour, and slip them into the pan. Turn the heat up to high and cook the meat for about 5 or 6 minutes, turning it until it becomes colored a dark brown over most of its surface.

6. Transfer the veal rolls to a plate using a slotted spoon or spatula. Add the wine to the pan and, as it bubbles, scrape loose the cooking residues with a wooden spoon. Boil the wine down to about half its original volume to obtain a fairly dense, dark juice.

7. Return the veal rolls to the pan, turn them over and over in the pan juices for about 1 minute, then transfer the entire contents of the pan to a very warm platter and serve at once.

AHEAD-OF-TIME NOTE: This dish does not take long to prepare, and it tastes quite a bit better when done from start to finish just before serving. You could pound the *scaloppine* a few hours earlier, if you like. Or, if you must, cook the *scaloppine* all the way through to the end of step 5, transfer them to a platter, cover with plastic wrap, and hold for up to 1 hour before resuming cooking. Do not clean the pan. When finishing the recipe, the veal rolls may have shed some liquid in their plate. Pour this into the skillet and boil it down before reheating the meat in the pan juices.

Breaded Veal Patties with Bell Pepper, Scallions, and Tomato

POLPETTE DI VITELLO CON PEPERONE, CIPOLLOTTI, E POMODORO

1 medium red or yellow bell
  pepper

4 medium scallions

3 tablespoons butter

1 pound ground veal

1 egg

1 cup freshly grated
  Parmigiano-Reggiano
  cheese

1¼ cups milk

½ cup broken-up fresh
  crumb—the soft,
  crustless part of bread—
  torn into small pieces

Salt

Black pepper ground fresh

1 cup fine, dry, unflavored
  bread crumbs, spread on
  a plate

1 tablespoon vegetable oil

2 cups canned imported
  Italian plum tomatoes,
  coarsely chopped, with
  their juice

6 veal patties

1. Wash the pepper, split it in half, remove the white core and all seeds, and cut the pepper's flesh into the finest possible dice.

2. Trim the root away from the scallions and remove any blemished outer leaves. Cut about 1 inch off the tops, wash the scallions in cold water, and slice them into thin rounds.

3. Put into a small skillet 1 tablespoon of butter, the diced pepper, and the scallion rounds, and turn on the heat to medium. Cook for a few minutes, stirring occasionally, until the vegetables are tender and have become lightly browned.

4. Put the meat, egg, and grated Parmesan in a mixing bowl.

5. Put the milk in a small saucepan and warm it over gentle heat. Don't let the milk come to a boil. As soon as you see the first little pearly bubble forming at the edge, take the pan off heat. Add the broken-up soft crumb, mashing it down until it is thoroughly soaked in milk.

6. Add the milk-soaked crumb to the meat, along with the cooked pepper and scallions, salt, and a few grindings of black pepper. Work the mixture with your fingertips until all ingredients are evenly combined. Shape the resulting veal mixture into six hamburger-shaped patties about 1 inch high.

7. Dredge each patty on both sides in the bread crumbs spread on a plate.

8. Choose a skillet broad enough to accommodate all the patties on one layer without overlapping. Put in the remaining 2 tablespoons of butter and the vegetable oil, and turn on the heat to medium high.

9.   When the fat is hot enough so that a little piece of meat dropped into it will sizzle, slip in all the patties. Brown them quickly on one side and as soon as that is done, turn them over with a flat metal spatula and do the other side.

10.   Add the chopped tomatoes with their juice, turn the patties over once or twice, lower the heat, and cook the tomatoes at a steady but gentle simmer for about 15 or 20 minutes, until they thicken into sauce and the fat begins to separate from the sauce, as described in the Note on page 133. Bits of the pepper and scallion may come loose, but this is no cause for concern because they become part of the sauce. Serve piping hot.

AHEAD-OF-TIME NOTE: You can cook the pepper and scallions in advance, several hours before making the patties.

VEAL PATTIES

Veal is lean meat; if we want to keep it moist and tender, we must keep in mind its lack of fat. This is particularly important when dealing with ground veal, which can dry out even faster than a solid piece. The surest way to produce a juicy veal patty is to bread it and fry it quickly over fairly high heat, and this is the method common to this recipe and the one that follows. That similarity aside, the two dishes are quite different.

For the first one, I sauté diced pepper and scallions and combine them with the ground veal, adding egg, grated Parmesan, and hot milk-soaked bread. Once the patties are breaded and fried, I braise them in tomato, simmering the tomato down to the density of sauce. To make the most of the sauce, I would serve them with lightly grilled crusty bread or, if there is no first course, with rice pilaf.

The simple patties of the second recipe owe their zestful flavor to capers. The coupling of capers and veal—the best-known example of which is the classic cold dish *vitello tonnato*, veal with tuna and caper sauce—is one that invests this meat with a sprightliness that it wears gracefully, without sacrificing any of its natural delicacy and finesse.

Simple Breaded Veal Patties with Capers

POLPETTINE DI VITELLO AI CAPPERI

½ pound ground veal

¼ teaspoon very, very finely
    chopped garlic

1 tablespoon chopped
    capers

1 tablespoon chopped
    Italian flat-leaf parsley

Salt

Black pepper ground fresh

1 egg

Fine, dry, unflavored bread
    crumbs, at least 1 cup,
    spread on a plate

Vegetable oil, enough to
    come at least 1 inch up
    the sides of the pan

For 4 persons

A wire rack set over a
heatproof tray

1. Combine the veal, garlic, capers, parsley, salt, and pepper in a bowl and mix thoroughly with a fork, distributing all ingredients uniformly.

2. Shape the mixture in your hands into round patties about 3 to 4 inches in diameter and 1 to 1½ inches thick. Work the mixture firmly but gently, without squeezing.

3. Break the egg into a shallow plate and beat it lightly with a fork.

4. Dip one of the patties in the beaten egg, lift it to let all excess egg flow back into the plate, then turn it in the bread crumbs. While it is lying in the bread crumbs, press it down firmly on one side with the palm of your hand, then turn it over and press the other side. Place the breaded patty on a platter and do another one, proceeding thus until they are all done.

5. Heat up the oil in a skillet. When the oil is hot enough to sizzle if tested with the edge of a patty dipped into it, slip in, using a spatula, as many patties as will fit loosely. As soon as the underside has formed a golden crust, turn the patties and brown the other side; then transfer them, using a slotted spatula, to the wire rack. If not all the patties fit into the pan at one time, as you remove one or two, replace them with those that have been left out. Avoid leaving the pan completely empty until you are finished frying.

AHEAD-OF-TIME NOTE: The patties are most enjoyable if served immediately when fried, but they are also quite nice a few minutes later, as long as they are still lukewarm. They can be breaded, however, and made ready for frying several hours in advance. If refrigerating them, let them come completely to room temperature before frying.

IL MANZO

Beef Stew with Peppers, Potatoes, and Milk

SPEZZATO DI MANZO AL LATTE CON PATATE E PEPERONI

⅓ cup vegetable oil

3¼ pounds beef chuck in cubes of about 2 inches

6 or 7 large onions, peeled and cut into wedges 1 inch thick, about 5 to 6 cups

Salt

3 tablespoons extra virgin olive oil

1 red and 1 yellow bell pepper, peeled and cut into 1-inch strips

Black pepper ground fresh

1 cup whole milk

6 boiling potatoes, peeled and cut into 4 or 5 pieces

For 8 persons

1. Choose a skillet or sauté pan in which you'll be able to brown all the beef cubes without overlapping. If you have no pan quite that large, plan to do the meat in two stages. Put in the vegetable oil, turn on the heat to high, and when the oil is quite hot, slip in the meat. It should sizzle as it goes in if the oil is hot enough. Turn the meat over to brown it evenly on all sides, then use a slotted spoon or spatula to transfer it to a bowl.

2. Into the pan put the cut-up onion and some salt. Cook, always at high heat, for 2 or 3 minutes, stirring occasionally, until the onion becomes colored a tawny gold. When the onion is partly cooked—it must not become tender at this stage—transfer it with a slotted spoon or spatula to the bowl containing the browned meat cubes.

3. Choose a large lidded saucepan or casserole made of heavy ware, such as enameled cast iron. Put in the olive oil, the meat and onions, the bell peppers, salt, and liberal grindings of black pepper. Turn on the heat to low and cover the pot. Cook at a steady but very gentle simmer for 1 hour.

4. Add the milk and cut-up potatoes, cover, and cook at a slow simmer for another 30 minutes, turning the contents of the pot over from time to time. Reposition the lid, setting it slightly askew, and continue cooking at a steady simmer for an additional 30 minutes. When done, the meat should feel very tender when tested with a fork; and the peppers and onion and some of the potatoes will have dissolved into a dense, creamy mixture.

AHEAD-OF-TIME NOTE: The dish can be cooked through to the end even a day or two in advance. Reheat gently but thoroughly just before serving.

TWO BEEF STEWS

Stews spring out of a hunger for meat and out of having to make do with humble cuts. Necessity is the mother of their flavor, and a very good mother it has been. From the list of ingredients in this and the preceding stew, one can compose the eternal Italian farmhouse scene: vegetables from the garden, pickles put up the previous summer, fresh milk, wine, a little cooking fat. And equally perennial is the ability of the dishes to supply comfort and warmth.

Like all stews, these are as kind to the one who makes them as to those who eat them. For most of the time they are cooking they do not need much looking after, and they can be made at any time that is convenient and served on another day.

Stewed Beef Cubes with Pickles, Capers, and Red Wine

SPEZZATO DI MANZO AL VINO ROSSO CON CETRIOLINI E CAPPERI

2 tablespoons vegetable oil

1½ pounds beef, preferably chuck, cut into 2-inch cubes

½ cup flour, spread on a plate

¼ cup extra virgin olive oil

⅔ cup finely chopped onion

¼ pound pancetta, cut into thin strips

A medium to thick carrot, chopped fine, about ½ cup

A medium celery stalk, chopped fine, about ½ cup

3 tablespoons very finely chopped small cucumber pickles such as *cornichons*, about 4 pickles

2 tablespoons capers, chopped very fine

Salt

Black pepper ground fresh

⅔ cup not too tannic red wine such as Barbera or a young Chianti or Merlot

For 4 persons

1. Put the vegetable oil in a small skillet and turn on the heat to high. Dredge some of the meat cubes in flour, no more at one time than can fit loosely in the pan; and as soon as the oil is hot enough to sizzle when a piece of meat is slipped into it, put the cubes that you dredged in flour into the skillet.

2. Turn them for a minute or so until they become colored a dark brown on all sides, then transfer them to a bowl, using a slotted spoon or spatula. Dredge some more of the beef cubes in flour, and repeat the procedure until you have browned all the meat. (The reason you don't want to turn it in flour all at one time in advance is that the coating would become soggy and prevent you from obtaining a crisp surface on the meat.)

3. Choose a saucepan that can easily contain all the beef cubes; put into it the olive oil, the chopped onion, and the pancetta strips, and turn on the heat to medium. Cook, stirring from time to time, until the onion becomes colored a rich gold; then add the carrot, celery, pickles, and capers. Cook, stirring from time to time, for 3 or 4 minutes.

4. Add the browned beef cubes, salt, and several grindings of black pepper, and turn the meat over two or three times. Add the wine, let it simmer for about 1 minute, then lower the heat to minimum and set a cover slightly ajar over the pan. Cook, occasionally turning the ingredients over, until the meat feels very tender when prodded with a fork, about 1 hour. Serve piping hot.

NOTE: To save time, you can chop the carrot, celery, pickles, and capers all together in a food processor.

AHEAD-OF-TIME NOTE: You can cook the dish several hours in advance, or even the day before. Warm up over moderate heat, adding 1 or 2 tablespoons water to keep the meat from drying.

Seasoned Sliced Grilled Beefsteaks

TAGLIATA DI MANZO

Italian beefsteak is rarely, if ever, quite as tender as the best of the American, but what it lacks in mere tenderness it more than makes up through the taste of its preparation. An Italian cook understands that grilling alone, is not sufficient to produce good flavor. Flavor is coaxed from the meat by a confident sprinkling of salt while it is cooking—not after it is served—by good olive oil, by pepper, and on occasion, by a judiciously restrained use of garlic and herbs.

In order to distribute the condiments more thoroughly, Italians often cut a large grilled steak into several thick slices, thereby producing many more surfaces to coat with seasoning. A steak served thus is called a *tagliata*, from the Italian for "to cut," *tagliare*.

Over-the-Stove Version

⅓ cup extra virgin olive oil

1 dozen medium garlic cloves, peeled

A sprig or two of fresh rosemary

2 boneless rib or strip steaks, cut 2 inches thick

Salt

Black pepper ground fresh

For 4 persons

A cast-iron skillet OR stove-top grill

1. Put the olive oil and the whole garlic cloves in a large skillet or sauté pan and turn on the heat to medium high. Cook, stirring two or three times, until the garlic becomes colored a pale gold. Turn off the heat and add the rosemary, turning it over a few times.

2. Turn on the heat under the cast-iron skillet or the stove-top grill to very high. When the pan or grill surface is very hot put on the meat, which should sizzle instantly and quickly begin to smoke. Cook it for 2 or 3 minutes until it is a very dark brown on one side; then turn it over, sprinkle with salt, and do the other side.

3. Transfer the steaks to a cutting board and cut them on an angle into slices about ½ inch thick. The meat should be quite, quite rare.

4. Turn on the heat to medium high under the pan containing the oil, garlic, and rosemary. As soon as the oil begins to heat up, put in the steak slices together with any juices they may have shed on the cutting board. Cook for about 1 minute at very lively heat, turning the meat over frequently and adding liberal grindings of black pepper.

5. Transfer the meat to a warm platter and pour over it all the oil and juices in the pan, but hold back the rosemary and garlic. Serve piping hot.

Outdoor Version

6 or 7 whole garlic cloves, peeled

¼ cup extra virgin olive oil

1 tablespoon chopped fresh rosemary

Four 1-inch-thick strip or rib beefsteaks

Salt

Black pepper ground fresh

For 4 persons

A charcoal or gas-fired outdoor grill

A serving platter kept hot

1. Twenty minutes in advance of grilling the meat, light the charcoal or turn on the gas grill to high.

2. Put the garlic and olive oil in a small saucepan, turn on the heat to medium high, and cook the garlic, stirring from time to time, until it becomes colored nut brown. Add the chopped rosemary, stir once or twice, then remove from heat.

3. Cook the meat to the degree of doneness you prefer: for rare, which is my preference, about 3½ minutes on one side and 2 minutes on the other. When turning over the steaks, season them with salt and liberal grindings of black pepper and, at the same time, put the saucepan over a corner of the grill to reheat the oil and garlic.

4. When the steaks are done, transfer them to the hot platter and cut them into several thick slices, detaching the meat from the bone, should it have any. Pour the contents of the saucepan over the meat, and serve at once.

Boiled Beef and Its Broth

IL LESSO DA BRODO

---

1 medium potato, washed
   and peeled

1 whole ripe tomato

1 medium carrot, peeled

1 stalk celery, with some of
   its leaves

¼ red or yellow bell pepper,
   seeds and white pith
   removed

8 cups water

4 pounds beef chuck or
   plate or brisket, with
   some bone in

Salt

---

*Boiled beef for 4, and 6 cups
degreased broth*

A pot in which the water will
cover the meat by 2 inches;
see step 1 below

There are two reasons why you should make boiled beef. The first is
for the beef itself. Slow cooking in abundant moisture softens beef's
toughest tissues and produces meat with a succulence and a fine, delicate flavor that no other method can approach. A perfectly boiled piece
of beef, however plain the description may sound, is as fine a dish of
meat as you can bring to the table.

The second reason is for the collateral product of boiling—the
broth. No risotto or soup can equal the finesse of one made with
homemade beef broth. It is, moreover, so practical. It cooks with very
little supervision, and you can freeze broth and use it weeks later.

When I say broth, I do not mean stock. The dense aromas of stock
are hostile to light-handed Italian cooking. Broth is water in which
solid meat and a few vegetables have cooked, nothing more. The vegetables I use, and subsequently discard, are carrot, celery, and onion. I
add to them a peeled potato that soaks up the flavor of the fat, a piece
of bell pepper that brings a whiff of freshness, a tomato whose acidity
prevents the broth from becoming cloying. I do not put in an herb
bouquet, because I don't want those fragrances interfering with any
dish in which I will be using the broth. I do not roast bones, and I no
longer make broth with chicken. Chickens today make distractingly
harsh broths.

Making Boiled Beef

1. The meat must cook covered by 2 inches of water, so you need a
pot that not only can contain the meat and vegetables and 8 cups water
but is narrow and tall enough to keep the water level high. Before you
begin to cook, you can try several pots, if you are not sure, with all the
ingredients.

2. Put all the vegetables and the water in the pot, bring to a slow boil,
and cook for 10 minutes.

3. Add the meat, cover the pot, and turn up the heat to high in order to return to a boil as rapidly as possible. When the water has begun to boil again, adjust heat so that it simmers steadily, but very gently.

4. After 1½ hours, add 2 tablespoons salt.

5. Cook another 1½ to 2 hours, depending on the thickness of the meat. It should feel tender when prodded with a fork.

6. Serve the meat while it is still hot with one of the condiments in this chapter or dressed simply with very good extra virgin olive oil and a few drops of lemon juice, or with the red or green sauces in my previous book, or with horseradish or mustard, as you prefer.

7. If you are not going to eat the beef at this time, slice it thin. Lay the slices in a flat refrigerator container, moisten each layer of meat, as you put it in the container; with olive oil, lemon juice, and salt; close the container tightly; and refrigerate. This is marvelous as a cold luncheon dish with salad.

NOTE: In a laboratory, broth at room temperature could well be used as a culture for growing bacteria, so you must either use it immediately or freeze it quickly.

Keeping the Broth

1. Having removed the meat and discarded all the vegetables, pour the broth through a large strainer lined with a single-ply paper towel into a broad bowl. Cover with plastic wrap and keep it in the refrigerator one day, or at most two.

2. When you take it out you will see that the fat has congealed in a thick yellow layer on top. Lift the fat out a piece at a time with a large, flat spatula, and discard it.

3. Pour the clear, degreased broth into ice cube trays and put them in the freezer. When it has solidly frozen, unmold the cubes, put them into airtight plastic freezer bags, label them, and return them to the freezer. If you are keeping the broth longer than 2 months, boil it again for 15 minutes, and refreeze it. Do not keep longer than another month.

Lamb

L'Agnello

Roast Boned Leg of Lamb Abruzzi-Style with Potatoes

COSCIOTTO D'AGNELLO ARROSTITO ALL'ABRUZZESE

5 medium garlic cloves, peeled and cut into thin wedges

A 4½- to 5-pound leg of lamb, boned and butterflied

Salt

Black pepper ground fresh

3 tablespoons extra virgin olive oil

½ cup grated Romano cheese

2 pounds potatoes, washed, peeled, and cut into 1-inch dice

5 to 6 sprigs fresh rosemary OR 2 teaspoons chopped dried leaves

For 6 persons

The foothills of Abruzzi, a ruggedly handsome and mountainous region that marks the southern limit of what mapmakers designate as central Italy, are home to shepherds and their flocks. Lambs are raised for meat and their mothers are milked to produce pecorino cheese. The recipe for roast leg of lamb given here combines both products of this sheep-tending culture.

Roasting a whole leg does not happen every day or even every month, but it can replace the customary stewed or fricasseed shoulder and loins on a holiday, or when celebrating a happy private event; a communion, a wedding, the birth of a child. I have seen it done in a wood-fired pizza oven, a departure from the usual over-the-stove method; but aside from that, the flavor foundation is that of nearly every Italian roast, garlic and rosemary. A delicious accessory to the dish is the potatoes, which are diced small and cooked along with the meat, each little nugget becoming engorged with the rich flavor of this roast.

1. Turn on the oven to 500°.

2. Force all the garlic wedges into the meat, distributing them broadly and poking them in as deeply as you can with a fingertip.

3. Sprinkle the lamb with salt and generous grindings of pepper.

4. Choose a baking pan that can contain the leg lying flat and all the potatoes. Put in the meat and use a brush to coat it evenly on all sides with the olive oil. Rub the grated cheese over the lamb, coating all

sides and patting it down firmly with the palm of your hand. Surround the leg with the diced potatoes, spreading the rosemary sprigs or sprinkling the chopped dried leaves over both meat and potatoes.

5. Place the pan in the upper-middle level of the preheated oven. After 20 minutes, sprinkle salt and pepper over the potatoes and turn these and the meat over. Then return the pan to the oven for another 20 minutes. Transfer the entire contents of the pan to a very warm platter and serve at once. The plates at table should be warm too.

NOTE: Lamb, when cooked Abruzzi-style, is tender and juicy but done medium-well. If you prefer to have it rarer, put the pan in the oven with just the potatoes and the rosemary, roast them for 15 minutes, sprinkle with salt and pepper, turn them over, make room for the lamb in the center, and return the pan to the oven. After 15 minutes, turn the meat over on its other side and continue cooking for another 10 minutes, or to taste. Make a small cut in the thickest part of the leg to see whether it is done to suit you or needs to be cooked slightly longer.

AHEAD-OF-TIME NOTE: You can peel and dice the potatoes a few hours in advance, if you want to, keeping them wrapped in a dishcloth; but you would not want to cook the lamb ahead of time deliberately. If a last-minute emergency compels you to put the roast aside after it's done, reheat it in a moderate oven covered with aluminum foil.

The three lamb stews that follow come from as many regions: the pastoral Marches, a former papal dominion in central Italy; Apulia, the ancient Greek colony in the southeast; and the remote island of Sardinia. Their landscapes, their histories, and their dialects are completely dissimilar, and so are their food cultures, except that for all three a major source of meat is lamb.

Reading the ingredients list of the recipes is equivalent to taking a brief tour of regional cooking styles. In the stew from the Marches, a generous dose of tomatoes helps to generate a sunny, fruity taste. The Apulian stew is sweetened by a large helping of onion and scented with oregano. In both, potatoes play a familiar role, sucking in and releasing a concentrated sampling of flavors. The Sardinian dish, one of several which I owe to that gifted cook from Olbia, Rita D'Enza, is spiked with the aromatic accents of the island, represented here by orange zest and fennel seeds. The cauliflower is a brilliant touch, moderating through its mildness the gamy taste that lamb sometimes has.

In all three stews, the cut employed is the shoulder, a choice originally prompted by frugality, but then confirmed by its fuller and juicier flavor.

Rita D'Enza's Fricasseed Lamb Shoulder with Cauliflower

STUFATO D'AGNELLO COL CAVOLFIORE ALLA MODA DI RITA D'ENZA

2 tablespoons extra virgin olive oil

3 pounds lamb shoulder cut into 2-inch pieces

½ cup chopped onion

1 tablespoon chopped garlic

1½ teaspoons chopped rosemary leaves

1½ teaspoons fennel seeds

Salt

1. Choose a sauté pan that can later accommodate all the meat and the cauliflower, put in the olive oil, and turn on the heat to medium high. As soon as the oil is hot enough that it sizzles instantly when you put in a piece of meat, slip in the lamb, a few pieces at a time. Brown the meat on one side, then turn it, and when it has browned well on all sides, transfer it to a platter using a slotted spoon or spatula.

2. Add the chopped onion to the pan and cook it, stirring frequently, until it has become colored a medium gold. Add the garlic and cook it, stirring, just until its scent begins to rise. Before its color deepens, return all the lamb pieces to the pan.

Black pepper ground fresh

¾ cup dry white wine

A head of cauliflower, about 1 pound

½ cup canned imported Italian plum tomatoes, cut up, with their juice

The zest of 1 orange peel

For 4 persons

3. Add the rosemary, fennel seeds, salt, and liberal grindings of black pepper. Using a wooden spoon, turn over all ingredients two or three times to coat them well.

4. Add the white wine, let it bubble briskly for a few seconds, then turn the heat down to very low and put a lid on the pan. Cook, turning the contents of the pan over from time to time, for about 1½ hours at a very gentle but steady simmer, until the meat feels very tender when prodded with a fork.

5. While the lamb is cooking, trim away the tough outer leaves of the cauliflower, wash the head in cold water, then cut it into little clumps about the size of a small potato.

6. When the meat is tender, add the cut-up cauliflower, sprinkle it with salt, add the tomatoes, turn over all the ingredients two or three times, then cover the pan again and continue cooking for about 8 minutes or so, until the cauliflower feels tender when tested with a fork. If at any time during the entire cooking cycle you find that the pan juices have dried up and the food is likely to stick to the bottom, add 2 tablespoons of water. If, on the contrary, when the meat and cauliflower are both done you find that the cooking juices are too runny, uncover the pan, turn up the heat, and boil them down.

7. When the cauliflower is done, add the orange zest, turn over the contents of the pan once or twice, then transfer to a warm platter and serve at once.

AHEAD-OF-TIME NOTE: You can cook the lamb all the way through several hours in advance, but add the cauliflower only when you are ready to resume cooking and complete the dish for serving.

Stewed Shoulder of Lamb Marches-Style with Potatoes, Rosemary, and Chili Pepper

UMIDO D'AGNELLO ALLA MARCHIGIANA

1 pound fresh ripe
  tomatoes OR 2 cups
  canned imported Italian
  plum tomatoes, cut up,
  with their juice

2 tablespoons extra virgin
  olive oil

3½ pounds lamb shoulder
  with the bone in, cut up
  into 3-inch pieces

6 whole garlic cloves, peeled

2 sprigs fresh rosemary OR
  1 tablespoon dried
  leaves, chopped fine

Salt

Chopped chili pepper,
  ¼ teaspoon or to taste

1 pound new potatoes,
  washed, peeled, and cut
  into 1½-inch wedges

For 4 to 6 persons

1. If using fresh tomatoes, skin them using a swivel-bladed vegetable peeler, and cut into fine pieces without removing their seeds.

2. Choose a sauté pan large enough to contain all the meat and potatoes later, put in the olive oil, and turn on the heat to medium.

3. When the oil is hot, slip in as many pieces of lamb as will fit loosely, brown them on all sides, transfer them to a bowl using a slotted spoon or spatula, put in more lamb pieces, and proceed thus.

4. Put the garlic and rosemary in the pan, stir once, then quickly return all the meat to the pan. Add salt, turning the meat over two or three times.

5. Add whichever tomato you are using, fresh or canned; put in the chili pepper; turn over the lamb pieces once or twice; then lower the heat to minimum and cover the pan.

6. Cook for about 1 hour, turning the meat over from time to time. Whenever it should become necessary to replenish the cooking juices to keep the meat from sticking, add ¼ cup water.

7. As soon as the lamb feels tender when prodded with a fork, add the cut-up potatoes and some salt. Turn over all the ingredients, cover the pan, and continue cooking for approximately 30 more minutes until the potatoes are done, testing them with a fork. While the potatoes are cooking, occasionally turn them and the meat over, adding a little water whenever necessary.

8. Transfer the contents of the pan to a warm platter and serve at once.

AHEAD-OF-TIME NOTE: You can cook the stew until done even the day before. Reheat gently in a covered pan on top of the stove, turning the meat and potatoes and adding a little water if necessary.

Pan-Roasted Lamb Apulian-Style with Onions and Potatoes

AGNELLO IN TEGAME ALLA PUGLIESE

3 tablespoons extra virgin olive oil

3 pounds lamb shoulder with the bone in, cut into 4-inch pieces

2 large yellow onions, cut into ½-inch-thick slices, about 3 cups

Salt

Chopped hot chili pepper, ¼ teaspoon or to taste

½ cup dry white wine

4 or 5 medium potatoes, peeled, washed, and cut into 1-inch pieces

Oregano, 1½ teaspoons if fresh, ½ teaspoon if dried

For 4 persons

1. Put the oil in a sauté pan large enough to contain all the ingredients and turn on the heat to medium high. When the oil is hot enough, it sizzles instantly when a piece of meat goes in. When that heat is reached, put as many pieces of lamb as will fit loosely in a single layer without overlapping. When the meat has browned deeply on one side, turn it to do the other side. When it is browned on all sides, remove it from the pan using a slotted spoon or spatula. If you did not have enough room in the pan to do all the meat at one time, proceed in batches until you have browned it all.

2. Put the sliced onions in the pan and add salt. Turn the onions over to coat them well, lower the heat, and cook at a slow pace so that the onions become limp before they become colored pale nut brown.

3. Return all the meat to the pan, sprinkle with salt, add the chili pepper, and adjust heat to cook at a lively simmer.

4. When the contents of the pan are simmering, add the wine, let it bubble gently for at least 1 full minute, then add the potatoes and the oregano. Turn all ingredients over to coat them well, put a lid on the pan, and turn the heat down to low. Cook until both the lamb and the potatoes feel very tender when prodded with a fork, about 40 minutes. If during the cooking the pan juices should become insufficient to keep the food from sticking to the pan, add up to ⅓ cup water. Taste and correct for salt, and serve piping hot.

AHEAD-OF-TIME NOTE: The entire dish can be cooked several hours or even a day in advance. Reheat very gently and thoroughly, adding a little bit of water if necessary.

Il Maiale

Pan-Roasted Pork Tenderloin Wild Boar–Style with Shiitake Mushrooms

FILETTO DI MAIALE ALLA MODA DEL CINGHIALE CON FUNGHI DI BOSCO

2 pounds pork tenderloin, cut into 2 pieces

¼ cup extra virgin olive oil

1 cup very thinly sliced onion

3 large garlic cloves, peeled and lightly mashed with the flat side of a knife blade

4 or 5 whole bay leaves

½ cup finely cut celery, both stalk and leaves

Rosemary leaves, 1 tablespoon if fresh, ½ tablespoon if dried, coarsely chopped

1 cup red wine; see headnote for suggestions

1 pound fresh shiitake mushrooms

What I like about game is the method by which it is prepared, the long marinade with wine and herbs that produces dense, sumptuous flavor. What I don't particularly like is the undomesticated taste of game itself, especially the furred varieties.

Boar are plentiful in Italy, especially in Tuscany and Umbria, for whose vineyards they are something of a menace, feeding on the young plantings. Grape growers retaliate by turning the pests into boar sausages, boar prosciutto, and dishes such as the one below.

Instead of boar, I have used pork, whose tenderloin is so much more succulent. Otherwise I have followed the classic procedure, marinating the meat overnight in olive oil, onion, garlic, herbs, and red wine. My husband suggests that the ideal wine to use would be Rosso di Montalcino. Like its sibling, Brunello di Montalcino, it is made from the *sangiovese* grape, whose juicy, fruity quality is exactly what you want in a marinade. Other Italian red wines from that same grape, such as Chianti or Vino Nobile di Montepulciano, would be good choices, or you may turn with comparably good results to a Rhône, a California merlot, or an Australian shiraz, among others.

Had I fresh porcini mushrooms available I would unquestionably use those, but when there are none in the market, I am content with fresh shiitake caps. I cook the shiitake in butter because it gives them a luscious mouth feel recalling that of porcini, but if you'd rather use olive oil, as in the rest of the recipe, you may.

1 tablespoon butter; see
    headnote

Salt

Black pepper ground fresh

For 6 persons or, if no first
course is served, for 4

1. Choose a deep rectangular or oval dish that can contain the meat and all the other ingredients except for the mushrooms, and put the pork tenderloin into it along with 3 tablespoons of olive oil and the onion, garlic, bay leaves, celery, rosemary, and red wine. Turn the meat over several times to coat it well, then cover the dish with plastic wrap and put it in the refrigerator overnight. Take it out occasionally whenever convenient to turn the pork over, basting it with its marinade.

2. The following day, take the meat out of the refrigerator at least 1 hour before proceeding with the preparation of the dish. Turn it over and baste it when you take it out of the refrigerator, and once every half hour thereafter.

3. Detach the mushroom caps from the stems, discarding the stems. Wash the caps quickly in running cold water without letting them soak. Pat them dry gently but thoroughly with a cloth towel, and cut them into thin slices.

4. Lift the tenderloin out of the deep dish, pick out any bits of the vegetables from the marinade that may be sticking to it, and pat the meat dry with kitchen towels.

5. Choose a skillet that can accommodate the two pieces of pork without their overlapping, put in the remaining tablespoon of olive oil, and turn on the heat to high. When the oil is hot enough to sizzle when you put in the meat, slip in both pieces. Turn the meat over to brown it evenly all around, then transfer it to a platter.

6. Pour all the marinade from the deep dish into the skillet, turn the heat down to low, and cover the pan. Cook, stirring occasionally, until all the vegetables are very soft or almost dissolved.

7. While the marinade is cooking, put 1 tablespoon of butter in a medium skillet, turn the heat on to medium, and add the sliced shiitake caps with some salt. Cook, turning the mushrooms over occasionally, until the liquid they shed evaporates completely and they have become very tender.

(continued)

8. When the vegetables of the marinade are very soft, add the cooked shiitake, cooking them together for about a minute or two. Add both pieces of pork, sprinkling them with salt and several grindings of black pepper, and raise the heat to high. Cook the meat for 10 minutes on one side, then turn it over and cook the other side for another 10 minutes.

9. Transfer the meat to a cutting board, cut it into slices about ⅓ inch thick, and place the slices on a very warm serving platter. Remove the bay leaves from the marinade—and the garlic cloves, if you can find them—then cover the meat with the cooked marinade and mushrooms and serve at once.

AHEAD-OF-TIME NOTE: When the overnight marinating of the meat is complete, it would be desirable to proceed at once through all the succeeding steps, but if you wish you can stop a few hours in advance right after the start of step 8, when the shiitake and the cooked-down marinade have been combined. Cook the meat, however, only when ready to serve, because it may dry out and become stringy if reheated.

Pork Strips with Broccoli and Carrots

FETTUCCE DI MAIALE STUFATE CON BROCCOLI E CAROTE

A bunch of broccoli, about
1½ pounds

4 or 5 medium carrots

3 flat anchovy fillets,
preferably the ones
prepared at home as
described on page 148

1 pound pork loin

2 tablespoons flour

3 tablespoons extra virgin
olive oil

2 teaspoons chopped garlic

⅓ cup dry white wine

Salt

Black pepper ground fresh

4 ample or 6 moderate portions

It has always intrigued me to note that of all the cuisines of the world the Italian has far less in common with those of its Latin neighbors Spain and France than it does with that of China. Both Italy and China make pasta, for example, to cite one of the most obvious parallels. But their culinary paths draw close in so many other ways: in their direct handling of ingredients, in the many quick-cooked dishes, in the integration of vegetables with meat or fish, in pairing sweet with sour.

When I first saw strips of pork with broccoli stems and carrots cut into thin sticks in this dish I wondered who the Chinese cook was in the kitchen. But it was the kitchen of my mother's house in Cesenatico and there was no one there but my mother's devoted companion Romana, the woman from Bari who looked after her during the last years of her long life. When I told Romana what my impression had been she didn't know what to make of it. "*Ma va!* Go on! Do the Chinese really eat pork and anchovies?" I couldn't say. Do they, I wonder?

1. Detach the largest stems of the broccoli. Using a sharp paring knife, pare away their hard, dark green rind, exposing the tender, paler core. Cut them into sticks about ½ inch thick and 2 inches long. You should get about 1½ cups. Soak briefly in cold water and drain well. (You can boil what remains of the bunch and dress it with olive oil and vinegar for a warm salad or use it in a soup; see pages 82 and 90.)

2. Peel the carrots and trim them down into sticks the same size as the broccoli. You should have about 1½ cups.

3. Chop the anchovies very, very fine, to a pulp.

4. Cut the pork into strips about ½ inch wide and thick and 3 inches long. Put them in a bowl, pour the flour over them, and turn them over to coat them evenly.

(continued)

5. Choose a skillet that will contain all your ingredients in a single layer with little overlapping, put in the olive oil and garlic, and turn on the heat to medium. Cook the garlic, stirring frequently, just until tiny bubbles appear in the pan and the garlic's scent begins to rise.

6. Turn the heat up to high and put in all the meat. As soon as you have browned one side, turn it over and do the other side. Add the broccoli and carrot sticks, and turn them over several times to coat them well. Add the chopped anchovies and the white wine. Let the wine bubble a few seconds, briskly stirring the contents of the pan, then turn the heat down to medium low and cover the pan. Cook at a gentle but regular simmer for about 15 or 20 minutes, occasionally turning over the contents of the pan, until the vegetables feel quite tender when tested with a fork. During that time, you will probably need to replenish the cooking juices to keep the food from sticking to the pan. Add up to 3 tablespoons of water whenever it becomes necessary. Taste to adjust for salt, add liberal grindings of black pepper, turn all ingredients over once or twice, then transfer to a warm platter and serve at once.

AHEAD-OF-TIME NOTE: All the preparatory steps—trimming the vegetables, chopping the anchovies and garlic, slicing (but not flouring) the pork—can be done several hours in advance. When cooked, the meat must be served at once because if reheated it would become tough.

Stuffed Pork Rolls with Pickles and Sage Braised in Tomatoes and White Wine

INVOLTINI DI MAIALE AL POMODORO CON SALVIA E CETRIOLINI

1 to 1¼ pounds boneless pork loin, sliced and beaten thin like veal *scaloppine*

¼ pound pancetta, sliced paper thin

A dozen or more small cucumber pickles in vinegar, such as *cornichons*

3 tablespoons extra virgin olive oil

4 to 5 peeled garlic cloves

6 whole fresh or dried sage leaves

⅓ cup flour, spread on a plate

Salt

Black pepper ground fresh

⅓ cup dry white wine

⅔ cup peeled and seeded fresh, ripe tomatoes OR canned imported Italian plum tomatoes, chopped coarse, with their juice

For 4 persons

Round wood toothpicks

Pork is the meat that responds better than any other, perhaps, to lively seasoning. Not for nothing is it chosen to make the tastiest sausages and salamis. And lively is the word for the seasoning of pickles and sage that makes these pork rolls so easy to like. Pancetta, the delicately peppery and spiced Italian bacon, has an important part too. It not only weighs in with its flavors but bastes the meat as it cooks and keeps it from drying, a not uncommon fate of many pork dishes.

1. Cover each slice of pork with sliced pancetta and a pickle, or half a pickle if it is not very small. Roll up the meat and fasten each roll by skewering it lengthwise with a toothpick.

2. Choose a skillet or sauté pan that can later accommodate all the pork rolls in a single layer without overlaps; put in the oil, garlic, and sage leaves; and turn on the heat to medium. Cook, stirring frequently, until the garlic becomes colored deep nut brown, then remove it from the pan.

3. Dredge the pork rolls in flour one at a time, slipping each into the pan the moment it is coated with flour. Turn the rolls over in the pan, cooking them until their surface acquires a rich brown color.

4. Add salt and several grindings of pepper, turn the rolls over once or twice, then add the wine. Let the wine simmer for about 1 minute, then add the chopped tomatoes with their juice. Turn the heat down, cover the pan, and cook at a gentle simmer for 30 to 35 minutes, turning the rolls over occasionally, until the meat feels tender when prodded with a fork. Serve promptly.

AHEAD-OF-TIME NOTE: Pork can become dry when reheated, so it is desirable to cook these rolls just before serving. Should it be necessary to prepare them in advance, you can do so several hours earlier. Warm them up in a covered pan, adding a tablespoon or two of water, over very slow heat.

Pork Balls with Beans and Tomato

POLPETTINE DI MAIALE E FAGIOLI BORLOTTI

1 cup dried cranberry
  beans, soaked overnight,
  OR 1 pound unshelled
  fresh cranberry beans

4 garlic cloves, 2 lightly
  mashed and peeled, 2
  peeled and chopped

10 medium sage leaves, 4
  whole and 6 chopped

Salt

Black pepper ground fresh

½ cup milk

½ cup crumb, the soft,
  crustless part of bread

¾ pound ground pork

⅓ cup very finely chopped
  onion

3 tablespoons finely
  chopped Italian flat-leaf
  parsley

1 egg

1 cup fine, dry, unflavored
  bread crumbs, spread on
  a plate

4 tablespoons extra virgin
  olive oil

Hah, you are making pork and beans!" said my raised-in-America son when he saw me working on this recipe. In responding I allowed as how it could be described as pork *with* beans, but I begged him please never to call it pork and beans. No offense intended, my Boston friends.

The ground pork is mixed with chopped onion, parsley, an egg, and milk-soaked bread, and shaped into the tiniest of meatballs. These are cooked with a family garlicky tomato sauce, and then combined with beans that have been cooked with sage and mashed garlic.

My own favorite way of serving this dish is with the soft, fine polenta from the recipe on page 237.

1. If you are using dried beans that have been soaking overnight, drain and rinse them. If using fresh beans, shell them and wash them in cold water. Whichever kind you are using, put them in a saucepan with 2 mashed and peeled garlic cloves, 4 whole sage leaves, a pinch of salt, a grinding or two of black pepper, and enough water to cover by 2 or 3 inches. Cover tightly, bring to a gentle but steady simmer, and cook them over very low heat until tender, about 45 minutes to 1 hour.

2. Warm up the milk in a small saucepan, but do not bring to a boil. When warm, take off heat and add the soft crumb.

3. In a bowl combine the ground pork, onion, parsley, egg, milk-saturated crumb, and salt and mix gently with your hands until all ingredients are uniformly distributed.

4. Make small, walnut-size balls from the pork mixture and roll them in the dry bread crumbs.

5. Put the olive oil in a 12-inch skillet and turn on the heat to medium high. When the oil is hot enough to sizzle when a meatball is slipped in, put in all the meatballs. Brown them for about half a

2½ cups imported canned
Italian peeled tomatoes,
cut up with their juice

Chopped chili pepper, ⅛
teaspoon or to taste

---

*For 6 persons if served with a
liberal portion of soft polenta or
preceded by soup or pasta, for 4
if served alone with a salad*

minute, then add the chopped garlic and sage. Turn the meatballs, browning them all over.

6.   When you smell the scent of garlic rising and the pork balls have been browned on all sides, add the chopped tomatoes with their juice and the chili pepper. With a wooden spoon, turn over the contents of the pan two or three times, cover the pan, and turn the heat down to low to cook at a slow simmer. After about 10 minutes, add the drained cooked beans.

7.   Cook until the fat begins to separate from the sauce, as described in the Note on page 133, about 20 minutes or so. While the meatballs are cooking, should it become necessary to replenish the liquid in the pan to keep them from sticking, add 3 or 4 tablespoons of water. When the tomato has cooked down to sauce density, however, there should be no water left in the pan.

AHEAD-OF-TIME NOTE: The dish can be cooked through to the end 3 or 4 days in advance and refrigerated in a tightly sealed container. Reheat gently but thoroughly, adding a tablespoon or two of water if needed.

Sautéed Pork Scallops with Scallions and Capers

FETTINE DI MAIALE CON CIPOLLINE E CAPPERI

15 scallions

1½ tablespoons capers, drained if packed in vinegar, rinsed and drained if in salt

1 pound sliced boneless top pork loin chop

2 tablespoons vegetable oil

2 tablespoons butter

Flour, spread on a plate

Salt

Black pepper ground fresh

For 4 persons

This is the last recipe that I worked on for this book. I had left Venice after completing the rest of the manuscript to recuperate for a few winter weeks under the tender sun of Longboat Key, Florida, on the Gulf of Mexico. As I was browsing through the meat counter of the local Publix market I saw pork loin that had been sliced almost as thin as scaloppine. My father used to cut it that way and cook the slices quickly in a pan in which he softened some cut-up young spring onions with a few capers. I never see here those sweet young onions which in Italy come to the market with their edible green tops on, but there are scallions available, a variety of onion that Italian farmers seem to ignore. Their flavor is even richer than that of onions, and not at all unsuited to this dish.

1. Wash the scallions in two or three changes of cold water, and slice them into ½-inch pieces, bulb and green tops included. You should get about 2½ cups.

2. Chop the capers.

3. Using a meat pounder, or the flat side of the blade of a heavy knife, lightly pound the pork scallops to a thickness of about ⅓ inch.

4. Put all the oil and 1 tablespoon of butter in a 12-inch skillet and turn on the heat to high.

5. When the oil is hot, turn both sides of the pork scallops in the flour and slip them into the pan. Brown them well on both sides; then, using a slotted spoon or spatula, transfer them to a warm plate.

6. Turn the heat down under the skillet to medium low and put in the cut-up scallions, add salt and pepper, and cover the pan. Cook, stirring from time to time, until the scallions are very, very soft, about 20 minutes.

7. Uncover the pan and add the chopped capers, turning them over once or twice.

8. Put the remaining tablespoon of butter in the pan and put the meat back in. Sprinkle with salt and pepper, and turn the meat over once or twice. Cook just a few minutes until the scallops have been thoroughly reheated—but not much longer, or the meat may become tough. Turn the contents of the skillet out onto a warm serving platter and bring to the table at once.

AHEAD-OF-TIME NOTE: You can prepare everything through step 7, up to the time when you would return the meat to the skillet, several hours in advance. Reheat the scallions and capers thoroughly over moderate heat before putting in the meat. Cover the browned pork with plastic wrap, if refrigerating, and bring to room temperature before warming it up.

Two Condiments for Meat

Except for pasta sauces, Italians usually don't make sauces separately. When they cook meat they prefer to let the cooking juices form a small amount of natural sauce. Among the few departures from this practice are a variety of condiments, as I prefer to call them, that are intended for warm or cold boiled meats or for cold cuts.

A platter of mixed boiled meats, when carefully made, has long and rightly been considered a triumph of the table. But an Italian cook rarely boils just enough meat for one meal, unless she or he is feeding a very large family. The objective is to obtain from the making of boiled meat a lot of good broth that can be used for soups and risottos. What meat is left over is delicious and can be served on one or more subsequent occasions.

The two condiments given below are fine examples of the great variety of those preparations that are designed to accompany either freshly made or leftover boiled meats. Neither requires any cooking. The second is the more zestful of the two, containing such vivaciously flavored ingredients as capers, anchovies, and garlic. It is also, because of the red or yellow pepper, brightly colored.

The first is a recipe given me by Gianni Cosetti of Tolmezzo in Friuli, as genial a cook as I have ever had the good fortune to know. The combination of green apple and basil is a ravishing one, so good you hate to put it on anything—you just want to eat it alone. But it gives a marvelous lift to a boiled piece of chicken or a slice of veal. It is splendid too on grilled meat of any kind, on a pork or veal chop especially, but also on hamburger or steak.

Apple and Basil Condiment for Meats

SALSA DI MELE VERDI E BASILICO

---

2 Granny Smith apples,
peeled, cored, and cut up

⅔ cup basil leaves, stripped
of their stems

Salt, 1 teaspoon or to taste

2 tablespoons extra virgin
olive oil

Approximately 1 heaping cup
green apple condiment

Put all ingredients in the bowl of a food processor and chop, pulsing on and off, to a grainy consistency.

AHEAD-OF-TIME NOTE: You can use this condiment 2 or 3 days after making it. Refrigerate sealed airtight, but bring to room temperature before serving.

Raw Savory Condiment for Warm or Cold Meats

SALSA A CRUDO PER LE CARNI

A red or yellow bell pepper

3 flat anchovy fillets, preferably the ones prepared at home as described on page 148

1 heaping tablespoon capers

2 tablespoons chopped flat Italian parsley

½ teaspoon very, very finely chopped garlic

⅓ cup extra virgin olive oil

1½ tablespoons freshly squeezed lemon juice

4 to 6 servings of savory condiment for meats

1. Wash the pepper, split it in half lengthwise, scoop away the pulpy white core and all the seeds, and chop it into very fine dice.

2. Chop the anchovies very, very fine, to a pulp.

3. Chop the capers coarsely.

4. Combine all the ingredients in a bowl, beating them with a fork or whisk. Taste and adjust for salt.

CHOPPING NOTE: You may do all the chopping in a food processor, but you will lose most of the textural interest that comes from the varying consistencies that you obtain from ingredients chopped by hand. If you do use the processor, try not to process everything to a pulp, and if possible, do the garlic by hand and add it afterward to the mixture.

AHEAD-OF-TIME NOTE: You can chop and combine all the dry ingredients a few hours in advance. Mix with the olive oil and lemon juice when ready to use.

Vegetables

VEGETABLES

La Verdura

Assunta's Beans

Sautéed Cauliflower with Green Olives
and Tomato

Baked Eggplant with Peppers, Tomato,
and Mozzarella

Escarole Sautéed Apulian-Style with Olive
Oil, Garlic, Anchovies, and Chili Pepper

Celery Root Puree with Black Olive Paste

Boiled Fava Beans with Olive Oil and Sage

Breaded and Fried Portobello
Mushroom Cutlets

Sautéed Mushrooms and Jerusalem
Artichokes with Olive Oil and Garlic

Mashed Potatoes with Sautéed Zucchini

Cooking Radicchio with Other Vegetables

Radicchio and Finocchio Sautéed in
Olive Oil

Sautéed Radicchio and Jerusalem
Artichokes with Olive Oil
and Garlic

Baked Mixed Vegetables with Mozzarella,
Basil, and Parmesan

Roman Spring Vegetable Casserole with
Artichokes, Peas, Fava Beans, and
Romaine Lettuce

Zucchini Cooked in Tomato
and Olive Oil

Zucchini, Tomatoes, and Pancetta
in the Marches Style

Zucchini, Green Beans, Bell Pepper,
and Basil

Vegetable Bundles

Baked Eggplant Rolls with Mozzarella
and Pecorino Cheese, Topped
with Cherry Tomatoes

Baked Swiss Chard Stalks Wrapped
in Bacon

Vegetable Pies and Molds

Baked Cauliflower Tuscan-Style

Baked Leek Pie

Artichoke and Swiss Chard Pie

Stuffed Vegetables

Baked Stuffed Peppers

Stuffed Zucchini Pesaro-Style with
Ground Veal, Tomatoes, Parmesan,
and White Wine

Is there anything, I wonder, that Italian cooks don't know about working with vegetables? Not a single procedure in the full repertory of cooking techniques has been overlooked in preparing vegetables for the Italian table. They can be blanched, boiled, fried, baked, gratinéed, grilled, stewed, sautéed in olive oil or in butter with garlic or onion or with both, stuffed, made into pies, used as wrappers, cooked singly, or mixed with several others.

Vegetables can animate every course of an Italian menu short of dessert. Their flavors, their textures, their seasonal accents bring variety to soups, pasta sauces, *risotti*, and meat dishes beyond counting. They may constitute a full course of their own that shares importance with, or even replaces, the meat or fish course. At an Italian meal, vegetables are not just dutifully tacked on as an afterthought. They are, if anything, a *before*thought.

The Italian word for edible vegetables is *verdura*, whose closest translation would be "greens," although it describes leafy vegetables of any color as well as all edible roots, tubers, and legumes. I like the sound of the word, "vehr-doo' rah," so cool and reassuring. It evokes, for an Italian on the way to the market, sensations of delight that cannot be aroused by the words for meat, for fish, or for any of the staples. The seller of *verdura* is called *verduraio*, "vehr-doo-rah' yoh." Another good sound, happy and exclamatory. The *verduraio* is the most significant purveyor an Italian cook has, and a visit to his stall can have more influence on what goes on the table for dinner than the stop one makes at the butcher or the fishmonger.

Are the zucchini irresistible this morning—small, firm, and glossy, with bright orange blossoms attached that show how recently they have been picked? They may lead to thoughts of sautéed zucchini, calling in turn for a roast of veal or a simple chicken fricassee. Are they somewhat larger, but fresh nonetheless? Perhaps we should consider slicing them for a pasta sauce or hollowing them out to make zucchini stuffed with ground meat.

Are the asparagus standing as erect as the queen's guard, and are the tips of the spears tightly clustered? If the stalks are slim, we may want to chop them up for a risotto, or if they are meaty we'll want to keep them intact, blanch them, and bake them with butter and grated Parmesan.

We find pea pods that snap crisply in the hand, exposing peas as tiny and dewy as freshwater pearls. If we sauté them with prosciutto cut into small dice, we will need a nice grilled chop or steak. Or we may decide to use them to sweeten a stew of fish fillets cooked in tomatoes.

Is it the moment of winter vegetables? Then it is time for a soup followed by meat rolls, or perhaps by a marinated tenderloin of pork. Or we may decide to take home some chard, a head of Savoy cabbage, and several stalks of *broccoletti di rape*; blanch them; chop them, sauté them with lots of olive oil and garlic; and serve them with pork ribs or browned sausages.

There are *finocchi*, so plump and crisp and clear white that we just cannot leave them behind. How lovely it would be to braise them and serve them with a roast bird.

The vegetables that come into an Italian kitchen, and that are put on an Italian family's table, have an implicit meaning for us, if we cook in that kitchen and eat at that table, that cannot be explained solely in terms of taste. They align our pace with the dependable motion of the seasons, giving everyday life a sane sense of continuity and a hopeful one of renewal. The pleasures we take when we choose them, prepare them, and eat them do not begin and end with those moments. They connect with sensations we have known and expect to know again as our earth continues to turn toward a new cycle of growth.

Keeping Vegetables

If they are very fresh to begin with, you can extend the life of basil, asparagus, and artichokes by placing their stems in an inch or two of cold water. Basil will keep fresh an extra day, asparagus two or three, artichokes a week. Store in a cool place but not in the refrigerator.

Assunta's Beans

I FAGIOLI DI ASSUNTA

———————— ✿ ————————

1 pound unshelled fresh
    cranberry beans

⅓ cup extra virgin olive oil

⅔ cup water, to start

4 to 6 fresh sage leaves

3 garlic cloves, lightly
    mashed with a knife
    handle, and peeled

Salt

Black pepper ground fresh

Extra virgin olive oil to
    serve at table; see step 4
    below

————————————————————

8 small or 4 to 6 large servings

A 5-cup heavy-gauge casserole,
preferably enameled cast iron

What do you want to eat today?" I ask my husband. It seems to me a very sweet, solicitous question for a wife to pose, but it never fails to irritate Victor. "I can't think about it now," he usually snaps. But on this day he says, "How about Assunta's beans?" It was said not without mischief, I am sure, because we hadn't had Assunta's beans since she had made them last, 45 years earlier.

Before we were married Victor had come to Italy to write and he had found, on a hill bristling with ancient olive trees, a villa that had once been glorious, from whose terrace one enjoyed an unobstructed, if distant, view of Florence. There he had taken an apartment. The villa's impoverished owners had a housekeeper, a very tall, gaunt woman with glowing black eyes and the largest feet I have ever seen on man or woman. When Victor asked her if she had time to look after the apartment for him her face shone as though she had just been awakened from a long bad dream by the good prince. It turned out she was rarely paid and infrequently fed. In exchange for a small but regular monthly stipend and an occasional shirt she stole for her husband Pasquale, Assunta did everything for Victor: cook, wash, iron, gather firewood for the stoves, and, in season, scour the woods for wild mushrooms and asparagus; and bring in for his breakfast every morning, from one of the few trees remaining in the orchard, fresh figs oozing honey, dark green outside, blood red inside. And she made sensational beans, the most wonderful I had had up to then or ever since.

Assunta didn't use a *fiasco*, a glass wine flask, as much later I learned was common practice in Tuscany. She had an old cast-iron pot, which she nearly filled with fresh *cannellini* beans. She then poured olive oil and water over them; added salt, pepper, garlic, and sage; covered the pot with a thick, damp napkin; put a lid over it; and cooked them for 2 hours or more over hot embers from a wood fire. How we had forgotten about those beans? But when Victor mentioned them, it was as though Assunta had just poured a ladleful onto my plate.

When Victor brought up Assunta's beans, we were in Venice, where they don't sell fresh *cannellini* beans. But we have something just as marvelous, Lamon beans, mountain-grown fresh cranberry beans. Theirs is a different taste from that of *cannellini*, denser, deeper, reminiscent of chestnuts. I won't say they are better than *cannellini* because it would be chauvinistic, the sort of claim I leave to Tuscans to make.

The fundamental principle of this recipe is to cook the beans with a minimum of water to concentrate their taste. But the little water you put at the beginning must be replenished in small measure from time to time; otherwise, the beans will dry out.

Serve the beans on their own as a side dish or as a rich appetizer, or do as we did on the day I made them for Victor: Toss them with very good tuna packed in olive oil and lots of sliced raw onion.

1. Shell the beans; if full and ripe you should get about 2 cups.

2. Put the beans and all the other ingredients in the pot. Moisten a cloth towel and use it to cover the pot. Put a lid on the towel and fold the towel back over the lid. Turn on the heat to very low. The beans should cook at the barest suggestion of a simmer. If necessary, put a flame tamer between the pot and the burner to reduce heat.

3. Stir the beans from time to time. After 45 minutes, add 2 tablespoons warm water, stir, and close the pot again. Add 2 tablespoons of water two more times at 20-minute intervals. Check the beans; depending on the heat of the fire, they may need additional water more frequently. They should never be soaking in water but should have just enough to keep from sticking. The beans should be done after about 1 hour and 45 minutes. Taste them. They should be firm but tender, and the skin should have remained whole without cracking.

4. Drizzle with fresh olive oil when serving.

AHEAD-OF-TIME NOTE: They are better the moment they are done, but you can cook them through to the end even a day in advance. Refrigerate in a tightly sealed container and reheat them gently with a tablespoon or so of water.

Sautéed Cauliflower with Green Olives and Tomato

CAVOLFIORE CON OLIVE VERDI E POMODORO

A head of cauliflower, about 1½ pounds

¼ cup extra virgin olive oil

⅓ cup very thinly chopped onion

16 green olives in brine, pitted and quartered

Salt

Black pepper ground fresh

1 cup really ripe fresh tomatoes, peeled raw, seeds scooped away, and cut into fine dice

For 4 persons

I don't think of myself as a fancy cook. Presentation is not one of my first thoughts, but I am not insensible to an attractive-looking dish as long as its appearance signals the flavors I am about to experience. The tomato dice and the green olive sections look very pretty in this Apulian-style cauliflower, but they are there for reasons of taste. Cauliflower, if it hasn't been around too long, can be quite mild, sometimes tediously so. Here, however, the residual bitterness of the olives and the acidulousness of the tomato help the cauliflower's potential sweetness make taste impressions that, by contrast, are both more intense and more lively. Bear in mind that cauliflower is one vegetable that wants to be cooked thoroughly—not until it is mushy, of course, but it has to be decidedly tender; otherwise, it will always retain a disagreeable trace of sourness.

1. Trim away the cauliflower's green leaves and wash it in cold water.

2. Choose a saucepan that can amply contain the whole cauliflower head, fill it three-quarters full with water, and bring the water to a boil. Drop in the cauliflower and cook until it feels very tender when tested with a fork, about 20 to 25 minutes. Drain and, as soon as the cauliflower is cool enough to handle, cut it into pieces about 1½ inches big.

3. Put the olive oil and the chopped onion in a 10- or 12-inch skillet, and turn the heat on to medium high. Cook the onion, stirring once or twice, until it becomes colored a pale gold, then add the cut-up cauliflower, the olives, salt, and a liberal grinding of black pepper.

4. Cook over lively heat for 2 to 3 minutes, occasionally turning over the contents of the pan with a wooden spoon. Add the diced tomato, turn all the ingredients over, and continue cooking for another 5 minutes or so. Serve at once when done.

AHEAD-OF-TIME NOTE: You can boil the cauliflower a few hours in advance, keeping it at cool room temperature, but preferably out of the refrigerator.

Baked Eggplant with Peppers, Tomato, and Mozzarella

MELANZANE AL FORNO CON PEPERONI, POMODORO, E MOZZARELLA

2 eggplants, about 1½ pounds each

4 to 7 garlic cloves, depending on their size, peeled and sliced very thin

Salt

Black pepper ground fresh

⅓ cup vegetable oil

1 red or yellow bell pepper

2 tablespoons extra virgin olive oil

⅔ cup canned Italian plum tomatoes, drained and cut up, OR fresh, ripe tomatoes, peeled and cut up

½ pound mozzarella, cut into thin slices

8 or 10 basil leaves

¼ cup freshly grated Parmigiano-Reggiano cheese

2 tablespoons fine, dry, unflavored breadcrumbs

1½ tablespoons butter

For 4 persons

An oven-to-table baking dish

Insofar as it is baked with tomato, basil, and mozzarella, this dish resembles eggplant *parmigiana*. It diverges, however, from the classic *parmigiana* version in several significant ways. There is a lusciously fleshy quality to the consistency of the eggplant itself because it is cut in half instead of in slices. In the *parmigiana* style the eggplant is fried before the dish is assembled and baked; here it is sautéed with slivers of garlic buried within it. When you are slicing and frying eggplant it's advisable to steep the slices in salt before cooking so that they shed their bitter juices. Whole eggplants, on the other hand, or even eggplant halves, seem to purge themselves of their astringency as they cook, so I have omitted that preliminary salting step. And I have put in a peeled bell pepper to add a secondary layer of flavor. To obtain a full measure of the pepper's distinctive aroma and sweetness, you must free it of its skin by peeling it raw as the recipe describes.

1. Wash the eggplants, slice off their green stems, and cut them lengthwise in half. With a sharp paring knife, deeply score the flesh side of the eggplant in a crosshatched diamond pattern. Cut down close to the skin, but not through it. Slip some of the garlic slices into the cuts, about 6 or 7 slices into each eggplant half. Sprinkle with salt and pepper.

2. Choose a lidded skillet or sauté pan that can accommodate the eggplants in a single layer. Put in the vegetable oil. Arrange the eggplant halves in the pan with their flesh side facing up, turn on the heat to medium, and cover the pan. Cook until the skin side begins to wrinkle and soften, then turn the eggplant over. When the flesh side becomes colored a golden brown, turn them over again. Continue cooking until the eggplant flesh feels thoroughly tender and creamy when tested with a fork.

3. Using a slotted spoon or spatula, lift the eggplants out of the pan and place them, flesh side facing up, in the baking dish.

4. Turn on the oven to 400°.

5. Split the pepper open; remove the core and all seeds; and, using a swivel-bladed peeler, skin the pepper raw. Cut it lengthwise into strips.

6. Put the 2 tablespoons of olive oil in a little saucepan, add the remaining garlic slices, turn on the heat to medium, and cook the garlic, stirring occasionally, just until it becomes colored a pale gold.

7. Put in the pepper and cook it for 2 or 3 minutes, then add the cut-up tomatoes, salt, and several grinding of black pepper. Cook at a steady simmer, stirring from time to time, until tomatoes lose all their watery liquid and turn into a dense sauce.

8. Cover the eggplants in the baking dish with mozzarella slices, sprinkle the basil leaves over the mozzarella, then top with the tomato and pepper sauce, distributing it uniformly over each eggplant half. Over the sauce, evenly sprinkle the grated Parmesan and the bread crumbs. Dot with butter, and place the dish in the uppermost level of the preheated oven. Bake for 20 minutes and and let the dish rest 15 minutes or so, until it is no longer very hot, before serving.

AHEAD-OF-TIME NOTE: You can cook the eggplants or make the sauce or do both several hours in advance of baking the dish.

Escarole Sautéed Apulian-Style with Olive Oil, Garlic, Anchovies, and Chili Pepper

ESCAROLA SALTATA CON L'ACCIUGA

1½ pounds escarole

Salt

Vegetable oil for frying the bread

4 slices good quality white bread, cut into ½-inch squares

4 tablespoons extra virgin olive oil

4 to 6 garlic cloves, depending on their size, lightly mashed and peeled

4 anchovy fillets, chopped very fine

Chopped chili pepper, ⅛ teaspoon or to taste

For 4 persons

Had I paid closer attention, I could have filled a book with the dishes that the Apulian woman who was my mother's companion used to cook. Among the things I remember best was her way of cooking wild chicory, *broccoletti di rape*, and other bitter vegetables. She blanched them and sautéed them in olive oil. In the oil she dissolved anchovies that served to take some of the edge off the vegetable's bitter bite. She served the vegetable with fried bread squares that lengthened the tastefulness of the dish and made it more substantial.

Escarole, which is not all that bitter, has never tasted better to me than when prepared this way. Even sweeter greens, such as spinach and Swiss chard, can benefit from this savory treatment.

1. Pull off all the escarole's leaves, discarding any bruised or wilted ones. Wash the leaves in several changes of cold water.

2. Pour 3 to 4 inches of water into a medium saucepan and bring it to a boil. Put in 1 tablespoon salt and all the escarole leaves. Cook until the escarole feels fully tender when prodded with a fork, then drain and let cool.

3. Put enough vegetable oil in a small skillet to come 1 inch up its sides. Turn on the heat to medium. When the oil is hot enough to sizzle when you test it by dropping in one of the bread squares, put in the bread. Do not crowd the pan. Fry as much bread at one time as will fit loosely; and when it is nicely browned transfer it, using a slotted spoon or spatula, to a plate lined with paper towels. Repeat the procedure batch by batch until all the bread is done.

4. Chop the escarole rather coarse, into pieces about 1 inch wide.

5. Put the olive oil and garlic in a 10-inch skillet and turn on the heat to medium. Cook the garlic, stirring it, until it becomes colored a pale creamy brown, then remove it.

6. Add the chopped anchovies, mashing them against the bottom of the skillet with a wooden spoon to help dissolve them.

7. Add the escarole and the chili pepper, turn the heat up to medium high, and turn the escarole over for a minute or two to coat it thoroughly in the flavored oil.

8. Add the fried bread squares, turn over all ingredients once or twice, then serve at once.

AHEAD-OF-TIME NOTE: You can boil and chop the escarole a few hours in advance, but do not refrigerate it. The bread squares can be fried ahead of time and, when cold, stored in a cupboard for a day or two.

Celery Root Puree with Black Olive Paste

PUREA DI SEDANO DI VERONA CON LA PASTA DI OLIVE NERE

1½ pounds celery root

2 tablespoons black olive paste

¼ cup extra virgin olive oil

Salt

Black pepper ground fresh

---

6 to 8 servings celery root puree

There are few purees of anything that I like, because purees obliterate the textural values of food. There are some notable exceptions, one of them being the mashed potatoes on page 356, and another any partly or wholly pureed bean, such as the kind that I add to soups or the dried fava bean puree with *broccoletti rapa* in one of my previous books.

Celery root I had never liked in any form, let alone mashed, because it is usually so bland. Yet, during an exchange of gastronomic ideas I had once with a wine producer at the annual wine fair held in Verona, the description he proffered of this celery root puree with olive paste seemed worth acting upon. I have now made it several times for the family and included it occasionally when I had guests for dinner, and each time I taste it with surprise and pleasure in equal measure. It has to be the black olives, an example of the catalytic effect an ingredient can have on another, inducing it to release qualities one never suspected it possessed.

1. Trim away a slice from the root end of the celery root and cut off any rootlets and spindly protuberances. With a paring knife, peel the entire knob of the root. Wash in cold water and cut it into four parts.

2. Put the root in a saucepan with enough water to cover amply, bring to a moderate boil, and cook until it feels very tender when prodded with a fork. Drain, put it back into the pan, and heat it for a few seconds to dry it somewhat.

3. Put the cooked root in a food processor with the olive paste, the olive oil, salt, and generous grindings of black pepper. Chop to a creamy consistency. Serve as you would mashed potatoes.

AHEAD-OF-TIME NOTE: This puree tastes best when combined with the olive paste and other seasonings just before serving. You can cook the root a few hours in advance, keeping it in a covered bowl at room temperature.

Boiled Fava Beans with Olive Oil and Sage

FAVE BOLLITE

---

3 pounds fresh, young fava beans in their pods

4 tablespoons extra virgin olive oil

Sage, 4 or 5 leaves if fresh, 1 teaspoon chopped if dried

Salt

Black pepper ground fresh

About 3½ cups beans and juices

There is no bean whose flavor is so gently pleasing as the fava bean, and there is no method that elicits that flavor so purely as boiling them with olive oil and sage. My husband and I have a passion for fava beans, a passion that in Italy can be requited only for a brief period in the spring. For Easter I make them Roman-style, with olive oil and cured pork jowl or pancetta, and serve them with baby lamb or, when both artichokes and peas are very young, in that other extraordinary dish, *vignarola* (see the recipe on page 364). But I keep my eyes open for the first, small, tender fava of the year, and then this is the recipe I would use, the one that brings me closest to their essence, undistracted by other ingredients.

1. Shell the beans, discarding the pods, and put them in a saucepan with half the olive oil, all the sage, and enough water to cover by 1 inch. Cover and turn on the heat to low. Cook for 30 to 40 minutes until they are tender to the bite.

2. When the beans have been cooking for 25 minutes, add salt and liberal grindings of black pepper, and stir thoroughly.

3. Before serving, swirl in the remaining 2 tablespoons of olive oil. Serve with all their juices and crusty bread.

AHEAD-OF-TIME NOTE: Although their taste is most alluring when lukewarm, the beans can be served several hours later at room temperature. If by some mishap you must serve them the day after, refrigerate them in their juices, then reheat very gently but thoroughly.

Breaded and Fried Portobello Mushroom Cutlets

COTOLETTE DI FUNGHI PORTOBELLO

4 to 6 portobello
  mushrooms, depending
  on size, but with the
  largest caps possible

1 teaspoon very, very finely
  chopped garlic

1 tablespoon finely chopped
  Italian flat-leaf parsley

1 whole egg

Salt

Black pepper ground fresh

2 cups fine, dry, unflavored
  bread crumbs, spread on
  a plate

Vegetable oil

For 4 persons

A wire drying rack set over a
tray

As I have related in the introduction to Assunta's Beans on page 342, during his last bachelor year my husband lived in a villa on a hill that overlooked Florence. The villa's housekeeper, Assunta, had a husband, Pasquale, under whose tutelage Victor learned to identify *pinaroli*, a delicious mushroom that grew only close to pine trees. Assunta breaded and fried those mushrooms, a treat that I used to look forward to when, during my fall school holidays, I was able to come down and visit.

Pinaroli is not a variety that is brought to the produce market, and I have never had it since. When I began working with portobello mushrooms, and found they had more flavor than the cultivated white button ones, I thought they might be susceptible to the breading and frying method I had seen Assunta use. As it turned out, they tasted even better than I had hoped.

The more than 45 years that have passed since I had Assunta's cooking may be blurring my memory a little, but it seems to me that in flavor and texture these portobello mushrooms come rather near the pine-loving ones from that Tuscan hill.

1. Separate the mushroom caps from the stems and wash both rapidly under running water. Pat dry with kitchen towels.

2. Cut the stems lengthwise into slices about ⅓ inch thick.

3. Choose a flat-bottomed bowl or another deep dish with a bottom that can subsequently accommodate the largest of the mushroom caps lying flat. Put in the garlic, parsley, egg, salt, and black pepper and beat thoroughly with a fork.

4. Dip the mushroom caps and stems, one piece at a time, in the egg batter. Make sure each piece absorbs batter on both sides, lift it, and pause to let excess batter flow back into the bowl; then lay it flat over the bread crumbs, turn it over, and pat it down with the flat of your hand to cause the bread crumbs to stick firmly to both surfaces of the mushroom. Place the breaded pieces on a clean, dry plate.

5. Put enough vegetable oil in a 10-inch skillet to come ½ inch up the sides, and turn on the heat to high. When the oil is hot enough so that it sizzles instantly when tested with a piece of mushroom, slip in the breaded caps and stems, but do not crowd the pan. Cook until a nice golden crust forms on one side, turn them and do the other side, then transfer them to the drying rack using a slotted spoon or spatula. Continue thus until all the mushrooms are done. Serve promptly.

Sautéed Mushrooms and Jerusalem Artichokes with Olive Oil and Garlic

FUNGHI E TOPINAMBUR TRIFOLATI

1 pound Jerusalem
    artichokes

1 pound fresh, firm
    cultivated mushrooms

¼ cup extra virgin olive oil

1 tablespoon chopped garlic

3 tablespoons finely
    chopped Italian flat-leaf
    parsley

Salt

Black pepper ground fresh

For 6 persons

It puzzles and saddens me to witness the obscurity to which Jerusalem artichoke, one of the finest of tubers, has been relegated. In America it is used only raw, for salads; and in Italy, except for a few districts in the northwest, it is neither known nor heard of, despite the fact that the plant it is the root of, a variety of sunflower, is widely grown. But it is cultivated for its oil-bearing seeds and the delicious root is discarded.

Near my hometown, there are acres and acres of those sunflowers, whose sight once led to an amusing incident. As we passed them I pointed them out to the driver who had picked me up in Venice to take me to my mother. "*Guarda*—look!" I said. "*Quanti topinambur*—how many *topinambur!*" *Topinambur* is the Italian for Jerusalem artichoke, but *topi* alone means mice, and that was the only part of the word the man heard. "Mice?" he asked, while braking abruptly. "Where?"

In the recipe below the artichokes and mushrooms are *trifolati*; this means that for cooking they are sliced wafer-thin like truffles, which are sometimes called *trifola*. The cooking procedure could not be much simpler. Olive oil is heated up with garlic and parsley, and the sliced artichokes and mushrooms are cooked in that scented oil. The mushrooms shed liquid that helps to cook the firmer artichoke, but at the end the only liquid left is the fragrant oil. The Jerusalem artichoke, which is reticently sweet, coaxes the cultivated mushrooms, by contrast, to express their latent flavor of the woods. It tastes just wonderful, take my word.

1. Skin the Jerusalem artichokes using a small paring knife or a swivel-bladed peeler, wash them in cold water, then slice them into the thinnest possible disks. You can use the fine slicing disk, not the blade, of a food processor or, if you have one, a mandoline, being careful to grasp the tuber with a pusher rather than with your fingers, or you will end up slicing those too.

2. Wash the mushrooms rapidly under running water. Pat thoroughly dry with kitchen towels, then cut them lengthwise, from cap to bottom of the stem, into the thinnest slices you can.

3. Choose a sauté pan or skillet that can later accommodate all the mushrooms and artichokes. Put in the oil and garlic, turn on the heat to medium high, and cook the garlic, stirring frequently, until it becomes colored gold. Add the parsley, stir quickly two or three times, then put in both the artichokes and mushrooms. Turn them over a few times to coat them well, add salt and generous grindings of pepper, turn the heat down to low, and cover the pan.

4. The mushrooms will shed a fair quantity of liquid. Cook, turning the pan's contents over from time to time, until the mushroom water has completely evaporated and the artichokes feel tender when poked with a fork. If, once the artichokes are done, there is still liquid left in the pan, uncover it, raise the heat, and boil all the liquid away.

AHEAD-OF-TIME NOTE: The dish can be cooked completely several hours in advance. Reheat gently but thoroughly, turning over the mushrooms and artichokes with a wooden spoon from time to time.

Mashed Potatoes with Sautéed Zucchini

PURÉ DI PATATE CON ZUCCHINE SALTATE AL BURRO

1 pound boiling potatoes

¾ pound young, glossy zucchini, small, but not miniatures

3 tablespoons butter, softened at room temperature

Salt

¾ cup milk

½ cup freshly grated Parmigiano-Reggiano cheese

4 ample or 6 small portions

Once you've had a taste of *puré*—Italian mashed potatoes made from good boiling potatoes with butter, milk, and Parmesan cheese—you'd be likely to think they need no improvement. And my family and I would agree. We are so fond of them and have them so often, that I decided the time had come to try something slightly different.

On a morning that I had just got some lovely zucchini, I cut them into thin sticks and sautéed them in butter; and when the mashed potatoes were ready, I stirred in the zucchini. Thereafter, our new version of mashed potatoes became such a favorite that when eventually I returned to making them the original way my husband asked, "What happened? Didn't you find any zucchini today?"

1. Wash the potatoes, put them in a saucepan with cold water, cover, and bring to a boil. Cook approximately 30 minutes at a steady but not too fast boil, until they feel tender when prodded with a fork.

2. While the potatoes are boiling, soak the zucchini for about 20 minutes in a basin of cold water and clean as described on page 162. After trimming away their ends, slice them lengthwise in half; then cut them into thin sticks, ½ inch wide or less.

3. Choose a skillet, preferably nonstick, that can contain all the zucchini sticks more or less on one layer without much overlapping. Put in 1 tablespoon of butter and the zucchini, sprinkle with salt, and turn on the heat to medium high. Cook, turning the zucchini over from time to time, until they are tender but not mushy. Take the pan off the heat.

4. When the potatoes are done, drain them and peel them while still hot. Mash them through a food mill or a potato ricer directly into a medium saucepan. Mix into them 2 tablespoons of butter, stirring until the butter is entirely dissolved.

5. Heat the milk in a small saucepan until the first pearly bubbles form at its edge, but do not let it boil. Add the hot milk to the potatoes, swirling it in vigorously and thoroughly.

6. Add the grated Parmesan, mixing quickly to incorporate it smoothly. Add salt to taste, mixing to distribute it evenly.

7. Add the zucchini to the mashed potatoes in the pan, turning the mixture over several times. Transfer to a very warm serving bowl and bring to the table at once.

AHEAD-OF-TIME NOTE: Mashed potatoes are meant to be eaten the moment they are done, when they are still hot and creamy. If they are ready before you are, place the saucepan with the mashed potatoes into a larger one containing simmering water. Keep the water simmering, and stir the potatoes from time to time. If they appear to be drying out, stir in 1 or 2 tablespoons warm milk.

COOKING RADICCHIO WITH OTHER VEGETABLES

The tonic bitterness of radicchio is a highly prized quality in the cooking of northeastern Italy. Venetian taste buds thrill to its bracing presence in fish dishes, in risotto, in pasta sauces, somewhat with the readiness with which central and southern Italian palates respond to the excitement of chili pepper in some of the specialties of their regions.

The least bitter of all radicchios, the late-harvest Treviso, can be cooked alone, liberally basted with olive oil and grilled over a slow charcoal fire or baked in the oven. It's a method that accentuates bitterness and hence it is less suitable to the standard long-leaf Treviso or to the variety best-known abroad, the red cabbage–shaped Chioggia radicchio. But these last are splendid when cooked with mellow-tasting vegetables and become an ideal accompaniment for virtually any meat dish.

In the first of the two following recipes, the radicchio's astringency is tempered by the mild anise aroma of *finocchio* and by onion that is cooked slowly until very soft to bring out all its sweetness. In the second recipe I have used Jerusalem artichokes. Their natural sweetness does not need an assist from onion—in fact, it calls for a headier accent, which is supplied by a whiff of garlic. In both instances, all the cooking is done with olive oil, for which radicchio has a strong affinity.

In making either of these dishes, or any other that calls for radicchio, you may replace radicchio with Belgian endive, a milder member of the same chicory family.

Radicchio and Finocchio Sautéed in Olive Oil

RADICCHIO E FINOCCHIO SALTATI ALL'OLIO

2 large *finocchi*

4 heads long-leaf Treviso radicchio OR 1 medium head round radicchio OR 1 pound Belgian endive

⅓ cup very thinly sliced onion

⅓ cup extra virgin olive oil

Salt

Black pepper ground fresh

For 6 generous or 4 small servings

1. Cut off the *finocchio* tops where they meet the bulb and discard them. Trim away any outer part of the bulb that may be bruised or withered. Slice away ⅛ inch or so from the butt end of the bulb. Cut the bulb into very thin vertical slices. Wash the sliced *finocchio* in several changes of cold water.

2. Slice off and discard the root or butt end of the radicchio. Pull off and discard any of the outer leaves that are wilted, discolored, or bruised. Cut the radicchio into very thin shreds, and wash in several changes of cold water. Spin or shake thoroughly dry.

3. Put the sliced onion and the olive oil in a medium skillet or sauté pan, turn the heat on to medium, and cook the onion, turning it over occasionally, until it is completely wilted.

4. Add the *finocchio* and radicchio, salt, and liberal grindings of black pepper; cover the pan; and turn the heat down to very low. Cook until the *finocchio* feels very tender when tested with a fork, about 30 minutes. If you should find, while the vegetables are cooking, that there is not sufficient liquid in the pan to keep them from sticking to the bottom, add 2 or 3 tablespoons of water whenever it becomes necessary. When the vegetables are done, however, there should be no runny liquid left in the pan.

AHEAD-OF-TIME NOTE: The taste of this dish is sweetest at the moment the vegetables are cooked, but if necessary you can complete the cooking several hours in advance—but not overnight, and do not refrigerate. Reheat gently in an uncovered pan, adding just a little water, which you must allow to evaporate completely.

Sautéed Radicchio and Jerusalem Artichokes with Olive Oil and Garlic

RADICCHIO E TOPINAMBUR SALTATI CON OLIO E AGLIO

½ pound Jerusalem artichokes

4 heads long-leaf Treviso radicchio OR 1 medium head round radicchio OR 1 pound Belgian endive

3 tablespoons extra virgin olive oil

2 medium garlic cloves, peeled and sliced very, very thin

Salt

Black pepper ground fresh

For 6 generous, 4 small servings

1. Skin the sunchokes using a small paring knife or a swiveling-blade peeler, wash them in cold water, then slice them into disks about ¼ inch thick.

2. If you are using the long Treviso radicchio with an extended root, pare it down to a short nub. If the root has been cut off, as it is in the endive, trim away a thin slice from the butt end. Detach the leaves from the radicchio or endive, discarding any blemished ones, shred them lengthwise into narrow strips about ¼ inch wide, soak briefly in cold water, and drain. If you are using a round, cabbage-like head of radicchio, shred it very fine, soak briefly in cold water, and drain.

3. Put the olive oil and garlic in a medium sauté pan, turn on the heat to medium strength, and cook, stirring frequently, until the garlic begins to sizzle. Quickly put in the sliced sunchokes and shredded radicchio or endive, adding salt and liberal grindings of pepper. Cover the pan; turn the heat down to low; and cook, turning over the vegetables from time to time, until the sunchoke feels tender when prodded with a fork, about 40 minutes.

AHEAD-OF-TIME NOTE: You can cook the dish all the way through to the end several hours in advance. Do not refrigerate. Reheat over medium heat in a covered pan, turning over the vegetables from time to time, until they are fully warm again.

Baked Mixed Vegetables with Mozzarella, Basil, and Parmesan

MISTO DI VERDURE AL FORNO

½ pound eggplant

1 pound potatoes

Salt

⅝ cup grated mellow pecorino sheep's milk cheese OR equal parts Romano and Parmigiano-Reggiano cheeses

¼ cup extra virgin olive oil

¾ pound ripe, firm, fresh tomatoes

2 yellow bell peppers

Chopped red chili pepper, ¼ teaspoon or to taste

6 small basil leaves or 3 large ones, torn by hand into small pieces

2 tablespoons fine, dry, unflavored bread crumbs

For 4 to 6 persons

An 11 by 7-inch oven-to-table baking dish or any rectangular dish of equivalent capacity

When Victor and I were much younger, we thought nothing of having a liberal portion of a mixed vegetable dish such as this alongside some breaded veal cutlets, which would have been preceded by pasta or risotto. Who would have believed then that, some decades later, we would look forward to making a whole meal out of just vegetables? And a satisfying meal it can be in all respects. It is a cheery combination of colors, the potatoes supply ample bulk, and the chorus of flavors—sweet and fragrant, ripe and pungent—entertains the palate from the first bite to the last. The juices produced are so delicious that it would be a regrettable oversight not to provide some good crusty bread, possibly lightly grilled, to help sop them up.

When I have too many guests to serve sitting down, this is one of the dishes I am likely to put on the buffet table, and it is unfailingly one of the first to disappear.

1. Turn on the oven to 400°.

2. Slice away the eggplants' green tops. Wash the eggplants and cut them lengthwise into slices ¼ inch thick or less.

3. Set a pasta colander over a bowl or deep dish; line it inside with one layer of eggplant slices, placing them vertically; sprinkle lightly with salt; place another layer of eggplant over the first and sprinkle a tiny bit more salt over it; and proceed thus until you have used up all the slices. Let stand for at least 30 minutes to allow the eggplant to shed some of its astringent liquid.

4. Peel the potatoes, wash in cold water, and slice very thin. Put them in a bowl; add 2 tablespoons of the grated cheese, 1 tablespoon of olive oil and salt; and toss several times to coat each slice well.

5. Use a swiveling-blade vegetable peeler to peel the tomatoes. Cut them in half, scoop out the seeds with a spoon (do not squeeze them), and cut into ⅓-inch-wide strips.

6. Peel the peppers by the same method used on the tomatoes, split them open, remove the white pith and all the seeds, and cut the peppers lengthwise into strips ½ inch wide.

7. Combine the tomatoes and peppers in a bowl, adding salt, 6 tablespoons of grated cheese, chopped chili pepper, and the basil leaves. Toss several times to coat well.

8. Evenly coat the bottom of the baking dish with 1 tablespoon of olive oil. Spread half the sliced potatoes over the bottom of the dish.

9. Distribute half the pepper and tomato combination over the potatoes and top with the sliced eggplant. Spread the remaining peppers and tomatoes over the eggplant, and top with the remaining sliced potatoes.

10. Combine 2 tablespoons of grated cheese with an equal amount of bread crumbs and sprinkle the mixture over the potatoes. Over them drizzle 2 tablespoons of olive oil, distributing it evenly. Bake in the uppermost level of the preheated oven for 45 to 50 minutes until the top becomes colored a tawny gold. Allow to settle for 10 minutes before serving.

AHEAD-OF-TIME NOTE: The most time-consuming portion of this dish is peeling and slicing the vegetables, and you can do that several hours in advance. Do not toss them with salt, however, until you are ready to assemble and bake the dish, because that would cause them to shed liquid.

CLEANING ARTICHOKES

The simple fact about an artichoke is this: Part of it is so tender you can slice it and eat it raw, as Italians do in salads; part of it is so tough that no cooking will ever tenderize it. There is nothing wonderful about sitting at table and scraping your teeth against an artichoke leaf to glean a minute amount of edible matter or spitting out an unchewable pellet. The Italian point of view is, if you can't cut it, why cook it? When you are cleaning artichoke you must be absolutely ruthless and leave nothing on it that might be capable later of bringing you anything but untroubled pleasure. Always keep a lemon or two cut in half by your side while you work. It will keep the artichoke from discoloring and your hands from becoming stained. The procedure described below is applicable to any variety of artichoke, from the globes grown in California to those available in Italy, such as the ones I cleaned for the photographer in the accompanying illustrations.

1. Begin by bending back the outer leaves, pulling them down toward the base of the artichoke, and snapping them off just before you reach the base (*photo A*). Do not take the paler bottom end of a leaf off because at that point it is tender and quite edible. As you take more leaves off and get deeper into the artichoke, the tender part at which the leaves will snap will be farther and farther from the base. Keep pulling off single leaves until you expose a central cone of leaves with a pale whitish base that may be about 1½ inches high (*photo B*).

2. Cut off the central cone of leaves down to the tender, whitish base (*photo C*). Take a half lemon and rub the cut portions of the artichoke, squeezing juice over them to keep them from discoloring.

3. Turn the artichoke bottoms up and, at the place where you have snapped off the outer leaves, pare away the tough green part that

A

B

C

D

E

F

G

H

remains (*photo D*). Detach, but do not discard the stem.

4. Cut the trimmed artichoke in half (*photo E*), and then into as many wedges as the recipe calls for.

5. Cut away the fuzzy inner choke of leaves from each of the wedges (*photo F*). As you trim each wedge, place it in a basin of cold water into which you have squeezed the juice of half a lemon (*photo G*).

6. Picking up the stem, you will notice, looking at the bottom, a whitish core surrounded by a layer of green. The green part is tough, the white, when cooked, soft and delicious. Pare away the green, all the way around, leaving the white intact (*photo H*). If very thick, cut it lengthwise in half. Add it to the basin with the lemony water and later cook it along with the rest of the artichoke.

Roman Spring Vegetable Casserole with Artichokes, Peas, Fava Beans, and Romaine Lettuce

LA VIGNAROLA

½ lemon

4 to 5 medium globe
   artichokes

2 pounds fresh, young peas
   in their pods, about 2
   cups shelled

2 pounds fresh, young fava
   beans in their pods,
   about 2 cups shelled

1 large head of romaine
   lettuce

2 to 3 fresh spring onions,
   about 2 to 2½ inches
   across (see headnote) OR
   2 cups very thinly sliced
   medium white onions

½ cup extra virgin olive oil

Salt

For 8 persons

Any moderately adept, reasonably patient, and attentive cook can follow directions and achieve complexity by complex means. The very greatest cooking, however, attains complexity through the most transparently simple means. *Vignarola*, a Roman dish in which the flavors of several spring vegetables are mingled and magically transmuted, and a startlingly similar Sicilian preparation, *frittedda*, are, to my mind, products of the very greatest cooking.

The recipe for *vignarola* could be summed up in a single sentence: Sliced onion is cooked in olive oil until quite soft, then the trimmed and shelled vegetables are put in and cooked slowly in that oil until they are tender. By the standards of our glossy food magazines, the result does not look very impressive; it is a rather murky dish in which all the vegetable shapes have become jumbled. But the taste, ah, the taste! There is nothing jumbled about that. It is the clear taste of sweet spring itself.

It's hard not to get carried away, particularly if the dish is on the table before you. I don't remember ever having had enough of it, ever having felt replete no matter how much of it I have managed to eat. Unhappily, it doesn't work with just any vegetables; there is no room for accommodation. Every vegetable has to be young and uncompromisingly fresh. You really have to pare down those artichokes because the slightest tough fragment of a leaf will undo the magic. In Rome they use the young onions that come to the market in spring. These have green shoots and look like scallions except that their bulbs are much larger than those of scallions. If you cannot get them, use small white onions or other sweet onions.

If you can get yourself to Rome in the spring, forget the Michelangelos, pass up the fountain with the coins, don't ask the way to the Colosseum. Ask the way to a simple Roman trattoria where they make *vignarola*.

(continued)

1. Squeeze the juice of ½ lemon into a bowl of cold water.

2. Prepare the artichokes as described on pages 362–63, trimming away all the tough, inedible portions. Cut the trimmed artichokes lengthwise into wedges about ½ inch thick. Drop the wedges into the bowl containing the water and lemon juice.

3. If any shelled fava bean is more than 1 inch in length, cut away the thick green skin that sheaths it.

4. Detach the leaves from the lettuce head, discarding any bruised, wilted, or discolored ones. Soak the leaves in two or three changes of water, drain, and shred them fine. You should have approximately 4 cups, but a bit more or less won't matter too much.

5. If using fresh spring onions, cut off all the green tops and the root ends, then slice them very thin.

6. Choose a saucepan that can subsequently accommodate all the ingredients. Put in the sliced onions, the olive oil, and a large pinch of salt, and turn on the heat to low. Cook the onions, turning them over from time to time, until they have become completely wilted.

7. Drain the artichokes, rinse them in cold water, and put them in the pot, together with the shelled peas, fava beans, and shredded romaine lettuce. Sprinkle liberally with salt and turn over all ingredients several times to coat them well.

8. Put a lid on the pot and cook, always at low heat, turning the contents of the pot over from time to time, until the artichokes, peas, and beans are tender. It may take up to 2 hours, depending on the freshness and youth of the vegetables. Add ⅓ cup water whenever the cooking juices appear to be insufficient to keep the vegetables from sticking to the pot. You should need no more than 2 cups of water all together.

9. Taste and correct for salt, and serve warm, but not piping hot, from a shallow bowl or deep platter.

AHEAD-OF-TIME NOTE: You may cook the dish 2 or 3 days in advance, refrigerating it in an airtight container. Reheat gently but thoroughly before serving, adding a tablespoon or two of water if necessary.

ZUCCHINI COOKED IN TOMATO AND OLIVE OIL

ZUCCHINE IN UMIDO

I don't know if there is an exact equivalent in English of the Italian expression *in umido*. Translated literally, *umido*—"oo'mee.doh"—is "moist," and, as a culinary term, it is used to describe something stewed in a moist environment consisting specifically of tomatoes and olive oil. Usage allows the adjective *umido* (moist) to turn into a noun, thus becoming *un umido*, "a moist," in the same way that something fried—*fritto*—becomes *un fritto* and anything roasted—*arrosto*—is referred to as *un arrosto*. People will say, "I love an *umido* of chicken," or lamb, or potatoes, or zucchini as the case may be.

In both the recipes that follow, the *umido* is of zucchini. In the first of the two, done in the style of the Marches region, with garlic, onion, and pancetta, you will note that I slice the zucchini into rounds and let them steep in salt for a while. This is to draw off much of their liquid so that they will stay firm and retain their shape while they cook.

The second *umido* is a recipe devised by me, but its taste would not be unfamiliar to a cook from my native Romagna. Besides zucchini, there are two other vegetables—green beans and yellow bell pepper—and the dish is finished off with a fistful of shredded basil. Note how the beans and pepper are sautéed alone before adding the zucchini, so that each can become impregnated with the lightly garlic-scented olive oil. I slice the zucchini into thin sticks and do not steep them in salt as for the preceding recipe. I want them to retain all their natural moisture and become very soft when cooked, not minding if they even partly dissolve.

Also contributing to the distinct difference in flavor of these two *umidi* is the way the garlic is handled. For the first dish, it is sliced wafer-thin and it is steamed in the cooking juices, rather than sautéed. It develops a sweetness that is reinforced by the onion, but then contrasted by the savoriness of the pancetta. In the second zucchini recipe, the garlic is chopped and allowed to become lightly colored, and there is no onion to buffer its presence.

Zucchini, Tomatoes, and Pancetta in the Marches Style

UMIDO DI ZUCCHINE, POMODORI, E PANCETTA ALLA MARCHIGIANA

2 pounds zucchini OR
2½ pounds if small

Salt

3 tablespoons extra virgin olive oil

1½ cups very thinly sliced onion

4 garlic cloves, peeled and sliced very thin

6 ounces pancetta, cut into very narrow strips

3 tablespoons chopped Italian flat-leaf parsley

2 to 2¼ cups fresh, ripe, firm tomatoes, peeled and chopped, with all their seeds and juice OR canned imported Italian plum tomatoes, chopped, with their juice

Black pepper ground fresh

For 4 persons

1. Soak and clean the zucchini as described on page 162, trim away their ends, and slice them into the thinnest possible rounds.

2. Set a pasta colander over a bowl or deep dish, put the zucchini slices into it, and sprinkle them liberally with salt. Turn them over two or three times, and let them steep for at least 3 hours, allowing them to shed a substantial amount of liquid. Before cooking them, rinse off the salt with cold water and pat them dry with a kitchen towel.

3. When the zucchini have steeped 3 hours or more, choose a skillet or sauté pan that can subsequently contain them without piling them up too deep; put in the olive oil, onion, garlic, and pancetta; and turn on the heat to medium high. Cook, stirring a few times, until the onion becomes colored a light gold.

4. Add the parsley, stir quickly, then put in the zucchini. Turn them over thoroughly for several seconds, then put in the tomatoes and the ground pepper. Turn over all ingredients, turn the heat up to high, and cook, stirring occasionally, until the tomato juices are no longer runny and the fat begins to separate from the sauce, as described in the Note on page 133, about 10 to 15 minutes.

AHEAD-OF-TIME NOTE: You can cook the dish through to the end several hours in advance, and reheat it gently in the skillet before serving.

Zucchini, Green Beans, Bell Pepper, and Basil

UMIDO DI ZUCCHINE, FAGIOLINI, E PEPERONE CON IL BASILICO

1 pound young, small
   zucchini

1½ pounds green beans

1 meaty, large yellow bell
   pepper OR 2 smaller ones

½ pound fresh, ripe, firm
   tomatoes OR 1 cup
   canned imported Italian
   plum tomatoes, cut up
   with their juice

¼ cup extra virgin olive oil

1 tablespoon chopped garlic

Salt

Black pepper ground fresh

About 20 basil leaves, fewer
   if very large, shredded
   fine with a chopping
   knife

For 4 to 6 persons

1. Soak the zucchini for at least 20 minutes in a basin of cold water and clean as described on page 162. After slicing away their ends, cut them lengthwise in half, then into long, thin sticks, ½ inch wide or less.

2. Snap both ends off the green beans, then soak in a basin of cold water until ready to cook them.

3. Split the pepper in half, scoop away the pith-like core and seeds, skin it raw with a swiveling-blade peeler, then cut it lengthwise into ½-inch-wide strips.

4. If using raw tomatoes, wash them in cold water, skin raw with a swiveling-blade peeler, split them in half, scoop out the seeds without squeezing the tomato, and cut them up in small pieces.

5. Put the olive oil and garlic in a 12-inch sauté pan, turn on the heat to medium, and cook the garlic, stirring from time to time, until it becomes colored a very, very pale gold.

6. Retrieve the green beans from their soak, add them to the pan with a sprinkling of salt, then put a lid on and turn the heat down to low.

7. When the beans have cooked for 5 minutes, add the strips of pepper, turn, put the lid back on, and cook for another 5 minutes.

8. Add the zucchini, the tomatoes, and several grindings of pepper; turn over all ingredients to coat them well; and cook, uncovered, at a steady simmer, turning occasionally, for 15 or 20 minutes. Taste for doneness—the beans should be firm but tender, and the pepper and some of the zucchini will have partly dissolved. Taste and correct for salt.

9. Off heat, swirl in the shredded basil, and serve.

AHEAD-OF-TIME NOTE: The vegetables can be cooked several hours in advance. Reheat in a 250° oven for about 30 minutes. Add the basil just before serving.

Baked Eggplant Rolls with Mozzarella and Pecorino Cheese, Topped with Cherry Tomatoes

INVOLTINI DI MELANZANE CON MOZZARELLA E PECORINO

4 medium eggplants, about
 2½ pounds

Salt

1 inch of vegetable oil in a
 frying pan

8 ounces mozzarella, sliced
 very thin

About ¼ cup aged pecorino
 sheep's milk cheese,
 whittled into slivers

Black pepper ground fresh

1½ teaspoons chopped
 garlic

3 tablespoons finely
 chopped Italian flat-leaf
 parsley

Extra virgin olive oil for
 greasing a baking pan

20 cherry tomatoes

*For 4 persons if served as a
vegetable course, for 8 if served
as an appetizer or buffet dish*

1. Slice away the eggplants' green tops. Wash the eggplants and cut them lengthwise into slices ½ inch thick.

2. Set a pasta colander over a bowl or deep dish; line it inside with one layer of eggplant slices, placing them vertically, and sprinkle lightly with salt; place another layer of eggplant over the first and sprinkle a tiny bit more salt over it; and proceed thus until you have used up all the slices. Let stand for at least 30 minutes to allow the eggplant to shed some of its astringent liquid.

3. Pour enough vegetable oil into a 12-inch skillet to come 1 inch up the sides of the pan, and place over high heat. When the oil is hot enough to sizzle when tested by dipping one end of an eggplant slice into it, slip in as many slices as will fit very loosely, without crowding. Fry the eggplant to a rich golden brown, and use a slotted spatula to transfer to a platter lined with a double thickness of paper towels. Lay the slices flat without overlapping too much. Add more slices to the pan. When they are done transfer them to the platter, after having covered the previous layer with a double thickness of paper towels, and proceed thus until all the eggplants are done. Let cool completely.

4. Turn on the oven to 400°.

5. Divide the mozzarella and the pecorino slivers into as many portions as you have eggplant slices. Lay the slices flat on a counter, place on the center of each a portion of mozzarella and pecorino, and sprinkle with pepper. Combine the chopped garlic and parsley and distribute it evenly over the two cheeses. Roll up each slice tightly.

6. Choose a baking pan that can accommodate all the eggplant rolls in one layer without overlapping. Lightly grease the bottom of the pan with olive oil, and put in the rolls, arranging them so that the folded-over edge of the eggplant faces down.

7. Wash the cherry tomatoes, cut them in half at their middle, toss them in a bowl with a pinch of salt, then place them over the eggplant rolls, their cut side facing down. Bake for 20 to 25 minutes in the upper third of the preheated oven. Let settle down to lukewarm temperature before serving.

AHEAD-OF-TIME NOTE: You can fry the eggplant several hours in advance before proceeding with the rest of the preparation.

VEGETABLE BUNDLES

INVOLTINI

In a vegetable roll, the vegetable can be either the wrapper or what the wrapper encloses. The two recipes below are examples of both approaches and represent, respectively, southern and northern cooking styles.

In the first of these instances, the bundle to be baked is composed of two cheeses, garlic, and parsley and bound by fried eggplant slices. One of the cheeses, mozzarella, is required for its melting quality; the other, pecorino—sheep's milk cheese—for its savory bite. The most widely available pecorino is the starkly rustic Romano, but if you can find a firm Tuscan sheep's milk *caciotta* or the Sardinian *fiore sardo*, their more restrained pungency would make them a better choice.

In the other roll, bacon is wrapped around a sheaf of Swiss chard stalks cut into thin strips. This is a lovely Piedmontese confection employing butter, milk, béchamel, and Parmesan. Before the dish is fully assembled for baking, the chard leaves are cooked separately in milk and butter. In the baking dish, little mounds of the sautéed leaves fill the spaces between the sheaves of bacon-circled stalks. Béchamel and grated Parmesan top the luscious composition.

Baked Swiss Chard Stalks Wrapped in Bacon

INVOLTINI DI COSTE DI BIETE

—————— 🌿 ——————

2 pounds mature Swiss
   chard with broad stalks

Salt

1½ tablespoons butter plus
   butter for smearing a
   baking dish

2 tablespoons milk

Black pepper ground fresh

8 thin slices bacon

A béchamel sauce made as
   described below, using 1
   tablespoon butter, 1 cup
   milk, 1 tablespoon flour

⅛ teaspoon grated nutmeg

5 tablespoons freshly grated
   Parmigiano-Reggiano
   cheese

———————————

*For 4 persons if served as a
vegetable course, for 8 if an
appetizer*

An oven-to-table baking dish,
13 by 9 inches, or any
rectangular shape of similar
capacity

1. Detach the Swiss chard stalks from the leaves. Wash both in several changes of cold water.

2. Trim the stalks into pieces 5 to 6 inches long and cut these into strips about ⅓ inch wide.

3. Bring water to a boil in a saucepan, then put in the stalks. Cook until very tender, about 25 to 30 minutes after the water resumes boiling. Drain with a colander spoon—do not empty the water from the pan—and set aside to cool.

4. Bring the water in the saucepan back to a boil; add a liberal quantity of salt to it; and, as it begins to boil again, put in the Swiss chard leaves. Cook until tender, about 8 minutes at a steady boil. Drain.

5. Turn on the oven to 400°.

6. Put 1½ tablespoons of butter in a skillet, turn on the heat to medium high, and when the butter foam begins to subside, add the drained chard leaves together with 2 tablespoons of milk, salt, and a generous grinding of pepper. Cook the leaves, turning them over frequently, until they are no longer sopping, about 2 to 3 minutes.

7. Thinly smear the bottom of the baking dish with butter.

8. Divide the chard stalks into eight equal bunches. Sprinkle lightly with salt. Wrap each bunch in a slice of bacon and place the bunches in the baking dish, leaving space between.

9. Divide the chard leaves into small mounds about 2 inches thick, and place these in the baking pan in the spaces between the stalk bundles.

10. To make the béchamel sauce, put the milk in a saucepan, turning on the heat to medium low. Cook until the milk is just short of boiling, reaching the point when it begins to form a ring of small, pearly bubbles.

While you are heating the milk, put the butter in a medium saucepan, turning on the heat under it to low. When the butter has melted completely, stir in all the flour, using a wooden spoon. Continue to cook, stirring constantly, for about 2 minutes. Do not allow the flour to become colored. Remove from heat.

Add the hot milk from the other pan, 2 tablespoons at a time, to the flour-and-butter mixture. Stir continuously. As soon as the first 2 tablespoons of milk have been incorporated into the mixture, add 2 more, continuing to stir. When, through this procedure, you have put in ½ cup milk, you can add the remaining ½ cup of milk at one time, stirring steadily, smoothly amalgamating the milk with the flour and butter.

Place the pan over low heat and cook, stirring constantly, until the sauce is as dense as thick cream. If you find any lumps forming, dissolve them by beating the sauce rapidly with a whisk.

Into it stir ⅛ teaspoon grated nutmeg and 2 tablespoons of grated Parmesan.

11. Spread the béchamel over the chard stalks and leaves. Sprinkle over it the remaining 3 tablespoons of grated Parmesan, and place the dish in the uppermost level of the preheated oven. Bake until the top becomes colored a light gold, about 20 minutes. Let settle down to room temperature before serving.

AHEAD-OF-TIME NOTE: You can assemble the dish and make it ready for baking several hours in advance. Cover with plastic wrap, but do not refrigerate if you want to keep the greens from acquiring a metallic taste.

Vegetable Pies and Molds

TORTE DI VERDURA

———— ❧ ————

Pies are one of the most ingenious things Italian cooks do with vegetables. When baked in a pastry crust they are called a *torta*; when unmolded from the baking dish they are known as a *sformato*. They are adaptable to various menu plans. They greatly enrich a buffet table set for a party; they become a luxurious appetizer that launches an elaborate holiday dinner; a single wedge is a fine vegetable accompaniment to a meat course; or they can be the whole meal when it consists of just one course.

The three recipes that follow come from Tuscany, Piedmont, and the Veneto, in that order. Just to read them, which I hope will lead to cooking and tasting them, should communicate a sense of the unmistakably distinct flavor values on which is founded the cooking of those regions.

Baked Cauliflower Tuscan-Style

SFORMATO DI CAVOLFIORE ALLA TOSCANA

———— ❧ ————

2 to 2½ pounds cauliflower or broccoflower

2 tablespoons butter plus butter for smearing the baking dish

A béchamel sauce (see page 372) made with 1 tablespoon butter, 1½ tablespoons flour, and 1 cup whole milk

2 extra-large eggs

As the wife of a man who writes about wine I have come to realize that there is no group of people so hospitable as wine producers. Accompanying Victor on his visits to Italy's wine districts has earned me a place at a broad variety of regional tables.

At a densely attended bibulous occasion in Montalcino—the southern Tuscan town where one of the world's most fascinating red wines, Brunello, is produced—a large spread was served buffet-style at midday. A vegetable pie was served that tasted better at each bite. I returned for seconds, and for thirds. One of the guests at my table, a woman of about my years, smiled after my third trip back from the buffet. "I am happy to see you like the cauliflower *sformato*," she said. "It's irresistible," I replied. "I wish I knew how to make it." "I can tell you," she said. "I am the one who made it."

Optional (see headnote):
   ¼ pound boiled,
   unsmoked ham, cut into
   narrow strips
Salt
Black pepper ground fresh
⅛ teaspoon grated nutmeg
⅔ cup plus 2 tablespoons
   freshly grated
   Parmigiano-Reggiano
   cheese

For 4 persons or, if served as a small appetizer, for 6
A 7 by 11-inch oven-to-table baking dish or any other format of comparable capacity

1. Trim away most of the cauliflower's outer leaves, keeping just the layer of tender leaves close to the head. Cut off a thin slice from the butt end and cut a cross into the root. Wash the cauliflower in cold water. Bring to a boil enough water to amply cover it and drop in the cauliflower. Cook about 20 minutes. Drain when it feels tender but firm when prodded with a fork.

2. When the cauliflower is cool enough to handle, cut into small pieces, the root end into smaller pieces than the rest.

3. Choose a skillet that can subsequently accommodate the cauliflower pieces in a single layer without overlapping, put in 2 tablespoons of butter, and turn on the heat to medium high. When the butter foam begins to subside, add the cauliflower pieces, turning them over for about 1 minute to coat them well. Transfer the cauliflower to a bowl and let it cool completely.

4. Turn on the oven to 400°.

5. Make a rather firm béchamel as described on page 372.

6. Break the eggs into a deep dish and beat them lightly with a fork.

7. Put all but 3 or 4 tablespoons of béchamel into the bowl with the cold cauliflower. Add the beaten eggs, the optional strips of ham, salt, liberal grindings of black pepper, grated nutmeg, and ⅔ cup grated Parmesan. Turn over all ingredients thoroughly with a spoon.

8. Thinly smear the inside of the baking dish with butter. Empty into it the contents of the bowl with the cauliflower pieces, leveling them off with a spatula. Spread the remaining 3 or 4 tablespoons of béchamel over the top, and sprinkle with 2 tablespoons of grated Parmesan.

9. Bake in the upper middle level of the preheated oven until a light golden crust forms on top, about 30 minutes. Let it settle for several minutes after removing it from the oven to serve it lukewarm.

AHEAD-OF-TIME NOTE: You can prepare the dish a few hours in advance up to the time it is ready for baking. Cover with plastic wrap and, if refrigerated, bring to room temperature before putting it in the oven.

Baked Leek Pie

TORTA DI PORRI

FOR THE DOUGH

1⅓ cups flour

5 tablespoons butter

⅓ cup water

½ teaspoon salt

FOR THE FILLING

3 to 3½ pounds leeks

3 tablespoons butter, cut
    into small pieces

Salt

2 eggs plus 2 yolks

Black pepper ground fresh

1 cup freshly grated
    Parmigiano-Reggiano
    cheese

½ cup heavy cream

⅛ teaspoon nutmeg

1 tablespoon butter for the
    pan

For 6 persons

A 9 by 2-inch round heavy cake
pan

Those who have had some acquaintance with Piedmont's cooking will recognize it in the textural sumptuousness and rich flavor of this torte. The leeks for its batter are cooked very slowly in a covered pan with butter and a little salt, a procedure that concentrates this vegetable's distinctive sweet-and-sour quality. Piedmontese cooks love egg yolks, and they are used liberally here, together with cream and Parmesan. Yet the dish compels our attention not purely for the richness of its components but, once tasted, for the grace with which they are balanced.

Making the Pie Dough

Pour the flour, butter, water, and salt into a food processor, and run the processor, pulsing it, until the ingredients form a ball of dough. Knead the dough briefly by hand, then wrap it in foil and put it in the refrigerator for 40 minutes or more.

Making the Leek Filling

1. Turn on the oven to 425°.

2. Trim the root end away from the leeks and slice away about an inch from the green tops. Cut both the bulbs and tender green tops of the leeks into very thin rounds. Soak in several changes of cold water, drain, and pat dry in a towel.

3. Put the leeks into a 12-inch skillet or sauté pan together with 3 tablespoons of butter and a pinch of salt. Put a lid on the pan and turn on the heat to medium low. Cook, occasionally turning the leeks over with a wooden spoon, until they wilt and are considerably diminished in bulk, about 30 minutes or more.

4. Put the leeks in a bowl to cool down.

5. Into another bowl, break open the eggs, separating and discarding the whites, and adding the yolks together with black pepper, grated

Parmesan, cream, and nutmeg. Beat the ingredients until they form a homogeneous mixture.

6. Smear the inside of the baking pan with 1 tablespoon butter.

7. Spread flat on a work surface a sheet of aluminum foil a bit larger than the diameter of the baking pan. Take the dough out of the refrigerator, put it on the foil, and roll it out very thin, trying for less than ¼ inch, and wide enough to cover nearly all the foil. If it sticks, sprinkle a little flour over it and on the rolling pin. Pick up the foil and turn it upside down over the baking pan. Lift away the foil, and press the dough into the pan. Cut away any excess and use that excess, if necessary, to patch any place in the pan that has remained bare.

8. Put the leeks into the pan, topping them with the egg and Parmesan mixture. Bake in the upper middle level of the oven for about 30 minutes. Let it settle for at least 10 minutes before serving.

AHEAD-OF-TIME NOTE: The leek torte is very appetizing when still hot, but it is also excellent lukewarm or several hours later at room temperature. It is not quite so lovely after a night in the refrigerator, but if you must keep it that long, let it come to full room temperature before serving.

Artichoke and Swiss Chard Pie

TORTA DI CARCIOFI E BIETE

——————— ✦ ———————

FOR THE PIE DOUGH

1¼ cups lukewarm water

A pinch of granulated sugar

1½ teaspoons active dry
    yeast

3½ cups all-purpose flour

¼ cup extra virgin olive oil

2 teaspoons salt

Some extra virgin olive oil
    for greasing a bowl

Venice is recognized as a source of a dazzling variety of seafood and seafood dishes, but what is not so generally known is that, for its light-handed cooking, it also draws on the riches of the vegetable gardens that cover the farm islands of its lagoon. Most prominent among these islands is S. Erasmo, whose fields benefit from exposure to the savory, salt-laden breezes of the Adriatic. S. Erasmo's most famous product is artichoke. In the spring it is copious in the market, whence it finds its way into risotto, into pasticcio — the Venetian version of lasagne — into fish and vegetable combinations; raw, into salads; and, most elegantly perhaps, into pies such as this one.

Here artichokes are combined with Swiss chard, another S. Erasmo specialty. A Venetian cook would have the option of buying young spring chard before it has grown a large stalk, when it looks like spinach, but I have rarely seen chard that young abroad. If you have only mature chard available, use just the leaves for this recipe, keeping the stalks for a soup or for gratinéing or for other chard recipes that you find in this and in my previous books.

With the young vegetables of the lagoon, olive oil is the cooking medium of choice, and that is what I have used here. The taste impressions this dish makes, light in weight yet deep in satisfaction, evoke the spirit that animates Venetian cooking at its freshest.

Making the Pie Dough

1. Put ¼ cup lukewarm water in a small cup together with a pinch of sugar and the dry yeast. Let the yeast dissolve and come to life for about 2 minutes.

2. Put the flour, ¼ cup olive oil, 2 teaspoons salt, 1 cup lukewarm water, and the dissolved yeast in a food processor and run the steel blade for 45 seconds to 1 minute until the dough masses.

1 lemon

4 globe artichokes

¼ cup extra virgin olive oil

3 tablespoons chopped
    onion

Salt

Black pepper ground fresh

1 pound Swiss chard

½ pound ricotta

1 cup freshly grated
    Parmigiano-Reggiano
    cheese

2 eggs

Some extra virgin olive oil
    for filming the baking pan

---

*8 appetizer or side dish portions,
or 4 to 6 portions if served as a
full course*

A 9½-inch springform pan

3. Remove the dough and knead it briefly by hand.

4. Grease the inside of a bowl with a thin film of olive oil, put in the dough, cover with plastic wrap, and set aside to rise in a warm corner of the kitchen for at least 2 hours.

Making the Artichoke and Chard Filling

1. Squeeze the juice of 1 lemon into a bowl of cold water.

2. Prepare the artichokes as described on pages 362–63, trimming away all the tough, inedible portions. Cut the trimmed artichokes lengthwise into the thinnest possible slices. Drop the slices into the bowl containing water and lemon juice.

3. Put the olive oil and chopped onion in a 12-inch skillet, and turn on the heat to medium. Cook the onion, stirring frequently, until it begins to be colored a pale gold.

4. Drain the artichokes, rinse them in cold water, and put them in the skillet, adding salt and black pepper. Turn the artichokes over three or four times to coat them well; then add ¼ cup water, turn the heat down, and cover the pan. Cook, turning the vegetable over occasionally, until it feels very, very tender when tested with a fork, from 15 to 30 minutes, depending on its freshness and youth. If during the cooking the pan juices should prove insufficient to keep the artichokes from sticking, add 2 tablespoons of water whenever necessary. When done, however, there should be no liquid left in the pan and the artichokes should become deeply colored. If there are watery juices left, uncover the pan, raise the heat, and boil them away.

5. While the artichokes are cooking, detach the thick stalks on the Swiss chard and set them aside to use in other dishes as described on pages 88 and 372. Wash the leaves in several changes of cold water until the water runs completely clear. Bring a quart or more of water to boil in a saucepan; add 1 tablespoon salt, which serves to keep the chard green; and put in the chard leaves. Cook a few minutes, until very soft, drain, and when cool enough to handle, chop coarsely.

(continued)

6. When the artichokes are done, add the chopped chard to the skillet, turn the heat up to medium high, and with a wooden spoon, turn the full contents of the pan over several times to coat them well. Transfer the artichokes and chard to a bowl and let the vegetables cool off completely.

7. Turn the oven on to 375°.

8. When the vegetables in the bowl are cold, add the ricotta, the grated Parmesan, and the eggs, holding back about ½ teaspoonful of egg. Turn the ingredients over for as long as it takes to produce a uniformly distributed mixture, then taste and correct for salt and pepper.

Assembling and Baking the Pie

1. Lightly film the inside of a springform pan with olive oil.

2. Divide the risen dough into two parts, one slightly larger than the other. Roll out the larger half into a disk about 14 inches in diameter and use the disk to line the bottom and sides of the baking pan. If the pan shows through in one or two places, pull the dough over, patching it together with thumb pressure.

3. Pour the vegetable filling into the pan, leveling it off.

4. Roll out the remaining dough into a disk large enough to cover the pan. Place it over the filling and press the two edges of the dough together to make a tight seal.

5. Pierce the dough covering the filling in several places to allow steam to escape during the baking. Brush the top with the reserved ½ teaspoon of egg.

6. Place the pan in the upper middle level of the preheated oven and bake for about 1 hour, until the top of the pie becomes colored a light gold. Let settle for 15 minutes or more before serving.

AHEAD-OF-TIME NOTE: The pie is also excellent when served several hours later at room temperature. Do not refrigerate, because that will alter the flavor of the chard.

Stuffed Vegetables

VERDURE RIPIENE

Hollowing out and stuffing vegetables is a delicious game that Italian cooks like to play. It is fun to do because you can make up most of the rules as you go along and nearly always end up with a winner. The stuffed peppers and stuffed zucchini in the recipes that follow illustrate how varied can be the combinations of ingredients that make congenial stuffings. Also see the stuffed peppers and stuffed tomatoes in Appetizers (pages 57–62).

Baked Stuffed Peppers

PEPERONI RIPIENI

4 meaty yellow or red bell peppers, about 2½ pounds

¾ pound eggplants, preferably the long, skinny variety

Salt

6 flat anchovy fillets, preferably the ones prepared at home as described on page 148

2 tablespoons Italian flat-leaf parsley

1 tablespoon capers

1 medium garlic clove, peeled

3 tablespoons fine, dry, unflavored bread crumbs

What makes these peppers particularly succulent is that they are stripped of their skin before they are stuffed and baked. You must char the skin to loosen it from the pepper, as the recipe describes. Once flayed, the pepper needs to be hollowed out—and this is where you want to use care, because if you tear the now tender pepper, it would become useless as a container.

1. Wash the peppers, then place each over a gas flame. If you don't have gas, put them under your oven's broiler. Turn them just until their skin is charred on all sides, but do not overcook them; they must remain very firm. As each pepper is done, put it in a sturdy plastic bag, closing the bag tightly. When all the peppers are done, set the bag aside to allow its contents to cool completely.

2. Wash the eggplants and cut off the green tops. Dice the eggplants into cubes of approximately ⅓ inch. Put them in a colander set over a bowl, and sprinkle salt over them. Let the eggplants steep thus, shedding their bitter juices, for at least 30 minutes.

3. Chop the anchovies, parsley, capers, and garlic all together, using a food processor if you like, but taking care not to puree them, and put them in a medium bowl.

⅛ teaspoon oregano

2 tablespoons extra virgin olive oil

A fresh, ripe, firm tomato, preferably the plum variety

Vegetable oil, enough to come 1 inch up the sides of the skillet

Black pepper ground fresh

For 4 persons as a full course, for 8 as an appetizer

4. Add 2 tablespoons of bread crumbs, the oregano, and 1 tablespoon olive oil. Mix thoroughly.

5. Using a swiveling-blade vegetable peeler, peel the tomato raw, cut it in half, scoop out the seeds without squeezing it, and cut it into ½-inch squares. Add the tomato to the bowl containing the other ingredients, and toss well.

6. Turn the oven on to 400°.

7. Retrieve the eggplant cubes from the colander and pat them dry with kitchen towels. Pour enough vegetable oil into a 10- to 12-inch skillet to come 1 inch up the sides, and turn on the heat to medium high. As soon as the oil is hot—if you hold your hand palm downward just above the pan, the air rising from it should feel quite hot—slip in the eggplant cubes. Fry them to a pale golden brown, then transfer them with a slotted spoon to the bowl containing the mixture of other ingredients and toss well.

8. Remove the peppers from the plastic bag and, using a little paring knife, pull away their charred skin, taking care to keep the peppers whole. Take a thin slice off the top of each pepper to create an opening. With the knife blade, gently detach the pepper's core and seeds without cutting through the flesh. Use a teaspoon to scoop out any seeds remaining. Stuff the peppers with the mixture from the bowl.

9. Choose a baking dish which can accommodate the peppers standing as straight as possible, their tops facing up. Sprinkle over the tops the remaining tablespoon of bread crumbs and of olive oil. Bake in the upper middle level of the preheated oven for 15 to 20 minutes. Allow to settle when done, and serve no hotter than lukewarm or, even better, at room temperature.

AHEAD-OF-TIME NOTE: They will never taste quite so wonderful as when freshly made, but you can keep the baked peppers in the refrigerator for 3 or 4 days. Bring to room temperature before serving.

Stuffed Zucchini Pesaro-Style with Ground Meat, Tomatoes, Parmesan, and White Wine

ZUCCHINE RIPIENE DI VITELLO ALLA PESARESE

7 or 8 medium zucchini

1 pound fresh, firm tomatoes OR 1 cup canned imported Italian plum tomatoes, cut up, with their juice

¼ cup extra virgin olive oil

10 ounces ground veal or pork

2 garlic cloves, peeled and lightly mashed with the handle of a knife

⅔ cup freshly grated Parmigiano-Reggiano cheese

Salt

Black pepper ground fresh

A medium yellow onion, chopped fine, about ½ cup

½ cup dry white wine

For 6 persons

From my earliest efforts as a cook, I have enjoyed exploring the potential of a hollowed zucchini and have found it can contain a diversity of good things: ground pork and such pork products as prosciutto and pancetta, ground lamb and rice, or rice with wholly vegetarian accompaniments such as onions, tomatoes, and herbs. You can adapt the procedure described below to produce combinations of your own devising. These are the zucchini I have been making lately, a dish I had in the Marches seaside town of Pesaro. I find them very fine because they contain veal—the meat most delicate in taste—which within its moist vegetable cocoon stays unusually juicy. You may also use pork, although for the fine, sweet taste of its meat, veal is my first choice.

1. Soak the zucchini for at least 20 minutes in a basin of cold water and scrub clean as described on page 162. Slice off both ends. If you have very large zucchini, cut them in half to obtain pieces about 4 to 5 inches long.

2. Use a narrow-bladed knife or other suitable tool to hollow out the zucchini, scooping out their center to make tubes with thin walls that will later contain the meat stuffing. Be careful not to pierce the skin. Chop the scooped-out zucchini flesh rather fine and set aside.

3. If using fresh tomatoes, skin them raw with a swivel-bladed vegetable peeler, cut them in half, scoop out the seeds with a spoon without squeezing the tomatoes, and cut them up in several pieces.

4. Put 1 tablespoon of olive oil in a small skillet and turn the heat on to medium high. As soon as the oil is hot enough to sizzle instantly on contact with the meat, put in the ground veal and cook it to a light brown color, turning it a few times. Use a slotted spoon or spatula to transfer it to a bowl. Do not clean out the skillet.

5. Put 1 tablespoon of olive oil in the same skillet, add the mashed garlic cloves, and cook them at medium high heat, stirring frequently, until they become colored a light gold. Remove them from the pan with a slotted spoon or spatula and discard.

6. Put the chopped zucchini flesh in the skillet and brown it lightly at medium heat for 5 to 6 minutes, turning it from time to time.

7. Put the browned zucchini flesh in the bowl containing the ground veal; add the grated Parmesan, salt, and black pepper; and mix all ingredients, combining them smoothly and uniformly.

8. Stuff the hollowed-out zucchini with the mixture. It doesn't matter if the stuffing is not sufficient to fill them tightly.

9. Put 2 tablespoons of olive oil in a 12-inch sauté pan or skillet and turn the heat on to medium high. As soon as the oil is hot, put in as many zucchini as will fit loosely in a single level without overlapping. Turn them, browning them on all sides, then use a slotted spoon or spatula to transfer them to a platter. If in the process a little bit of the stuffing should fall out, it's of no consequence. If the zucchini did not all fit comfortably into the pan in a single batch, do another batch, repeating the procedure. Do not clean out the pan when they are done.

10. Put the chopped onion in the pan where you browned the zucchini, and cook it over medium high heat, stirring, until it becomes colored a light gold.

11. Return all the zucchini to the pan, squeezing them in tightly if necessary, and add the wine. While the wine bubbles away, use a wooden spoon to scrape loose the browning residues from the bottom of the pan. Sprinkle lightly with salt, put in the cut-up tomatoes with their juice, turn over the contents of the pan once or twice, then put a lid on and turn the heat down to low. Cook at low heat for about 30 or 40 minutes, gently turning the zucchini from time to time. When done, allow their heat to subside for about 5 minutes before serving.

AHEAD-OF-TIME NOTE: The dish can be cooked through to the end several hours in advance. It can even be done overnight, but after a night in the refrigerator the vegetables won't taste quite so sweet.

Salads

SALADS
Le Insalate

———— ✿ ————

Raw Zucchini Salad with Mint
  and Tomato Dice

Arugula and Finocchio Salad

Roman Puntarelle Chicory Salad

  Belgian Endive Salad Puntarelle-Style

Potato Salads

  Potato Salad with Onions and Pickles

  Pierino Jovine's Amalfi-Style
    Potato Salad

Capri-Style Tomato
  and Buffalo-Mozzarella Salad

  Victor's Capri-Style Tomato
    and Mozzarella Salad

Salads with Beans

  Warm Cime di Rapa Salad
    with Cannellini Beans

  Raw Boston Lettuce Salad
    with Warm Chickpeas

Shrimp and Scallop Salad
  with Orange Sections

Sardinian Salad with Seafood
  and Couscous

Turkey Breast Salad with Pomegranate

*Preceding photograph (clockwise from top right):
Pierino Jovine's Amalfi-Style Potato Salad, Turkey Breast
Salad with Pomegranate, Raw Zucchini Salad with Mint
and Tomato Dice, Arugula and Finocchio Salad*

When I was growing up, a salad meant raw seasonal greens that were tossed with salt, olive oil, and vinegar. Most frequently it was a single green, the freshest lettuce that was available that morning. In a more festive mood, to mark a holiday or simply to celebrate the good taste of life, my mother would fill the bowl with raw young artichokes sliced very thin, with red-rimmed disks of radishes, spindly carrot sticks, diced celery, *finocchio* slices, sliced onion that had been sweetened by soaking in many changes of cold water, the wild pungent *rucola*—arugula—and an assortment of wild chicory—*misticanza*. For such a salad, I could hardly wait to get past the meal that was served before it.

In the summer we had tomatoes that, in addition to the obligatory olive oil, my father sometimes dressed with a few drops of vinegar in which he had previously steeped a mashed clove of garlic and dissolved the salt. It made a ripe tomato taste even sweeter. In the winter, we also used garlic to scent a piece of bread with which we tossed shredded Savoy cabbage. Otherwise, we rarely flavored salads with garlic.

All these were what we called *l'insalata*, "the" salad, a dish that had an unvarying place and function in the meal. It came always after the meat or fish course that had in turn followed the pasta, risotto, or soup. It freshened and lightened the palate by sweeping away and replacing the weightier impressions that had been stamped on it by the preceding courses.

Then there were all the other salads, no longer identified as *l'insalata*, but called "*un'insalata di . . .*"—"a salad of . . . "—followed by the name of whatever each contained. Thus we had *insalate di verdura cotta*, salads made with boiled vegetables such as zucchini, green beans, or potatoes, either singly or together, always tossed with salt, liberal quantities of good olive oil, and vinegar. The boiled vegetable could also be asparagus or cauliflower or a leaf vegetable such as chard. In the latter case we would substitute lemon juice for vinegar and call it *all'agro* from the Italian for citrus fruit, *agrume*. We would try to serve such salads still lukewarm, and often they would turn into a major course of their own, possibly accompanied by cheese, particularly at the light evening meal.

Those plain, and to me insuperable, salads have since been joined by a growing throng of dishes that bear the name "salad." As our lives and eating habits have changed so has their place at table. They can be appetizers, party dishes, a luncheon course. On a hot summer day or evening some could well be the whole meal. If I had them too often, I would feel deprived of the profoundly restorative power that only a fully structured Italian meal of small but substantial courses can generate. But there are times when one cannot rise to the challenge of a large spread, and the sparkling freshness of a salad like the Sardinian seafood with couscous, the scallops with oranges, or the turkey with pomegranate, which you will find in these pages in addition to a few simple vegetarian salads, may be just what the taste buds need to revive their forces.

Raw Zucchini Salad with Mint and Tomato Dice

INSALATA DI ZUCCHINE CON LA MENTA E DADOLATA DI POMODORO

½ pound small, very fresh
   zucchini

A stalk of celery

½ cup ripe, fresh tomatoes,
   their seeds scooped out,
   cut into small dice

1 tablespoon chopped fresh
   mint leaves

2 garlic cloves, peeled and
   tied up in cheesecloth

Salt

The freshly squeezed juice
   of ½ lemon

2 tablespoons extra virgin
   olive oil

Black pepper ground fresh

For 4 to 6 persons

All that this wonderfully aromatic and comely salad asks of you is that you select very young, small, but not miniature, zucchini with tiny seeds. You want raw zucchini that will taste sweet and firm, not stale and spongy. The tomato too should be chosen at the season's peak when it is firm and sugary. So many kinds of mint are available, from mild to spicy, that you can opt for the kind you find most pleasing.

1. Soak the zucchini for about 20 minutes in a basin of cold water. Scrub them under running cold water using a brush or rough cloth. Cut off both ends, then cut the zucchini into 2- to 2½-inch lengths. Slice the zucchini very, very thin using a swiveling-blade vegetable peeler. As you near the end of each piece, turn it to hold it better while you continue slicing. You should end up with very thin julienne-style strips. When all the zucchini strips are done, put them in a salad bowl.

2. Snap one end of the celery stalk to pull away the strings, wash it in cold water, and cut it into ¼-inch dice. You should end up with about ¼ cup. Add it to the salad bowl.

3. Put the tomato dice and the chopped mint into the bowl.

4. Smash the tied-up garlic cloves using the flat side of a large knife blade, then add them to the bowl without undoing the cheesecloth.

5. Add salt, lemon juice, olive oil, and several grindings of black pepper, and toss thoroughly. Invert a pasta colander over the bowl—or a strainer large enough to cover—and refrigerate for 1 hour.

6. Before serving, pick out and discard the garlic bundle.

AHEAD-OF-TIME NOTE: You can keep the salad in the refrigerator for several hours, but in that case do not add salt until just before serving; otherwise, the zucchini will shed too much liquid.

Arugula and Finocchio Salad

L'INSALATA CON RUCOLA E FINOCCHIO

½ pound arugula

1 large *finocchio*

3 tablespoons extra virgin olive oil

Salt

1 tablespoon freshly squeezed lemon juice OR wine vinegar

Black pepper ground fresh

For 6 persons

The fresh, lively, cleansing effect that this salad has on the palate comes from the way the two ingredients act upon each other. The mellow, licorice-like quality of the *finocchio* picks up briskness from the arugula's pungency, which is even more accentuated if you can obtain the sharp-edged leaves of wild arugula. In the event you are using wild arugula, you might want to use a little less of it. The softness of arugula's leaves contrasts with *finocchio's* crispness, just as the dense green color of the former dapples the bright white flesh of the latter.

1. Trim away the larger stalks of the arugula and soak it in two or three changes of cold water. Drain and shake dry in a salad spinner or in a cloth towel. Put into a salad bowl.

2. Discard the *finocchio's* outer leaves if bruised and discolored. Trim away all protruding top stalks and slice off a thin disk from the root end. Wash under cold running water. Cut in half lengthwise, then slice it crosswise as thin as possible with a sharp, sturdy knife or a mandoline if you have one. Add the sliced *finocchio* to the salad bowl.

3. Toss with olive oil, salt, lemon juice (or vinegar), and generous grindings of black pepper, and serve at once.

Roman Puntarelle Chicory Salad

LE PUNTARELLE

A 1½- to 2-pound head of *puntarelle* chicory

Ice cubes

4 medium garlic cloves, lightly mashed with a knife handle and peeled

2 tablespoons red wine vinegar

Salt

4 tablespoons extra virgin olive oil

4 anchovy fillets, preferably the ones prepared at home as described on page 148, chopped very fine

Black pepper ground fresh

For 6 persons

*P*untarelle is a variety of chicory grown for the Roman market; it is used primarily for raw salads. A head of the full-grown vegetable weighs about 1½ to 2 pounds. A crown of long, slender, dark green outside leaves resembling those of *catalogna* chicory cradle within them a mass of white, twisted, hollow stalks. It is from these stalks that *puntarelle* salad, the crispest and possibly most refreshing of all salads, is made.

Puntarelle chicory is just becoming available in America; past experience suggests that its day will come as it did for other Italian vegetables: arugula and radicchio. If you want to grow it, seeds are available from The Cook's Garden, Box 535, Londonderry, VT 05148.

1. Pull off all the outer green leaves of the chicory, exposing the inner clump of gnarled, white stalks. Put the green leaves away to use as described in the Note at the end of this recipe.

2. Detach the white stalks from their base and cut each lengthwise in half. You will see that the stalk is hollow. Keep cutting it lengthwise to obtain strips ¼ inch wide.

3. Put several ice cubes in a large bowl, fill with water, and put in the *puntarelle* strips. Let them soak in the ice water for at least 1 hour. Do not refrigerate. The strips will curl into ring-like shapes.

4. Put the mashed garlic and vinegar in a very small saucer.

5. When ready to toss the salad, drain the *puntarelle* and shake them dry in a salad spinner or gathered up in a dry towel. Put them into a salad bowl; add the vinegar, holding back the garlic, a pinch or two of salt, the olive oil, the chopped anchovies, and liberal grindings of black pepper. Toss thoroughly, taste and correct for salt, vinegar, and oil, and serve at once.

NOTE: You can keep the outer green leaves in the vegetable drawer of the refrigerator up to 3 or 4 days before cooking them. Wash them, drop them in abundant boiling salted water, cook until tender, drain, toss with olive oil and lemon juice, and serve lukewarm either as a salad or as a side dish.

Belgian Endive Salad Puntarelle-Style

While waiting for the *puntarelle* you have planted to grow, you can cut and toss Belgian endive in the same style. You will come remarkably close to the *puntarelle* salad's taste, if not its texture.

1. Substitute 1 pound of Belgian endive, about 4 thick heads, for the one head of *puntarelle* chicory.

2. Trim away a thin slice from the butt end of each head of endive and detach the leaves, discarding any blemished ones, shred them lengthwise into the skinniest possible strips, soak briefly in cold water, and drain. Shake thoroughly dry in a cloth towel or a salad spinner, and put into a salad bowl.

3. Except for the ice cubes (and the ice-water soak), use all the other ingredients and follow the steps in the recipe for puntarelle salad on page 392.

Potato Salads

INSALATE DI PATATE

———————— ✦ ————————

To me, and I do not hesitate to say to all Italians, "potato salad" means creamy, new potatoes, boiled slowly in their skins, drained, peeled, sliced thin, and dressed while warm with salt, wine vinegar, and a large amount of olive oil. It is so devastatingly satisfying that, in a country where practically every family has a different idea of what is good to eat, it can claim to be perhaps the one universal example of comfort food.

You can use the description above as the basic potato salad recipe: What more does a cook need to know? Following, however, you'll find two variations for vivacious alternatives to a familiar theme.

Potato Salad with Onions and Pickles

INSALATA GUSTOSA DI PATATE E CETRIOLINI

———————— ✦ ————————

1¼ pounds boiling or new potatoes

Salt

¼ cup red wine vinegar; see headnote

⅓ cup extra virgin olive oil

⅓ cup very finely chopped onion

Black pepper ground fresh

1½ tablespoons finely chopped *cornichons* (small vinegar pickles)

1½ tablespoons roughly cut-up Italian flat-leaf parsley

For 4 to 6 persons

1. Wash the potatoes, put them in a saucepan of cold water with their skins on, cover, bring to a boil, and cook at a steady but moderate boil until they are tender enough to be easily pierced by a fork. Drain.

2. Peel the potatoes while they are hot and cut them right away into ¼-inch slices. Try to keep the slices whole, if possible, using a fine, sharp knife, but do not worry if they break apart—it won't affect the taste.

3. Put the sliced potatoes in a warm ceramic or glass serving bowl, sprinkle salt on liberally, drizzle immediately with vinegar, and toss gently. They should still be quite warm when you add the vinegar. Add the olive oil, onion, black pepper, chopped pickles, and parsley; turn the potatoes over several times; let them steep in their seasonings until they come to room temperature; then serve.

AHEAD-OF-TIME NOTE: If it eases the pressure, you can have the onion and pickles and parsley chopped as many hours in advance as you like, but the vinegar must hit the potatoes while they are still hot. They can be kept a little while—but not in a refrigerator—after they have been tossed and have reached room temperature.

Pierino Jovine's Amalfi-Style Potato Salad

INSALATA DI PATATE ALL'AMALFITANA

1½ pounds new potatoes

1 tablespoon capers

4 black, round Greek olives

2 tablespoons extra virgin olive oil

4 anchovy fillets, preferably the ones prepared at home as described on page 148

2 tablespoons chopped Italian flat-leaf parsley

½ teaspoon very finely chopped garlic

Salt

Black pepper ground fresh

1 tablespoon red wine vinegar

For 4 to 6 persons

1. Wash the potatoes thoroughly in cold water, put them in a saucepan with their skins on, and add enough water to cover amply. Bring to a boil and cook at a moderate boil until tender when pricked with a fork, about 25 to 30 minutes, depending on the potato. Drain, but save some of their water.

2. As soon as you are able to handle them, peel the potatoes while still hot. Cut them into slices—it doesn't matter if some of the slices break up—and put them in a salad bowl. Pour 2 tablespoons of the reserved cooking water over them.

3. Add all the other ingredients, taking into account, when salting, that the capers, olives, and anchovies are salted. Toss thoroughly and serve.

AHEAD-OF-TIME NOTE: You must toss the potatoes while they are still hot, but you can allow them to cool down afterward and serve an hour or two later. Keep at room temperature, covering the bowl with a dinner plate.

CAPRI-STYLE TOMATO
AND BUFFALO-MOZZARELLA SALAD

LA CAPRESE DI BUFALA

This salad, which bears the name of the island of Capri, is so simple that it requires no recipe: It consists of slices of tomato, mozzarella, and basil leaves arranged alternately on a plate and seasoned with salt, pepper, and extra virgin olive oil. That's it. Anyone can make it. Anyone, that is, who has sweet basil, very ripe, firm, sugary, locally grown summer tomatoes, and fresh mozzarella made from the milk of the water buffalo.

That last word irritates purists from Capri, who object that there are no milk-producing buffalo on the island. A former mayor of Capri, and a Venetian acquaintance of mine, the Marchese Antonio Pisani Massa Mormile, a.k.a. Totò, insists that the mozzarella has to be the one known as *fior di latte*, from cow's milk. That is what they use on Capri because they have nothing better, and besides, if you are having it in Capri, even rubber might taste heavenly. But in more earthbound locations, for me the choice is imperative: buffalo mozzarella or nothing.

It's not impossible but it isn't easy. Basil is plentiful, and suitable tomatoes, however short their season may be, are available nearly everywhere. The problem is the mozzarella.

If all you can lay your hands on is that plastic substance in the supermarket or even the so-called fresh mozzarella supposedly made in the back room of an Italian food shop, then don't bother—because when you put it into your mouth, nothing will happen. For something to happen, the mozzarella has to be made from the uniquely rich and savory milk of the water buffalo, long ago domesticated across the bay from Capri in the Neapolitan plains.

Difficult? Certainly. Unattainable? Hardly. Sometimes it requires just a little cunning. I happened to be sojourning briefly in a city on the East Coast, and out of curiosity I entered a food shop that displayed products of various ethnic origins, Italian among them. In the refrigerated cheese locker I was startled to find buffalo mozzarella produced by the same dairy that supplies my cheesemonger back in Venice. There was but one package of it; I squeezed and it felt tough. Too old. A clerk approached me and said, "If you have never tried that cheese, I really recommend it; it's wonderful, and we get it fresh from Italy every two weeks." "Every two weeks? When is the next shipment coming in?" I asked. "Day after tomorrow," was the reply. "Thank you," I said, "I'll be back." And I was, and my husband and I had it in the hotel, and it was tender and juicy and terrifically good.

Victor's Capri-Style Tomato and Mozzarella Salad

LA CAPRESE ALLA MODA DI VICTOR

1 pound ripe, sweet cherry
tomatoes

A 10-ounce ball of
imported fresh buffalo-
milk mozzarella

15 to 20 basil leaves,
depending on size

Salt

Black pepper ground fresh

2 teaspoons red wine
vinegar; see Note below

3 tablespoons extra virgin
olive oil

Good crusty bread

For 4 to 6 persons

Buffalo mozzarella comes in a ball about the size of a large fist, and the tomatoes for a Capri salad are round and usually about the same size so that the diameter of a slice of tomato is more or less equal to that of a slice of mozzarella. My husband came home once from the market with some mozzarella freshly arrived that morning. In the kitchen there was a basketful of very ripe, delicious cherry tomatoes. Victor pondered the difference in dimensions and, since he could not match the tomato to the mozzarella, he decided to reverse the procedure, matching the mozzarella to the tomato. He dropped the two into a bowl, adding a fistful of torn-up basil leaves. What we discovered was that when the salad is tossed, diced-up fresh buffalo mozzarella discharges a considerable quantity of milky whey, which merges with the juices released by the tomatoes. Together with the oil and vinegar of the seasoning, these juices form a delectable pool that, in between bites of the salad, you sop up with a crusty piece of bread. It is almost better than the salad itself.

1. Wash the tomatoes and slice them in half horizontally, across their middle. You should get about 3¼ cups.

2. Cut the mozzarella into ½-inch dice, approximately 1½ cups.

3. Tear the basil leaves into smaller pieces by hand. You should have about ⅓ cup.

4. Put the tomatoes, mozzarella, and basil in an ample salad bowl. Add salt, toss once; add the pepper and the vinegar, toss again; add the olive oil, and toss thoroughly several times. Let rest for 20 minutes, but no more than 30, before serving with crusty, and possibly grilled, slices of bread.

NOTE: In the classic *caprese* there is no vinegar, but Victor insists it is a required part of the juices in his version.

SALADS WITH BEANS

INSALATE CON I LEGUMI

Beans and other legumes add weight to a salad and turn it into a more substantial course. Although it can be served precisely as you would any simple raw vegetable salad, it can be—along with good cheese, a hard-boiled egg, and a glass of young, fruity red wine—a satisfying little meal on its own.

I cannot overemphasize the importance of cooking the beans until they are very tender. *Al dente* beans are an abomination perpetrated by people who measure taste solely by the criterion of crunch. You can grind flour from uncooked beans, but we don't want flour; we want cream.

When cooked thoroughly, the floury substance becomes creamy, it tastes sweet, and part of it leaves the bean to envelop the other ingredients.

The first of the two recipes that follow is for a fully cooked salad in which the slightly bitter tang of the *broccoletti di rape* conducts a lively exchange with the mellow flavor of the presumably thoroughly cooked and creamy *cannellini* beans. In the second salad, the green—Boston lettuce—is raw and the chickpeas with which it is paired are partly mashed to bind the salad and thicken the consistency of the dressing. Both salads should be served somewhat warm.

Warm Cime di Rapa Salad with Cannellini Beans

INSALATA TIEPIDA DI CIME DI RAPA E CANNELLINI

1 cup dried *cannellini* beans
OR 3 cups drained
canned beans, liquid
reserved

2 pounds *cime di rapa*, also
known as *rapini* or
broccoletti di rape

Salt

⅓ cup extra virgin olive oil

Black pepper ground fresh

For 4 persons

If Using Dried Beans:

1. Put them in a bowl, cover with lukewarm water, and soak them overnight or no less than 6 hours before cooking them. Drain them, put them in a saucepan with enough water to cover by about 3 inches, put a lid on the pot, and bring to a slow boil. Cook at a steady but slow boil for 40 to 50 minutes.

AHEAD-OF-TIME NOTE: You can prepare the beans a day in advance, storing them in the refrigerator covered by their cooking liquid.

If Using Canned Beans:

Before tossing the beans in the salad, heat them in a saucepan with the liquid from the can until they are lukewarm. Drain well.

2. Using a paring knife or a peeler, trim away the tough outer skin of the thicker stalks of the *cime di rapa*. Wash the vegetable in several changes of cold water. Bring a pot of water to a boil, add salt, put in the *cime di rapa*, and cook until tender. Drain well when done and transfer to a salad bowl. The vegetable should be at room temperature for the salad, and when cooked may be kept thus for a few hours before serving, but do not refrigerate.

3. If using cooked dried beans that were prepared in advance, reheat them in their liquid until lukewarm, drain well, and add to the salad bowl. Or put in the warm, drained canned beans. Add the salt, olive oil, and liberal grindings of black pepper. Toss thoroughly, taste and correct for seasoning, and serve.

Raw Boston Lettuce Salad with Warm Chickpeas

INSALATA COTTA E CRUDA DI CECI E CAPUCCINA

1 head of Boston lettuce

1 cup drained canned chickpeas OR ⅓ cup dried chickpeas, soaked overnight and boiled as described on page 401

3 tablespoons extra virgin olive oil

Salt

1 tablespoon red wine vinegar

Black pepper ground fresh

For 4 persons

1. Detach the leaves of the lettuce from their head, discarding any blemished ones. Wash them in cold water, shake thoroughly, and dry in a cloth towel or in a salad spinner. Lay a few leaves one on top of the other and cut into thin longitudinal strips, about ¼ inch wide.

If Using Drained Canned Chickpeas:

2. Squeeze off the skin from every pea, put the chickpeas in a saucepan with enough water to cover, and warm them up at a gentle simmer for 2 minutes.

If Using Cooked Dried Chickpeas:

Drain them, reserving the water in which you have boiled them. Squeeze off the skin from every pea, put the chickpeas in a saucepan with enough of the reserved water to cover, and warm them up at a gentle simmer for 2 minutes.

3. Retrieve about ¼ cup of the warm chickpeas, using a slotted spoon, and put them in a salad bowl. Mash them to a pulp with the back of a spoon, then trickle in the olive oil, beating it in with a fork. Add the salt, vinegar, and black pepper, continuing to beat with the fork to incorporate the condiments smoothly.

4. Drain the remaining chickpeas and add them whole to the bowl together with the shredded lettuce. Toss thoroughly and serve at once.

AHEAD-OF-TIME NOTE: You must put the salad together just before serving, when the chickpeas are very warm. If using dried chickpeas, after you have reconstituted them by soaking overnight and boiling, you can store them in the refrigerator, in the water in which you have cooked them, for as long as 2 or 3 days. The lettuce can be washed and shredded a few hours in advance, and kept crisp in the refrigerator.

Shrimp and Scallop Salad with Orange Sections (page 404)

Shrimp and Scallop Salad with Orange Sections

INSALATA DI MARE CON ARANCE

Salt

¼ cup white wine vinegar

1 pound raw medium
    shrimp in their shells

1 pound bay scallops or sea
    scallops cut in half

5 medium oranges

1 head of romaine lettuce

¼ cup extra virgin olive oil

Salt

Black pepper ground fresh

For 6 persons

Anyone whose acquaintance with Sicilian food is limited to restaurant fare would be puzzled by the claim that this is one of the world's most refined and elegant cuisines. If I hadn't had the good fortune to eat splendid home-cooked meals in Sicily, I would have been disinclined to learn more about the island's food, but the flavors I experienced at such good tables as those of Tommaso d'Alba and Anna Lanza encouraged me to broaden my knowledge of the cooking. In the search for local dishes I often employed one of the best recipe-hunting techniques I know, questioning chance acquaintances at the source.

Actually, Antonino Tamburello was not that much of a chance acquaintance; he was my taxi driver for a week in Palermo. As soon as he realized I was more interested in the address of a good cassata place than in the Norman chapel, he began to describe the dishes his wife made. One of them is this seafood salad with oranges. I tried it the moment I got home, I have made it several times since, and each time I am astonished at its beauty and at its ambrosial Garden-of-Eden freshness of taste.

Antonino had said, Make sure you use the scallops' coral. I couldn't bear to tell him that in America scallops are not brought to the market live in their shell. Only the white, pluglike muscle is shipped, and the shell, along with the bivalve's delicious—but very perishable—ovary sac is discarded. Instead of slicing the orange, as I had been instructed, I separated it into sections and peeled each section, and, if not the taste, at least I had the look of the scallop's crescent-shaped, orange-colored egg sac.

1. In two separate saucepans bring water to a boil with 1 tablespoon salt and 2 tablespoons vinegar in each pan. (If you don't have two saucepans, you can execute this step in two stages using the same saucepan twice.)

2. When the water comes to a boil, drop the shrimp into one pan and the scallops into the other. Cook the shrimp for 1 to 2 minutes, depending on their size, and the scallops for about 1 minute, until their color turns a flat white. Drain immediately.

3. Shell the shrimp, remove the vein that runs down the center of their back, and put them in a bowl together with the drained scallops.

4. Peel four oranges. Slip the blade of a sharp paring knife in between the sections to detach from the pulp the thin membrane that encloses each section. Lift out the membrane-less sections and remove any seeds. Set aside.

5. Detach the lettuce leaves from the head, discarding any bruised or wilted leaves. Wash the leaves in several changes of cold water and shake dry in a towel or in a salad spinner. Cut the leaves into strips about ½ inch wide.

6. Cut the remaining orange in half and squeeze it.

7. Combine the shrimp, scallops, and orange sections in a bowl, add the orange juice, salt, olive oil, and liberal grindings of pepper, and toss thoroughly.

8. Choose a shallow—neither too deep nor too flat—serving platter. Line it with the strips of lettuce and top them with the shrimp, scallops, and orange sections, distributing evenly over them all the seasoning in the bowl. Serve at once.

Sardinian Salad with Seafood and Couscous

PANZANELLA SARDA CON FREGOLA E FRUTTI DI MARE

½ pound fresh scallops, preferably bay

Salt

Wine vinegar

8 medium shrimp in their shells

½ pound whole small squid OR 6 ounces sliced small squid rings

A ¼-pound slice of fine, white-fleshed fish such as striped bass

¼ cup plus 1 tablespoon extra virgin olive oil

⅓ cup couscous (precooked medium-grain semolina)

6 green olives in brine, pitted and coarsely chopped

6 Greek-style black olives, pitted and coarsely chopped

I like to call this Sardinian salad *panzanella* after the Tuscan bread salad of that name. In this instance, Sardinia has gone Tuscany one better by using *fregola*, Sardinians' word for what we know as couscous. The bread Tuscans use in *panzanella* really must be good, stale, authentically compact Tuscan bread; otherwise, it doesn't crumble as it should and the salad leaves something to be desired. Couscous, on the other hand, is available everywhere and is amazingly easy to make.

The other ingredient that makes this salad distinctive is the seafood. The flavor of seafood, which in Sardinia is remarkable, varies from one patch of sea to the next, and my choices are a free interpretation of the original components using what was available to me on the Atlantic coast. If, wherever you happen to be, different fish is available, use my ingredients list as a guide, and assemble a comparable assortment drawn from your local resources. Striped bass, which is difficult to buy by the slice even on the East Coast, can be replaced by any firm, white-fleshed fish with good flavor, such as monkfish or grouper or cod. If you have no scallops, use crabmeat or lobster or both. If you are comfortable using them, add boiled octopus tentacles, as long as they are tender. Strive for an interesting and balanced mix of textures, but stay away from strong-flavored, dark-fleshed fish and from fish with a flaky consistency, such as American sole.

1. Look the scallops over and cut away any remaining bits of the tough tendon that once attached them to their shells. Wash the scallops in cold water. Put water, a pinch of salt, and 2 tablespoons of vinegar in a small saucepan and bring to a boil. Put in the scallops. If they are bay scallops, cook for 30 seconds after the water returns to a boil; cook for 1 minute if they are the larger sea scallops; then drain immediately.

2. If you are using sea scallops, cut them all into ½-inch pieces; if you are using bay scallops, cut only the larger ones into two pieces. Put them into a salad bowl and set aside.

1 tablespoon chopped
Italian flat-leaf parsley

1 tablespoon sliced scallions
(sliced into very thin
rings)

1 cup firm, ripe tomato,
peeled, seeded, and cut
into fine dice

Black pepper ground fresh

For 6 persons

3. Wash the shrimp in cold water, and boil them, cooking them for just 1 minute, following precisely the same procedure used for the scallops, above. When they have cooled off, shell them, remove the dark vein under their back, and cut them into six to eight small pieces, about ⅓ inch each. Add them to the bowl containing the scallops.

4. If you are using whole squid, clean them as directed on page 262, separating the sacs from the tentacles. Divide the tentacles into two parts, cut the sacs into thin rings, and wash in cold water. If you are using prepared squid rings, wash them in cold water. Boil, following the basic procedure used for the scallops above, but omitting the salt. Cook for no more than 1 minute, draining them the moment their color turns from translucent to flat white. Add them to the scallops and shrimp.

5. Boil the fish slice in water with salt and vinegar, following exactly the procedure used for the scallops. Cook for 5 to 6 minutes; drain; and when it has cooled off completely, remove the skin, cut the fish into ¼-inch pieces, and add it to the salad bowl.

6. Put ½ cup of water in a small saucepan together with a pinch of salt and 1 tablespoon olive oil, and bring it to a boil. Add the couscous, cover the pan, and remove from heat. After 5 to 6 minutes, uncover the pan and stir the couscous.

7. Put the olives, parsley, couscous, scallions, and tomato in the salad bowl. Add salt, 1½ tablespoons of vinegar, ¼ cup olive oil, and liberal grindings of black pepper; toss thoroughly but gently; and taste and correct for salt and other seasonings. Serve at room temperature.

AHEAD-OF-TIME NOTE: The bright taste of the salad would be dulled by refrigeration. Try to make it as close as possible to the time you are going to serve it. If I were to cook it 3 to 4 hours in advance, I would keep it in a very cool place, but not refrigerated. If you'd rather refrigerate it, bring to room temperature and toss with the seasonings only when ready to serve it.

Turkey Breast Salad with Pomegranate

INSALATA DI PETTO DI TACCHINO CON IL MELOGRANO

1 carrot

1 celery stalk

½ medium yellow onion, peeled

1 pound turkey breast, in a single piece

Salt

2 or 3 pomegranates

1 head of Boston lettuce

3 tablespoons extra virgin olive oil

½ lemon

For 4 persons

Some years ago, on our anniversary, Victor and I decided to revisit Sirmione, the peninsula at the southern tip of Lake Garda where, many winters before, we had had our brief honeymoon. Sirmione is a short morning's drive from Venice and we thought we would stop there for lunch. The excursion buses at the town's gate were a signal that the romantically deserted Sirmione of our youth no longer existed, and after a disconsolate walk past the souvenir stalls and down the main street lined with tourist trade shops, we decided to have our anniversary lunch elsewhere.

The lunch, at the Vecchia Lugana restaurant on the lakeshore just east of Sirmione, saved the day. It began with this turkey breast with pomegranate, an old Lombard recipe, served as an appetizer. It was beautiful to see, the vermilion of the pomegranate seeds studding the turkey's creamy flesh. But more wonderful yet was the taste. As each one of the crunchy seeds burst under one's teeth it released a few drops of juice that was tart and sweet at once, mingling with bitefuls of the breast, injecting life into the mild flavor of the turkey.

1. Peel the carrot and wash both the carrot and the celery stalk. Put the carrot, celery, and onion in a medium saucepan with enough water to cover the turkey later. Bring to a boil and cook at a moderate but steady pace for 15 minutes.

2. Add the turkey. Cook at a gentle boil for 30 minutes, and add salt. Cook for 10 minutes longer, then take off heat, letting the turkey steep in its broth.

3. While the turkey is cooking, split open the pomegranates and pick out all the vermilion-colored seeds from the spongy pith that surrounds them. Use as many pomegranates as you need to make about ⅔ cup of seeds.

4. Pull off the ten largest leaves of the lettuce, wash them, and pat them thoroughly dry. Cut them into very thin strips. You should get about 6 cups. When ready to serve, spread the lettuce over a platter.

5. The turkey should still be warm, but if you have made it ahead and it is cold, warm it up gently in its broth. Drain (you can freeze the broth in cubes and use it on other occasions in a soup or a risotto) and cut the turkey into very thin slices. Arrange the slices over the lettuce in the platter. Drizzle oil over them and squeeze on a little bit of lemon juice. If the half lemon is very juicy, do not use it all, because you don't want to make the seasoning too acidic. Scatter the pomegranate seeds over the turkey and serve while still lukewarm.

AHEAD-OF-TIME NOTE: The salad should be served warm, but you can cook the turkey several hours in advance, refrigerate in its broth, and reheat gently but thoroughly just before composing the dish.

Desserts

DESSERTS
I Dolci

———— ❧ ————

Peaches, Raspberries, and Blueberries with
  Prosecco

Marisa's Piedmontese Apple Timbale with
  Cinnamon and Cloves

Asti-Style Apple Tart with Honey, Orange,
  Lemon, and Grand Marnier

Almond and Pine-Nut Tart

Orange Cake, Ancona-Style

Yogurt and Sambuca Cake

Ligurian Ladyfingers Dessert with Cocoa
  and Espresso Cream, Rum, and Marsala

Venetian Raisin and Polenta Cookies

Nadia's Morning Coffee Cake with Winter
  Fruits

Lunigiana's Confirmation Cake

Burano's Sugar Cookies

Heavy Cream Custard with Hazelnuts

Heavy Cream Custard

Zabaglione Frozen Dessert with
  Amaretto Cookies

Semifreddo with Nuts and Dried Fruit

Apricot Gelato

Rita D'Enza's Sardinian Rice Gelato

Tangerine Sorbet

Granny Smith Apple Sorbet with Muscat
  Wine and Grappa

Do Italians have a sweet tooth? One might think so on noticing the displays of pastries in every coffee bar; on regularly meeting one's neighbor at the local espresso counter, cappuccino in one hand and a *cornetto*—croissant—in the other; on observing the irresistible spread of gelato shops. But if they are tempted by sweets, Italians yield to that temptation at a café, at a *gelateria*, at a restaurant, seldom at home.

At a family dinner, the first course of pasta, risotto, or soup begins to tip the scales of one's interest and capacity. Once one has progressed through the meat or fish course, accompanied by vegetable and salad, there is little interest in or capacity for anything of substance. In fact, most meals in Italy end on a light note. It is likely that even an enterprising Italian cook will bake no more than one cake or batch of cookies during the whole year. Nor would it be surprising if in a lifetime of cooking she (because it is almost always "she") produced nothing more elaborate for dessert than a bowl of fruit.

Fruit usually satisfies what yearnings an Italian palate may still have left at the conclusion of a meal. Very good ripe native fruit—juicy pears, aromatic peaches, sugary canteloupes, honeyed figs, fragrant grapes, succulent persimmons, crisp apples—is plentiful and needs no special presentation. But it also lends itself to one of those refreshing preparations, such as the peaches and berries in white wine described on page 414, that are as lovely to see as they are effortless to produce.

Fresh fruit is also the key ingredient in most of the baked desserts that people would buy on festive occasions, or that they would be likely to be drawn to when eating out. I believe, however, that the most triumphant use of fruit Italians make is in their frozen desserts, in the various gelati, sorbetti, and *semifreddi* that, for visitors to Italy, have made a stop at the *gelateria* an essential part of the itinerary. I am loath to clutter my kitchen with bulky equipment, but I gladly make an exception for my solid, dependable electric ice cream freezer. I would make room for it even if it were to produce only the green apple sorbet with muscat wine that you will find later on in these pages.

You will find fruit in some form in most of the desserts of this chapter. I have stayed away from elaborate confections, choosing to leave those to born bakers or to the good commercial bakeries that most people have access to. Many of those who are reading this could no doubt display more disciplined baking prowess than I can. I would prefer to bake as I cook, intuitively, allowing myself to be seduced by an ingredient's siren call, unfazed by a teaspoon more here or a tablespoon less there. I have, however, tried to tame the rebelliousness and impetuosity that are my nature in order to make these recipes as trustworthy as I could. There are simple, homey things here, such as my orange cake, that I am rather pleased to have done. You probably won't find them elsewhere; they work, and I hope you will like them. I think you may.

Peaches, Raspberries, and Blueberries with Prosecco

PESCHE E FRUTTA DI BOSCO CON IL PROSECCO

2 pounds peaches,
    preferably the aromatic
    white-fleshed variety

⅔ cup granulated sugar

1⅛ cups Prosecco or other
    young, fruity, dry white
    wine; see headnote

½ pint raspberries

½ pint blueberries

The zest of ½ lemon

Serves 6 to 8

A little sugar, a little wine, some lemon zest or mint leaves or other aromatics, and you can transform even less than perfectly ripe peaches into a bowl of luscious, refreshingly fragrant fruit.

I made this dessert on a summer day in Long Island when my thoughts had turned to Venice. Summer visitors to Venice find every bar celebrating the season with a mixture of peach juice and wine called a Bellini. I imagined this as a solid version of that drink.

The wine Venetians use is Prosecco, a young, lightly sparkling, appetizing white wine. Prosecco is exported, but it may not be available near you. You can use any other sparkler, the simpler and less pretentious the better—or even a still white wine, as long as it is young and fruity.

When I was buying the peaches, there were beautiful berries on the farmstand that beckoned, so I got those too to add to the bowl.

1. Wash the peaches, peel them, pit them, and cut them into slices about ¼ inch thick.

2. Put the peaches in a serving bowl, add the sugar and wine, and stir thoroughly.

3. Wash the raspberries and blueberries and add them to the peaches.

4. Grate the thin, yellow skin of half a lemon, being careful not to dig into the bitter white pith beneath, and add it to the bowl. Turn over the bowl's contents several times. Refrigerate at least 1 hour before serving, or even as far ahead as early morning of the day in which you intend to serve the fruit.

Marisa's Piedmontese Apple Timbale with Cinnamon and Cloves

TIMBALLO DI MELE

2 to 2¼ pounds crisp, juicy cooking apples; see headnote

A dozen cloves

Cinnamon, two 1 inch pieces

¾ cup granulated sugar plus another ¾ cup to make caramel

3 tablespoons cognac or other grape brandy

4 egg whites

Salt

¼ cup water

6 to 8 servings

A small piece of cheesecloth

An 8-cup loaf pan, 9 by 5 by 3 inches

Whenever we are in the Piedmontese town of Alba we try to have at least one meal in the cool, neat dining room of the Porta San Martino restaurant. The unlabored yet carefully prepared food of Porta San Martino has a quality I prize greatly, the perceptible presence of a real person at the stove. It is cooking that expresses the warmth and sincerity of the talented woman who produces it, Marisa Pavesi, a co-owner of the restaurant.

It's hard to say what makes this apple timbale of Marisa's so good. It is so simple that it is nearly impossible to sabotage. It doesn't even have any pastry crust to struggle against. It is basically a puree of apples cooked with cloves and cinnamon, laced with brandy, plumped up with beaten egg whites, and baked in a loaf pan.

In Italy I use a homely but flavorful apple called *renetta*, squashed in shape with a dull, mottled yellow skin. Although it is described as a Canadian apple, I have never found it in North America. What I do find and would use is the always reliable Golden Delicious. You may choose any other cooking variety you favor, as long as it is juicy and more sweet than tart.

1. Wash the apples, peel and core them, and slice them as thin as possible.

2. Cut the cheesecloth into two pieces, and use them to make two equal bundles of cloves and cinnamon, tying them with some kitchen string. You could make just one bundle, but two separate ones will better distribute the aromas of the spices while the apples are cooking.

3. Put the sliced apples in a saucepan together with the spice bundles and ¾ cup sugar. Turn the heat on to very low and put a tight-fitting cover on the pan. Cook, stirring from time to time, until the apples are reduced to a pulp, about 40 minutes.

4. Transfer the apples to a food processor and puree them. Put the pureed apples into a bowl and add the brandy, stirring thoroughly.

5. Turn on the oven to 325°.

6. Beat the egg whites in a bowl with a pinch of salt until they form stiff peaks. Fold them gently into the apple puree, working patiently to incorporate them uniformly without deflating them.

7. Put the remaining ¾ cup sugar and ¼ cup water into the loaf pan and place the pan over a burner, turning on the heat to medium. Bring the sugar to a boil, resisting the temptation to stir it. Tilt the mold forward and backward to move the melted sugar around until it becomes colored a light nut-brown. Take off heat immediately and quickly tip the pan in all directions, while the caramelized sugar is still liquid, to coat its bottom and sides evenly. Keep turning the pan until the caramel congeals, then set aside to cool.

8. When the caramel is cold, pour the apple mixture into the pan, leveling it off evenly.

9. Choose a saucepan with oven-safe handles that can subsequently accommodate the loaf pan. Pour enough water into it to come 1 inch or 1½ inches up the sides and bring the water to a simmer over the stove. Lower the loaf pan into it and place the whole thing in the preheated oven. Bake for 1 hour, then remove from the oven, lift out the loaf pan, and let it cool off.

10. When cool, turn the pan over with all its contents onto a serving platter. The caramel should be completely liquefied and ought to pour out easily, but if there is still some sticking to the bottom of the pan, place the pan over a burner, loosen the caramel over gentle heat, and pour it over the apple timbale. Refrigerate for at least 24 hours, or up to 4 days, before serving.

Asti-Style Apple Tart with Honey, Orange, Lemon, and Grand Marnier

TORTA DI MELE PROFUMATA ALL'ASTIGIANA

FOR THE DOUGH

The ingredients for the sweet pastry used in the Almond and Pine Nut Tart on page 420

FOR THE FILLING

5 Golden Delicious apples, peeled, cored, and cut into 1-inch pieces

⅓ cup honey

The grated peel of 1 small lemon

The grated peel of ½ orange

The freshly squeezed juice of 1 lemon

The freshly squeezed juice of 1 orange

¼ cup Grand Marnier liqueur

---

8 to 10 servings

An 8-inch quiche pan with removable bottom, preferably nonstick, plus butter to grease the pan and flour to dust it

O n his return from a wine producers' convention in Piedmont, my husband, Victor, brought back for this tart he had in the restaurant of Giuliano Zonta's Hasta Hotel in Asti. As he is not known for his fondness for honey, his admiration for this dessert led me to believe that there had to be something unusual about its flavor. There is indeed. The apple filling is cooked in a skillet with a fascinating mélange of lemon and orange aromas in the form of zest, juice, and liqueur that chase away the cloying effect of honey's presence.

1. Prepare the sweet pastry as described in steps 1 through 3 of the Almond and Pine Nut Tart recipe on pages 420–21. Remove the dough from the processor's bowl, cover it with plastic wrap, and store it in the refrigerator for 1 hour.

2. Put all the filling ingredients into a 10- to 12-inch skillet. (If the honey does not pour easily, warm the jar briefly in a small saucepan of simmering water.) Turn the heat on under the skillet to high and cook, stirring frequently, until the apples are tender, but not reduced to a pulp. They should be dry when done. Transfer the contents of the skillet to a bowl, setting them aside to cool completely.

3. Remove the pastry dough from the refrigerator, unwrap, cut off two-thirds of it, rewrap the remainder, and return it to the refrigerator.

4. Turn on the oven to 375˚.

5. Keeping the dough that is out of the refrigerator under plastic wrap, let it come to cool but malleable room temperature—about 45 minutes. Roll it out on a floured work surface as described in step 5 of the recipe on page 421, thinning it into a disk no more than ¼ inch thick.

6. If the bottom of the quiche pan is not of the nonstick variety, cut a disk of wax paper to line it. Grease the pan thinly with butter and

dust lightly with flour, turning the pan over and tapping it on the counter to shake off excess flour.

7. Gently lift the dough from the work surface, possibly helping yourself with thin metal spatulas, and lower it into the pan, lining the bottom and sides with it, pushing the dough out with your fingers to make it fit. Lightly rub your hands with flour when working with the dough to keep it from sticking to them.

8. Place the pan in the middle level of the preheated oven and bake it for about 10 minutes, until the dough loses its glossiness and begins to set, forming a dun-colored crust. Should blisters appear after it has been in the oven a few minutes, pierce the dough with a fork in several places to let it settle back into the pan.

9. Remove the pan from the oven and turn the thermostat to 350°.

10. While the pan is in the oven, take the remaining dough out of the refrigerator. Let it come to cool room temperature—about 45 minutes—and roll it out, as described above, this time to a thickness of about ⅓ inch. Cut the flattened dough into strips about ½ inch wide.

11. Pour the apple filling into the pan, leveling it off. Over it place the ½-inch strips of dough, in a latticework pattern. Return the pan to the 350° preheated oven and bake in the middle level for about 45 minutes until the top has formed a rich golden crust.

12. When the tart has cooled, slip a knife under the bottom to loosen it from the pan, and transfer it to a serving plate. It will taste best while still slightly warm, but it is also delicious at room temperature.

AHEAD-OF-TIME NOTE: The apple filling can be cooked many hours in advance, or even the day before making the tart if stored in an airtight container in the refrigerator. The unthinned pastry dough can be stored in the refrigerator overnight, but not longer. Take it out a full hour before rolling it out. You must bake the tart the moment you have topped the shell with the apple filling.

Almond and Pine-Nut Tart

TORTA DI MANDORLE E PIGNOLI

For the Sweet Pastry

2 cups all-purpose flour

1 cup granulated sugar

8 tablespoons (1 stick)
   chilled unsalted butter

1 egg

A pinch of salt diluted in
   ¼ cup ice water

The grated peel of ½ lemon

For the Filling

3 eggs

⅓ cup granulated sugar

⅓ cup freshly squeezed
   lemon juice

The grated peel of 2 lemons

½ cup shelled and peeled
   almonds, chopped fine

½ cup whole pine nuts

Butter for greasing the pan
Flour for dusting the pan

---

6 to 8 portions

A 9½-inch springform pan

Almond blossoms ushering in the spring, almond nuts drying in the Sicilian sun of late summer, almond pastries in the windows of Venetian bakers remind us that for most of its desserts Italy looks toward the balmy eastern Mediterranean rather than to the mass of the European continent to which it is attached.

My husband loves almond cake, which his mother, who was born in the Middle East, used to make so well. He is also insatiably fond of pine nuts—he can eat a sackful. From time to time in Venice he comes home with a tray of almond and pine nut pastries that he claims he has bought for me, but in whose consumption he plays the larger role. There seemed to be nothing daunting about the composition of these little tarts, sweet pastry crust topped with almonds and pine nuts and scented with lemon, so I decided to make him a large one.

I don't often bake cakes for the two of us, but when Victor returns from his morning excursions with a tray of almond and pine nut tartlets, I know it's time for me to make him another one of these. He is very sweet and complimentary and never fails to say my tart couldn't be any better, "But"—he adds after a pause—"if you wanted to, you could always put in more pine nuts, couldn't you?"

1. Mix the flour and sugar in a food processor.

2. Cut the chilled butter into ½-inch dice, drop it into the bowl of the processor, and run the steel blade, pulsing on and off, until the mixture achieves a granular consistency. Don't let it mass.

3. Break one egg into a small bowl and beat it with a fork until it becomes foamy. Swirl into it the salt and the grated peel of half a lemon. Add the mixture to the food processor, running the steel on and off until the ingredients are evenly combined, but still grainy, not massed hard.

4. If the bottom of the springform pan is not of the nonstick variety, cut a disk of wax paper to line it. Grease the pan thinly with butter and dust lightly with flour, turning the pan over and tapping it on the counter to shake off excess flour.

5. Roll the pastry dough out into a disk about ½ inch thick, giving it a full half turn each time you turn it. Line the pan's bottom and sides with it, pushing the dough out with your fingers to make it fit. Cover with plastic wrap and refrigerate for up to 1 hour, but no less than 30 minutes.

6. Turn on the oven to 400°.

7. Beat 3 eggs and ⅓ cup sugar in a bowl until they foam and form yellow ribbons. Swirl in the lemon juice in a thin stream, and add the grated peel of lemons, mixing it in uniformly.

8. Remove the pan from the refrigerator, discard the plastic wrap, and pierce the dough in many places with a fork. Spread the chopped almonds over the bottom; add the beaten egg and lemon mixture, leveling it with a spatula; and top with the pine nuts, distributing them evenly. Bake in the upper middle level of the oven for 30 minutes, until the top has become a light golden brown.

AHEAD-OF-TIME NOTE: You can prepare the pastry dough, line the pan, and refrigerate as described in step 5, keeping it in the refrigerator overnight, but not longer. The cake itself, when finished, will keep for several days covered with tinfoil in a dry, cool place.

Orange Cake, Ancona-Style

TORTA DI ARANCE ALL'ANCONETANA

———— ❧ ————

2 cups plus 2 tablespoons
   all-purpose flour, plus
   flour for dusting the pan

3 eggs

The grated peel, avoiding
   the spongy white pith,
   of 3 oranges

4 tablespoons (½ stick)
   butter, softened to room
   temperature, plus butter
   for greasing the pan

1 cup plus 3 tablespoons
   sugar

2 tablespoons ouzo liqueur;
   see headnote

1 tablespoon whole milk

2½ teaspoons baking
   powder

2 cups freshly squeezed
   orange juice with
   3 tablespoons sugar
   dissolved in it

———————————

8 to 10 servings

A tube pan with loose bottom

Of all the cakes that I have worked on for this and for my previous books, none has been more gratifying than this tribute to the orange. It is so soft, so juicy, so tenderly aromatic, so easy to make.

I call it *all'Anconetana* because I had it and obtained the recipe for it in Ancona, the large port town in the Marches. But I understand it is made elsewhere in this happy central Italian region between the mountains and the sea. One ingredient of the original recipe is apparently native to the Marches. It is *mistrà*, the driest of the anise-based liqueurs. I have tried such Italian and French alternatives as Sambuca and Pernod, but they are too cloying, too stickily anise-tasting. I was about to abandon trying to duplicate this wonderful cake until I was prompted to try ouzo, which works very nicely.

Another ingredient you may want to replace is the Sicilian blood oranges that one would use in Italy. The Italian blood orange is full of juice and exceptionally fragrant. The ones from California I have tried are stingy with juice, short on fragrance, and, considering the amount of liquid that is required here, extravagantly expensive. You'd be better off forgoing the drama of the red juice and employing an orange such as the tangelo or the temple or any other comparably fragrant variety.

1. Turn on the oven to 350°.

2. Put flour, eggs, grated orange peel, 4 tablespoons softened butter, sugar, and liqueur in a food processor and run until all ingredients are evenly amalgamated.

3. Add the milk and baking powder, and process again to incorporate into the mixture.

4. Thickly smear the tube pan with butter and dust with flour. Put the cake mixture in the pan and place the pan in the upper level of the preheated oven. Bake for 45 minutes or slightly longer, until the top of the cake becomes colored a rich gold.

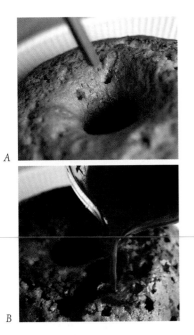

A

5. When the cake is done, place the bottom of the pan over a tumbler or tall mug, using pot holders, and push down to raise the loose bottom. Take the tube with the cake out of the hoop, work the cake loose from the bottom with a knife, and lift it away from the tube. Place it on a plate with a slightly raised rim.

6. While the cake is still warm, poke many holes in it using a chopstick (*photo A*) or any similar narrow cylindrical tool. Into each of the holes slowly pour some of the orange juice (*photo B*). At first the hole fills to the brim with juice, but this is subsequently—in about 1 hour—absorbed by the cake. Always serve at room temperature.

NOTE: You can keep the cake for up to 1 week in the refrigerator, fully covered by plastic wrap.

B

Yogurt and Sambuca Cake

TORTA DI YOGURT CON SAMBUCA

¾ cup whole-milk plain
   yogurt

1½ cups granulated sugar

¾ cup corn oil

3 eggs

1½ cups flour plus some
   flour for dusting the cake
   pan

¾ cup cornstarch

2½ teaspoons baking
   powder

3 tablespoons Sambuca
   liqueur

Butter for smearing the pan

One cake serving at least 8

A 9-inch springform cake pan

The sixteenth century brought tomatoes to the Italian table; the late twentieth, yogurt. Although the gastronomic implications of the latter are hardly as momentous, cakes made with yogurt have quickly become universally popular with home cooks in Italy. They are certainly easy to make and nearly foolproof—only deliberate mischief is likely to cause a failure, and because they are made with yogurt they wear an aura of dietetic respectability, without much justification I suspect. Most important to me is that they taste light and delicious. My favorite version of this genre is the one with Sambuca, which I give below.

As a reluctant baker, I enjoy making it because the measurements of its principal ingredients—the sugar, oil, flour, and starch—are easy to remember: They are all multiples of the cake's basic component, the yogurt, and can be measured out of the same container. The only struggle you are likely to face is in looking for whole-milk yogurt, which has been all but pushed off the supermarket shelves by the fashionably "lite" and lean varieties, which are unsuitable for this recipe.

1. Turn on the oven to 350°.

2. Combine the yogurt and sugar, mixing them in a bowl until you obtain a homogeneous consistency.

3. Trickle the oil into the mixture, stirring it in thoroughly.

4. Add the eggs, one at a time, mixing thoroughly before adding the second and the third.

5. Separately, mix the flour, cornstarch, and baking powder, then add them, a little at a time, to the yogurt batter, stirring constantly until any lumps have dissolved.

6. Swirl in the Sambuca liqueur. At this point the consistency of the batter should be that of a thick cream.

7. Lightly smear the bottom and sides of the cake pan with butter. Sprinkle with flour, then turn the pan upside down and rap it against the counter to shake off excess flour.

8. Pour the batter into the pan, level it off, and bake in the upper middle level of the preheated oven for 45 minutes. Let cool down to room temperature before serving.

AHEAD-OF-TIME NOTE: The yogurt cake will keep well for 3 to 4 days if wrapped in heavy aluminum foil and refrigerated.

Ligurian Ladyfingers Dessert with Cocoa and Espresso Cream, Rum, and Marsala

DOLCE PIEVANO

8 eggs, at room temperature

6 ounces (1½ sticks) butter, softened at room temperature

½ cup plus 1 tablespoon granulated sugar

3 tablespoons full-strength espresso coffee, cooled to room temperature

2 tablespoons rum

10 ounces ladyfinger biscuits, about 36

1⅓ cups dry Marsala wine poured into a deep oval dish

⅓ cup unsweetened cocoa powder

---

10 portions

A mortar-shaped round-bottomed bowl, 4 to 6 inches high and about 8 inches in diameter at top

Cheesecloth

Many summers ago, my husband and I had taken an apartment in Sori, a small town on the Italian Riviera. During our explorations of the area we stopped in a nearby hamlet named Pieve Ligure, where, at the local pastry shop, we bought a dessert to take home. We were told it was adapted from a sweet that was made in the town as far back as the Renaissance. I can't vouch for the historical accuracy, nor do I care, but what is certain is that it was luscious. Recently, as I was cleaning out some old Italian food magazines, I came across the recipe for a dessert called *dolce pievano*, and as I read it I recognized it as the one I had picked up more than 20 years ago in Pieve Ligure.

This is just the kind of dessert-making I like, calling for a minimum investment of labor and skill, and paying off with a large return in taste. Whatever baking was involved was done by the makers of the ladyfingers you buy in the store. The other steps consist of assembling the components and then waiting for their flavors to come together overnight in the refrigerator.

The dome-shaped look of *dolce pievano* comes from the mold in which you put the ingredients. Any round-bottomed metal, plastic, or ceramic bowl of the approximate dimensions indicated will do the job. The original implement, called *polsonetto* in Italian, would have been of unlined copper, with a stubby handle, and used mainly for cooking custards.

1. Put the eggs in a saucepan, add enough water to cover by at least 1 inch, and turn the heat on to medium. Cook the eggs for 10 minutes after the water comes to a boil. Retrieve from the pan and set aside to cool completely.

2. Cut off a piece of cheesecloth large enough to line the bowl and have enough left over to cover. Moisten it with cold water, line the bowl with it, centering it and letting the surplus cloth hang down over the bowl's rim.

3. Put the softened butter and sugar in another bowl and mix to a smooth consistency.

4. Remove the yolks from the eggs, discarding the white, and, with a fork, mash the yolks in a small bowl or dish.

5. To the butter and sugar mixture add the mashed egg yolks, the espresso coffee, and the rum, and mix to a smooth, creamy consistency.

6. Soak the ladyfingers, one at a time, in the Marsala wine, and place them, arranging them vertically, along the sides of the cheesecloth-lined bowl. Use portions of wine-soaked ladyfingers to fill in any gaps and completely line the bottom of the bowl.

7. Pour one third of the creamy egg yolk and coffee mixture over the ladyfingers, leveling it off with a spatula. Top the cream with a layer of wine-soaked ladyfingers, using portions of them to fill in, patchwork-fashion, any gaps.

8. Add the cocoa powder to the remaining egg and coffee cream, and mix thoroughly. Pour it all over the layer of ladyfingers in the bowl and level it with a spatula.

9. Top the contents of the bowl with one last layer of wine-soaked ladyfingers, patching as before where necessary to fill in gaps.

10. Pull the cheesecloth over the top, making sure it covers the top completely. If it does not, moisten another piece of cheesecloth to complete the job.

11. Cover the top of the bowl with plastic wrap and refrigerate overnight.

12. To serve, remove the plastic wrap, unfold the cheesecloth, letting it hang over the sides of the bowl, turn the bowl over onto a round platter, lift it away from the dessert, and carefully pull off the cheesecloth.

AHEAD-OF-TIME NOTE: Once made, *dolce pievano* can be kept in its bowl in the refrigerator and served up to 1 week later.

Venetian Raisin and Polenta Cookies

ZALETTI VENESSIANI

———— ❧ ————

4 ounces (¾ cup) black raisins, soaked ahead of time; see below

1 tablespoon rum

½ pound (2 sticks) butter plus 1 tablespoon, softened at room temperature; plus butter for smearing the baking pan

1 scant cup confectioners' sugar

4 eggs

1 cup plus 2 tablespoons flour for the raisins, plus flour for dusting the baking pan

1 cup yellow cornmeal (polenta flour)

1 teaspoon baking powder

Salt

————

About 3 dozen Venetian zaletti

The largest rectangular baking pan that will fit your oven

When I was teaching and living in Bologna, the baker Margherita Simili, who was assisting me at the school, showed me how to make a Bolognese polenta cookie called *zalett*, which she explained meant "little yellow ones" in the dialect of Bologna. I included the recipe in one of my earlier books.

When I came to live in Venice and, like everyone else in the city, spent a good part of the day walking, every time I looked in a baker's shop I saw trays of cookies identified as *zaletti*. They didn't look the least bit like the flat bright yellow *zalett* of Bologna. They were darker; they were lumpy with raisins; and when I tasted one, unlike the crisp Bolognese polenta cookie, it was soft.

As I soon learned, Venetians called them "za-eh'tti," dropping the "l," as is their custom; and these were the local version of cookies with polenta. Again there was an expert friend, Mara Martin of the restaurant Da Fiore, willing to show me how to make them. If you like the graininess and fragrance of polenta and the sweetness of raisins, you should find these cookies very agreeable.

1. Put the raisins in a bowl and add 1 tablespoon of rum and enough warm water to cover. Let soak a minimum of 1 hour, but if you can let them steep thus overnight they will puff up even more.

2. Turn the oven on to 350°.

3. Put the softened butter and the confectioners' sugar in a bowl and mix for about 10 minutes, using any hand or electric mixing tool, until the mixture swells visibly.

4. Break the eggs open into the bowl; mix well; then add both the flour and the cornmeal, the baking powder, and a pinch of salt, and continue mixing until you obtain a smooth, puffy batter.

5. Drain the raisins, pat them dry with kitchen towels, and dust them with 2 tablespoons of flour. Add them to the bowl stirring them thoroughly into the batter.

6. Smear the bottom of the baking pan with butter, sprinkle with flour, and then turn the pan over, giving it a tap or two against the work counter to shake off excess flour.

7. Shape the batter into little mounds about the size of a large walnut, and place them in the pan about 2½ to 3 inches apart.

8. Bake in the preheated oven for 15 minutes or until they become colored a rich gold.

AHEAD-OF-TIME NOTE: You can refrigerate the batter covered in plastic wrap for up to 3 days before baking the cookies. You can serve *zaletti* when still warm, but they will keep for weeks in a biscuit tin.

Nadia's Morning Coffee Cake with Winter Fruits

LA TORTA DI NADIA CON FRUTTA D'INVERNO PER IL CAFFELATTE

3 eggs

1⅓ cups sugar

⅛ teaspoon salt

2 tablespoons extra virgin olive oil

The grated peel of 2 oranges

A large pear, about ½ to ¾ pound, or 2 smaller ones

1 crisp, juicy apple

1 banana

2 tablespoons freshly squeezed lemon juice

2¾ cups flour

2½ teaspoons baking powder

½ tablespoon butter for greasing the pan

8 to 12 portions

A 10-inch springform pan

Caffelatte is what Italians of all ages have for breakfast at home. For small children it is a cupful of warm milk lightly stained with coffee, the ratio of coffee to milk increasing with one's years. It is often accompanied by some store-bought biscuits, but not in my assistant Nadia's family. She lives on her father's farm outside Venice with her husband and small boy, and for her son Tommaso she bakes wholesome cakes with fresh fruit. He has some with his *caffelatte* and takes another piece to school to eat for *merenda*, recess.

I was particularly taken with the cake Nadia makes when there is no more summer fruit on the farm. She uses pears and apples and always adds a banana she buys in town. The proportions of one fruit to another may vary, and indeed Nadia says they always do, but nothing much can go wrong or affect the cake's plainspoken, engagingly fresh taste.

1. Turn on the oven to 375°.

2. Choose a mixing bowl that can subsequently contain all the ingredients. Put in the eggs and sugar and beat them until they are foamy and form yellow ribbons.

3. Add the salt, olive oil, and grated orange peel—making sure you haven't grated any of the bitter white pith beneath the orange skin—and mix thoroughly.

4. Peel all the fruit. Core the pear and apple and cut them into thin ½-inch pieces. Slice the banana very thin. Put the fruit into a separate bowl and toss with the lemon juice.

5. Combine the flour and baking powder and mix them into the beaten eggs, incorporating them thoroughly.

6. Add the fruit to the bowl with the eggs and flour, mixing well to distribute it evenly.

7. Smear the bottom and sides of the springform pan with butter, then pour into it the fruit batter. Level off by shaking the pan from side to side; do not press down on the batter.

8. Bake on the middle level of the preheated oven for 50 to 55 minutes, until the top of the cake becomes colored a light gold.

AHEAD-OF-TIME NOTE: The finished cake will keep fresh for about 5 days, wrapped with foil and refrigerated.

Lunigiana's Confirmation Cake

BUCCELLATO DELLA LUNIGIANA

3 cups flour plus flour for dusting the baking pan

2½ teaspoons baking powder

Salt

3 eggs

1½ cups granulated sugar

8 tablespoons (1 stick) butter plus butter for greasing the cake pan

The grated peel of 1 lemon

2 tablespoons freshly squeezed lemon juice

1 cup milk

---

8 to 10 portions

A 9 by 2-inch round cake pan

Lunigiana is an area that encloses the mountainous districts of three regions, Tuscany, Emilia-Romagna, and Liguria. *Buccellato* is a Tuscan cake that accompanied the ritual celebration of a child's confirmation. It is a good, simple cake.

1. Turn the oven on to 350°.

2. Combine in a mixing bowl the flour, the baking powder, and a pinch of salt.

3. Break the eggs into a food processor bowl, add the sugar, and run the metal blade until the eggs swell and become colored a pale yellow.

4. Put the butter in a small saucepan and melt it over very low heat. Do not let it come to a simmer.

5. Add the flour and baking powder mixture to the processor bowl and run the blade to combine it thoroughly with the eggs and sugar.

6. To the processor, add the melted butter, the grated lemon rind, and the lemon juice, and run the blade.

7. With the processor blade running, slowly add the milk until it is fully incorporated in the *buccellato* batter.

8. Smear the inside of the baking pan liberally with butter, sprinkle all over with flour, then turn over the pan, tapping it against a work surface to shake off excess flour.

9. Pour the batter, which will have a rather runny consistency, into the pan; give the pan a shake to level off the batter; and bake in the upper middle level of the preheated oven for 50 minutes, or until the top of the cake has become colored a deep gold.

Burano's Sugar Cookies

I BUSSOLAI DE BURAN

½ pound (2 sticks) butter, softened at room temperature, plus butter for smearing the baking pan

1¼ cups sugar

Pinch of salt

The grated peel of 1 lemon

½ teaspoon vanilla

5 egg yolks

4½ cups flour, plus flour for dusting the baking pan

2 tablespoons milk

About 2 dozen bussolai

A large rectangular baking pan

Burano is an island in the Venetian lagoon famous for its gaily colored houses, its handmade lace, and these cookies. The cookies are highly prized in Venice, where the pastry shops sell them at a high price. Their name comes from *buso*, Venetian for hole, and they are called that when shaped into a circle. They can also be made into an "S" shape, and then they are simply called *buranei*, after the island they come from.

I have worked with several batters, some with less flour, but I found this the easiest to handle. Once you have tried them, you can adjust the proportions to suit your way of dealing with batter.

1. Put all the ingredients for the batter into a food processor and run the blade until they come together without forming a hard mass.

2. Transfer the batter to a container that you can tightly seal and refrigerate it for 2 hours.

3. Turn on the oven to 400°.

4. Smear the bottom of the baking pan with butter, sprinkle with flour, then turn the pan over, giving it a tap or two against the work counter to shake off excess flour.

5. Sprinkle flour on a marble counter or another work surface. Pull off from the batter a piece about the size of a very large egg and roll it on the counter into a cylinder about 8 inches long and slightly less than 1 inch thick. Curl it into a circle, overlapping the two ends, and place it on the baking pan. Proceed thus, spacing the circles at least 2 inches apart, until you have used up all the batter.

6. Bake in the upper middle level of the preheated oven for 10 to 15 minutes, until they become colored a very light gold. They will keep well in a tightly closed biscuit tin for 2 to 3 months.

Heavy Cream Custard with Hazelnuts

PANNA COTTA CON LE NOCCIOLE

---

8 ounces whole shelled
  hazelnuts

1 cup granulated sugar

½ cup confectioners' sugar

2 cups heavy cream

1 cup whole milk

1¼-ounce envelope gelatin
  plus 1 teaspoon

FOR THE CARAMEL

1 cup granulated sugar

¼ cup water

---

6 hazelnut custards

6 custard ramekins

I learned how to make this version of *panna cotta* from one of Piedmont's gifted young cooks, Walter Ferretto of Cascinale Nuovo, the superb restaurant on the main road that leads from Asti to Alba. If you compare it with the basic recipe that precedes this one, you will see that the procedure is identical, but for one thing. This one contains a cream of toasted hazelnuts, the most delectable of nuts. If you liked the plain *panna cotta*, you may find this one, as I do, even more delicious.

1. Turn on the oven to 400°.

2. Spread the hazelnuts on a baking sheet and put them in the uppermost level of the preheated oven. If they have already been skinned, toast them briefly, about 7 or 8 minutes. If they still have their skin on, toast them longer, for about 30 minutes, turning them once or twice; then put them into a wire strainer and chafe away most of the skin by rubbing the nuts against the sides of the strainer.

3. Put the hazelnuts in a food processor with 1 cup granulated sugar and chop to the creamiest possible consistency.

4. Put the confectioners' sugar, cream, and milk in a saucepan, turn the heat on to medium high, and stir steadily.

5. Remove the pan from heat the moment its contents begin to bubble, before they start to boil. Continue stirring, and as you do so, drizzle in all the gelatin. Stir for 5 minutes, then empty the pan into a bowl.

6. Add the pureed hazelnuts, stirring them thoroughly to keep them from forming lumps. Let the mixture cool, giving it an occasional stir.

7. Make a caramel by putting 1 cup granulated sugar and ¼ cup water into a small, preferably lightweight, saucepan. Melt the sugar over medium high heat without stirring it, but tilt the pan occasionally. When the melted sugar becomes colored a dark brown, pour it into the

ramekins, tipping them just enough to distribute the caramel evenly on their bottom.

8. When the hazelnut and cream mixture has cooled down completely to room temperature, stir it thoroughly one last time, then pour it into the ramekins. Refrigerate overnight.

9. When ready to serve, bring water to a simmer in a small skillet. Loosen the custard from the sides of the ramekin using a knife blade. Put the ramekin bottom down in the skillet for 1 or 2 seconds, then turn it over onto an individual serving plate, shake to unmold the custard, and serve. If there is caramel left in the ramekin and you'd like it on the custard, put a teaspoon of the simmering water into the ramekin to loosen the caramel so that you can pour it easily.

AHEAD-OF-TIME NOTE: You can keep the custards in their ramekins for 1 week in the refrigerator.

Heavy Cream Custard

PANNA COTTA

¾ cup confectioners' sugar

2 cups heavy cream; see headnote

1 cup whole milk

1¼-ounce envelope gelatin plus 1 teaspoon

---

6 custards

6 custard ramekins

Panna cotta is the most weightless of custards. It has a soothingly silky feel on the palate, it is just sweet enough, and I have never known anyone who didn't like it. For a short period, however, when I was working with it in an American kitchen, I hated it.

Panna cotta means cooked cream, and that is the way I make it in Italy, allowing the cream to boil. At home in Venice it came out perfectly, but on each of my first attempts in the States, I ended up with a gummy residue on the bottom, even before adding the gelatin. One day, as I picked up the container to hurl it into the trash can, my eye was caught by the fine print, and I discovered that it contained a density enhancer that, at high heat, hardens and precipitates. The solution became clear: Do not let the cream boil.

1. Put the sugar, cream, and milk in a saucepan, turn the heat on to medium high, and stir steadily.

2. Remove the pan from heat just as its contents begin to bubble, but before they boil. While stirring, drizzle in all the gelatin. Continue to stir for 5 minutes, then empty the pan into a bowl. Stir occasionally while the mixture cools.

3. When cold, pour the mixture into the ramekins and place them in the refrigerator for at least 8 hours, or even better, overnight.

4. When ready to serve, bring water to a simmer in a small skillet. Loosen the custard from the sides of the ramekin using a knife blade. Put the ramekin bottom down in the skillet for 1 or 2 seconds, then turn it over onto an individual serving plate, shake to unmold the custard, and serve.

SERVING SUGGESTION: Marinate raspberries or blueberries or strawberries, or a mixture of them, in a small bowl with 1 or 2 tablespoons of sugar for at least 30 minutes—an hour or two would be better—and pour over each custard before serving.

Zabaglione Frozen Dessert with Amaretto Cookies

SEMIFREDDO DI ZABAGLIONE CON GLI AMARETTI

4 egg yolks

¼ cup granulated sugar

½ cup dry Marsala wine

10 pairs of imported Italian amaretto cookies

1 cup heavy cream

6 to 8 portions

A double boiler

A loaf pan

Wax paper

Semi, in Italian as in English, means half or partially; *freddo* is Italian for "cold." A *semifreddo* is not whipped in an ice cream freezer, but it is frozen packed in either a rectangular or a round container. It becomes firmer than a gelato and it is served sliced if it comes out of a loaf pan or cut into wedges if unmolded from a pie pan. Among its ingredients there are always some that will not freeze—components such as biscuits, candied fruit, pound cake, and whipped cream, which produce palate sensations less frosty than those of gelato.

The *semifreddo* below starts out as a conventional zabaglione, and if you have never had zabaglione before, you might want to stop before adding the powdered amaretto cookies and whipped cream and taste it warm, when it is the frothiest of all desserts. Freezing it, with cookies and whipped cream, reduces most of its sugary impact and converts its richness into an elegant refreshment.

NOTE: The upper half of your double boiler must be large enough to accommodate the egg yolk mixture, which swells considerably in volume when beaten and cooked. If your double boiler is a small one, you can easily improvise one of greater capacity by using two good-size saucepans, one somewhat larger than the other, placing on the bottom of the larger pan a metal trivet or a similar object on which you'll subsequently rest the smaller of the two pots.

1. Put the egg yolks and sugar in the upper half of the double boiler or the smaller of the two saucepans and, using either a whisk or an electric mixer, beat them until they are creamy and colored a pale yellow.

2. In the lower half of the double boiler or in the larger of the two saucepans bring some water to the brink of a simmer.

(continued)

3.   Fit the halves of the double boiler together or place the smaller of the two saucepans into the larger, resting it on a trivet or other supporting object placed on the bottom of the larger pan. Add the Marsala wine to the egg mixture, beating the mixture uninterruptedly. It will begin to foam, then swell into a frothy mass. When it has formed soft mounds, in 15 minutes or less, the zabaglione is done. Ladle it into a bowl and set it aside to cool completely.

4.   Chop the amaretto cookies to a very fine consistency in the food processor, then mix them gently into the zabaglione.

5.   Whip the heavy cream to a stiff consistency, then fold it carefully into the zabaglione.

6.   Line the loaf pan with wax paper, then pour the zabaglione mixture into it. Freeze overnight or for up to 3 or 4 days. Unmold the dessert onto a serving platter. Serve frozen.

Semifreddo with Nuts and Dried Fruit

SEMIFREDDO ALLA FRUTTA SECCA

———— ❧ ————

¼ cup (2 ounces) shelled, unpeeled hazelnuts

¼ cup (2 ounces) shelled, unpeeled almonds

⅓ cup (2 ounces) raisins

4 extra large eggs

¼ pound granulated sugar

¼ cup (2 ounces) dried apricots

¼ cup (2 ounces) candied citron

1 tablespoon grappa

1 cup fresh heavy cream

Salt

————————————

Serves 6 to 8

An 8-cup loaf pan

Wax paper

When Giorgio Rocca, the owner-chef of one of Piedmont's most illustrious restaurants, Da Felicin in Monforte d'Alba, comes over to your table and suggests you try something he made, however unlikely the dish may sound to you, you suspend judgment until you taste it. Skepticism comes as naturally to an Italian as breathing, and I was skeptical about a frozen dessert loaded with dried fruit, but Giorgio was right—it's good. I tinkered with it at home, eventually omitting the dried figs he uses and adding candied citron, one of my favorite flavors, but it is basically the same extraordinary dish, the most opulent of *semifreddi*.

1. Turn on the oven to 300°.

2. Spread the hazelnuts on a baking sheet and when the oven reaches the preset temperature, put them in and roast them lightly for about 10 to 15 minutes. Transfer them to a medium-size wire strainer and rub them against the sides of the strainer to remove as much of the peel as will slip off.

3. In a small saucepan, bring water to a boil and drop in the almonds. Moisten a dish towel with cold water. When the almonds have simmered for 1 or 2 minutes, drain them and gather them in the wet dish towel. Rub the almonds briskly with the towel to remove their peel.

4. Fill a cup or small bowl with warm water and put in the raisins to soak.

5. Separate the eggs, putting the whites in a bowl where you'll later beat them, and the yolks in the upper part of a double boiler or in a metal bowl that can fit into a pot of water. Add the sugar to the yolks.

6. Turn the heat on to medium under the double boiler (make sure you have water in the lower half), or under the pot in which you have put the bowl with the egg yolks. Beat the yolks with a whisk or a portable mixer until they form firm, pale ribbons. Separate the top half

of the double boiler from the lower half, or remove the bowl from the pot of simmering water, and continue to beat the yolks until they have cooled off.

7. Drain the raisins and squeeze all the moisture you can from them. Put them in a food processor together with the hazelnuts, almonds, apricots, candied citron, and grappa. Process to a fine but not creamy consistency.

8. Add the fruit and nut mixture to the egg yolks and mix thoroughly.

9. Whip the heavy cream until it stiffens and fold it into the fruit, nut, and egg yolk mixture.

10. Add a pinch of salt to the egg whites, beat them until they form stiff peaks, then fold them gently into the ingredient mixture.

11. Line the loaf pan with wax paper, then pour the mixture into it. Freeze for at least 8 hours or up to 4 days; unmold when ready to serve.

Apricot Gelato

GELATO DI ALBICOCCA

1 pound ripe, sweet apricots

1 cup water

1 cup granulated sugar

½ cup heavy cream

1 tablespoon Grand
   Marnier liqueur

2 pints apricot gelato

Gelato is Italian for ice cream, any kind of ice cream. Whenever I see the term *gelato* used in the United States, it appears to be with the intention of describing a particular style of ice cream, one that is often dense and rich. In Italy, however, there is less fat, less cream, less sugar, and less weight than in the so-called Italian-style ice creams that are dispensed elsewhere. *Gelato* ought to be light and not filling; one should look to it for refreshment rather than nourishment. All flavors are its province, but it is particularly triumphant with fruit, as in the apricot gelato that follows.

1. Wash the apricots and slice away any blemished part of their skin. Split them and remove the pits.

2. Put the apricots, water, and sugar in a food processor and process to a runny consistency.

3. In a mixing bowl, whip the cream to the consistency of thick buttermilk.

4. Fold the apricot mixture into it, together with the liqueur.

5. Freeze the mixture in your ice cream maker, following the manufacturer's instructions. Serve when done or transfer to suitable containers and store in the freezer.

Rita D'Enza's Sardinian Rice Gelato

IL GELATO DI RISO DELLA RITA

———— ❧ ————

2 cups milk

3 heaping tablespoons
   granulated sugar

3 long strips lemon rind,
   just the outer skin
   without the white pith
   beneath

⅓ cup *arborio* or other
   imported Italian risotto
   rice such as *carnaroli* or
   vialone nano

Salt

3 egg whites

────────────

1 pint gelato

This recipe and I have had several contentious encounters, but I refused to give up on it. I well remembered its taste and consistency from the time I had it in Rita D'Enza's restaurant Gallura in Sardinia, so different from those of any other ice cream. It's an ice cream you can chew on because bits of the rice kernels remain firm enough, and it has a flavor that, like the aftertaste of a fine wine, keeps lengthening after you have swallowed.

My error, I found after many irritatingly unsatisfactory trials, was that I cooked the rice as I do for the Bolognese rice cake in my first book—I cooked it, that is, until it had absorbed all the milk. When frozen, it became a leaden mass. A phone call to Sardinia set me right. Cook the rice in the milk just until the kernels are tender, but not mushy. There should still be milk left in the pan. Puree the rice and milk, and you are safely on the way to making a gelato like no other.

1. Put the milk, sugar, and lemon rind in a saucepan, turn on the heat to medium, and bring to a boil.

2. Add the rice and a tiny pinch of salt, cover the pan, turn the heat down, and cook at a very, very gentle simmer. Stir frequently, making sure there is no rice sticking to the bottom of the pan. Cook until the rice is tender, about 25 minutes.

3. As soon as it is done, remove the lemon rind and puree the rice, with what milk remains in the pan, in a food processor for a minute or two. It should become creamy, but it will be punctuated throughout by a few firm bits of rice kernel. Transfer to a small bowl and let it cool completely.

4. When the pureed rice is cold, whip the egg whites with a tiny pinch of salt until they form stiff peaks, then fold them gently but thoroughly into the rice.

5. Freeze the mixture in your ice cream maker. This is a mixture that is likely to mass and freeze faster than other ice creams. Serve when done or transfer to suitable containers and store in the freezer.

SERVING SUGGESTIONS: If stored in the freezer, let it soften in the refrigerator for about 20 minutes before serving. It is excellent served alone, but you can top it with pureed raspberries or strawberries.

Tangerine Sorbet

SORBETTO AL MANDARINO

¾ cup sugar

½ cup water

1 cup freshly squeezed tangerine juice

The freshly squeezed juice of ½ lemon, about 1 tablespoon

The grated peel of 1½ tangerines, about 1 teaspoon

¼ cup Grand Marnier or other orange or tangerine liqueur

1 cup muscat wine (see headnote on page 444)

About 2 pints tangerine sorbet

An ice cream maker

Tangerine is the citrus fruit I am fondest of, and what I most like about it is its blossom-like aroma. When I was younger I used to crush its pliant skin under my nose and inhale the scent as I might have that of a flower. It is that scent, present through both the juice and the skin's zest, that makes this sorbet so appealing. The lemon that you find here, and in many fruit desserts, is used for its acidic drive, which helps propel the fragrance of other ingredients.

1. Put the sugar and water in a small saucepan and bring to a slow boil, stirring frequently.

2. Combine the sugar and water syrup with all the other ingredients in a bowl, making sure you haven't grated any of the bitter white pith beneath the tangerine skin. Stir thoroughly to obtain a uniform mixture.

3. Freeze to a very firm consistency in your ice cream maker. Serve when done or transfer to suitable containers and store in the freezer.

Granny Smith Apple Sorbet with Muscat Wine and Grappa

SORBETTO DI MELA VERDE

3 Granny Smith apples

1 tablespoon honey

1 cup granulated sugar

1 cup water

The freshly squeezed juice
of 1 medium lemon

1 cup muscat wine (see
headnote)

2 tablespoons grappa

About 2 pints sorbet

An ice cream maker

Superlatives are always suspect. If you want to be credible you should scrupulously avoid them, but I am going to use them anyway now. This is the most exhilarating and deliciously fresh sorbet I know. What makes it so is the felicity with which the ingredients act upon each other. The Granny Smith and the grappa both have bite, but grappa isn't all bite. It is packed with the aromatic esters of the pomace, the grape skins left over after making wine, from which it is distilled. The honey is all suavity with its characteristically musky aftertaste. The muscat wine brings its own soft touch and the scent of peaches and apricots. None of these qualities stand apart but all coalesce to produce this sorbet's unique, scented, zephyr-like refreshment.

If you have all the choices in the world, the wine you would use would be the low-alcohol Moscato Naturale d'Asti, a shyly sweet muscat from Piedmont. Only slightly less desirable, but far more available, is Asti Spumante, which you must beat lightly with a fork or a swizzle stick to drive away some of the bubbles. If you must look for something else, there are California moscatos and other sweet wines, as well as a number of similarly off-dry German wines. Do not use an intensely sweet wine in the late-harvest, Sauternes, or Beerenauslese category.

1. Peel and core the apples, and cut them into pieces about the size of a walnut.

2. Put the honey, sugar, and water in a small saucepan and bring to a slow boil over low heat. Cook down to a syrup half its original volume.

3. Put the apples, the honey and sugar syrup, the lemon juice, the muscat wine, and the grappa in a food processor and puree to a creamy consistency.

4. Freeze to a very firm consistency in your ice cream maker. Serve when done or transfer to suitable containers and store in the freezer.

Afterword

As I look back at the preceding pages, I am prompted to say that this book has written itself. I do not say it wholly without misgivings, fearing the simplistic interpretations to which such a statement is subject. I certainly did not just sit back while it happened. When I was not teaching or traveling, I spent most of the past three years in the kitchen working on dishes whose recipes I could turn over to you in the reasonable hope that they could be replicated and prove satisfying. There were many more recipes left behind in the workbooks that I keep by the stove than the ones collected between these covers. Some dishes, I felt, were subject to too many imponderables; some were the result of intuitions that I myself was unable to recapture in succeeding trials; some did not seem to justify the effort; others did not taste good enough to me or to my husband.

What I mean when I say that the book wrote itself is that it is not the product of a predetermined plan. It was not mapped out like a military campaign, so many objectives to reach, so much territory to cover, so many positions to hold. It advanced, unforced, day by day, and the features of the cooking it describes have been shaped by the life that my husband and I live. There can be no doubt about its being a cookbook, but when here and there it decided to step over the line into autobiography I allowed it to have its way.

The photographs that Allison Harris took, in collaboration with Joel Avirom, the genial designer of this book, are themselves drawn from life. They were all shot either in the Rialto market where I shop or in our house in Venice. No stylist brought in props. All the crockery, all the containers, every pot, every tool, came out of my cupboards or my kitchen. The light, in all but a few instances when we had to augment it with flash, is the natural Venetian light that falls on our terraces and our courtyard or comes through our windows. Except for the handmade pasta that I had a friend from Bologna roll out, I alone made the bread and every dish shown, scrupulously following my own manuscript's recipes.

When Craig Claiborne, then the food editor of the *New York Times*, came home to lunch more than 25 years ago and set off the process by which I was propelled into the food world, my cooking had been simply of the wifely and motherly kind. I cooked to please myself, my husband, our son, our friends, without pausing to reflect on questions that were not directly related to accomplishing the specific task at hand. I learned to cook by cooking, by discovering what had to be done to produce the results I wanted. As I came to face the world that lay beyond my kitchen, however, and as I was confronted with the aims and achievements of many other cooks of diverse backgrounds, it became necessary for me to define to my own satisfaction what were the fundamental principles by which a good cook, and in particular a good Italian cook, ought to be guided.

Out of the long discussions on this subject that I had with my husband over the years, three general attributes emerged above all others: passion, clarity, sincerity.

Like many others, I sometimes speak of loving to cook, but it is a glib and facile expression. As Tina Turner might say, What's love got to do with it? I love my husband, my son, my house, my native town, my adopted country, America; and there are a few friends whom I love. That is not the emotion I feel toward the making of a sauce, or when I yield to the temptation of a recently caught fish, glistening and bright-eyed, or contemplate the perfection of a well-cut piece of meat, or respond to the allure of glossy young zucchini or the ripeness of tomatoes. This is emotion of another kind, specific to the object of the moment: it is ardor, desire, lust, if you will. It is passion. To cook without abandoning one-self to that excitement, to fail to take intimate possession of one's ingredients, to go merely by the book and work by rote, is to circumvent the sensual nature of cooking, to produce food that may pacify the taste buds but does not arouse them.

Clarity is about letting ingredients speak for themselves. It is not a quality as essential to all cuisines as it is to the Italian or, say, the Japanese. It isn't the absence of technique, but rather its transparency. It is for clarity's sake that we use clear meat broth rather than stock to make risotto, that we toss pasta with just enough sauce to coat it, that we refrain from swamping our dishes with too distracting a use of herbs or chili pepper or garlic or cream. Protecting the integrity of the individual flavors and textures is the reason we do not make purees out of our soups. It is for clarity that our meat and fish dishes are usually presented with no other sauce than the juices they have produced in cooking, and that they are rarely piled on the same plate with vegetables or other courses. We reach for clarity when we judge how long or how briefly we need to cook something so that it explicitly releases its flavor: very little for a truly ripe tomato in a simple sauce, longer for green beans and asparagus so that they can bring more of their properties to the mouth than mere crunch, at considerable length for poultry so that the savor of its juices saturates every fiber of the flesh.

Sincerity means speaking with your own true voice. Its flip side is mimicry. Of course we make dishes that we have reason to think will please others, but to carry conviction the taste of those dishes must express the genuinely felt convictions of the cook. The recipes we read, the foods we taste at other tables, need to be recast in the foundry of our senses. Cooking is a far more self-centered act than has been generally admitted. It is we who must, first and last, be satisfied with how we cook. The applause that may greet us is help-ful encouragement, but it will ring hollow if it does not resonate within us. We need to rec-ognize ourselves in the dishes we prepare. Good cooking is not fantasy, it is reality; it's not theater, it is life. If the table to which one's dishes come is a stage at all, it is the kind where, uncostumed, one plays just one character—oneself.

Venice, January 1997

Index

Noto – leggero gustoso nutriente va bene per patate
raffinati e uno suppo primaverile

Noto – Se le fave sono molto fresche e dure togliere
la pelliccina

(+)

per 6 persone __Zuppa di broccoli e patate.__ (+)

(4) 2 lb di broccoli

(1) 1 cipolla grossa a fettine sottili (1 e $\frac{1}{2}$ cup)

(5) 1 spicchio a fettine sottili di aglio

(2) $\frac{1}{4}$ cup di olio d'oliva (io ho fatto con olio di semi $\frac{1}{3}$ cup)

dado (3) 3 Tb di burro

(6) 4 patate piuttosto grosse
pelate, lavate e tagliate
a dadini piccoli.

(10) $\frac{1}{2}$ cup di parmigiano reggiano

(9) 6-8 foglie di basilico a pezzetti

(7A) sale (8) pepe

– Mettere la cipolla, tutto l'olio d'oliva e 1 Tb di
burro in una pentola con coperchio e a fuoco piuttosto
basso cuocere la cipolla con un pizzico di sale
fino a che sia ben cotta ed abbia preso un colore
marciola.

– Nel frattempo prendere le fiorette dai broccoli
e lavarle (i gambi pelati si potranno usare un'altro
giorno per insalata).

– Quando la cipolla è pronta mettere l'aglio e
insaporire per 1-2 minuti in esso (non deve essere
colorato)

– Poi mettere le fiorette e un altro po' di sale